Courtroom Discourse

Practical Insights from Legal Linguists

EDITORS
Zakeera Docrat
Annelise de Vries
Russell H Kaschula
Paul Svongoro

SUN PRESS

Courtroom Discourse: Practical Insights from Legal Linguists

Published by African Sun Media under the SUN PReSS imprint
Place of publication: Stellenbosch, South Africa

This publication was subjected to an independent double-blind peer evaluation.

First edition 2025

ISBN 978-1-991260-94-9
ISBN 978-1-991260-95-6 (eBook)
https://doi.org/10.52779/9781991260956

Set in Warnock Pro Light 10/14.5

Typesetting and production by African Sun Media
Cover design by African Sun Media

SUN PReSS is an imprint of African Sun Media. Scholarly, professional and reference works are published under this imprint in print and electronic formats.

This publication can be ordered from:
orders@africansunmedia.co.za
Takealot: bit.ly/2monsfl
Google Books: bit.ly/2k1Uilm
africansunmedia.store.it.si *(e-Books)*
Amazon: amzn.to/2ktL.pkL

Visit africansunmedia.co.za for more information.

CONTENTS

Part 3 | COURT INTERPRETING AND POLICE STATEMENT TAKING

Part 4 | CUSTOMARY LAW, LEGAL LANGUAGE POLICIES, AND LEGISLATION

LIST OF TABLES

LIST OF FIGURES

SERIES FOREWORD

Series Editors

Monwabisi K. Ralarala (South Africa)
Russell H. Kaschula (South Africa)
Georgina Heydon (Australia)

Studies in Forensic and Legal Linguistics in Africa and beyond (SF&LLA) is an exciting series of books on forensic linguistics and language and the law. The role of language in the legal process in establishing a just society cannot be overemphasised, particularly in a multilingual/multicultural African context. The series, therefore, intends to explore, by means of case studies as well as through empirical research, issues of relevance in forensic linguistics and in language and the law. This series distinguishes itself by encompassing specific disciplines in the domains of humanities and social sciences. A research programme of this nature is highly interdisciplinary, involving scholars from linguistics, interpreting and translating, languages, migration, psychology, criminology, policing, and law. The series' peculiarity is its centering of African linguistic and legal contexts, with the inclusion of research from around the world that resonates with the African experience. These volumes not only strive towards contemporary relevance, but also share research findings that have the potential to effect positive change in people's lives. The series is also meant to discuss the various theoretical frameworks and methodological choices and their applicability in a variety of contexts. In this way, the series will provide a global audience with a unique analysis of the benefits gained through these studies, as well as the challenges encountered. To this end, we wish to encourage scholars who have a keen interest in this field to submit book proposals for consideration to the series.

Published

1. Ralarala, MK., Kaschula, RH. & Heydon, G. (2019). *New Frontiers in Forensic Linguistics: Themes and Perspectives in Language and Law in Africa and beyond.* African Sun Media.
2. Docrat, Z., Kaschula, RH. & Ralarala, MK. (2021). *A Handbook on Legal Languages and the quest for linguistic equality in South Africa and beyond.* African Sun Media.
3. Ralarala, MK., Kaschula, RH. & Heydon, G. (2022). *Language and the Law: Global Perspectives in Forensic Linguistics from Africa and Beyond.* African Sun Media.
4. Kaschula, RH., Ralarala, MK. & Heydon, G. (2023). *Language, Crime and Courts in Contemporary Africa and Beyond.* African Sun Media.
5. Ralarala, MK., Kaschula, RH., Docrat, Z., Satia M. & van den Berg, K. (2025). *Documenting Forensic Linguistics in the African Context: Perspectives in Language and Legal Practice.* African Sun Media.

ACKNOWLEDGEMENTS

Peer review is central to academic scholarship. As the editors of this volume we would like to express our sincere gratitude to the anonymous peer reviewers who took time to engage with the manuscript. Your contributions in the form of comments and recommendations are acknowledged and appreciated.

Mrs Grace Naidoo, our project administrator, is deserving of our utmost gratitude. Her meticulous project administration was invaluable.

Finally, we wish to express our gratitude to Ms Davida van Zyl, Ms Arin Barry, Mr Glenn Hekma, and his team from African Sun Media, who answered our many questions and guided the publication process.

ABOUT THE EDITORS

Zakeera Docrat is a forensic and legal linguist, author, and researcher. She is presently a post-doctoral research fellow under the auspices of the Research Chair in Forensic Linguistics and Multilingualism, University of the Western Cape. Zakeera was awarded three post-doctoral research fellowships by the National Research Foundation, the Andrew W Mellon Foundation, and the National Institute for the Humanities and Social Sciences. Zakeera holds the following degrees: BA, BA Honours (cum laude), LLB, MA (cum laude), and a PhD; and she was awarded full academic colours. She has published widely in national and international journals and books. She has presented at international and national conferences. She has been interviewed on national media. Zakeera's research has been referred to and referenced in judgments emanating from South African courts. Her research was used in the pleadings of a language rights case at the UN Human Rights Committee. She is the Chairperson of the Indigenous Languages Action Forum (ILAF). Zakeera is the first scholar from outside of Europe to be appointed to the board of the Austrian Association for Legal Linguistics. She is an international advisory board member for the International Journal for the Semiotics of Law. Zakeera was one of the Mail & Guardian 200 Young South Africans (Justice and Law category) and received numerous awards, including Most Outstanding Master's Thesis (African Languages Association of Southern Africa); the Women in Science Award – Albertina Sisulu Doctoral Fellowship (Department of Science and Technology), recognising her outstanding academic and research ability; Phenomenal Heroic Woman in Science Award (Sunday World and Department of Science and Innovation); the African Language Association of Southern Africa (ALASA) emerging researcher award; and the Quote This Woman+ Voice of the Year Award for 2022. Her ORCID number is: 0000-0003-1444-9768

Annelise de Vries is a distinguished language planner, academic, and forensic linguist, currently serving as the CEO of the South African Academy of Science and Arts. Her career spans various fields, including language rights, legal language, forensic linguistics, and academic language planning. She holds a PhD in Applied Linguistics from the University of Johannesburg and specialises in multilingualism in legal practice, language policy, and legislative language transformation. De Vries has a broad academic and professional background, having served as a lecturer, researcher, and language planning specialist. She previously led the Afrikaans Language Board as Chairperson, is the Vice-Chair of the African Association of Forensic and Legal Linguistics (AAFLL), and serves as a board member of the Virtual Institute for Afrikaans. Her research focuses on the impact of language as access to justice, legislation, and jurisprudence, significantly contributing to policy development and the promotion of multilingualism in South Africa. As a respected academic and expert witness in legal cases, she has produced numerous academic publications, conference papers, and contributions toward advancing language rights and language transformation. Her work remains dedicated to language as a tool for justice and inclusive social development.

Russell H Kaschula holds a PhD from Rhodes University. He is HOD and Professor in the Department of African Language Studies at the University of the Western Cape. He also holds the Institutional Chair in Forensic Linguistics and Multilingualism. He has published widely in the field of Applied Language Studies, including Forensic Linguistics, Intercultural Studies, Education, and Multilingualism more generally. In 2021 he published a book with Routledge in London and New York titled *Languages, Identities and Intercultural Communication in South Africa and Beyond.* He also co-edited *A Handbook on Legal Languages and the quest for linguistic equality in South Africa and beyond,* published by African Sun Media (2021), and co-edited a book titled *Language and the Law: Global Perspectives in Forensic Linguistics from Africa and Beyond,* published in 2022. In 2023, Russell co-edited *Language, Crime and Courts in Contemporary Africa and Beyond* (African Sun Media). Russell acts as an international advisor to the *Journal of Semiotics and Law* as well as a number of other journals. He has a B1 rating with the National Research Foundation. Russell has taught at five South African universities and a liberal arts college in the USA. He has supervised 36 MA students and 35 PhD students to completion. He has also acted as a postgraduate examiner for many universities both in South Africa and abroad. His ORCID number is: 0000-0002-54816748.

Paul Svongoro holds a PhD from the University of the Witwatersrand, South Africa. Currently, Paul works as a senior lecturer in Language Education in the Faculty of Education at the University of Botswana. He is also a research fellow in the Department of African Languages of the University of South Africa. For three consecutive years, Paul Svongoro served as a post-doctoral research fellow at the University of the Western Cape. The fellowship, which ended in May 2024, was sponsored by the the Andrew W. Mellon Foundation. Paul conducts research and publishes in the areas of legal interpreting, multilingualism and diversity, language rights, translanguaging, and academic literacies. Some of Paul's publications appear in such journals as *Perspectives in Education, South African Journal of African Languages,* and *Southern African Linguistics and Applied Language Studies.* One of his latest publications is a co-edited book published by Routledge titled *Discrimination and Access to Justice in Africa: Language, Vulnerability and Social Inclusion in Southern and Eastern Africa* (2025). Apart from being a member of the African Association of Forensic and Legal Linguistics (AAFLL), African Languages Association of Southern Africa, and the Southern African

Association for Language Teachers (SAALT), Paul is also an International advisory board member of *The Namibian Journal of Linguistics, Literature and Communication Studies.* To date, Paul has supervised and graduated seven MA students. Currently, he co-supervises three PhD students and has acted as an external examiner for four universities in Africa. His ORCID number is: 0000-0002-3186-339.

FOREWORD

In a relative world and specifically in the judicial sphere in a multilingual state, the Cinderella is the linguistic competencies and qualifications of the role players: Victims of crime, accused persons, witnesses, and the parties involved are on the receiving end of the still unrecognised and underestimated systemic problem of linguistic injustices. A colonised-minded approach ignores the challenges in the system, whilst linguistic justice cries out for a better approach. This book introduces the discipline of legal linguistics to South African and African legal practitioners and judicial officers. Improving access to justice through language is one of the primary objectives of *Courtroom Discourse: Practical Insights from Legal Linguists*. In doing so, the editors have meticulously sought varying contributions from court intermediaries, legal practitioners, and academics. The contributing chapters shed light on legal linguistic issues affecting various legal systems.

The book comprises 18 contributing chapters across 4 parts. The compilation of contributions appropriately commences with 3 chapters providing critical insights into the role of language within various courtroom and legal settings. The role of the legal linguist as an expert witness is important in the South African and broader multilingual jurisdictions. This issue is specifically addressed in chapters 2 and 3 of this book.

The power of language within courtroom discourse is often underestimated or overlooked to the detriment of victims, accused, witnesses, and litigants. The book explicates the importance of understanding courtroom proceedings and being understood. Any person summoned to court is already stressed, and not knowing the procedure aggravates this stressful experience. Chapter 1 highlights this aspect. It also focusses on a global issue of violence against women and children, offering practical solutions, ensuring language is not an impediment when providing evidence. The golden aim is to present accurate and truthful evidence in a case without a linguistic limitation which can obscure a just outcome.

As a legal practitioner, I can attest to the power of language during examination in chief and cross-examination. The challenge is to listen to an interpretation of the evidence of the witness and then instead of concentrating on the contents, your focus is detracted by wrong interpretations which you must rectify, if you are fortunate to understand the language of the witness. The role of the legal practitioner is critical in ensuring the client is represented and fully understood in the courtroom, which is an additional burden as they should only be obliged to communicate and present their client's case with the applicable law to the court. The language of legal education remains a challenge where the focus is on pursuing a monolingual education programme. The results of which are linguistically ill-equipped legal practitioners in multilingual societies. These discussions surrounding the impact of the monolingual LLB (Legum Baccalaureus/ Bachelor of Laws) degree in the South African and broader African context is discussed in Part 2 of this book.

At the core of discussions relating to language and law is courtroom interpretation and police statement taking. These central facets of courtroom discourse and criminal law cannot be overlooked. The lack of linguistic training for police officers affects the quality of statement taking and investigations. The government's failure to appoint police officers in accordance with the language demographics of specific regions exacerbates this, and the demand that English or the dominant official language be used in completing the statements. Within South Africa, the statements directly impact witness credibility where discrepancies are prevalent between the written statement and oral testimony: they are consequently made liars in court. Witnesses are therefore reluctant to appear in court and provide oral testimony. Interpreters are appearing to be filling terminology and cultural voids while trying to ensure the witness's oral testimony correlates with the lack of language mastery apparent in the written police statement. Interpreters' qualifications, training and competencies are constantly scrutinised especially in multilingual contexts where legal systems function in one language. The presiding officers are a controlling mechanism for the accuracy for interpreters where those presiding officers can understand the witnesses' languages, but there is not a policy that presiding officers be appointed in areas where their language competencies are relevant. The research advanced in Part 3 of this book, provides solutions and recommendations in relation to ongoing high profiled cases, and the need to produce terminology in all official languages of the specific country. The different creative vocabularies, which interpreters use, related to technical legislative terminology, creates challenges, which this book highlights.

Legislation and policies need to support the implementation and application of the language rights for all speakers of the official languages on an equitable basis. The language rights violations remains a cause for concern. The politicisation of the language question for legal systems favour an elitist approach where colonial languages are dominant on the African continent. Indigenous languages are pitted against each other in a struggle to compete with the hegemonic dominance of colonial languages. The failure to utilise the translation of legislation into the official languages undermines the potential role as a social practice for the intellectualisation of African languages. In the South African context the policy related decisions and legislative drafting where two languages are included favour the default English and previously also Afrikaans approach, but the latter is currently down leveled to the disadvantaged level of the

9 African official languages. Part 4 of the book outlines the shortcomings of various legislation and policies that consciously marginalise indigenous languages and the speakers thereof.

With a global phenomenon of language hegemony and the growing extinction of indigenous languages, victims, accused witnesses and litigants are left to their own devices or are solely reliant on poor quality interpretation. The scales have been tipped in favour of an English elite in the South African legal system, where the indigenous language voices are lost. Notwithstanding that, the majority as citizens speak an official language without real content, whilst their language rights are relegated to interpreting rights only, the legal system left them in the lurch until now. The need for research that identifies issues, and proposes solutions and recommendations is ever more important and is put forward in this book.

Legal linguists have an integral role to play in transforming the system from a point of language to ensure a more equal and just system. The editors of this book together with the contributing authors have challenged the narratives as part of their continued efforts to create a linguistically inclusive legal system in order to attain linguistic justice. The editors who are activists in their own right have demonstrated that academic research must be coupled with practical insights. Hopefully magistrates, judges and justices will take notice of this sensitising publication as justice can only be done if linguistic justice manifests itself in the legal process. Hopefully the heads of courts together with government will initiate integrated language plans and protocols for the taking of police statements. This book is a must read for legal practitioners aiming to support legal language initiatives globally.

Mr. Cerneels J.A. Lourens

South African Practicing Attorney and Language Rights Activist

INTRODUCTION

Zakeera Docrat,
Annelise de Vries,
Russell H. Kaschula &
Paul Svongoro

Since 2015, there has been a significant increase in the production of research within the discipline of forensic linguistics in South Africa and the broader African continent. In addition to the body of research, the growth of this book series, *Studies in Forensic Linguistics in Africa and beyond*, has resulted in the publication of six volumes. The series serves as a consolidated reference for our growing number of postgraduate students, legal practitioners, judicial officers, and researchers.

As the Global South, we are finding and proposing practical solutions to language related issues plaguing our legal systems, with the overarching aim of ensuring access to justice is attainable for speakers of all official languages. The increased number of collaborations among African and international researchers continues to grow, ensuring the collective growth of the discipline. This has resulted in the 17th Biennial Conference of the International Association for Forensic and Legal Linguistics being hosted for the first time on the African continent, in Cape Town, South Africa, in 2025. The conference will address the theme of *Transformative Justice through a Forensic and Legal Linguistics Lens*. The conference will ensure further collaborative interdisciplinary research between African and international scholars while directly addressing the language issues facing legal systems globally.

Given the interdisciplinarity of forensic and legal linguistics, research from linguists and legal researchers focused on the legal system and legal practices must be coupled with practical insights from legal professionals. These insights go beyond empirical studies and offer informed approaches to proposed solutions while highlighting real life challenges within the profession and courtroom discourse. The language question for courtroom communication is gaining momentum among legal professionals, who acknowledge the need for forensic and legal linguistics research and expert evidence in transforming the system to ensure linguistic inclusivity. Judicial officers are using indigenous languages in South Africa by writing bilingual judgments and publicly expressing their support for using indigenous languages equally alongside English. This, in turn, contributes to the South African Constitutional mandate of promoting and using the languages in high status domains. Although restrictive language legislative provisions and policies remain in place, the tide is turning in favour of a linguistically inclusive and equal system. The research can no longer be overlooked in favour of restrictive legislative provisions, policies, decisions, and reasoning.

Volumes II, *A Handbook on Legal Languages and the quest for linguistic equality in South Africa and beyond* (Docrat, Kaschula & Ralarala, 2021), and IV, *Language, Crime and Courts in Contemporary Africa and Beyond* (Kaschula & Ralarala & Heydon, 2023) offered consolidated research on the issues plaguing our legal system and profession while offering solutions and recommendations. Building on this research, this volume contributes new knowledge and critical insights from legal linguists. The practical, professional voice is coupled with researched approaches and methods to address current issues, where this volume focuses on legal linguistics.

Research produced in the discipline of forensic and legal linguistics on the African continent contributes to the achievement of the transformational agenda, where the role of language is often overlooked. This volume not only contributes to the transformational agenda; it lays the groundwork for further research in legal linguistics.

Outline and summary of chapters

The book comprises four interconnected themes:

Part I: The language of complainants and witnesses;
Part II: Courtroom discourse and legal education;
Part III: Courtroom interpreting and police statement taking;
Part IV: Customary law, legal language policies and legislation.

Part I: The language of complainants and witnesses

The chapters in this section explore the language of complainants and witnesses and how this language use affects court role players, either positively or negatively.

Chapter 1 is by Fiona van Wyk and Tasneemah Nordien. The chapter seeks to create an understanding about the challenges child witnesses face in multilingual South African courtrooms, where the language of record remains a monolingual, English-only approach. Intermediary services in South African courts are essential support services for the child witness. This is important because the child witness is not only vulnerable, but also offers testimony of a very sensitive nature. The chapter finds that this vulnerability is exacerbated by the rigidity of the court and the fact that the South African legal system operates only in English, thus making it a monolingual system within a multilingual country. The chapter finds that this issue of language is relevant in the Cape Winelands (Boland) judicial areas of the Western Cape where most child witnesses are either Afrikaans or isiXhosa speakers.

Chapter 2 of the book, by Annelise de Vries and Karien Brits, looks at dispute resolution cases and it analyses linguistic analysis as part of the testimony that is provided. It is argued that language is inevitably a part of the arsenal of a legal practitioner. The linguist can, as an expert witness, assist in cases dealing with language in order to restore fairness and justice. In this chapter, the focus is aimed at the linguistic testimony in a dispute resolution case heard by the Education Labour Relations Council (ELRC). The trade union, Solidarity, appealed on behalf of a high school teacher, Anneke Smit, against inter alia the verdict that she had shown inappropriate conduct by calling a learner a 'police monkey' when she used the word 'polisiemannetjie'. The authors specifically exercised methodological choices with the purpose of rendering reliable, independent, and accountable testimony in the case. Research questions were formulated to guide the linguistic analysis, and the chapter closes with the findings in answer to these questions. The principal question was as follows: what is the probability that the applicant had offensively referred to a learner as a monkey or a male animal by using the word 'polisiemannetjie'? Two sub-questions arising from this were: a) what is the probability that 'polisiemannetjie' sounded like 'police monkey'? and b) what is the probability that if a person is referred to as a 'mannetjie', the person is by default equated to a male animal? The chapter centres around the theoretical linguistic analysis of these utterances mentioned in the sub-questions. The study adopts an interpretivist paradigm due to its ontological belief in multiple realities and epistemological, holistic understanding. Grounded theoretical methodology is chosen for its qualitative nature. External data sources aid in a sociolinguistic approach, employing cross-cultural and theoretical linguistic analyses to examine expressions within South African language contexts. The findings based on the analysis demonstrated that the probability that the applicant had referred to a learner in an offensive way as a monkey or a male animal in her statement 'polisiemannetjie' was very small.

In chapter 3, Stanley Madonsela looks at the notion of deception and whether it can be considered a catalytic agent of lies. The legal implications of this process in the courtroom are further critiqued. Whereas deception is commonly viewed as an unethical action, some people consider certain lies to be more detrimental than others. In this chapter, several deception theories have been integrated to arrive at the intentional element that this concept has in the legal system. This is considered within the elements of social, psychological and communication contributions that have been built into this concept. It is the overarching vehicle of deception which is mostly the language and its associated agent that are used in deception. Considering the diverse views of the scholars studying deception, there is still some debate about what aspects should be considered deceptive communication in courts of law. While this chapter is not an attempt to provide a universal definition of 'deception', it tries to provide the elements of prototypical deception.

Part II: Courtroom discourse and legal education

The chapters in this section of the book address the important role of legal education and its far-reaching impacts on courtroom discourse, where learning and teaching practices directly affect the relationship between language, law, and power in courtroom proceedings. Empirical studies offer critical insights and inform the recommendations.

Chapter 4, by Wellman Kondowe, Paul Svongoro and Gerald Nthala, titled 'Until when shall "ignorance of the law be no defence"? Practical insights from the discursive strategies used by offenders in seeking mitigation in Malawian criminal trial', engages with the legal maxim 'ignorance of the law is no defence' in the Malawian context. They argue that from a theoretical perspective the law provides for equal protection, however from a point of practice offenders are uninformed of their rights. Relying on collected empirical data, they explain that there are high levels of 'legal illiteracy', where urgent reformative measures need to be implemented. They recommend that the law, legislation, and other policies governing the legal system be made available in indigenous languages. The need for legal education and rights-awareness programmes is proposed to ensure citizens are well equipped to understand the law and defend themselves. This, in turn, would reverse the historical discrimination and marginalisation currently being perpetuated in Malawian courts.

Chapter 5, by Precious Lungu, is titled 'Knowledge and Perception of Forensic Linguistics by Linguists in Malawi'. The chapter presents an empirical study where the views of linguists on using and teaching forensic linguistics in Malawian tertiary institutions are presented. The study shows that linguists are reluctant to teach forensic linguistics. An overwhelming majority of linguists stated that pure linguists should not be replaced by the teaching of forensic linguistics. The chapter advances the importance of teaching forensic linguistics at universities with the aim of using forensic linguistics and related research to improve the Malawian legal system and legal education.

Chapter 6, by Keneilwe Radebe, titled 'Culture and Language: Discussing the under-use of indigenous languages in legal education and legal practice', is important within the African context, where language and culture directly affect access to justice. The chapter provides examples of cultural terms and practices that, when interpreted, have no English equivalences, often requiring the interpreter to fill a cultural vacuum in courtroom discourse. The chapter provides extensive recommendations of using indigenous languages within legal education and developing law glossaries to assist African-language speaking students and legal practitioners. The chapter focusses on a specific linguistic provincial model that can be adopted for all indigenous South African languages.

Chapter 7, by Precious Lungu, titled 'Manifestation of Power in the Discourse of Lawyers and Witnesses in the Malawian Courtroom', is concerned with language, law, and power within courtroom discourse. The chapter examines the power disparities between legal practitioners and witnesses during examination and cross-examination in courts. The chapter is based on a study conducted in two comparative civil and criminal cases in Malawi. The study provides critical insights into the influence of power of legal practitioners during questioning and how this impacts court proceedings.

Part III: Courtroom interpreting and police statement taking

The chapters in this section deal with some of the challenges confronting the court interpreting practice and profession in African countries and beyond. Using authentic, contemporary data from different legal contexts, the chapters focus on the challenges faced by court interpreters as language mediators, language rights issues during the recording of statements by police officers, and the lack of legal terminology in African languages, among other issues. The chapters also offer practical solutions to address some of the language challenges related to language mediation during court trials and police interrogations.

Chapter 8, by Paul Svongoro, is based on a systematic literature review to explore the difficulties faced by court interpreters. The chapter, titled 'An exploration of researchers' views regarding difficulties faced by court interpreters and how they affect the delivery of justice', brings to the fore some of the challenging conditions court interpreters work in all over the world and how these challenges impact the administration of justice. The chapter highlights the skills and abilities that court interpreters can enhance to overcome challenges and improve access to justice. It suggests policies and practices to enhance interpreters' skills, knowledge, and preparedness, addressing the changing legal, socio-economic, and linguistic landscapes in which they work. These insights are crucial for enhancing their performance.

In chapter 9, Natasha Venter analyses language use in the South African Police Service (SAPS) with a bias towards language rights, the language of record, and criminal investigations. The chapter, titled 'Language usage in the SAPS in relation to language rights; the language of record policy and criminal investigations: Linguistic challenges regarding A1 statements, and the implications of poorly constructed statements', challenges the use of English as the only language of record in South Africa's justice system. To address some of the challenges posed by the choice of English as the language of record in a highly multilingual country like South Africa, the chapter suggests viable options that could be implemented to enable a multilingual model in courts and police stations, which would not require too many resources. The chapter also argues that designating English as the only language of record does not advance nor develop other official indigenous languages. Rather, the opposite has occurred in South Africa.

In chapter 10, Mabilo T. Jonas, Josephat Mutangadura, Tebogo J. Rakgogo, and Corle Smith explore presiding officers and court interpreters' experiences with multilingualism in the Limpopo province of South Africa. The title of the chapter is 'Presiding officers and courtroom interpreters' experiences on multilingualism within South African Courtrooms'. Put more succinctly, the chapter explores the impact of multilingualism on courtroom discourse in Limpopo Province. It identifies indigenous and immigrant languages in courtrooms and examines how multilingualism influences courtroom interactions. The chapter also assesses whether multilingualism has an impact on case outcomes. The chapter, therefore, contributes to discussions on linguistic rights, legal fairness, and the need for improved interpretation services in South African courtrooms.

Chapter 11, by Mabilo T. Jonas, Tebogo J. Rakgogo, Josephat Mutangadura, and Corle Smith, titled 'Language Challenges in Courtroom Interpreting: A Study of Courtroom Discourse in the Limpopo Province' extends research into court interpreting by examining the language challenges experienced during court interpreting. The chapter identifies and discusses six main language challenges in courtroom interpreting: idioms, metaphors, figurative speech, lack of word equivalence due to dialects in Limpopo province, influence of IsiNdebele in the province, and the presence of foreign nationals in South Africa who chose to use their home language during the trial. These challenges complicate the communication between the accused and court interpreters. The chapter also established that the movement of people across provinces and nationalities has increased the need for interpreters who can speak multiple languages to minimize language challenges, and linguists are needed by courts to expedite cases often hindered by language issues.

In chapter 12, Nomfundo Mali uses the ongoing Senzo Meyiwa trial as a case study to explore the issue of inclusion and exclusion of interpreting during court proceedings. The Senzo Meyiwa trial has drawn international attention from language researchers and legal minds. The chapter is titled '"...to have the proceedings interpreted in that language": Probing the inclusion and exclusion of interpreting during court proceedings, a case study of the Senzo Meyiwa Murder Trial'. By investigating court interpreter inclusion and exclusion phenomena during the Senzo Meyiwa trial, the chapter shares insights into interpreting practice and how court interpreter inclusion and exclusion may hinder the provision of complete interpreting during court proceedings.

In chapter 13, Nomfundo Mali together with Aliziwe Sidiki, Qhamani Masiki, Lindile Mali, and Indiphiwe Mxakaza explore one of the challenges which faces multilingual courtrooms in Africa – the lack of terminology for legal and technical terms in indigenous languages. Focusing on the South African context, the chapter, titled 'Exploring the development of legal terminology in indigenous languages as a tool to justice for all in South African courts', explores the general shortage of accurate legal terminology in African languages and suggests possible ways to develop legal terminology for African languages to address some of the language challenges faced by court interpreters. By so doing, the chapter also attempts to elevate the status of previously marginalised African languages by developing them to the level where they can be used more effectively in justice delivery systems of African countries.

Part IV: Customary law, legal language policies and legislation

This part explores how language, legal frameworks, and customary law shape access to justice, legal interpretation, and policy development, highlighting challenges in multilingual legal contexts and legislative reforms.

Chapter 14, by Donovan Pitt and Lloyd Matenga, examines the impact of language policies in South Africa's legal system, comparing them to Arizona and Virginia in the USA. It explores historical language dominance, constitutional protections, and linguistic rights in courts and education. Despite multilingual policies, English remains dominant, affecting jurisprudence and governance. The chapter highlights challenges in achieving true linguistic equality within South Africa's legal and educational frameworks.

Chapter 15, by Endurance K.M. Dissake, explores the role of oral legal traditions as an effective peacebuilding mechanism, using the customary court proceedings of the Banen community in Cameroon as a case study. The chapter critiques Western peacebuilding models, arguing that customary laws, deeply embedded in African culture and language, were historically more effective in conflict resolution. Through ethnographic and linguistic analysis, the study highlights five key peacebuilding themes – Spirituality, Brotherhood, Endorse, Conciliation, and Deference – demonstrating how indigenous legal traditions foster social harmony and sustainable peace.

Chapter 16, by Happyness Nokwatu Raselabe, critically examines language barriers in South African courtrooms, using the 1959 trial of Sityodana Mseswa under the Witchcraft Suppression Act (WSA) of 1957 as a case study. The chapter explores how misinterpretation and linguistic exclusion during legal proceedings disadvantaged indigenous language speakers, undermining justice. By analysing archival records, lexicographical gaps, and cultural misunderstandings, the study highlights the Eurocentric bias in South African law, advocating for forensic linguistics and language transformation in the judiciary to ensure equitable legal representation for all linguistic communities.

Chapter 17, by Hlohlolo Sephiri, explores the translation of legally drafted wills into Indigenous African Languages (IALs) in South Africa. With most wills written in English or Afrikaans, many beneficiaries struggle to comprehend legal terminology, leading to misinterpretation and disputes. Through a mixed-methods study, the chapter highlights the need for multilingual legal documentation to ensure language equity and accessibility, aligning with constitutional language rights and the Use of Official Languages Act 12 of 2012 for greater legal inclusivity.

Chapter 18, by Daniel Green, analyses public legal discourses on the amendment of the Austrian Nazi Prohibition Act of 1947. Through a qualitative corpus-assisted discourse analysis of 51 statements from legal scholars, institutions, NGOs, and private individuals, the chapter explores differing perspectives on the law's effectiveness, fairness, and implementation. Key themes include legal consistency, resource constraints, and ideological criticism. The study underscores the law's role in combating Nazi ideology, hate speech, and extremism, reinforcing democratic safeguards in Austria. The chapter provides parallel examples relating to South Africa and the discriminatory laws of Apartheid and the far reaching effects into the democratic period.

Concluding remarks

Appropriately, this book commences with practical insights of court intermediaries. The first chapter highlights the linguistic barriers and challenges imposed on child witnesses, focusing specifically on sexual crimes. The chapter sets the tone for the book, while also focusing on the gender-based violence scourge and the role of language therein.

With almost all chapters contributing practical insights, the chapters grounded in theory are aimed at highlighting the legal linguistic challenges from a historical to contemporary perspective. These chapters offer new approaches to ensuring linguistic equality in African and international legal systems.

With this book focusing on the African continent, international case studies are included to ensure broader research applicability and growth of the discipline.

The book will appeal to legal professionals, forensic and legal linguists, and researchers and students with a particular interest in advancing the rights of all persons equally within legal systems and professions.

PART I

The Language of Complainants and Witnesses

1 SERVICES TO THE CHILD WITNESS IN A MULTILINGUAL SOUTH AFRICA WITH A MONOLINGUAL LEGAL JUSTICE SYSTEM: A PRACTICAL PERSPECTIVE

Fiona van Wyk & Tasneemah Cornelissen-Nordien

Introduction

It is an unfortunate fact that South African children are frequently exposed and subjected to high levels of crime and violence, particularly of a sexual nature. Consequently, there is an ever-increasing number of child victims and witnesses who must testify about these crimes in court. Alarmingly, the age of child victims and witnesses before the courts is decreasing (Bekink, 2018), thus sometimes subjecting very young children to the secondary trauma which testifying may cause. The highly adult-orientated, confrontational, and adversarial justice system applied in South African courts is gruelling and traumatic for child victims and witnesses (Muller & Hollely, 2000), therefore aggravating secondary trauma. This is particularly so because 'children are by their very nature ill-equipped to deal with the court setting and its demands' (Bekink, 2018: 39). Not only are children naturally ill-equipped to manage the court proceedings – they also do not have the necessary mother-tongue vocabulary to express themselves clearly and unambiguously. Child witnesses often reside in communities in which colloquial language is spoken which is riddled with words and phrases unfamiliar to the court, thus making them less likely to be understood. The issue of being understood (as faced by child victims and witnesses) was further complicated in 2017 by a directive by the then-chief justice, that English alone should be the language of the courts. This is despite rendering services in a multilingual country with eleven official languages, notwithstanding sign language and colloquial languages. Thus, 'complicated' language and the use thereof add to the burden and trauma experienced, in addition to the physical, mental, and intellectual disabilities that are risk factors which led these child victims and/or witnesses to be in court (Cornelissen-Nordien, 2019). All these factors highlight the need for support services to the child witness.

Victim empowerment and support

Fortunately, much progress has been made to support child victims and witnesses and to make testifying in court a less harrowing experience. This is evident in policy documents, including the National Policy Guidelines for Victim Empowerment (VEP) (RSA, 2009). In accordance with the VEP, various victim empowerment and support programmes are implemented at court which provide court preparation services, debriefing, and pre- and after-care services to witnesses and their caregivers (RSA, 2009). These programmes aim to empower the child with skills and knowledge of court processes which enables them to understand and participate in the process of testifying. However, these services do not adequately address the use of language by the child, which is at the core of communication during testimony.

The empowerment services, which are mainly court readiness preparation for children, are offered by Court Preparation Officers (CPOs) employed by the National Prosecuting Authority and court supporters, who are volunteers trained and managed by NGOs such as Childline, LifeLine, RAPCAN, and Jelly Beanz. These NGOs provide referral services, victim empowerment, court-readiness preparation, and the teaching of stress-relief and coping mechanisms to support and empower the child witness. These services are used as resources and coordinated at the various courts so as to offer support and not overwhelm the child witnesses with the plethora of role players in the court system. In fact, the coordination of these services is aimed at offering a multidisciplinary, integrated, and holistic service to promote the overall well-being of the child witness (RSA, 2009). Great care is taken to prevent the infliction of secondary trauma, or possibly influencing or manipulating the witness; thus, the merits of the case are avoided and issues related to the use of language are not addressed. This is of importance to avoid secondary trauma and to retain the focus on empowering the child with the knowledge of the court procedures and the functions of the various role players in the court, including that of the intermediary.

Court intermediary

The court intermediary provides empowerment and support services to the child witness/victim who testifies in camera, by comforting and supporting the child witness during testimony and facilitating the communication between the court and the child testifying via closed circuit television facilities (Criminal Procedure Act 51, of 1977).

According to section 170A of the Criminal Procedure Act 51 of 1977, the appointment of intermediaries to support children is indicated specifically 'whenever criminal proceedings are pending before any court and it appears to such court that it would expose any witness under the biological or mental age of eighteen years to undue mental stress or suffering if he or she testifies at such proceedings, the court may, subject to subsection (4), appoint a competent person as an intermediary in order to enable such witness to give his or her evidence through that intermediary.'

This support service was further extended on 28 January 2022 as an amendment was made to section 51 of The Magistrate's Courts Act, 1944, by the insertion of sections 51A, 51B and 51C after section 51 in Act 32 of 1944, which permits 'evidence through intermediaries in proceedings other than criminal proceedings' and furthermore makes provision for a wider category of vulnerable witnesses by including adults who suffer from physical, psychological, mental, or emotional conditions as well as older persons as defined in section 1 of the Older Persons Act 13 of 2006 (Older Persons Act 13, 2006) (Government Gazette, 2022). It is thus evident that victim empowerment is highly regarded and acknowledged in policy and legislative documents. With these amendments, the role of intermediaries is validated as not only necessary for assisting witnesses but also as invaluable to the courts, as it promotes improved participation and a positive and expedient testimony process to those who might otherwise experience difficulty in the harsh and formalistic court environment.

Currently, court intermediaries are mainly social workers and former teachers who are experienced in working with children, have knowledge about childhood development, and, more specifically, child language development. Understanding childhood development and language learning processes are essential in establishing rapport with the child during the relationship-building phase. The timeframe within which court intermediaries have to build rapport is often very limited which puts them under pressure to make quick and accurate assessments of the linguistic ability and comprehension level of the child witness. This role is one almost exclusively fulfilled by the intermediary who is usually the only role player in the court formally qualified in childhood development. This can be argued as problematic within court proceedings, due to the limited role of the intermediary. The main focus of the intermediary, although not legally trained, is to deal with children in the court environment with special emphasis on court language (legalese), the child's understanding thereof, and how to simplify what is said in a manner acceptable to all role players. Emphasis within courts is placed on court language and the understanding thereof and not on the child witness' use of language. Despite this disjuncture, the intermediary retains a key role in the court process as a linguistic support service to the child witness.

Essentially, the role of intermediaries is two-fold. Firstly, intermediaries are a resource mandated by the court to assist child witnesses during the testimony process and to mitigate and shield the child witness from secondary traumatisation or re-victimisation, which refers to excessive stress or 'undue mental stress' they may experience from retelling and thus reliving the traumatic event (Maniglio, 2009; Schoeman, 2006). While listening to how and what a child testifies, an intermediary is able to gauge and form an understanding of the impact of the trauma suffered. They may afterwards attempt to promote the well-being of the child witness by providing a support and referral service to professional help and counselling where necessary.

The second important task of an intermediary is to facilitate the interaction which takes place between the court and child witness. The intermediary interprets and simplifies messages from the court, which may be difficult for the child to understand given their developmental level, into language suitable for the child's level of understanding in order to encourage and facilitate more effective testimony. However, the intermediary is not at liberty to interpret or clarify the child's testimony, even if the child witness is misunderstood by the court. This is particularly notable, given that the child testifies in their mother-tongue (i.e. mainly Afrikaans or isiXhosa) and is interpreted to the court via court-appointed interpreter, who may not have an understanding of the colloquial or slang language spoken by the child witness. It is usually during cross-examination that this becomes of particular relevance, and it is expected that this part of the testimony is more difficult for a child witness. However, the child's lack of understanding will be evident right from the onset of proceedings, depending on the development of the child or merely the nature and the complexity of the use of language in court.

For example, when the presiding officer attempts to ascertain whether the child will be a truthful witness, one of the questions often posed is:

> 'Do you know the difference between truth and lies?'

If the child answers 'No', he/she is not required to explain further because then the presiding officer will enter into a line of questioning which determines the child's understanding of this concept. However, should the answer be 'Yes', the very next question is usually:

> 'What is the difference?'

Very few young children are able to verbalise an answer to this question regardless of the fact that they might know what lies are and what telling the truth means. Although the presiding officer will usually clear this up, the young witness may be left feeling stressed and anxious, thinking that they were not able to answer even simple questions. One could achieve this part of competency testing by merely simplifying the questions to 'Do you understand what lies are?'; 'Do you know what telling the truth means?'; 'Can you give an example of a lie or truth?'; or the court could provide simple examples and ask the child witness to say whether it is a lie or truth. According to Bekink (2018) attempts are made towards 'meaningful legal reform' especially with regards to competency testing; however, court intermediaries have yet to see this achieved in a more child-friendly yet effective manner.

Intermediaries assist the communication process by simplifying, clarifying, smoothing over, and straightening out, so to speak, although they themselves are not really active participants in the court dialogue in the true sense of the word. The role of intermediaries is restricted to conveying the general purport of what was said or asked and they may not enter into any clarifying line of questioning or conversation with the child witness themselves. They, thus, rely on prosecutors to be alert to misunderstandings, miscommunications, or misinterpretations which arise; keeping in mind, as will be discussed later, that the child is not privy to how his/her words are received or understood inside the courtroom. This break in communication, too, may be stressful to the child witness and a potential cause for anxiety, as the child is essentially in the dark. This sense of being uninformed of the communication inside the courtroom may not always be in the best interest of the child as is intended. The intermediary is ideally positioned to mitigate any anxiety which might potentially arise, however, given the limited nature of their role, this is not always fully possible.

Acting in the best interest of the child as per the South African Constitution (RSA, 1996) is often riddled with obstacles as not all court role players are holistically in agreement about how to protect the delicate psyche of the child witness. This is despite an array of policy and legislative documents acknowledging the vulnerability of children in South Africa such as (the) White Paper for Social Welfare (RSA, 1997); WHO, 2003; Children's Act 38, of 2005; ISDM, 2006; Framework for Social Welfare Service, 2013. Furthermore, the appointment of an intermediary is done at the discretion of the presiding officer. This decision may be based on several factors including a desirability report, victim impact statement, and possible objections from opposing counsel amongst others. Therefore, whether the child, in their opinion, will experience undue mental stress when testifying in an open court in front of the alleged perpetrator or not is dependent on the decision of the presiding officer. Often in making this decision not enough consideration is given to the negative effects stress induces on speech, listening ability, concentration, and comprehension even in circumstances outside of the foreboding courtroom environment. It could be argued that this decision is based purely on a legal perspective with insufficient regard to and understanding of child and language development. Language is of particular relevance given the current directives for language use in South African courts.

Court language directive – 2017

In 2017 the then-chief justice, Mogoeng Mogoeng, issued a directive that English should be the sole language used for proceedings in the South African High Courts (Docrat et al., 2021). The multilingual context in which the court functions extends beyond the officially recognized languages of South Africa, as vernacular languages should also be granted due consideration. Consideration of other official, unofficial, and vernacular languages (including dialects and slang) is essential because it forms part of the everyday speech of many witnesses before the court and ignoring its use and value may place an additional burden on intermediary and interpretation services. Without due consideration to everyday spoken language and slang words, the true meaning of the evidence given by a child witness may be lost as children with limited vocabulary often do not know any other 'proper' words to use instead. This notion of 'proper' words is an important consideration, as meaning is often lost in testimony when utterances are incorrectly understood and incorrectly interpretated by the court. This is often without the knowledge of the child, given the 'in camera' testimony and from a separate room, the child is left in the dark, not knowing if the court's understanding is a true reflection of what they are saying. This is therefore not in the best interest of the child in accordance with section 28(2) of the Constitution (RSA, 1996) which stipulates that 'a child's best interests are of paramount importance in every matter concerning the child.' The intermediary may be best placed to ensure that the child's testimony is correctly understood and/or interpreted, but this is not their role.

Furthermore, this directive is seemingly oblivious to the linguistic ability and background of role players other than possibly assuming that legally trained parties should be proficient in English. The English language proficiency of interpreters, intermediaries, child, and other vulnerable witnesses was not taken into account and no consideration was expressed regarding the difficulties which might arise as a result. It becomes the responsibility of the interpreters, who by the very nature of their job are mainly non-mother tongue speakers of English, to make all court proceedings understandable to all parties involved.

It is apparent that the Cape Winelands district is particularly negatively impacted by the language directive, more specifically the lower courts, as the majority of role players including perpetrators and complainants are either Afrikaans or isiXhosa speakers, in line with the language demographics (South Africa Gateway, 2021). Until recently, court cases in the Cape Winelands area were conducted mainly in Afrikaans in the best interest of the Afrikaans-speaking child witnesses. It was considered more prudent and expedient to conduct cases in Afrikaans when the child witness is Afrikaans speaking. The directive to conduct all court cases in English directly impacts on court intermediaries who are expected to be equally fluent in both English and the language of the child in order to be able to assess whether the child's intent is correctly understood and interpreted back to the court. In addition to this, the court intermediary has to be au fait with legal jargon and be able to 'interpret' this into language suited to the child's level of understanding. This is a rather tall order considering that none of the 23 court intermediaries currently employed in the Western Cape, although fluent in English, are English mother-tongue speakers. It must be noted again that court intermediaries are not legally or linguistically trained, and the onus is upon them to familiarise themselves with court terminology and expressions, and much of this knowledge is gained through in-service training, experience, and self-education. The intermediary relies on the context, the prosecutor, and the court interpreter for clarification if they do not understand legal terminology. It is often found that prosecutors use much simpler, child-friendly language when addressing child witnesses, while opposing counsel use more legal terminology and formal language as part of their strategy, thus not acting in the best interest of the child.

Additionally, in areas such as the Western Cape where the majority of the population are Afrikaans (49.7%) with 24.7% isiXhosa speakers and the minority of 20.3% English (South Africa Gateway, 2021), language demographics in relation to the courts should be taken into consideration. This is particularly relevant as the vast majority of child witnesses before the Western Cape courts are either Afrikaans or isiXhosa mother-tongue speakers; therefore the use of interpreters became mandatory. The court intermediary must always be fluent in the language of the child witness, but other than in Zimbabwe, (Muller & Marowa-Wilkerson, 2011) the South African court intermediary is not sworn-in as a court interpreter as well and therefore does not perform a dual function.

A very concerning issue which appears to go unnoticed is when cases are for some reason not conducted in English and an interpreter is not employed, the records (before submission to the High Court for review or appeal purposes) are referred for translation into English to the outsourced party which offers the cheapest quotation. Such a translation service might potentially translate without due consideration to meaning or context or understanding of the colloquial language usage of the child witness. Before submission to the High Court, the translated records are rarely read, verified, or edited by any of the parties initially involved in the matter. There is thus no guarantee that the original meaning or intent of what was said was preserved in translation. The best interest of a child witness is therefore again compromised.

Court interpreters

Interpreters have become an integral part of court proceedings as cases must either be conducted in English or interpreted into English. As mentioned earlier, the vast majority of interpreters (Cape Winelands area) although fluent, are not mother-tongue speakers of either English or Afrikaans which are two of the main spoken languages in the area (except for isiXhosa, which was never regarded as an official language of the court). Apart from having to be fluent in at least two official languages and undergoing advanced training in court interpretation, it is not a requirement for court interpreters to possess any higher language training or understanding of child language development. Besides, unless living in the area where the child witnesses come from, interpreters cannot be expected to know and understand all of the slang words and strange forms of expression which seem to be made up and evolve daily.

Furthermore, interpreters act as language conduits and merely interpret what they hear,as it is being said by and to parties in court, and do not speak directly to the child witness or the intermediary. When an interpreter has little understanding of the dialect or slang of the child witness before the court, he is challenged to fully grasp the child's intended meaning and could therefore potentially incorrectly translate and cause misunderstanding in the court. Such an interpreter may simply translate or interpret the general purport of what is said and may lack the insight required to express the exact intent and impact of the words spoken by the child witness, often leaving it to the court to grasp the nuances in meaning, tone, and context.

It is often expected from the child witness to clarify what he/she means. If colloquial or slang is the only language known to the child, they are unable to offer clarity or provide the 'proper' words for what they mean or what is being described. This inability to clarify, explain, and describe by using more acceptable or sophisticated words places the child at a disadvantage during testimony and potentially causes feelings of inadequacy, undue distress, and further trauma.

The intermediary, through their lived experiences, become familiar with the dialect and slang words used by children in the area and are able to clarify and bridge the resulting linguistic gap with ease. Intermediaries may, however, not interpret (as in Zimbabwe) and have a limited speaking role in court proceedings. A child witness must deliver their testimony first hand. Intermediaries may indicate when the child is misunderstood but may only clarify or provide input when called upon to do so.

Serious miscomprehension problems arise when the presiding officer and/or other role players within the courtroom also do not speak or understand the child's language. The intended meaning of some colloquial Afrikaans or isiXhosa words simply do not have English equivalents and may take some time and effort to fully explain.

For example, if a child were to say in Afrikaans '*Ek was eers saam met my niggie en toe met my neef*', the direct English translation would be: 'I was first with my cousin and then with my cousin.'

In *S v Opperman* (2021), Paarl, PSB145/21, the interpreter interpreted this Afrikaans statement into English as follows: 'I was first with my cousin sister and then with my cousin brother.'

Although the interpreter understood the gender difference, English does not have separate words for male and female cousins, leaving the interpreter to make that distinction as it is done in isiXhosa. However, this might still cause confusion where people might think the interpreter means 'cousin's sister or cousin's brother' and the intended meaning would be completely distorted. The interpreter, in essence, is the most important language facilitator in the courts and their linguistic abilities may determine how well the child witness is understood by the court.

Misunderstanding and misinterpreting the child witness

As a practicing intermediary, the frequent lapses in understanding the intended meaning of a child witness are observed and is a constant source of concern. These issues are not always adequately addressed as and when they arise. Where misinterpretations and misunderstandings are left unclarified, it may potentially affect the outcome of a case.

Confusion often results from words child witnesses use for body parts, especially genitalia. Young children often do not know or refuse to utter the proper names for genitalia for various reasons including social taboos.

It is often experienced that when children are required to explain something for which they lack the proper words they use the slang or colloquial words which they are familiar with. The use of slang words can cause confusion and misunderstanding and could completely change the intended meaning.

To mention one example from Afrikaans: the Afrikaans word '*boude*' is 'buttocks' in English. However, the child witnesses who appear in the Cape Winelands courts use the slang word '*stêrre*' to refer to buttocks, and '*boude*' is used exclusively to refer to 'thighs'.

Questioning the child witness on an issue involving these words could potentially have the following result:

Child witness: '*Hy het aan my stêrre gevat.*' (i.e., He touched my buttocks.)

Defence: '*Bedoel jy hy het aan jou boude gevat?*' (Do you mean he touched your buttocks?)

Child: '*Nee, hy het nie aan my boude gevat nie.*' (No he did not touch my buttocks.)

Defence: '*Verstaan ons nou reg? Hy het nie aan jou boude gevat nie?*' (Do we understand correctly? He did not touch your buttocks?)

Child: '*Ja.*' (Yes.)

The child's meaning is misunderstood because of using words in a way other than what is commonly accepted as Standard Afrikaans and it is up to the interpreter to clarify the child's intended meaning (if the interpreter her/himself grasped the meaning of the slang words).

Intermediaries, although they may raise concerns in this regard, are mere instruments of the court and not really active participants in the dialogue (as illustrated in Figure 1.1 below) and as such have a very limited scope for intervening and explaining when the child's words, meaning, or intent has been misunderstood. Opposing counsel in particular may take issue with intermediaries becoming too involved and may view them as interfering and not as impartial as they should be. All the speakers within the courtroom, barring the interpreter whose only role is to interpret and translate, are legal experts; keeping in mind that intermediaries are not inside the courtroom but in the CCTV room with the child witness. This places the burden on the child witness to make themselves understood within the court action system, as illustrated below.

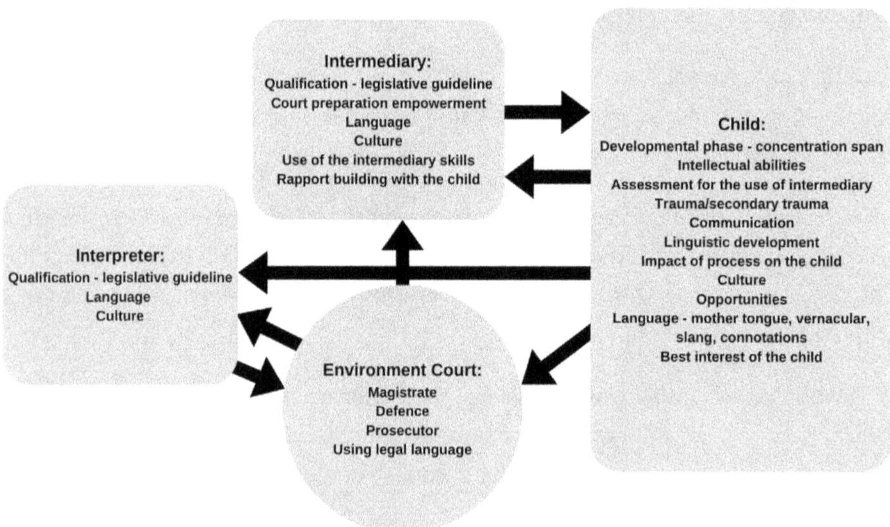

FIGURE 1.1: The court as an action system

Figure 1.1 illustrates the interactions within the court hearing process demonstrating various role players which form part of the action system. It is evident that there are many communication processes between role players, but the child witness, however, seems isolated. The court (referring to the presiding officer, the prosecutor, and the defence attorney) speaks to the child via the intermediary but in response the child speaks directly (into the microphone) to the court.

As the diagram illustrates, the child who testifies via closed circuit television with a court intermediary does not see or hear anyone except for the intermediary next to them. They do not receive direct feedback from the courtroom and the child witness does not know whether his/her message was received the way it was intended and therefore relies heavily on cues and feedback from the intermediary. The child witness has to trust the intermediary for reassurance, therefore building proper rapport with a child witness before testimony is essential. The intermediary in turn is very limited in terms of what feedback they may provide to the child witness, as side conversations while court is in progress is disallowed.

Regardless of having the intermediary as a comfort person, the child witness may feel very isolated and anxious as they must speak for themselves using their own words and may not ask the intermediary for assistance with what they want to say. Young children are expected to put into words that which they cannot yet fully comprehend and for which they might not yet have the vocabulary as is often the case in sexual offence matters. When the child is misunderstood, they are expected to explain and clarify themselves to the court. They have to do this by either using other words or using their words differently to how they used it initially which is extremely difficult for a child with limited vocabulary and means of expression. Whether they can make themselves understood is highly dependent on a variety of factors which includes developmental level, frame of reference, level of intelligence, schooling, culture, beliefs, and even taboos amongst others. Younger children may resort to pointing and gesturing which is usually not encouraged (unless demonstrating with anatomically detailed dolls) and even this may potentially be misunderstood.

This is an undue system which may be exploited by unscrupulous opposing counsel who may use this aspect to their advantage by showing little regard for the child's language developmental phase and aspects of diversity from which the child resides. Thus, the best interest of the child is seemingly irrelevant and disregarded.

Furthermore, the child witness gains no direct feedback from the court and relies solely on input, prompting and feedback from the intermediary. The intermediary hardly ever speaks as first-person during court proceedings, but rather relays the general purport of what is said or asked from inside the courtroom. With very young witnesses the intermediary might be able to keep up the pretence of direct conversation between her and the child only, but the stilted and unnatural flow of conversation is easily noticed by the child witness. It is the experience of this intermediary that the best practice is to openly and honestly explain the process of testimony and how the speaking turns work before testimony commences.

In considering that communication according to Johnson and Yanca (2010) and Hepworth, Rooney, Rooney, Strom-Gottfried, and Larsen (2023) is a process with a beginning, middle, and end as is illustrated in Figure 1.2 below, it is easy to see how the child witness, especially the younger ones, may become lost in the process.

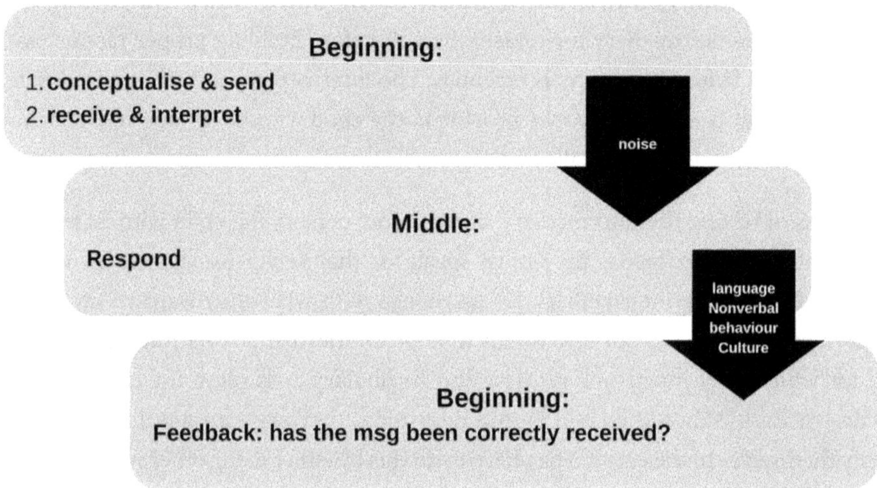

FIGURE 1.2: The communication process (Adapted from Johnson & Yanca, 2010)

Due to the monolingual court system, the communication process illustrated above takes place multiple times to relay a single message between role players. There is a back-and-forth turn-taking process between speakers of which the child is unaware. For example: the prosecutor asks a question to the child – the interpreter interprets the question – the intermediary then puts the question to the child in child-friendly language – the interpreter interprets what the intermediary said – the child answers the question – the interpreter interprets the child's answer; and the whole process repeats itself until the child's testimony is complete. The child who only hears the intermediary experiences these lapses in conversation as 'noise' during which he may become distracted or bored.

In understanding communication in line with childhood development it is evident that a response, feedback, acknowledgement, and the need to please authority are important aspects to consider when communicating with children. In the court process however, it would appear that the communication process only has a beginning for the child witness (a question is asked by the intermediary and the child answers into the microphone). There is no immediate acknowledgement of what was said and no immediate response or feedback (apart perhaps from the encouraging looks and nods from the intermediary). The communication process that takes place inside the courtroom cannot be heard by the child who may experience the unnatural silence as only 'noise' or an abrupt end to the communication. This could be seen as a pitfall within the process for the child as some child witnesses experience this peculiar flow of conversation particularly unnerving and the intermediary must reassure them by saying something like 'They are not talking to us now' or 'They are talking to one another.'

The intermediary is ideally placed and suited to provide feedback to the child witness, but the required impartiality and formality of court processes prohibits constant side conversations during proceedings. Intermediaries may often find themselves, especially after a rather long discussion by parties within the courtroom, repeating what was last said to or by the child to remind, recap, and regain the child's attention. The duty of the intermediary is constantly challenged with the need to remain impartial while at the same time retaining the child witness' attention and also offering comfort and support.

The complex nature of the communication process within the court can further be complicated by diversity elements including vernacular and legal language (legalese and courtroom jargon), which can be and is often misunderstood and therefore misinterpreted by the more inexperienced interpreter or one not au fait with that vernacular. Incorrect intermediary and interpretation processes may impede the smooth running of proceedings and may even interfere with the outcomes of a trial. Intermediaries and interpreters may convey the general gist of the question, but they have an extremely limited scope within which they can move and manipulate language so as not to change meanings or pose leading questions which may solicit incorrect answers or raise objections from within the courtroom.

Conclusion

Surely court proceedings and the intermediary process will have less hinderance if one particular language is not favoured as the only language to be used in courts. Children should not have to bear the responsibility of our monolingual court system, as it is not in their best interest and causes undue stress. The burden of understanding them and making sense of what they are saying should be on the adults within the court and not on the young child witness with limited vocabulary and no or very little knowledge of court proceedings. The Children's Act 38 of 2005 emphasizes the importance of children to South African society and that they should be placed at the centre of service delivery. More should thus be done in the South African legal system to support this goal by employing all of its adult resources to support a child witness, not just physically and emotionally but also linguistically. Court intermediaries are in the perfect position to get proper information from child witnesses; firstly, because they build a relationship of trust with them, and secondly, because they speak the same language and know most or all those slang words and expressions used by the children. This will enable the child to express him/herself freely without the pressure of feeling like he/she is doing an oral examination for marks. Proceedings will progress faster and more effectively if a child witness can relax and say what they want to say in their usual way of speaking without worrying that they would have to explain themselves later. To achieve this end, court intermediaries should be granted a greater role in child testimony than just being mere 'conduits.'

References

African Charter on Rights and Welfare of the Child. (1990). Available at: https://au.int/en/treaties/african-charter-rights-and-welfare-child [Date accessed: 2 May 2025].

Bekink, M. (2018). 'The Testimonial Competence of Children: A Need for Law Reform in South Africa.' PER/PELJ2018(21) https://doi.org/10.17159/1727-3781/2018/v21i0a3407

Cornelissen-Nordien, T. (2019). Empowerment services for sexually abused children offered by non-profit organisations in the Western Cape. [Doctoral dissertation] Stellenbosch University.

Docrat, Z., Kaschula, RH. & Ralarala, MK. (2021). *A Handbook on Legal Languages and the quest for linguistic equality in South Africa and beyond*. African Sun Media: Stellenbosch.

Government Gazette: Act no.12 of 2021 'Evidence through intermediaries in proceedings other than criminal proceedings.' No.45822, 28 January 2022.

Hepworth, DH., Larsen, J., Rooney, RH., Rooney, G., & Strom-Gottfried, K. (2023). *Direct Social Work Practice: Theory and Skills* (9th edition). United States: Brooks/Cole.

Hollely, K & Muller, K. (2000). *Introducing the Child Witness*. Port Elizabeth: Printrite.

Johnson, LC. & Yanca, SJ. (2010). *Social Work Practice. A Generalist Approach* (9th edition). Toronto: Allyn & Bacon Inc.

Maniglio, R. (2009). Severe mental illness and criminal victimization: a systematic review. Acta Psychiatr Scand.

Marowa-Wilkerson, T. & Muller, K. (2011). An innovative approach to the use of intermediaries: lessons from Zimbabwe. Child Abuse Research in South Africa, 12(2) 13-24.

Republic of South Africa (RSA). 1996. *Constitution of the Republic of South Africa*. Pretoria: Government Printer.

Republic of South Africa (RSA). 2006. *Integrated service delivery model (ISDM) towards improved social services*. Pretoria: Government Printer.Available at: https://www.gov.za/documents/other/service-delivery-model-developmental-social-welfare-services-01-jan-2006 [Date accessed: 2 May 2025].

Republic of South Africa (RSA). 2013. *Framework for Social Welfare Services*. Pretoria: Government Printer.

Republic of South Africa (RSA). (1977). *Criminal Procedure Act 51 of 1977*. Pretoria: Government Printer.

Republic of South Africa (RSA). (2005). C*hildren's Act 38 of 2005.* Pretoria: Government Printer.

Republic of South Africa (RSA). (2006). *Older Persons Act 13 of 2006.* Pretoria: Government Printer.

Republic of South Africa (RSA). (1997). *White Paper for Social Welfare.* Pretoria: Government Printer

Schoeman, UC. (2006). A Training Program for Intermediaries for the Child Witness in South African Courts. [Doctoral dissertation] University of Pretoria.

South African Gateway, 2021. What languages are spoken in South Africa's nine provinces? Available at: https://southafrica-info.com/infographics/animation-languages-south-africas-provinces/ [Date accessed: 2 May 2025].

S v Opperman (2021)

2

DO NOT LAY WORDS IN MY MOUTH: LINGUISTIC ANALYSIS AS PART OF THE TESTIMONY IN A DISPUTE RESOLUTION CASE

Annelise de Vries & Karien Brits

Contextualisation

In this chapter, the focus is on linguistic analysis as part of the testimony in a dispute resolution case. The authors of the chapter were approached during the first half of 2022 to act as expert witnesses. This case caused quite a sensation in the media when on 6 July 2022 the verdict was announced in favour of Solidarity, which had acted on behalf of the teacher Anneke Smit (Nanni, 2022; Netwerk24, 2022; Smit, 2022). Similar disputes involving linguistic interpretation in legal cases have been observed in other multilingual jurisdictions, such as Canada, Australia and the USA, where legal systems must navigate the complexities of language variation and interpretation in court proceedings (Borrows, 2001; Levi, 1994; McKerracher, 2023; Rusho, 2021; Solan & Tiersma, 2002: 226).

Background of the case

Background is briefly provided regarding the case *Solidarity obo Anneke Smit v Education Department of Gauteng* (2022) heard by the Education Labour Relations Council (ELRC). Solidarity acted as the applicant on behalf of Anneke Smit and the Gauteng Department of Education was the respondent.

The allegation (which is of importance for the chapter) against which Solidarity appealed in this case is that on 23 August 2019, Anneke Smit while employed as a teacher at Montana High School had displayed 'improper, scandalous or unacceptable conduct' by calling a learner a 'police monkey' (*Solidarity obo Anneke Smit v Education Department of Gauteng*, 2022: 2).

The disciplinary hearing was held on 21 and 22 October 2020 and 3 February 2021. The applicant was found guilty. The following, from the testimony summarised in the verdict rendered on 6 July 2022, is important for the analysis (*Solidarity obo Anneke*

Smit v Education Department of Gauteng, 2022:3-7). One of the learners testified that the applicant spoke English and Afrikaans intermittently, especially when admonishing someone.

One view was that 'police monkey' refers to a monkey in the police. According to this learner, 'monkey' was an offensive (rude) word, and 'police' was merely an adjective. Another learner testified that they had never before heard the combination of 'police monkey' as an insult to black people, but that 'monkey' is disparaging (derogatory) if white people use it regarding black people. The learner testified that it did not sound like '*polisiemannetjie*' until another learner pointed it out. The word '*mannetjie*' was also problematic for the learners because according to them it referred to a male animal.

The applicant often had disciplinary problems with the specific class. The class misbehaved again on 23 August 2019 when she used the word '*polisiemannetjie*'. The principal stood outside the class, and the applicant sent one of the learners to go and call him because it seemed as if the learners always required someone for policing them. She could not immediately think of the correct word in English and then used the word '*polisiemannetjie*', coming from a rhyme that she had known for many years. One of the learners in the class helped her explain what she was saying.

The learner who laid the charge comes from a home where Setswana is spoken (Du Plessis, 2022), but did not testify during the disciplinary hearing in 2019. The utterance 'can someone go and call the principal because this class always needs a polisie mannetjie [sic]' was according to the applicant directed to the whole class and not to a specific learner.

The figure below is a graphic exposition that summarises the events regarding the dispute resolution case in question:

Research questions

From the information made available to the two authors beforehand and briefly summarised above, the authors used the following questions to guide the analysis.

1) What is the probability that the applicant had referred to a learner in a derogatory way as a monkey or a male animal in her utterance '*polisiemannetjie*'?
    a) What is the probability that '*polisiemannetjie*' sounds like 'police monkey'?
    b) What is the probability that if reference was made to a person as a '*mannetjie*', the person would by default be compared to a male animal?

Controversy about expert testimony

It is important to highlight the controversy about expert testimony and specifically linguistic testimony, especially when it comes to methodology and possible interpretations. According to Leonard et al. (2017: 882), specialised linguists can offer expert testimony to provide insight into legally significant language data, in the same way that experts could use biology and physics to provide insight regarding medical or ballistic data. Solan and Tiersma (2002) and Leonard et al. (2017: 883) stated that nowadays linguists are, in certain dispute resolution cases, permitted to render expert testimony about possible interpretations of texts being scrutinised – regardless of whether these texts contain written or spoken data. The method by means of which the text is analysed when a linguist acts as an expert witness is not subject to standardised procedures but rather depends on the nature of the text. Various methods of analysis with reference to theoretical linguistic fields such as phonetics and phonology, morphology, syntax, pragmatics, semantics, semiotics, and discourse analysis can be employed. These texts can also be analysed by means of linguistic theories such as, for instance, the speech act theory, the appraisal system theory, frame semantics, or the prototype theory.

Although there are various methods of analysing linguistic data, such testimony should essentially still comply with the criteria of the so-called Daubert standard (Kotzé, 2012: 2). The case in the USA, Daubert v Merrell Dow Pharmaceuticals, Inc. (1993), gave rise to the implementation of this standard. The Daubert standard is aimed at determining whether the scientific testimony of an expert is based on a scientifically valid argument or methodology that can be applied to the relevant facts. The factors to be taken into account, include: 1) whether or not the relevant theory or technique can be tested; 2) whether or not it was subjected to peer assessment and peer publication; 3) the familiar potential error margin; and 4) whether or not it is accepted over a wide spectrum within an applicable scientific community.

Edmonds-Smith and Lewis (2014) mentioned that although the Daubert standard is generally used in the USA, no tests are at present specified in South African law according to which expert testimony can be gauged. There is indeed South African jurisdiction regarding the nature and quality of expert testimony, but the problem often arises in the South African courts that such testimony is not relevant or that it gives preference to the point of view of one party over the other in a dispute resolution case.

Belavusau (2014) wrote that harnessing the testimony of experts was by far the only neutral method to make sense of texts in a legal context, but it is not general practice that a linguist is employed as expert witness during dispute resolutions. The latter is not only a deficiency in the South African context, but also in international law (Picornell, 2022).

Against this background, the authors considered the fact that linguistic expert testimony was indeed used to assist the ELRC to reach a decision, as a significant step in the right direction. Although there were no specified tests according to which expert testimony could be gauged in a South African legal context, the authors acted in a self-regulatory way during the rendering of the testimony and, as far as possible, complied with the criteria of the Daubert standard.

Research methodology

As explained earlier on in this chapter, the effectiveness of the expert testimony depends on the scientific accountability of inter alia the methodology followed during the analysis of the relevant utterances. For this reason, this section provides a thorough exposition of the methodology followed during the linguistic analysis as part of the dispute resolution in question. The role of linguistic expertise in legal proceedings has been recognised beyond South Africa, with courts in multilingual countries like Canada increasingly considering forensic linguistics in cases involving language disputes (e.g., translation discrepancies, meaning interpretation, and sociolinguistic contexts of utterances in courtroom settings) (Borrows, 2001; Levi, 1994; Solan & Tiersma, 2002: 226).

An interpretivist research paradigm was followed during the linguistic analysis. There are four reasons for applying this paradigm: 1) the ontological reason; 2) the epistemological reason; 3) the rhetorical reason; and 4) the methodological reason.

Seen from the ontological point of view, the interpretivist paradigm was applied because the authors approached the linguistic analysis in question from the point of view that the only reality is that which is interpreted by the individuals involved in the research situation (Bakkabulindi, 2015: 23). Thus, the authors are of the opinion that there are multiple realities in any given situation and this view was therefore followed in the broad linguistic analysis (see Figure 2.1). When reference is made to the epistemological reason for the chosen research paradigm, the observation of Bakkabulindi (2015: 23) comes into question that interpretivists should, in a holistic way, give an account of their research subjects/context. Such holistic accountability of the research subjects/context includes objectives, culture, experience, and history. As regards the rhetorical reason for the chosen paradigm, the relevant linguistic analysis reflects the subjective personality of the authors. Lastly, the methodology followed during the linguistic analysis can also be ascribed to the choice of research paradigm. Analyses take place in an inductive way where the authors observed certain phenomena and based on this observation had reached specific conclusions.

The research subject forthwith symbolises this interpretivist paradigm because a grounded theoretical methodology (which is, by implication, of an inductive nature) was used. This methodology was followed because the authors described a concept/

phenomenon within a context where no absolute theoretical framework was in existence to understand the concept/phenomenon (Taole & Van Wyk, 2015: 176).

As regards the research design, the authors judged that the grounded theoretical methodology was the most suitable methodology to answer the research question in this study. The research question required that a qualitative method had to be followed to determine the probability of whether or not the applicant had in a derogative way referred to a learner as a monkey or male animal in her utterance '*polisiemannetjie*'.

No primary data was gathered during this study; use was rather made of secondary, external data sources. Gasa et al. (2015: 357) stated that external data sources encompass published or unpublished text and computerised databases, and can be disclosed to authors by various organisations. In the case of this study, Solidarity (in this organisation's capacity as a trade union), that acted on behalf of the applicant, provided information to the authors. Information was in the first place provided to the authors via email (Du Plessis, 2022) in which the context of the case, which had at that stage already been in progress, was explained. The email was followed up with a consultation in person between the legal representative of Solidarity and the authors of this chapter. Lastly, a recording of the first day of the proceedings during the dispute resolution on 22 March 2022 (which took place virtually) was provided to the authors (Du Plessis, 2022).

These external data sources were used for data analysis. The authors mainly made use of a holistic, sociolinguistic approach towards data analysis. Sociolinguistics is a field of linguistics that studies language in the community and the actual use of language in various social environments (Baldauf, 2012: 237).

Various methods of linguistic analysis were applied as part of the sociolinguistic approach to the linguistic analysis in question. The methods of analysis are separated into two categories: 1) a cross-cultural analysis – an analysis of the language context of the expressions in question; and 2) a theoretical linguistic analysis of these expressions (see Figure 2.1).

In the first category ('a cross-cultural analysis – an analysis of the linguistic context of the utterances in question'), reference was made to the context of South African language usage with a specific focus on the phenomenon of code-switching (see the discussion under 'Data analysis and discussion'). The three codes that came into question during this cross-cultural analysis are Setswana, English, and Afrikaans. There was further reference to two theories that form part of the study of semantics. These theories encompass the semantic frame theory and the prototype theory. Briefly explained, the semantic frame theory entails that one cannot understand the meaning of a single word without access to all the essential knowledge related to that word (Petruck, 1996: 1). As regards the prototype theory, this is part of the field of cognitive linguistics that deals with categorising, and which posits that there is no absolute meaning attached to words and that words are notorious for being ambiguous and vague (Bergh & Carney, 2016: 486).

In a broader sense, reference was also made to the implicit association test of Álvarez-Mosquera (2017) (Implicit Association Test – IAT). This test encompasses an innovative, mixed-method approach that sets up correlations between reaction times as opposed to selected accents. Reference is made to linguistic background, exposure to language, and social distancing levels.

It is important to mention that the authors did not do a full analysis of the relevant utterances on the basis of the semantic frame theory, the prototype theory, and the IAT, but rather broadly referred to the principles of those theories and approaches as part of the cross-cultural analysis.

Aside from this, an analysis was made on the basis of some of the aspects of a theoretical linguistic study (second category of analysis – 'a theoretical linguistic analysis of these utterances'). Firstly, the utterances were considered on the word level (morphology), during which lexicography and corpus analysis were employed to draw certain conclusions. According to Stubbs (1996) a corpus analysis encompasses the analysis of systematic or randomly gathered and electronically stored language expressions with the purpose to draw conclusions from these. At the time of this study, use was made of thirteen different databases of Afrikaans text or expressions in the language (see Addendum: Corpora applied for corpus analysis). Besides this, a brief analysis was made of morphology in the Sintu languages, of which Setswana forms part, as part of the cross-cultural analysis that was followed. Lastly, reference was made to the phonetic similarities and differences between the words 'monkey' and '*mannetjie*' to conclude the theoretical linguistic analysis.

Figure 2.1 is a graphic presentation of the research methodology that was followed.

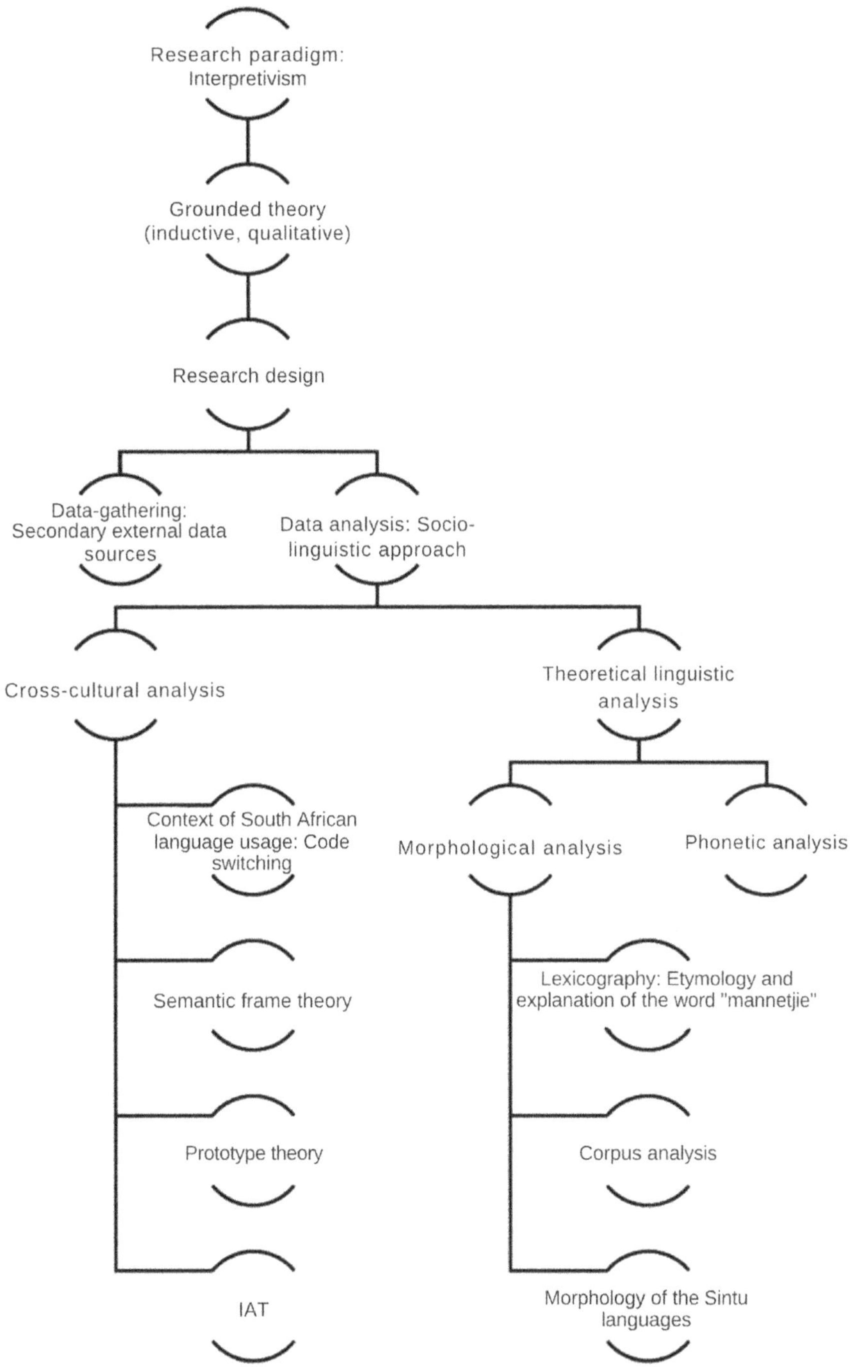

FIGURE 2.1: Graphic presentation of the research methodology

Data analysis and discussion

This section is handled in the same way in which the methodology was presented (see Figure 2.1). The findings and description of the cross-cultural analysis where the linguistic context of the expressions was calculated are first discussed, after which the findings of the theoretical linguistic analysis are explained.

- ### *Cross-cultural analysis: An analysis of the linguistic context of the expressions*
  - Code-switching and code-mixing

In reality, education in the broad South African context cannot be discussed without also referring to code-switching and code-mixing. It may not be the official policy of the Department of Education, but that is what takes place in practice. If we widen the lens, that which we see in schools is a reflection of the South African language landscape (Mabule, 2015). Code-switching, in the broadest sense, is the default position in South Africa. It is a kind of diglossia where permanent switching takes place among Sintu languages as well as Afrikaans and English (depending on the environment) as part of the language dynamics in South Africa. The focus of this chapter is not on attitudes towards code-switching and code-mixing (see more about this in Finlayson et al., 1998; Probyn, 2006; and Songxaba et al., 2017), but rather that it is a given in the language context within which the applicant found herself.

There are various definitions for code-switching and code-mixing and how these concepts can be differentiated, but for the purposes of this chapter it will be defined as follows: code-switching is the use of two or more linguistic varieties during the same conversation. It is when a speaker switches from language A to language B (Mabule, 2015). Linguistic varieties refer to different languages or varieties within one language. Code-mixing, according to Mabule (2015: 341), means expressions in which a mixture of the grammar of one language and another is used without altering the grammar of the first language that is used.

McCormick (2002: 217) differentiated between code-mixing and code-switching as follows: code-mixing means including shorter elements (often just a single word) and code-switching means including elements longer than one word of two different languages.

The applicant thus made use of code-mixing in this specific case, and it was in a broader context where code-mixing and code-switching are of the order of the day.

- Semantic frame theory (connotation and denotation)

As mentioned in the section regarding the methodology that was used, the semantic frame theory involves the idea that words/expressions cannot be interpreted in isolation, but that each word/expression rather represents a specific field of experience (Petruck, 1996: 1). In this instance, it is tantamount to denotation v connotation of a word/expression. When words/expressions are analysed by means of the semantic frame theory, the research objective is to reveal the reasons of a language community to create a specific reference represented by the word. To put it simply, the researcher must indicate what connotation a specific language community attaches to a specific word/expression and how it influences the reaction to the use of that word/expression. Lowe (1997: 18) explained that the semantic frame theory assumes that each word/expression contains a certain amount of own-world knowledge and that such knowledge can be set out in schematic form.

In the case of the first testimony that the respondent brought to the fore (see Figure 2.1: Graphic exposition contextualising the dispute resolution case. This figure illustrates the progressive stages of a dispute resolution case, moving from the initial conflict through structured steps toward a final resolution, as contextualised within a formal process).

, reference was made to the connotatively derogatory nature of the word 'monkey' – especially when a white person utters it to a black person. Therefore, when only this testimony is taken into account that the applicant had said 'police monkey', the conclusion can be made on the basis of the semantic frame theory that this statement was taken as derogatory or offensive by the black learners but was not necessarily intended as such by the white teacher.

When the respondent's testimony is taken into account that the teacher had not said 'monkey', but had indeed said '*mannetjie*', and that '*mannetjie*' is also derogatory or offensive because it equates the recipient of the message with a male animal, it can be concluded on the basis of the semantic frame theory that '*mannetjie*' elicits the connotative meaning of a male animal in view of the black recipient, but that the white sender of the message had not attached the same connotation to the word.

- Prototype theory

The prototype theory corresponds with the semantic frame theory in the sense that the actual knowledge of words/expressions ought to be unravelled and not just the dictionary meaning. The actual knowledge referred to here is influenced by inter alia the cultural and linguistic community of which we form part of. Carney (2016: 488) wrote that jurists often refer only to the dictionary meaning (lexical or denotative meaning) when establishing the most generally understood meaning of a word, but that the meaning most generally understood, and the dictionary meaning of a word/expression, are for the greater part not the same. The last-mentioned author suggests that the analysis of the words/expressions is, on the basis of the principles of the prototype theory, an effective method to determine the connotative meaning of the word/expression and that this method is not as one-sided as merely establishing the dictionary meaning of a word/expression.

In conjunction with the observation of Carney (2016: 488), the authors mention that the respondent's legal representative had, during the cross-examination of the expert testimony in the relevant dispute resolution case, physically looked up the word '*mannetjie*' in a dictionary and used it as the only method of determining the most generally accepted meaning thereof. In reaction to this, the experts rendered testimony that it is not academically and scientifically justifiable merely to refer to the lexical meaning of the word in order to draw significant conclusions. For this reason, the principles of the prototype theory are followed and form part of the cross-cultural and linguistic analysis in this study.

- Linguistic prejudice and the IAT

The usage of language is not a neutral event and thus the phenomenon of linguistic prejudice is discussed with reference to research by Kaschula (2021). In the literature study, quite some consideration was given to the role that accent plays in language prejudice. As already mentioned before, Álvarez-Mosquera (2017) and Álvarez-Mosquera and Marín-Gutiérrez (2018) did quite a lot of work by means of the implicit association test (or briefly, the IAT) in order to determine people's association with accent in the South African context. The IAT is widely considered as an effective method of establishing the strength of association between concepts and evaluations. It is especially a reliable method to assess attitudes towards language and to ascertain whether certain properties are associated with a social group due to the language variety they are using (Álvarez-Mosquera & Marín-Gutiérrez, 2018: 239).

Álvarez-Mosquera and Marín-Gutiérrez (2018) used the IAT inter alia to establish the language attitude of mother-tongue speakers of indigenous South African languages (the nine Sintu languages) in Cape Town towards the Afrikaans accent in English. The results indicated that the speakers of Sintu languages demonstrated more negative attitudes towards the Afrikaans accent than to the Standard South African English accent. The Afrikaans accent alone appears to trigger naturally negative attitudes (Álvarez-Mosquera & Marín-Gutiérrez, 2018: 246).

The IAT could of course not be undertaken with the learners, but the findings of the study should nevertheless be borne in mind in the context within which the utterances were analysed. The learners are speakers of Sintu languages, and the applicant is a native speaker of Afrikaans, who spoke in English to the learners. This could therefore have affected how they interpreted '*polisiemannetjie*'.

Theoretical linguistic analysis of the utterances

Morphological analysis

Lexicography: Etymology and explanation of the word '*mannetjie*'

As already mentioned in the contextualisation, one of the witnesses of the respondent testified that even if the applicant had said '*polisie mannetjie* [sic]' and not 'police monkey' (as one of the other witnesses had alleged), she had referred to the learner who laid the charge as a 'male animal' (see Table 2.1, block three 'witness 2'). This view was supported by the respondent's legal representative who had, during the cross-examination of the expert witnesses, read aloud from an outdated dictionary (see the discussion in this regard under 'Semantic frame theory').

To trump the view that if the word '*mannetjie*' is used during an interaction it by default means that the speaker equates the listener to a male animal, the authors did a lexicographic (dictionary) investigation. Four different types of authoritative sources were used to determine the etymology and explanation of the word '*mannetjie*':

1. The online version of the *Woordeboek van the Afrikaanse Taal* (WAT) (Botha, 2019) was used as encompassing dictionary.
2. The *Handwoordeboek van die Afrikaanse Taal* (HAT) (Luther et al., 2015) was used as a dictionary of definitions in a single volume.
3. The *Etimologiewoordeboek van Afrikaans* (Liebenberg et al., 2003) was used as specialised dictionary.
4. The *Pharos Afrikaans-Engels English-Afrikaans Woordeboek* (Pharos, 2010) was used as a bilingual dictionary.

A summary of the definition or translation of the word '*mannetjie*' is set out in the form of the table below. The definitions/translations are presented in the order of frequency of occurrence.

TABLE 2.1: Definition or translation of the word 'mannetjie' as sourced from four dictionaries

Definition/translation (according to frequency of occurrence)				
Freq.	WAT	HAT	Etymological dictionary	Pharos
1	Vkw. van man	[vkw.] klein(erige) man	Klein man	Male
2	Manlike dier, waaronder ook voëls, reptiele, visse, insekte, spinnekoppe, krappe. e.d., man-like plant	(geringskattend) kêreltjie	Manlike dier	Chappie, manikin, little fellow/man, (*infml.*) nipper
3	(dikw. as aanspreek- of verwysingsvorm wat irritasie uit-druk) Jong seun.	(biologie) man-like dier/plant	(as aanspreek- of verwysingsvorm om irritasie uit te druk) Jong seun	Young man

It appears from the above table that all four sources are in agreement about the three most frequent meanings of the word '*mannetjie*'. In all the sources there is consensus about the most frequent definition/translation of the lemma (diminutive of man). The second and third most frequent definition/translation of '*mannetjie*' vary in the sources. According to the WAT and the *Etimologiewoordeboek*, the second most frequent definition is a 'male animal', while the third most frequent definition in the above two sources refers to a form of address or a means of referring to something in such a way that it expresses irritation. The HAT and Pharos differ from the WAT and the *Etimologiewoordeboek* regarding the second and third most frequent definitions/translations of '*mannetjie*'.

It can be deduced that the word '*mannetjie*' occurs in Afrikaans more often in the context of a man of small stature and not necessarily as a male animal.

To support this conclusion even further, a corpus analysis of the word '*mannetjie*' was done.

- Corpus analysis of the word '*mannetjie*'

The table below contains an exposition of the lemmas in each of the corpora (see Addendum: Corpora applied for corpus analysis).

TABLE 2.2: Exposition of findings of corpus analysis

Lemma	ATKV	Comments	Leipzig	LAPA2	Maroela	NCHLT	PUK-Protea	RSG	Speech corpus	Taalgenoot	Language Commission	Wikipedia	WKJ	Total
All inflections and compositions with 'mannetjie'	117	1189	3903	907	479	2	2302	140	92	81	1466	1682	170	12530

The corpus search showed 12 530 hits for the lemma '*mannetjie*' as well as all inflections and compositions containing this lemma (see Table 2.2). The authors examined each of the lemmas to determine the context in which it was used. It was found that the word '*mannetjie*' is mostly used in the context of a man of small stature, a form of address, or a form of reference to express irritation.

The definition/translation of 'male animal' is mainly used in the context of the description of a phenomenon in nature and not as a form of reference to a human being.

It is apparent from the above that the assumption cannot be made that when the applicant said '*mannetjie*' she referred to a male animal, but rather to a man of small stature, or used it as a phrase to express irritation – as language users sometimes tend to do during communication.

- The role of morphology and phonology in Sintu languages

The learner who laid the charge, comes from a home where Setswana is spoken (Du Plessis, 2022b), and it was therefore also required to study the morphology and phonetics of Setswana to determine whether this could have any effect on the understanding and interpretation of '*polisiemannetjie*' or 'police monkey'. Setswana forms part of the Sintu languages (Cole & Moncho-Warren, 2012: 29–30). The principles highlighted in

Setswana are also relevant in the other Sintu languages (cf. Cole & Moncho-Warren, 2012: 24).

- Syllable structure and accent in Setswana

Setswana generally has an open syllable structure. This means that the characteristic pattern is that of consonant + vowel. There are indeed a few cases where vowels or consonants are syllables on their own (Cole & Moncho-Warren, 2012: 29).

The word 'stress' in Setswana is on the second last syllable of the word (Cole & Moncho-Warren, 2012: 29–30).

If anyone who speaks Setswana and does not have knowledge of Afrikaans or English, the syllable structure and word stress would look like this: in Afrikaans the accent would fall on the '*-ne-*' in '*po-li-sie-ma-n-ne-tjie*', and in English on '-n-' in 'po-li-ce mo-n-key'.

Because the learner who laid the charge had since primary school been exposed to Afrikaans and English (Du Plessis, 2022b), there is a very small probability that the learner would pronounce these words in this way.

There is, however, the possibility that because the '*-ne-*' in '*mannetjie*' bears less stress in Afrikaans than if it is pronounced quickly, it can sound like the word 'monkey' in English. That meaning was therefore also examined as regards its meaning in Setswana..

- Morphology
  - Classes of nouns

Nouns in Setswana are divided into different classes on the basis of the morphological structure of the word, specifically the prefix (Cole & Moncho-Warren, 2012: 30–37). The classes of importance here are class 1 and class 9. In class 1, mainly humans are found, and in class 9, mainly animals.

If we take the Setswana word for man – '*monna*', it falls in class 1 on the strength of the prefix mo- (this is incidentally also where the word for humans is, namely '*<u>mo</u>tho*'). The Setswana for 'monkey' is '*kgabo*'. It is interesting to note that '*kgabo*' is also used as a greeting (praise name) for humans of the Kgatle tribe (Cole & Moncho-Warren, 2012: 237).

- Diminutive

The diminutive suffix -ana, -nyana or -anyana is used in Setswana to indicate diminution. The truth is that the diminution can be even further diminished by adding the -anyana to the existing diminution (Brits, 2006: 86). The diminution of '*monna*' is '*monnanyana*', which means little man. The class does not change in the process and it thus still has the broad meaning of a human (a man who is small).

In Setswana, there is no equivalent for the Afrikaans '*-mannetjie*' that is added as a suffix to indicate gender, but there is, however, the feminine/augmentative suffix *-gadi*, that can be used to indicate the feminine gender. The same *-gadi* can also be used to indicate that something is very big or important (Brits, 2006: 92 and Cole & Moncho-Warren, 2012: 102).

The probability that '*monnanyana*' could refer to an animal is therefore negligible.

Conclusion

This chapter encompasses a linguistic analysis in order to determine the probability that the applicant referred in an offensive way to a learner as a monkey or a male animal in her utterance '*polisiemannetjie*'. The findings of this study align with international research on linguistic analysis in legal cases, particularly in multilingual legal systems such as Canada. These jurisdictions have also recognised the role of forensic linguistics in dispute resolution, underscoring the importance of linguistic expertise in maintaining fairness and accuracy in legal interpretations.

Various methods were used to determine the probability that '*polisiemannetjie*' sounded like 'police monkey' and the probability that if the learner was referred to as a '*mannetjie*', the learner was by default equated with a male animal.

It is important to mention that language analysis is not an absolute science, but if various methods of analysis are employed as transparently as possible, it increases the reliability of the findings, and the probability of certain questions can indeed be represented. For this reason, the authors set out the findings of the linguistic analysis on a probability continuum and then made significant conclusions from this continuum. The exposition on the left indicates a greater probability that the applicant referred to a learner in an offensive way as a monkey or a male animal in her statement '*polisiemannetjie*' and the exposition on the right indicates a smaller probability of this.

From the above figure the following summarising conclusions can be made:

- During the analysis of the linguistic context of the utterances (on the basis of the semantic frame and the prototype theory as well as the IAT) the probability is greater that the applicant referred to a learner in an offensive way as a monkey or a male animal by using the word '*polisiemannetjie*'.
  - Here it is important to mention that only the perspective of the respondent's witnesses was taken into account and that the connotative meaning of 'monkey' and '*mannetjie*' was based only on their perspective (see Table 2.1, block 3).
- As opposed to this, the theoretical linguistic analysis of the utterances demonstrated that the probability that the applicant had referred to a learner in

an offensive way as a monkey or a male animal in her statement *'polisiemannetjie'*, is much smaller.

- The purpose of this was to trump the findings of the analysis of the linguistic context by means of theoretical linguistic analysis.

The authors reached the conclusion that the probability that '*polisiemannetjie*' sounded like 'police monkey' and that if a person was referred to as a '*mannetjie*', that the person was by default equated to a male animal, is very small.

The commissioner who rendered the verdict in this dispute resolution case agreed with the expert testimony that the authors rendered and referred to the authors' analysis in the verdict:

> 'I am of the view that the findings and conclusions of Ms Brits and Dr de Vries as regards the non-existence of the phrase "police monkey" and the meaning which should be attributed to the phrase "*polisiemannetjie*" in the circumstances of this case, are more persuasive than the version of the respondent's witnesses. It is therefore concluded that the applicant has on the balance of probabilities, used the phrase "polisiemannetjie" as opposed to using the phrase "police monkey". It is also concluded that such language utterances were indeed intended to make an appeal for an intervention by someone in authority as opposed to being directed at Thembi because using the phrase towards Thembi would have served no logical purpose' (*Solidarity obo Anneke Smit v Education Department of Gauteng,* 2022: 29).

This confirms the importance of the scientific approach in expert testimony and the role of the linguist. Language is an essential part of a legal practitioner's arsenal and as indicated, the linguist can assist as an expert witness in restoring fairness and justice in cases dealing with language.

References

Álvarez-Mosquera, P. 2017. The Use of the Implicit Association Test (IAT) for Sociolinguistic Purposes in South Africa. Language Matters, 48(2), 69-90.

Álvarez-Mosquera, P. & Marín-Gutiérrez, A. (2018). Implicit Language Attitudes Toward Historically White Accents in the South African Context. *Journal of Language and Social Psychology*, 37(2): 238–248.

Ariani, MG., Sajedi, F. & Sajedi, M. (2014). Forensic linguistics: A Brief Overview of the Key Elements. *Procedia-Social and Behavioral Sciences*, 158: 222–225.

Baldauf, RB. (2012). Introduction-language planning: Where have we been? Where might we be going? *Revista Brasileira de Linguística Aplicada,* 12(2): 233–248.

Bakkabulindi, F. (2015). Positivism and interpretivism: Distinguishing characteristics, criteria and methodology. In: Van Wyk, M. (ed.) *Educational Research: An African approach.* Oxford University Press Southern Africa (Pty) Ltd. 19–38.

Belavusau, U. (2014). Experts in Hate Speech Cases: Towards a Higher Standard of Proof in Strasbourg? In: Gruszczynski, L., Werner, W. (ed.) *Deference in International Courts and Tribunals: Standard of Review and Margin of Appreciation.* Oxford University Press.

Borrows, J. (2001). Listening for a Change: The Courts and Oral Tradition. *Osgoode Hall Law Journal*, 39(1): 1–38.

Botha, WF. (ed). (2019). *e-WAT: elektroniese woordeboek van the Afrikaanse taal, A tot R.* http://www.woordeboek.co.za [Date accessed: 7 June 2022].

Brits, JH. (2006). *Outomatiese Setswana Lemma-identifisering.* [Unpublished Master's dissertation]. Potchefstroom: North-West University.

Carney, TR. & Bergh, L. (2016). Using Prototype Theory to Determine the Ordinary Meaning of Words. *Journal of Contemporary Roman-Dutch Law*, 79: 486–495.

Clarke, I. & Kredens, KJ. (2018). 'I consider myself to be a service provider': Discursive identity construction of the forensic linguistic expert. *International Journal of Speech, Language and the Law*, *25*(1): 79–107.

Cole, DT. & Moncho-Warren, L. (2012). *Setswana and English Illustrated Dictionary.* Northlands: Macmillan South Africa.

Coulthard, M. (2005). The linguist as expert witness. *Linguistics and the Human Sciences*, 1(1): 39.

Coulthard, M. & Johnson, A. (ed.) (2010). *The Routledge handbook of forensic linguistics.* London: Routledge.

Daubert v Merrell Dow Pharmaceuticals, Inc. (1993)

Du Plessis, L. (2022a). Request to provide expert evidence. Personal correspondence. Email to Annelise de Vries (annelise@akademia.ac.za). 24 May 2022.

Du Plessis, L. (2022b). FW: lelanie@solidarity.co.za sent you Day 1 – Held 22 March 2022 via WeTransfer. Personal correspondence. Email to Annelise de Vries (annelise@akademia.ac.za). 1 June 2022.

Finlayson, R., Calteaux, K. & Myers-Scotton, C. (1998). Orderly mixing and accommodation in South African codeswitching. *Journal of Sociolinguistics*, 2(3): 395–420.

Gasa, V., Mafora, P. & Maphalala, M. (2015). The literature review. In: Van Wyk, M. (ed.) *Educational Research: An African approach*. Oxford University Press Southern Africa (Pty) Ltd. (sixth edition).

Kaschula, RH. (2021). *Language identities and Intercultural Communication in South Africa and Beyond.* London: Routledge.

Kotzé, EF. (2012). *Forensic linguistics in commercial crime investigations.* Presentation at the First Annual Conference of the Institute for Commercial Forensic Practitioners, Johannesburg, 23–24 July.

Kotzé, E. (2018). Die klassifikasie van Afrikaans. *LitNet*. https://www.litnet.co.za/die-klassifikasie-van-afrikaans/ [Date of access: 31 August 2022].

Leonard, RA., Ford, JE. & Christensen, TK. (2016). Forensic Linguistics: Applying the Science of Linguistics to Issues of the Law. *Hofstra Law Review,* 45(3): 881–897.

Levi, JN. (1994). Language as evidence: The linguist as expert witness in North American courts. *The International Journal of Speech, Language and the Law,* 1(1): 1–26.

Lewis, C. & Edmonds-Smith, C. (2014). Forensic Science: The coming paradigm shift. *De Rebus.* Available at: https://www.derebus.org.za/forensic-science-coming-paradigm-shift/

Liebenberg, H., Lubbe, J., Cloete, A., Jordaan, A. & Van Wyk, G. (2003). *Etimologiewoordeboek van Afrikaans*. Stellenbosch: Buro van die Woordeboek van die Afrikaanse Taal.

Lowe, JB. (1997). A frame-semantic approach to semantic annotation. In *Tagging Text with Lexical Semantics: Why, What, and How?*. Association for Computational Linguistics.

Luther, J., Pheiffer, F. & Gouws, RH. (2015). *HAT: Handwoordeboek van the Afrikaanse taal*. Virtuele Instituut van Afrikaans (VivA) (sixth edition).

Mabule, DR. (2015). What is this? Is It Code Switching, Code Mixing or Language Alternating. *Journal of Educational and Social Research*, 5(1): 339–350.

McCormick, K. (2002). *Language in Cape Town's District Six.* Oxford University Press.

McKerracher, K. (2023). Relational legal pluralism and Indigenous legal orders in Canada. *Global Constitutionalism*, 12(1): 133–153.

Nanni, M. (2022). Onderwyser kan terug skool toe ná vals rassismeklag. *Maroela Media,* 12 July. Accessed @https://maroelamedia.co.za/nuus/sa-nuus/onderwyser-kan-terug-skool-toe-na-vals-rassismeklag/ [Date accessed: 31 August 2022].

Netwerk24. (2022). Ontslaan oor valse rassisme-klagte: Onnie terug skool toe. *Netwerk24,* 12 July. Accessed @https://www.netwerk24.com/netwerk24/nuus/aktueel/ontslaan-oor-valse-rassisme-klagte-onnie-terug-skool-toe-20220712.

Petruck, MR. (1996). Frame semantics. In Östman, J. & Verschueren, J. (ed.) *Handbook of pragmatics*. John Benjamins Publishing Company.

Pharos. (2010). *Pharos Afrikaans-Engels English-Afrikaans Woordeboek.* https://www.pharosaanlyn.co.za/tuis [Date accessed: 7 June 2022].

Picornell, I. (2022). *'There can only be one possible meaning' – linguistic experts and evidence in court*. Presentation at the International Association for Forensic Linguistics Conference, Porto 2022.

Probyn, M. (2006). Language and Learning Science in South Africa. *Language and Education*, 20(5):391-414.

Rusho, D. (2021). Cross-currents: Indigenous language interpreting in Australia's justice system. *The International Journal of Speech, Language and the Law*, 28(2): 281–288. https://doi.org/10.1558/ijsll.21607

Smit, J. (2022). Onnie oor rasklag: 'Ek is soos sleg hond daar weg'. *Rapport,* 17 July. https://www.netwerk24.com/netwerk24/nuus/aktueel/onnie-ek-gaan-met-oorgawe-terug-skool-toe-20220716 [Date accessed: 31 August].

Solidarity obo Anneke Smit v Education Department of Gauteng (2022).

Songxaba, SL., Coetzer, A. & Molepo, JM. (2017). Perceptions of teachers on creating space for code switching as a teaching strategy in second language teaching in the Eastern Cape Province, South Africa. *Reading & Writing: Journal of the Reading Association of South Africa*, 8(1).

Stubbs, M. (1996). *Text and corpus analysis: Computer-assisted studies of language and culture* (p. 158). Oxford: Blackwell.

Tiersma, P. & Solan, LM. (2002). The Linguist on the Witness Stand: Forensic Linguistics in American courts. *Language* 78(2): 221–239. https://doi.org/10.1353/lan.2002.0135

Van Wyk, M. (2015). *Educational Research: An African approach*. Oxford University Press Southern Africa (Pty) Ltd. (sixth edition).

Van Wyk, M. & Taole, M. (2015). Chapter 10: Research Design. In: Van Wyk, M. (ed.) *Educational Research: An African approach.* Oxford University Press Southern Africa (Pty) Ltd. (sixth edition).

Addendum: Corpora applied for corpus analysis

- Collection of newly written plays entered for the ATKV Teen Drama Competition.
- Collection of unedited user comments on web pages, arranged in subcorpora per web page.
- A subcollection of the Leipzig corpus.
- A corpus of Afrikaans books (mostly fiction) published by Lapa Publishers.
- Collection of news reports and blogs as published on the mediahouse Maroela Media's website up to and including 30 November 2020.
- A collection of government documents from the various web pages and electronic publications of the South African government.
- Corpus of Afrikaans books (fiction and non-fiction) published by the publisher Protea Boekhuis.
- Collection of news bulletins from 1 January 2005 up to and including 28 February 2021 as broadcast on Radio Sonder Grense and published on their website.
- Transcriptions of extracts from a variety of remaining spreech corpora, arranged in subcorpora per project.
- A stratified corpus as used by the Afrikaanse Taalkommissie (Afrikaans Language Commission) consisting of a variety of genres and domains, including: scientific journals, newspapers, literary works, and informal and formal writing material.
- Collection of articles published in the journal *Taalgenoot* from 2006 to 2012.
- A collection of documents from the various web pages available on the Afrikaans version of *Wikipedia* as on 28 February 2021.
- Collection of informal blogs as published on watkykjy.co.za up to and including 31 August 2020.

3 IS DECEPTION CONSIDERED A CATALYTIC AGENT OF LIES? THE LEGAL IMPLICATIONS IN THE COURTROOM

Stanley Madonsela

Introduction

Despite taking an oath to tell the truth, the whole truth, and nothing but the truth, witnesses can still give false testimony during legal trials. Some individuals may sincerely believe that their memory of an event is accurate, although it is factually erroneous (Laney & Loftus, 2013; Schacter & Loftus, 2013), while other witnesses may deliberately attempt to mislead trial judges by deception. For this chapter, it is prudent that a distinction be made between deception and perjury. Deception is carried out for the purpose of unfair or unlawful gain while perjury is the deliberate giving of false or misleading testimony under oath. However, unlike mistaken eyewitness identification, very few studies have been conducted on deception in courtrooms (Fawcett, 2014). This chapter draws on and expands existing theoretical models to explicate aspects of the context that inform deception production. Considering the divergent views among scholars and researchers on how 'deception' should be defined, an endeavour is made in this chapter to integrate these views to come to an understanding of what it entails and its implications in a court of law. The arguments on deception are raised in this chapter against the backdrop of attempts to use deception for the purpose of unfair or unlawful gain in court. These arguments are driven by, among others, Coleman and Kay's (1981) elements of the prototypical lie, and Miller's (1983) and Miller & Stiff's (1993) notions of deceptive communication. This chapter focuses on deception in the courtroom other than other contexts outside the courtroom environment where the issue of deception has been considered in terms of whether it successfully concealed or fabricated information.

There are two types of factors that are central to the philosophical discussion of lying to others and other forms of deception. The first type is conceptual and includes factors such as how lying or deceiving should be defined, and whether lying forms part of deceiving. The second type is based more on moral issues, including whether deception or lying is morally classified. The issue of deception is raised in this chapter against the backdrop of using testimony to establish the facts of a case and, because of which, a legal decision will be made. Judicial permission for the police to use deception based on allegations often carries over into the interrogation and testimony phases of the police's development of a case, since the latter becomes accustomed to using deception to secure the conviction of a defendant that they consider guilty (see John & Srivastava, 1999). Recent studies on deception have focused even more on individual-level characteristics to identify deception in a range of settings (see Taylor & Vrij, 2000, and DePaulo, 1992). Empirical researchers have considered the distinction between prolific lying and identifying prolific liars. Prolific lying involves deceptive tendencies during a single opportunity for gain. Prolific liars are individuals who demonstrate a repeated proclivity for taking up the opportunity for deception (Serota et al., 2021). Therefore, the number of repeated deceptions over a particular timespan may be informative for deception research as a moderator to enhance detection abilities.

Since there is usually a lack of forensic evidence in many criminal cases that are brought before the courts and considering that other types of information can be obtained only by means of questioning, interviewing becomes the only available option to discover the truth about what happened. Most people know that they should not act deceptively irrespective of the justification for doing so. Deception reduces the possibility that people's actions will result from their rational appreciation of the options that are available to them. False implicatures will also be discussed in this chapter as attempts normally used with a view to mislead the courts. This chapter considers the views raised by scholars such as Saul (2012), Horn (2017), and Skoczeń (2019) on false implicatures. However, the dissenting views of Meibauer (2014), Dynel (2011), and Weissman and Terkourafi (2016) are also explored. Deception and lies are presented in the form of a statement, and making a statement requires the use of language. In this case, the language used may include the different symbols, conventional signs or expressions that are used in courts. These language symbols may be used to determine whether there is any deception presented and may assist in determining the judgment.

Comprehending deception

Leach et al. (2016) believe that studying deception in courtrooms within an experimental court paradigm resembles investigative interview settings. There seems to be no universally accepted definition of 'deception', which makes it difficult to formulate a comprehensive and clear-cut definition. The point of departure could be Coleman and Kay's (1981) elements of the prototypical lie and Miller's (1983) and Miller & Stiff's (1993) notions of deceptive communication. Deception is a deliberate attempt to hide or fabricate the facts, using verbal and/or nonverbal means, to create or maintain in another person/other persons a belief that the communicator themselves considers false.

Most of the definitions of 'deception' provided by scholars and researchers indicate that there are two approaches to consider in defining deception, the first being the intention component and the second being the sender's belief that the information being conveyed is false. Emerging from these two approaches is the communicator's deliberate attempt to make others believe that what is communicated is true, or the objective falsity of information, or introducing a false belief (DePaulo & DePaulo, 1989; Hall & Pritchard, 1996).

Deception is 'a successful or unsuccessful deliberate attempt, without forewarning, to create in another a belief which the communicator considers to be untrue' (Vrij, 2008: 15). This definition does not preclude the element of a credible statement required by the court. This is because credibility incorporates competence, or the perceived ability to accurately recall an event, and trustworthiness, and the perceived ability to tell the truth (Tabak & Klettke, 2014). Confusion around lies and deception is not surprising since Leach et al. (2016) use 'lie' and 'deception' interchangeably, although the two terms are not synonyms (Galasinski, 2000). From the definition provided, it becomes apparent that several deception theories and a variety of social psychology and communication contributions have been integrated to formulate it.

Methodology

Apart from the theoretical abstractions, this chapter presents arguments and discussions with methods that lend themselves to application in the real world. This chapter employs a literature search method that reviews the readily available sources on deception and the elements of social, psychological, and communication contributions that have been built into this concept. In trying to provide the overarching elements of deception and its vehicle, which mostly comprise the language, this chapter examines court cases that dealt with deception and lies and everything associated with the concept of deception.

Theoretical framework

The need to incorporate new inventions in languages and expressions used in courts has become imperative in detecting deception. It has not been easy to identify a single theory that would focus on all the aspects of deception. Therefore, a combination of theories, including the leakage theory and the Contextual Organization of Language and Deception (COLD) framework, was considered. The latter considers how the context may influence the relationship between deception and communication behaviour, such as language. Another possible approach to representing deception is the leakage theory, as proposed by Ekman and Friesen (1969). This theory suggests that liars experience specific emotions that could reveal unknowingly their mental state through their facial expressions. Closely linked with non-verbal leakage, this theory manifests when a person expresses one thing but their body language suggests something else. Non-verbal leakage forms part of the study of body language. It originated around the 1960s and was followed up by several studies undertaken in the 1970s on the same topic. Even today, it is a valid/relevant theory.

The relevance of this theory to the discussion is that even if suspects in court try to suppress their own non-verbal leakage, certain aspects will still be expressed; despite suspects' efforts to say something different, this give-away body language happens involuntarily. In some cases, others can pick up incongruity between verbal and non-verbal messages, which could sometimes be confusing. Studies on the topic have revealed that deception and facial expressions manifest as emotional leakage to some extent when individuals are trying to conceal high-intensity emotion (Ekman & Friesen, 1969). The non-verbal leakage is relevant in this discussion as it focuses on several bodily and facial movements that are associated with it in the context of deception. In this theory, Ekman and Friesen (1969) describe parts of the body, such as the face, that have a high sending capacity, meaning that the signals that this body part sends are easily visible and quickly received by the observer. The sending capacity and clear visibility of the face makes non-verbal leakage obvious when expressed on the face. Often, emotions expressed on the face are discernible because of the complex musculature and movements of the face when compared with movements of the feet or hands, for example. Non-verbal leakage indicates that facial expressions are some of the first expressions to be masked when a person is telling a lie. Therefore, communication via the face becomes more visible if there is deception in what is being recounted. People become aware of how obvious their facial expressions are, so they are likely to mask those expressions first. This means that non-verbal leakage can be more obvious on the face. However, considering a person's awareness of their facial expression, the face can sometimes produce confusing non-verbal leakage.

Related literature on deception

Deception and the detection of deception are dependent phenomena. This means that the way in which people tell lies and what they lie about may vary and are dependent on several factors. This would also include how well people can detect lies in various settings. The lies that some people tell about potentially controversial opinions are considered here (Newman et al., 2003). These lies are considered different from the lies people tell during emergency calls in terms of their emotional content (Burns & Moffitt, 2014). The personality constructs of psychopathy, which are not only associated with the propensity to lie but also the amount of positive emotion experienced in deceiving others, have been explored (Baughman et al., 2014). Levine et al. (1999) researched lie-detection accuracy, which is also considered to be dependent on artifacts of truth-lie judgments. The accuracy for truth, which is greater than the accuracy for lies because people tend to guess true more often than false in detection tasks, is explored in detail (Levine, 2014 and 2020). In empirical research and several studies on deception, the common findings are that telling lies and detecting lies are influenced by the context (Luo et al., 2022). The theoretical conceptualisations of the context for deception research are considered uncommon (Blair et al., 2010, and Markowitz, 2022). However, empirical research provides for a better understanding of what deception entails. In all these studies, it seems that context determines how to describe why lie production or detection may differ across settings. This universal use of detection is considered the catalytic agent of lies, which this chapter explores.

In doing so, the focus is on identifying how aspects of the context inform our understanding of deception production and detection in the courtroom; this will influence empirical research and practice to distinguish lies from truths. Existing scholarship has articulated how contextual characteristics (e.g. pragmatic goals) inform the relationship between deception and language (Markowitz & Hancock, 2022).

Contextualising deception

Considering that deception scholarship has had a limited focus on the context, it has become imperative to consider how scholars have viewed the role of the context in empirical evidence and theory. Hauch et al. (2015) have observed that the relationship between deception and context has been systematic for many verbal dimensions (e.g. emotion, cognitive complexity), although the effects were minimal. The other observation has been that liars typically use fewer words than truth-tellers in their verbal utterances/expressions (Markowitz & Hancock, 2019). In addition to this, the effect regulated by the interaction level between those who are communicating should also be considered. The meta-analysis by Hauch et al. (2015) provides clear evidence that the context and contextual factors influence deception, yet our conceptualisations of the context are limited.

Considering the COLD framework and contrasting primary study effects for the same linguistic indicator can help to demonstrate the impact of psychological dynamics on language patterns for deception. Psychological aspects of deception are critical contextual factors that change how people communicate about lies, an idea supported by decades of deception research across multiple domains, lie types, stakes, and settings. Another aspect of the context for deception and language relates to pragmatic objectives. The ultimate objective of the things that witnesses want to achieve with their deception normally influences how falsely or truthfully they communicate. Scholars of deception have also realised that motivational attitudes and values help facilitate our understanding of when an individual may be most inclined to be dishonest (Levine, 2014).

A similar observation has been made by Lee et al. (2020), who found that neutralisation was the primary motivator for academic dishonesty. This evidence suggests a deeper consideration of how motives modify communication and deceptive patterns. Personality traits and individual differences have received limited treatment in deception literature. Past research indicates the role that certain dispositional traits may play in deceptive communication (Miller & Stiff, 1993), while recent work on deception has focused even more on individual-level characteristics to identify deception in a range of settings. Deception studies may indicate control for individual differences; however, such differences might serve as key moderators for lie production or detection. Some people may be more dispositionally honest or deceptive than others. Additional types of individual differences also need greater treatment in deception literature, since some research suggests that they influence detection. In interpersonal deception, most people lie when honesty is a problem (Levine, 2020), or when the opportunity for deception is available and facilitates some form of significant personal gain.

To detect lies efficiently, researchers should attempt to establish base rates of deception that can signal the probability of lying in each setting. If deception is improbable or implausible (Walczyk et al., 2014), detection efforts may be futile. Detection efforts with a more evenly distributed lie-truth base rate may be more effective.

Deception detection

Research in detecting deception offers a guide to the detection of deception with a focus on the ways in which new, cognitive, psychology-based approaches can improve practice and results in the field. Deception detection has become increasingly fashionable in the popular media since the American television show *Lie to Me* (Levine et al., 2010). Nevertheless, research on deception detection has been explored for centuries. At the core of deception detection are the techniques that are used to elicit differences between liars and truth-tellers. Deception detection involves certain behaviours that indicate that there is little or no truth in liars. For example, they usually show their dishonesty by evading answering questions, sometimes even rubbing their big toe on the ground, shivering, or rubbing the roots of their hair with their fingers.

However, in the recent past, the polygraph was introduced as a lie detection tool based on the widespread assumption that the act of lying is associated with physiological activity within the liar's body (Vrij, 2008). Research on deception revealed that statements derived from truthful individuals differ from those of deceptive individuals (Steller, 1989). Deception scholars subsequently began to focus more on the verbal responses of liars and truth-tellers. They also distanced themselves from traditional approaches to deception detection and focused on interactions to develop different techniques; this led to a significant improvement in deception detection accuracy. More recently, deception detection has provided several theoretical and practical approaches for law enforcement. However, there is still a lot of work to be done for justice to be served better.

Deception in the courtroom

Recent approaches to detecting deception have pointed to evidence-based techniques in questioning the suspects brought to court by the police and in investigative interviews. However, these are considered part of the initial stages of the judicial process that would eventually lead to the imprisonment of those who have been found guilty of criminal offences. Since there is limited understanding of deception detection research among the judges presiding over criminal cases (Strömwall & Granhag, 2003) and of the science of the deception (Chin & Dallen, 2016), the lack of empirical research on deception detection is a cause for concern. Even though evidence-based techniques are supported by sound empirical testing in the courtroom, such an important exercise becomes futile in the judicial process where guilty parties are acquitted and innocent persons are imprisoned because of inaccurate judgments by the judges based on credibility assessment and deception.

Adding to the complexities of deception in the courtroom is the fact that trials are conducted in a consistent manner, depending on how the investigating officer investigates the suspect. Moreover, different courts may have different approaches to certain types of questions, which could also mean that deception detection is prohibited. Policies and practices may also differ from one court jurisdiction to another, depending on the type of trial being held (Vauclair, 2016). The disclosure of evidence in criminal trials allows suspects to know beforehand the evidence that prosecutors have against them. This may have some drawbacks in deception detection and may provide suspects with enough 'ammunition' to deal with the crime that they are faced with.

However, unlike where the police conduct investigative interviews with suspects, many deceptive practices are common and accepted in courtrooms. There is a strong possibility of deception in the courtrooms. However, the acts of deception could be regarded as ill-intentioned when considered in the context of investigative interviews and what happens between the time when the police investigate or interrogate the suspects and the trials are conducted.

redibility is a matter that permeates most trials and it may amount to a verdict of guilty or innocent (*R v Handy*, 2002). Moreover, considering that those who are telling 'sincere' lies are likely to be believed more than the truth-tellers who are believed to have low credibility (Bond & DePaulo, 2008: 487), it has become crucial for deception researchers to discuss the legal scholarship in this field with the judiciary to help them come to an accurate understanding of the matching and contrasting roles including the scope of deception in courtrooms. When witnesses are asked to answer with only 'yes' or 'no' answers and lawyers argue to accentuate the good testimonies and depreciate the bad testimonies, such answers and arguments can be deceptive, even if they are accepted by law. Yet, presiding judges have an obligation to assess the credibility of witnesses and weigh up the evidence given by the witnesses, either accepting or rejecting it.

The case of *Segalo v S* (2017) involves an appeal against the conviction and sentence with leave of the trial court. The grounds for the appeal were that, during the trial, the court underplayed the discrepancies and contradictions in the complainant's evidence and emphasized the flaws in the appellant's evidence. It was submitted that the court a quo ignored the contents of the complainant's statement and overemphasized her testimony in court. The correct approach to the evaluation of evidence in a criminal trial was enunciated by the Supreme Court of Appeal as follows, in *S v Chabalala* (2003): the trial court's approach to the case was holistic, and rightly so; refer to *S v Van Aswegen* (2001). The correct approach is to weigh up all the elements that point to the guilt of the accused against all those that indicate their innocence, taking proper account of inherent strengths and weaknesses, probabilities and improbabilities, on both sides. Then, having done so, the judge must decide whether the balance weighs so heavily in favour of the state as to exclude any reasonable doubt about the accused's guilt.

The trial court has the advantage of observing witnesses as they testify, which the appeal court does not have. The following quotation from *S v Mafaladiso en Andere* (2003) sums this up:

> The juridical approach to contradictions between two witnesses and contradictions between the versions of the same witness (such as, *inter alia*, between her or his viva voce evidence and a previous statement) is, in principle (even if not in degree), identical. Indeed, in neither case is the aim to prove which of the versions is correct, but to satisfy oneself that the witness, could err, either because of a defective recollection or because of dishonesty. The mere fact that it is evident that there are self-contradictions must be approached with caution by a court. What the witnesses meant to say on the statements should be considered carefully. It must be considered that, not every error, contradiction or deviation affects the credibility of a witness. It also emerged that any contradictory versions must be considered and evaluated on a holistic basis. (*S v Mafaladiso en Andere*, 2003)

The judge presiding over the case has the responsibility to weigh up the statement against the oral evidence, to consider all the evidence and to decide whether it is reliable or not.

To establish whether there has been deception or lies told, there must have been indications other than a mere lack of detail in the witness' statement to conclude that what the witness said in court was unsatisfactory or untruthful. Unfortunately, the law does not compel a witness about what to say and what not to say in their statement. This makes it easy for the witness to deceive or tell lies in court even though an oath has been undertaken. If it happens that a witness, through a lapse of memory or any other valid reason, omits some detail which later could become important, they should not as a matter of course be considered as deceiving or being untruthful.

What should be considered is that, even though a witness may deviate in a material respect from what was said in a previous statement, that does not necessarily render all the evidence defective. The court will have to make a final analysis considering the evidence to determine in what respects the witness' evidence may be accepted and in what respects it should be rejected.

Conclusion

Few theoretical perspectives can address how context moderates the effects of lie production and lie detection. It has emerged from the above-mentioned court cases that many trials are not about who is lying and who is telling the truth, but about who is the most credible. It became apparent that there is a need for further research to test how individual differences, lie-truth base rates, and situational opportunities for deception and interpersonal dynamics can modify lying. The issue of credibility of witnesses, or those who are brought before the courts, seems to be the underlying factor in making a judgment. Therefore, the assessment of credibility must always be at the midpoint of the presiding judge's view of the diverse elements or aspects they have perceived at a given trial. Furthermore, the judge's experience and logic should be other determining factors to determine the credibility of a presented statement.

The evidence in deception research is often mixed and contingent on the studies involved. It can be argued that incremental theory-building related to the context is essential to understand how people tell lies and how deception detection accuracy might vary across different forms of deception.

References

Baughman, HM., Jonason, PK., Lyons, M. & Vernon, PA. (2014). Liar liar pants on fire: Cheater strategies linked to the Dark Triad. *Personal and Individual Differences,* 71, 35–38. https://doi.org/10.1016/j.paid.2014.07.019

Blair, J. P., Levine, T. R., & Shaw, A. S. (2010). Content in context improves deception detection accuracy. Human Communication Research, 36, 420-439.

Bond, CF. & DePaulo, BM. (2008). Individual differences in judging deception: Accuracy and bias. *Psychological Bulletin,* 134(4), 477–492. https://doi.org/10.1037/0033-2909.134.4.477

Burns, M. & Moffitt, K. (2014). Automated deception detection of 911 call transcripts. *Security Infomatics,* 3, 1–9. https://doi.org/10.1186/s13388-014-0008-2

Chin, J.M. & Dallen, S. (2016). R v Awer and the Dangers of Science in Sheep's Clothing. *Criminal Law Quarterly.*

Coleman, L. & Kay, P. (1981). Prototype Semantics: The English Word Lie. *Language,* 57, 26–44.

DePaulo, BM. (1992). Nonverbal behavior and self-presentation. *Psychological Buletin.,* 111, 203–243. https://doi.org/10.1037/0033-2909.111.2.203.

DePaulo, PJ. & DePaulo, BM. (1989). Can Deception by Salespersons and Customers be Detected through Nonverbal Behavioral Cues? *Journal of Applied Social Psychology,* 19(18), 1552 - 1577.

Dynel, M. (2011). A web of deceit: A neo-Gricean view on types of verbal deception. *International Review of Pragmatics*, 3, 139–167.

Ekman, P. and Friesen, WV. (1969) The Repertoire or Nonverbal Behavior: Categories, Origins, Usage and Coding. *Semiotica,* 1, 49–98. https://doi.org/10.1515/semi.1969.1.1.49.

Fawcett, HE. (2014). Witness, False testimony of. In Levine, T. (ed.), *Encyclopedia of Deception* (Vol. 2, pp. 937–940). Sage

Galasinski, D. (2000). *The Language of Deception: A Discourse Analytical Study*. Sage.

Hall, HV. & Pritchard, DA. (1996). *Detecting Malingering and Deception:. Forensic Distortion Analysis (FDA)*. St Lucie Press.

Hauch, V., Blandón-Gitlin, I., Masip, J. & Sporer, S. L. (2015). Are computers effective lie detectors? A meta-analysis of linguistic cues to deception. *Personality and Social Psychology Review,* 19, 307–342. https://doi.org/10.1177/1088868314556539.

Horn, L. (2017). What lies beyond: Untangling the web. In Rachel Giora and Michael Haugh (eds.), Doing Pragmatics Interculturally, 151-174. Berlin: de Gruyter.

John, OP. & Srivastava, S. (1999). The Big Five Trait Taxonomy: History, measurement, and theoretical perspectives. In Pervin LA. & John OP. (ed.), *Handbook of Personality: Theory and Research* (pp. 102–138). Guilford Press.

Laney, C. & Loftus, EF. (2013). Recent advances in false memory research. *South African Journal of Psychology*, 43(2), 137–146. https://doi.org/10.1177/008124631348423

Leach, AM., Ammar, N., England, DN., Remigio, LM., Kleinberg, B. & Verschuere, BJ. (2016). Less is more? Detecting lies in veiled witnesses. *Law and Human Behavior*, 40, 401–410. https://doi.org/10.1037/lhb0000189

Lee, SD., Kuncel, NR. & Gau, J. (2020). Personality, attitude, and demographic correlates of academic dishonesty: A meta-analysis. *Psychological Buletin,* 146, 1042–1058. https://doi.org/ 10.1037/bul0000300

Levine, TR. (2014). Truth-default theory (TDT): a theory of human deception and deception detection. *Journal of Language and Social Psychology,* 33, 378–392. https://doi.org/10.1177/0261927x14535916

Levine, TR. (2020). *Duped: Truth-Default Theory and the Social Science of Lying and Deception*. University of Alabama Press.

Levine, TR., Park, HS. & McCornack, SA. (1999). Accuracy in detecting truths and lies: Documenting the 'veracity effect'. *Communication Monographs,* 66, 125–144.

Levine, TR., Serota, KB. & Shulman, HC. (2010). The impact of *Lie to Me* on viewers' actual ability to detect deception. *Communication Research,* 37(6), 847–856. https://doi.org/10.1177/0093650210362686

Luo, M., Hancock, JT. & Markowitz, DM. (2022). Credibility perceptions and detection accuracy of fake news headlines on social media: Effects of truth-bias and endorsement cues. *Communication Research,* 49, 171–195. https://doi.org/10.1177/0093650220921321

Markowitz, DM. (2022). Toward a deeper understanding of prolific lying: Building a profile of situation-level and individual-level characteristics. *Communication Research,* https://doi.org/10.1177/00936502221097041

Markowitz, DM., and Hancock, JT. (2019). Deception and language: the ontextual Organization of Language and Deception (COLD) framework. In Docan-Morgan, T. (ed.) *The Palgrave Handbook of Deceptive Communication*. Backingstroke: Palgrave Macmillan, 193–212.

Markowitz, DM. & Hancock, JT. (2022). Lies and language: A context-contingent approach to verbal cues of deceit. In Dehghani, M. & Boyd, RL. (ed.) *The Handbook of Language Analysis in Psychology* (pp. 274–284). Guilford Press.

Meibauer, J. (2014). A truth that's told with bad intent: Lying and implicit content. *Belgian Journal of Linguistics*, 28, 97–118.

Miller, GR. (1983). Telling it like it isn't and not telling it like it is: Some thoughts on deceptive communication. In Sisco, JI. (ed.), *The Jensen Lectures: contemporary communication studies* (pp. 91–116). University of South Florida.

Miller, GR. & Stiff, JB. (1993). *Deceptive Communication*. Sage.

Newman, ML., Pennebaker, JW., Berry, DS. & Richards, JM. (2003). Lying words: Predicting deception from linguistic styles. *Personality and Social Psychology Bulletin,* 29, 665–675. https://doi.org/10.1177/0146167203029005010

R v Handy (2002)

Saul, J. (2012). *Lying, Misleading, and What is Said: An Exploration in Philosophy of Language and in Ethics*. Oxford University Press.

Schacter, DL. & Loftus, EF. (2013). Memory and law: What can cognitive neuroscience contribute? *Nature neuroscience*, 16(2), 119–123. https://doi.org/10.1038/nn.3294

Segalo v S (2017)

Serota, KB., Levine, TR. & Docan-Morgan, T. (2021). Unpacking variation in lie prevalence: Prolific liars, bad lie days, or both? *Communication Monographs.,* 89, 307–331. https://doi.org/10.1080/03637751.2021.1985153/SUPPL_FILE/RCMM_A_1985153_SM5737.docx

Skoczeń, Izabela. (2019). Post-Gricean implicature theories and their relevance for the legal realm. In I. Skoczeń (ed.), Implicatures within Legal Language, Chaper 3. Law and Philosophy Library 127, https://doi.org/10.1007/978-3-030-12532-5_3

Steller, M. (1989). Recent developments in statement analysis. In Yuille, JC. (ed.) *Credibility Assessment* (pp. 135–154). Kluwer Academic Publishers.

Strömwall, LA. & Granhag, PA. (2003). How to detect deception? Arresting the beliefs of police officers, prosecutors and judges. *Psychology, Crime & Law,* 9(1), 19–36. https://doi.org/10.1080/10683160308138

S *v Chabalala* (2003)

S v Mafaladiso en Andere (2003)

S v Van Aswegen (2001)

Tabak, SJ. & Klettke, B. (2014). Mock jury attitudes towards credibility, age, and guilt in a fictional child sexual assault scenario. *Australian Journal of Psychology,* 66, 47–55. https://doi.org/10.1111/ajpy.12035

Taylor, R. & Vrij, A. (2000). The effects of varying stake and cognitive complexity on beliefs about the cues to deception. *International Journal of Police Science and Management,* 3, 111–123.

Vauclair, M. (2016). *General treatise of penal evidence and procedure*. Yvon Blais.

Vrij, A. (2008). *Detecting Lies and Deceit: Pitfalls and Opportunities.* Wiley.

Walczyk, JJ., Harris, LL., Duck, TK. & Mulay, D. (2014). A social-cognitive framework for understanding serious lies: Activation-decision-construction-action theory. *New Ideas Psychology,* 34, 22–36. https://doi.org/10.1016/j.newideapsych.2014.03.001

Weissman, B & Terkourafi M. (2016). Are false implicatures lies? An experimental investigation. *Mind and Language* 34: 221–246.

PART II

Courtroom Discourse and Legal Education

4

UNTIL WHEN SHALL 'IGNORANCE OF THE LAW BE NO DEFENCE'? PRACTICAL INSIGHTS FROM THE DISCURSIVE STRATEGIES USED BY OFFENDERS IN SEEKING MITIGATION IN MALAWIAN CRIMINAL TRIAL

Wellman Kondowe, Paul Svongoro & Gerald Nthala

Introduction

Article 26 of the United Nations International Covenant on Civil and Political Rights states that 'all persons are equal before the law and are entitled without any discrimination to the equal protection of the law'. The concept of equality is further enshrined in section 20 (1) of the Constitution of the Republic of Malawi, which states that all persons are, under any law, guaranteed equal and effective protection against discrimination, regardless of the person's condition. Even though in theory, international laws and laws of Malawi have such provision to promote equality for every citizen, this does not really transpire in practice. For instance, as noted by Kondowe et al. (2022), most people who appear in court as witnesses or as accused persons are poor, uneducated, and not familiar with the law, and it raises doubts whether such a disadvantaged population can effectively receive equal protection under the law. Due to poor legal literacy, most people have poor access to law and legal information. This is widely evidenced when such people are called to respond to questions either as witnesses or as accused persons. They meet serious challenges in obeying courtroom culture and rules which are not only strange, but also intimidating (Kondowe, 2020 and 2024). They are further ignorant of their rights and how to execute them, and this makes it difficult for them to defend and protect themselves. Fairness and equality are endangered when only a few people know laws.

To further ensure equality and fairness, section 42 of the Constitution of the Republic of Malawi states that every person who is arrested or suspected of a crime has the right to a fair trial, which includes the right to be heard. One way of achieving this maxim is that when a person is convicted, he/she has the right to seek mitigation or leniency before the court passes its sentence. Section 260 (1) (2) of Criminal Procedure and Evidence code further states that 'the court may, before passing sentence, receive such evidence as it thinks fit in order to inform itself as to the sentence proper to be passed. Evidence that the court may receive under subsection (1) may, in addition to the evidence of the accused or the prosecution, include the evidence by or on behalf of the victim of the offence and any relevant reports to enable the court to assess the gravity of the offence'. These provisions, therefore, provide the offender with the opportunity to seek leniency and protect themselves as explained in *Rep. v Felix Madalitso Keke* (2010). This can be achieved by providing convincing reasons that the court should consider as mitigation factors which can either compel the court to lower the sentence below the maximum punishment as provided in the Penal Code. However, due to lack of legal literacy in Malawi, most people are ignorant of how they can protect themselves when seeking mitigation as both legal and linguistic engagements. It is further doubtful whether, as a country, there are effective awareness-raising campaigns put in place to enable people to become knowledgeable about their laws and courtroom procedures to safeguard equality, fairness, and protection of every citizen. Such powers are given to the Malawi Law Commission as stipulated in section 6(a)(iv) of the Malawi Law Commission Act. This chapter was therefore set to address the following objectives:

1) Identify awareness campaigns that can help people know about criminal procedure.
2) Assess the discursive strategies that offenders use in seeking for mitigation.
3) Examine mitigation discursive strategies which are effective and those which are not in moving the court towards leniency.

The vulnerable and the disadvantaged before the law

There are a number of influential studies that have documented vulnerable groups and those that are disadvantaged before the law (Gibbons, 2003; Aldridge, 2010; Ehrlich, 2010; Svongoro et al., 2012). These scholars provide a list of groups of people who meet serious challenges when called as witnesses or when they appear as accused persons before courts of law. Such groups include children, second-language speakers, witnesses with disabilities, women in sexual assault trials, the deaf, and the insufficiently educated (Aldridge, 2010; Kondowe & Svongoro, 2025). It has been observed that contrary to the traditional view that children are the most 'dangerous' of all witnesses, children's testimonies may not be fully trusted because they apparently lack credibility due to their inability to remember and relate their experiences accurately. Some child witnesses also do not understand the concept of numbers. Their ability to count numbers does not mean that they understand the value of such numbers (Aldridge, 2010; Gibbons, 2003). Furthermore, children are said to have serious challenges responding to lawyers' questions which often signify total communication breakdown. They are mostly victims of the court's interpersonal power of coercion, and the linguistic complexity and technicalities of legal language and courtroom pressure. They can easily be threatened and their stories can easily be destroyed (Kondowe, 2020).

Another disadvantaged group covered in prior studies is second-language speakers where the second language serves as the medium of communication during courtroom trial sessions. Second-language speakers are people who have less command of other languages which are not their first languages. This challenge is further compounded when second-language speakers have to deal with the language of the law. They express serious linguistic challenges during courtroom interactions, hence they are vulnerable. Gibbons (2003: 211) lists five possible indicators of linguistic incomprehension of second language speakers: 1) overt statements of incomprehension, 2) asking what to say, 3) responding with an apology ('sorry', 'I beg your pardon'), 4) clarification requests, and 5) absent or inappropriate responses. They often demonstrate very limited linguistic comprehension and production skills. People with intellectual and language disabilities, such as those with Down syndrome, have impaired phonological abilities, as well as those with cerebral palsy. Persons with Down syndrome have a slower word retrieval and they need more time to tell their story (Aldridge, 2010). Their vocabulary may also be less rich. Therefore, people with communicative difficulties are likely to have greater difficulty with grammar and vocabulary.

The deaf are also said to be highly disadvantaged before the law. These are people with an inability to hear and therefore understand verbal communication (Zoloni & Ndalama-Mtawali, 2025). Sign language does not always match precisely with spoken language, in many ways because it is considered a standalone language in its own right (Gibbons, 2003; Svongoro & Ralarala, 2023). Deaf people constitute a separate community with a special culture which differs significantly from that of the hearing population (Gibbons, 2003). This may pose serious challenges when the deaf encounter the law even when a sign interpreter is involved, taking into account the technicalities and complexity of the legal language right from police stations to courtrooms and even in prisons.

Finally, women become vulnerable when handling sexual assault cases. Scholars have argued that the language of rape trials is as harmful as the actual rape itself (Ehrlich, 2010). It is argued that women are publicly re-victimised once their complaints of rape enter the legal system. Some legal critics have referred to rape trials as 'judicial rape' and 'rape of the second kind' (Lees, 1996). Reporting in an African context, Svongoro et al. (2013) note that, in handling rape cases, court officials often demand sexually explicit register, notwithstanding the need to observe cultural appropriateness. This is argued to be a huge obstacle when victims of rape appear and express themselves in court. Victims of rape are sometimes traumatised by the style of questioning they are subjected to in court (Liebes-Plesner, 1994).

The poor and the uneducated groups also fall under the category of disadvantaged groups. Since laws are predominantly communicated in English, uneducated groups are left ignorant. Unfortunately, they are still expected to know the laws, legal procedures, and how they can protect and defend themselves once they are in conflict with the law. In addition, poor people often represent themselves during trials as they cannot afford legal representation. Consequently, they often become a defenceless target of the learned lawyers.

Access to law and fair trial

One parameter in addressing the question of access to law is described by Paul (1975), cited in Kishindo (2001), who points out that it is 'the individual's opportunity to defend himself when he is the target of [legal] claims or when proposed government action threatens his liberty or economic security' (2001: 9). Beqiraj (2016) notes that the right to be heard is a fundamental right which is included in Article 41 of the Charter of Fundamental Rights of the European Union, which stipulates that every person has the right to be heard before any individual measure which would affect him/her adversely is taken. Section 41 of the Constitution of the Republic of Malawi provides access to justice and legal remedies. Specifically, section 41(3) stipulates that every person has the right to an effective remedy by a court of law or tribunal for acts violating the rights and freedoms granted to him/her by the Constitution or any other law. Section 42 stipulates that every person who is arrested or detained (including those convicted) shall have the right to a fair trial.

Even though the law provides for equality and protection of everyone, including the above-mentioned vulnerable groups, these groups meet serious challenges when it comes to accessing the law and knowing procedures that protect them when they are targets of the law. Unfortunately, the ordinary citizens in Malawi are vulnerable. Most people have limited knowledge of the law, legal procedures, and the proper discursive strategies of seeking leniency in the court of law as a form of individual protection. What is more disturbing is that they cannot use ignorance as an excuse in a court of law. According to Gibbons (2003), this is an injustice caused by the justice system. If the courts are unaware of the existence of these challenges within various groups of people, then there is a weakness in legal education. But if the courts are aware of the existence of possible communication issues, and choose to exploit them to discredit such groups of people and their weaknesses, this represents an ethical clash of ensuring fairness and fair trial as provided for in the law.

The right to appeal for mitigation/leniency

The right to appeal for mitigation or leniency is a very important right. Even though this right is provided for in section 260 of Criminal Procedure & Evidence Code, most accused persons, who are unrepresented, find it difficult to exercise the right to seek leniency because they are not aware of the proper discursive strategies. At the mitigation stage of the trial, the offender is given the opportunity to make any statements they deem appropriate for the consideration of the judge prior to the imposition of the sentence. The right to plea for mitigation is also provided for in Magistrates' Court Sentencing Guidelines (2016). The plea may include an explanation as to what led to their actions or how they have changed since the crime. Mitigation pleas give the offender an opportunity to have the judge see the other side of their story, which should be considered as mitigation factors in the sentencing process as emphasised in *Rep. v Felix Madalitso Keke* (2010).

The legal maxim of 'ignorance of the law is no defence'

One of the key duties of a responsible citizen is to obey the law. This entails the duty to respect and obey the laws with all relevant regulations and refraining from engaging in illegal activities which could harm individuals and society. *Ignorantia legis neminem excusat* (Ignorance of the law is no defence) is an expression that has a very long tradition, and it is said to be a principle of Roman law. The principle says that you cannot defend your actions by arguing that you did not know they were illegal, even if your assertion is genuine. John Selden, in his book *Table Talk*, published posthumously in 1689, argues that not all people know the law, but because it is an excuse every person will plead, and no one can tell how to confute them, everyone must be presumed to know the law.

It would indeed be tricky to tell who is genuine and who is not. It would be too easy for people to break laws, sell drugs, have sex with minors, and ignore each other's rights by arguing that they did not know it was illegal. However, this maxim brings forth two key problems. First, our legal systems are complicated; there are a myriad of laws that even some lawyers do not know, yet the majority of citizens are not legal specialists. Second, the legal system has kept the laws within itself, and there are no clear mechanisms put in place to make laws available to ordinary people. It is unfortunate, therefore, that the maxim continues to be applied in full throttle, which raises a serious question about the fairness of the legal system.

We find weakness in the legal definition of the maxim. The agreed upon legal understanding of the 'ignorance of the law is no defence' maxim is concerned with people's prior knowledge of laws. The law deliberately ignores the reality that many people do not know the law, legal procedures, and how they can protect and defend themselves. This chapter extends the definition of 'ignorance of the law' to encompass people's ignorance of legal procedures and ignorance of how they can defend and protect themselves. As Kondowe (2020) notes, the majority of people in Malawi have never been to court and they have no knowledge of what they are expected to do once their matters enter the court of law either as witnesses or accused persons. Even though the law provides for the "the individual's opportunity to defend themselves", most ordinary people are not aware of the available discursive strategies and those which are effective. Therefore, in such a country where the laws are known by just a few people, for how long shall we live in pretence that ignorance of the law will be no defence?

Theoretical framework

The chapter applied the theory of transformative equality. The concept of transformative equality was developed to promote better understanding of the rights of persons who are vulnerable before the law and to address power relations within the institutions of law and the state (Minkowitz, 2017). Fredman et al. (2016) described four dimensions of substantive transformative equality: redressing disadvantage; addressing stigma, stereotyping, prejudice and violence; facilitating voice and participation; and accommodating difference. Minkowitz (2017) notes that there is a need for real transformation of opportunities in institutions such as justice systems so that they are no longer grounded in historical determinants of power and life patterns.

The theory is rooted in law and it is critical in understanding the forms that trigger discrimination and hinder people's participation, accessibility, and inclusion as a result of power imbalances (Goldschmidt, 2017). The approach, therefore, aims to transform the legal system into a more balanced structure to provide a language of rights that is capable of articulating the needs and entitlements of more individuals than just those who form the liberal archetype of the autonomous, self-sufficient individual. Transformative equality targets different systems to bring on board new measures that empower groups of people that are excluded and are treated unequally in the system.

The chapter argues that in such a system where the law operates within the confines of legal specialists who came to know the law after several years of training, it does not make any logical sense to leave out the rest of the population to understand the law by themselves. There is a great need to advocate for transformative equality approaches which meet people's realities and expectations. There are many people in Malawi who are arrested and serve jail sentences for crimes they never committed, and the police are aware of this as explained in *Rep. v officer in charge* (2018).

Data

Data for the study was collected using a combination of document analysis and key informant interviews to facilitate triangulation. Data for objective one was collected using document analysis. We selected Malawi Law Commission annual reports to see the kind of awareness activities they conduct to ensure that people are knowledgeable about laws, legal procedures, and the ways they can protect themselves before courts of law. Data for the second objective was collected from the *Weekend Nation* newspaper dating from March to October, 2023. The newspaper has a special page titled 'In the courtroom' which is dedicated to reporting crimes that occurred during that week. The data collected from newspapers comprise news headlines, the offender involved, the age, and the mitigation strategies the offender had used. Data for objective three was collected from four judicial officers as key informants who were asked to explain which discursive strategies (identified in objective two) are more effective in moving the court towards leniency.

Research findings

The collected data comprised of 26 newspaper articles drawn from the *Weekend Nation.* The newspaper reported 28 crime stories ranging from robbery, theft, rape, defilement, forgery, burglary, assault, illegal entry into the country, and possession of fake currency. Most of the crime suspects were male, with the youngest being 19 years old and the oldest being 50 years old. Only two cases had female suspects, whose ages were 20 and 24 years.

Awareness campaigns available to help people know criminal procedures

The powers to promote the awareness of the law and the Constitution by the public in Malawi is provided for in section 6(a)(iv) of the Malawi Law Commission Act. The Commission has the duty, through civic education, to make sure that every Malawian citizen is made aware of laws and the entire criminal procedure. To execute these functions, the Malawi Law Commission is empowered by the Act to sponsor, support or organise conferences, seminars, workshops, and meetings on any matter under its consideration. However, with the level of ignorance that most Malawians have regarding laws, it raised curiosity on the extent to which the Commission executes such a responsibility to ensure that the ordinary Malawian has access to information regarding the law.

During document analysis, the 2008 Annual Report indicated that the Commission organised a number of workshops and press briefings to publicise its various programmes and to consult the public (Annual Report, 2008). However, most of these activities were meant for the development of legislation such as the Gender Equality Statute; Legislation on HIV and AIDS; Trafficking in Persons Legislation; Declaration of Assets, Liabilities and Business Interest by Public Officers and Elected Officers; and Review of the Education Act (Annual Report, 2008). They also held workshops and conferences in order to enhance networking and collaboration with other institutions.

Similarly, in 2009, the Commission conducted a countrywide dissemination exercise on HIV and AIDS Legislation and Trafficking in Persons Legislation, and they provided information to both the print and broadcasting media on various law reforms (Annual Report, 2009). The Commission conducted a press briefing on the review of the Education Act and another one on the development of the Anti-Trafficking in Persons Legislation. In 2012, the Commission conducted workshops with different law enforcement institutions on the dispensation of justice and national duties on the proposed Firearms Acts, Local Courts Act, and other Acts (Annual Report, 2012). They also conducted information dissemination through various media stations on the proposed Acts (Annual Report, 2012).

The analysed documents do not mention anything on the activities the Commission undertook to educate the local people about the existing laws and criminal procedures. The same can be said about the 2016 Annual Report where the Commission only carried out sensitisation meetings on gender-related laws and an awareness campaign on the Penal Code (Amendment Act of 2016). What is also more interesting is that all these workshops and conferences were held in hotels to which ordinary people have no access. It is clear from the reports that the Commission does not undertake much outreach activities to serve the interests of local people in their communities. Furthermore, it seems that much of the work they do concerns law reviews and reforms. In view of the limited activities of the Commission, this chapter argues that depriving the poor and uneducated population of vital information means depriving them of a common voice which makes them somehow feel that the laws were not meant for them, but only for those who are educated and rich (Kondowe et al., 2022). In some cases, as Goldschmidt (2017) notes, they may be right to think in that way. Vulnerable groups continue to be ignorant about existing laws, and institutions which are entrusted to educate them are not performing their duties adequately, yet their ignorance cannot be considered as defence. Their rights regarding access to justice (equal protection and the opportunity to defend themselves) remains a nightmare.

Discursive strategies that offenders use in seeking mitigation

We define discursive strategies as deliberate linguistic planning, practices, and tactics which writers and speakers employ in discourses in order to reveal their ideas and persuade the audience. The chapter found that offenders used various discursive strategies for seeking mitigation as a way of protecting themselves from stiffer punishments. Results on the discursive strategies of mitigation were grouped into two broader categories. First, the offenders presented their current circumstances so that the court could pay attention to the offender's circumstances. This is where the accused stated that they are first offenders, breadwinners with family responsibilities, are of youthful age, on long-term treatment, breastfeeding, or that they regret their actions. In the second category, the offenders provided reasons that influenced them to commit the crime. Some mentioned that they were influenced by the devil, poverty, and hunger. Others still said that they did not know that what they were doing was wrong.

TABLE 4.1: Common discursive strategies used by the offender to seek leniency

S/N	Common mitigation discursive strategies	Frequency
1	First offender	15
2	Age	3
3	Breadwinner/family responsibilities: *(looking after wife, children, or old mother)*	12
4	Regret/work of the devil	3
5	Responsible person/asking for forgiveness	6
6	Long-term treatment	1
7	Breastfeeding	1
8	Poverty and hunger	3
9	They didn't know they were wrong	3
	Total	**51**

As Table 4.1 shows, the data revealed that there were nine different strategies that the offenders opted to use in seeking leniency when they are convicted in the court of law. The appeal as a first offender came top of the list, followed by the appeal that they are breadwinners with family responsibilities. Some mentioned that they are looking after a wife, children, and old parents. Other strategies were used by few people. The appeal for long-term treatment, and that the accused is breastfeeding, were rare and appeared only once in each case.

Discursive strategies which are effective in moving the court towards leniency

A simple questionnaire was designed which listed the above identified discursive strategies. The questionnaire was then circulated to four judicial officers who acted as key informants to assess which strategies can/do influence the court in deciding the quantum of the sentence. Results reveal that mentioning that one is a first offender and of youthful age are the most effective strategies as mitigation factors. This has also been emphasised in *Rep. v Felix Madalitso Keke* (2010). Even though the appeal for pleading guilty did not appear in the data, the key informants also mentioned it to be a very effective discursive strategy in seeking mitigation. However, it was discovered that the responses provided by the key informants were largely based on legal provisions. For instance, on imprisonment of first offenders, section 340 of the Criminal Procedure and Evidence Code states that where a person is convicted by a court of an offence and no previous conviction is proven against him/her, he/she shall not be sentenced for that offence unless the court finds good grounds for doing so after weighing all the available options. This clearly provides leniency towards first offenders. Therefore, accused persons who are knowledgeable of this provision find it safer to consider it as an effective discursive strategy. The courts, therefore, have no option but to consider such an appeal once it is raised.

It was also mentioned that courts give more leniency towards young offenders. It is usually appropriate for the court not to impose a sentence which involves a term of actual imprisonment. In *Rep v Mills* (1998), a young offender was sentenced for reckless assault and the defendants appealed the decision to the Victorian Court of Appeal. The appeal court recognised that young offenders are immature and may not understand the consequences of their actions. They also recognised that young people have their whole lives ahead of them and they should not have their prospects ruined by a youthful mistake. Such decisions have been handed down through case law and have influenced legal decisions in most common law countries including the case of *Rep. v Felix Madalitso Keke* (2010).

Similarly, it was mentioned by the judicial officers that offenders who plead guilty can also find solace in case law. Pleading guilty at the first available opportunity means that the offender accepts having committed the offence, and a reduction of one-third could be applied to the sentence (Brereton & Casper, 1981). The available sentence reduction for a guilty plea, therefore takes a sliding scale from a maximum to one-quarter. According to the Crown Prosecution Service's Annual Report, in 2018 and 2019, 78% of the cases in the magistrates' courts were resolved by a guilty plea. Similarly, in Malawi, the Magistrates' Courts Sentencing Guidelines (2016) also provide for a sentence discount for a guilty plea that has been provided timely. The courts showed leniency in *Flora Jeke v The Rep* (2008) Crim. Appeal No. 139. The court reduced the 18 months' custodial sentence of a woman who had pleaded guilty to the charge with a maximum of 7 years imprisonment with hard labour. The High Court substituted the appellant's sentence with an immediate release.

Even though the study discovered that the above are some of the effective mitigation strategies, the list is not exhaustive. The Magistrates' Court Sentencing Guidelines (2016) outline many other effective strategies for seeking mitigation that the offenders could have utilised if they were aware of them. Unfortunately, most of them were quick to point at being first offenders, not knowing that there are other, more effective options available. Some of the effective mitigation strategies include time already spent in custody, evidence of genuine remorse, cooperation with police, poor health, and previous good character. We are aware that these mitigation strategies are not enough on their own to influence a lenient outcome. The court still considers the aggravating and mitigating circumstances of the offender and the offence in totality and circumstances surrounding it (Magistrates' Court Sentencing Guidelines, 2016). Our central argument in this chapter is that it is of paramount importance that ordinary people should be made aware of these discursive strategies so that they know how they can protect and defend themselves well. Unfortunately, not many people have adequate knowledge of these available strategies. It is for this reason that most accused people are quick to mention that they are first offenders in isolation without considering these other available strategies which would add more weight to their narrative. People's ignorance of these opportunities to protect themselves defeats the maxims which state that everyone is equal before the law. Peoples' ignorance remains a big challenge in accessing the law and is a huge obstacle in yielding fairness and equal protection of the law in Malawi.

Discussion

The expectations of legal discourse and layperson's linguistic realities

Most laypersons who appear in court as accused or as witnesses are just ordinary persons from different social classes and language backgrounds, and without any formal training in the fields of language and law (Kondowe, 2020; Svongoro et.al. 2012). By contrast, legal professionals have at least a diploma or a degree in law. These imbalances in social classes and educational training pose challenges when it comes to courtroom interaction (Svongoro et al., 2012). As further noted by Heffer (2020), everyday conversational narratives naturally include point of view, evaluative reactions, emotions, and other subjective aspects. However, conversely, legal discourse attempts to be scientific, logical, based on analytical categories, and other objective criteria. Legal discourse insists on factual reports rather than emotive and suggestive stories. It forces people to shift from personal language to a neutral and objective style. Everyone is therefore expected to adhere to an objective mode rather than a subjective mode. There is a preference for using speech which is impersonal rather than personal, and a preference for facts rather than narratives. Many laypersons find these restrictions difficult to understand and comply with. Such practices can discredit genuine appeals, and vulnerable people can be traumatised. Fairness is therefore endangered (Gibbons, 2003). Such language restrictions only serve the interests of educated groups, who play an important role in the reproduction of inequalities between legal experts and laypersons, and this needs to be resolved by using transformational equality approaches.

Laypersons bring to court language ideologies which are socially, culturally, and historically conditioned. These language ideologies constitute their daily language use outside the court (Blommaert, 2005). When they come to court, the laypersons will bring all these acquired language practices and repertoires, and they do not leave such language practices by the doorway as they enter the court. These language practices and repertoires are part of their culture and, as argued by Patrick Devlin 'law should be used to enforce the norms of a society's culture' (Post, 2003: 485). Sumner (1906) further argues that if laws do not speak to the people's local realities and needs, such laws will meet stiff resistance and will be rejected. Common law must, therefore, embody the experiences and customs of the surrounding community. Unless deliberate efforts are put in place to ensure that everyone understands the culture of legal discourse, the law will continue to be alien and a myth to the common people. Some of the mitigation discursive strategies bear a very strong cultural relevance. For instance, when a male offender says, 'I committed a crime of theft because I am a breadwinner and I had nothing to feed my wife and children', this discursive strategy culturally takes into account the inherent societal roles a man is burdened with regardless of one's economic status. Further, if one says that it was 'poverty and hunger' that made them commit a certain crime, this strategy could also be justifiable considering the levels of poverty in African societies and the psychological pressures accompanied by poverty. There is no doubt that poverty and hunger can lead someone to take criminal action to secure some means of survival. However, this chapter does not in any way encourage the poor to commit crimes and use poverty as an excuse; rather, we are bringing to light the conflicts between discursive strategies that have cultural justifications which the law needs to consider.

Towards transformative equality approaches

Even though the United Nations International Covenant on Civil and Political Rights, the Charter of Fundamental Rights of the European Union, and the Constitution of the Republic of Malawi provide for equal protection under the law, fairness, and the creation of non-discriminatory legal environments, in practice remains nothing but an idea in theory. In practice, Malawi has not yet adopted serious implementation measures to enforce the provisions of statutory requirements to ensure that poor and uneducated populations are made aware of the law. In a country where the majority cannot comfortably read English, let alone understand the complexity of legal English, and with a literacy level of 62.14% among people above 15 years of age (Kondowe et.al. 2024), it is a mockery to continue upholding colonial and historically conditioned maxims that do not make much sense in reality. The legal maxims, such as 'ignorance of the laws is not a defence', need to be transformed to meet the realities in underdeveloped countries like Malawi. As Svongoro & Ralarala (2023) observe, the transformative equalities can be achieved by making reasonable physical and procedural accommodations, modifications, and adjustments to the justice system to ensure that all citizens enjoy equal rights.

To transform this maxim, we first need to expand its definition as it is currently confined within the prescribed law and leaves out the component of practice. As stated earlier, proponents of this maxim and the current legal understanding is that you cannot defend yourself before the court by arguing that you did not know that your actions were illegal. This would mean that everyone can make this excuse and it would be difficult for the court to tell who is genuine. This can, however, make sense if the country made deliberate efforts to make the law available to everyone by, among other strategies, ensuring that laws exist in (local) languages familiar to the bigger population. In its current state, we can argue that the justice system thrives on people's ignorance and punishes them for the same.

Furthermore, the definition of 'ignorance of the law' is narrowly defined. Knowing the law should extend further to include the law in practice, such as knowing the legal procedures both in criminal and civil cases, knowing how to defend and protect oneself when one is in conflict with the law, and knowing all the legal strategies that are effective and ineffective. As written earlier, lawyers acquired such knowledge through years of learning and mastering the law, yet ordinary citizens are expected to know the law by themselves, and failure to know the law cannot be said to be an excuse. This is legal hypocrisy which needs to be heavily revised through transformative approaches.

To ensure that there is equality, the legal system needs to be transformed into a more balanced structure by taking asymmetrical power structures into account to accommodate the majority of the population, which is poor and uneducated, and by incorporating Fredman et al.'s (2016) four dimensions of substantive equality. The dimensions call for the urgent need to redress disadvantage (the redistributive dimension) of the poor and the uneducated population by making sure that they are not left out in accessing the law and having knowledge about the law and legal procedures. The law needs to address stigma, stereotyping and prejudice (the recognition dimension) that some of these colonial maxims have on ordinary people. In addition, the law should be able to facilitate the voice and participation (the participative dimension) of all the people regardless of power and social class. Finally, there is also need to accommodate differences, including through structural change (the transformative dimension) for people of various social classes. Therefore, a country like Malawi needs to introspect to see how far it has gone in making sure that everyone knows the law and is protected before we continue embracing these inherited colonial maxims, and consider how unfair these maxims are to persons with disabilities, in particular those with visual, hearing, and intellectual disabilities when the information is inaccessible to them (Kondowe & Svongoro, 2025).

Malawi as a country needs robust awareness-raising campaigns in all corners of the country to reach out to as many people as possible. Apart from the Malawi Law Commission, there is a need to empower more institutions to join hands in a concerted effort to address these gaps if the information is to reach out to as many Malawians as possible. Some of these institutions include governmental and non-governmental organisations, universities, and human-rights defenders. We also agree with Kondowe et al. (2022) who recommend that law should be introduced as a compulsory subject in schools and should not be restricted to lawyers. To remove ignorance of the law, everyone must be taught basic components of the law at all levels of education. Furthermore, the law should be translated into local languages; languages which most Malawians can easily understand, read, and use to access information on legal matters. These are some of the transformative equality practices that can be introduced to bring different perspectives in the legal domain in a bid to curb challenges that emanate from the current legal circumstances which seem to be promoting selective justice.

We are aware of some of the advocacy measures taken by police through the Victim Support Unit which are largely meant to assist victims of violence and abuse, especially women and children. Lonsway and Archambault (2023) call this 'advocacy at an individual level' where the interest is on protecting the interests of the offender both inside and outside the criminal justice system. We argue that these measures are meant to treat a wound but not to prevent a wound from happening. Transformative approaches need to go beyond individual interests and check the available advocates at community and system levels to question some of the longstanding practices that continue to victimise the already vulnerable population.

Summary and conclusions

This chapter set out to question a longstanding legal maxim which states that 'ignorance of the law is no defence' by taking into account legal provisions, legal practice, and cultural realities in Malawi. The study used data from 28 news articles taken from one of the leading newspapers in Malawi, the *Weekend Nation* for the year 2023. The chapter problematised the extent to which Malawi's legal system has embraced the provision that 'all persons are equal before the law and are entitled without any discrimination to the equal protection of the law' which is stipulated in both local and international laws. We have therefore identified three objectives: 1) identify awareness campaigns that can help people know about criminal procedure; 2) identify the discursive strategies that offenders use in seeking mitigation; 3) assess mitigation discursive strategies which are effective and those which are not in moving the court towards leniency. We have discovered that the Malawi Law Commission as an institution entrusted to raise awareness in the country is not doing much to address the gap. The mitigation strategies which are made by the offenders demonstrate a lack of knowledge by most ordinary people who are not aware of the many available options that can be effective in moving the court towards leniency. There is clear evidence that most people are not aware of the legal procedures and how they can ably defend themselves.

In theory, the law states that it shall protect everyone equally, while in reality a lot needs to be done for equal protection to be realised. The chapter demands more transformative equality approaches that can enable poor and uneducated people to understand the law. The current legal maxim that 'ignorance of the law is no defence' is distanced from the cultural realities of most Malawians who do not have access to laws which exist in English. The chapter has proposed to introduce the law as a subject in schools, increase awareness levels of ordinary Malawians, and translate the laws into local language as some of the transformative equality practices that can change the way the legal system operates. Otherwise, the poor and the uneducated will remain vulnerable and disadvantaged. Equality and fairness for the poor are heavily endangered and justice can hardly come to the fore. Otherwise, until transformative equalities are implemented, the maxim of 'ignorance of the law is no defence' shall continue to victimise many people. It is legal hypocrisy to continue clinging to old traditions that are not in tandem with realities in underdeveloped countries like Malawi. These forms of injustice in the justice system need to be addressed if equality, fairness, and equal protection are to be realised.

Acknowledgements

I extend my deepest gratitude to Her Honour Thokozani Soko, Assistant Registrar of the High Court of Malawi, Lilongwe District Registry (Civil Division); and His Worship Paul Chiotcha, Chief Resident Magistrate (North) for providing very substantive feedback to my earlier drafts of this chapter.

References

Aldridge, M. (2010). Vulnerable witnesses in the Criminal Justice System. In Coulthard, M. & Johnson, A. (ed.) *The Routledge Handbook of Forensic Linguistics.* New York: Routledge. 296–314.

Annual Report (2008). *Malawi Law Commission: Expert provider of advisory services on law development, reform and status of the law in Malawi.*

Annual Report (2009). *Malawi Law Commission: Expert provider of advisory services on law development, reform and status of the law in Malawi.*

Annual Report (2012). *Malawi Law Commission: Expert provider of advisory services on law development, reform and status of the law in Malawi.*

Beqiraj, P. (2016). The Right to Be Heard in the European Union – Case Law of the Court of Justice of the European Union. *European Journal of Multidisciplinary Studies,* 1(1): 264–269.

Brereton, D. & Casper, JD. (1981). Does It Pay to Plead Guilty? Differential Sentencing and the Functioning of Criminal Courts. *Law & Society Review*, *16*(1), 45–70. https://doi.org/10.2307/3053549.

Ehrlich, S. (2010). Rape victims: The discourse of rape trials. In Coulthard, M. & Johnson, A. (ed.) *The Routledge Handbook of Forensic Linguistics.* New York: Routledge. 265–280.

Flora Jeke v The Rep (2008)

Fredman, S., Kuosmanen, J. & Campbell, M. (2016). Transformative equality: Making the sustainable development goals work for women. *Ethics & international affairs,* 30(2): 177–187.

Gibbons, J. (2003). *Forensic Linguistics: An introduction to Language in the Justice System.* Oxford: Blackwell Publishing.

Goldschmidt, JE. (2017). New Perspectives on Equality: Towards Transformative Justice through the Disability Convention? *Nordic Journal of Human Rights,* 35 (1): 1–14. https://doi.org/10.1080/18918131.2017.1286131.

Government of Malawi (2016). Magistrates' Court Sentencing Guidelines. Zomba: Government Printer

Heffer, C. (2020). Narrative in trial: Constructing crime stories in court. In Coulthard, M. & Johnson, A. (eds.), The Routledge handbook of forensic linguistics. London: Routledge. 199-217.

Kishindo, P. (2001). Language and the law in Malawi: A case for the use of indigenous languages in the legal system. *Language Matters: Studies in the Languages of Africa,* 32(1): 1–27.

Kondowe, W. (2020). *Insincerity and the Principle of Believability in Malawian courtroom trial: An inquiry into forensic discourse.* [Doctoral dissertation] Wuhan: Central China Normal University.

Kondowe, W. (2024). Insincerity in lawyers' questioning strategies in Malawian criminal courtroom discourse. *Text & Talk*, 44(6), 763-786.

Kondowe, W., Ngwira, FF. & Labanna, D. (2024). Unintended Mental Health Consequences of Media Framing During COVID-19. *COVID-19 and Psychological Distress in Africa.* London: Routledge, 89–100.

Kondowe, W., Liao, M. & Ngwira, FF. (2022). A study of intentional insincerity in Malawian criminal justice: Witnesses' discursive strategies. In Ralarara, MK., Kaschula, RH. & Heydon, G. (ed.) *Language and the Law: Global Perspectives in Forensic Linguistics from Africa and beyond.* Stellenbosch: African Sun Media. 241–260.

Kondowe, W.,& Svongoro. P. (2025). *Discrimination and Access to Justice in Africa: Language, Vulnerability and Social Inclusion in Southern and Eastern Africa.* New York: Routledge.

Lees, S. (1996). *Carnal Knowledge: Rape on Trial.* United Kingdom: Penguin.

Liebes-Plesner, T. (1994). Rhetoric in the service of justice: The sociolinguistic construction of stereotypes in an Israeli rape trial. *Text*, 4(1–3), 173–192.

Lonsway, KA. & Archambault, J. (2023). Effective Victim Advocacy Within the Criminal Justice System. *End Violence Against Women International* (EVAWI).

Malawi Government. (2010). *Criminal Procedure and Evidence Code.* Zomba: Government Printer.

Malawi Government. (2018). *Malawi's Constitution of 1994 with Amendments through 2017.* Zomba: Government Printer.

Malawi Government. (1998). *Malawi Law Commission Act.* Zomba: Government Printer.

Malawi Government. (2011). *Local Courts Act.* Zomba: Government Printer.

Minkowitz, T. (2017). CRPD and transformative equality. *International Journal of Law in Context*, 13(1): 77–86. https://doi.org/10.1017/S1744552316000483.

Post, R. (2003). Law and Cultural Conflict. *Chicago-Kent Law Review.* Vol 78: 485–508.

Rep. v Felix Madalitso Keke (2010)

Rep v Mills (1998)

Rep. v officer in charge (2018)

Sumner, WG. (1906). *Folkways: A Study of the Sociological Importance of Usages, Manners, Customs, Mores, and Morals*. Boston: Athenaeum Press.

Svongoro, P. & Ralarala, MK. (2023). Zimbabwe's constitutional safeguards for persons with communication disabilities: Implications for access to justice. In Kaschula, RH., Ralarala, MK. & Heydon. G. (ed.) *Language, Crime and Courts in Contemporary Africa and Beyond.* Stellenbosch: African Sun Media, 51–71.

Svongoro, P., Mutangadura, J., Gonzo, L. & Mavunga, G. (2012). Language and the Legal Process: A Linguistic Analysis of Courtroom Discourse involving Selected Cases of Alleged Rape in Mutare, Zimbabwe. *South African Journal of African Languages,* 32(2), 117–128.

Zoloni, M., & Ndalama-Mtawali, D. (2025). Legal status of Malawi Sign Language: Implications on language rights and access to justice for the hearing impaired. In Kondowe, W. & Svongoro. P. (ed.) *Discrimination and Access to Justice in Africa: Language, Vulnerability and Social Inclusion in Southern and Eastern Africa.* New York: Routledge (forthcoming).

5 KNOWLEDGE AND PERCEPTION OF FORENSIC LINGUISTICS BY LINGUISTS IN MALAWI

Precious Lungu

Background

Linguistics has various branches that have been researched for some time. One increasingly prominent area of applied linguistics, which has sprouted from a research-based understanding of language, is forensic linguistics (Ariani et al., 2014: 225). This branch of linguistics is intriguing because of numerous studies that are being carried out across the globe. One indication that an area is gaining ground is the extensive research that is carried out in that area, and this is the case with forensic linguistics. According to Coulthard and Johnson (2007: 5), the initial growth of forensic linguistics was slow; however, research in forensic linguistics has continued to grow, now reaching considerable proportions, making forensic linguistics a multi- and cross-disciplinary field, with many up-to-date bibliographies. This sharp rise shows that this field is making strides with each passing day. We can only envision an unstoppable growth of the field as more research is being conducted.

MacLeod and Wright (2020: 360) equally assert that one area of applied linguistics in which there have been increasing trends in both utilising technologies to assist in the analysis of texts and scrutinising digital data through the lens of traditional linguistic and discursive analytical methods is forensic linguistics. Thus, forensic linguistics has witnessed an increase in amalgamating linguistics and science in this digital era. The application of science in language use also brings on board the field of law, thereby leading to forensic linguistics. Eventually, the field of forensic linguistics is finding its feet, especially in Africa.

Furthermore, Tiersma and Solan (2012: 2) state that linguistics and related disciplines have blossomed into significant academic fields with impressive accomplishments. Scholars trained in law, those trained in language-related fields (including psychology, computer science, and the philosophy of language), as well as those trained in both, have seriously taken the openness of the legal system to new ideas by engaging in a broad programme of interdisciplinary research. Such openness has also accommodated forensic linguistics, which is unarguably one of the most freshly budding fields of linguistics. The amalgamation of law and language makes forensic linguistics a unique field, whose prowess cannot go unnoticed among legal experts and linguists.

However, it would be erroneous to assume that every linguist or legal expert is knowledgeable of forensic linguistics. Given that this is still an emerging field of linguistics, it would only be proper to assume that it is not well known in some parts of the world, especially in Africa, including Malawi. This is also evidenced by the extensive research that is still being carried out in the field.

As an emerging field of linguistics, forensic linguistics is yet to trend worldwide. Many scholars are carrying out research in this field as a way of contributing to scholarship and knowledge of forensic linguistics. To that effect, a study was also conducted in Malawi by Kondowe and Ngwira (2023) to investigate how knowledgeable legal experts are in forensic linguistics, and the need for linguists as expert witnesses. This study shows that forensic linguistics is still not well known in Malawi, even in some parts of Sub-Saharan Africa, especially to legal experts. The study also indicates that although legal experts can speak English competently, they are not language experts and therefore may not appreciate the impact of language on their legal decisions (Kondowe & Ngwira, 2023: 18). Since forensic linguistics merges the fields of law and language, it would only be proper to conduct research that also focuses on linguists or language experts. Hence, the current study aims to establish the knowledge and perceptions of forensic linguistics by linguists in Malawi.

To carry out this study, the following specific objectives were used as a benchmark:

1) to establish the extent to which linguists in Malawi are knowledgeable of forensic linguistics
2) to determine the perceptions that linguists in Malawi have on forensic linguistics.

Literature review

Forensic linguistics

According to Ariani et al. (2014: 223), linguistics Professor Jan Svartvik (1968) was the first person to use the term 'forensic linguistics', in his book *The Evans Statements: A Case for Forensic Linguistics*, in 1968. Coulthard and Johnson (2007: 7) add that, in this book, the Professor demonstrated that disputed and incriminating parts of a series of four statements which had been made to police officers by Timothy Evans about the deaths of his wife and baby daughter, had a grammatical style measurably different from that of uncontested parts of the statements, and thus, a new area of forensic expertise was born. Eventually, in the 1980s, Australian linguists discussed the application of linguistics and sociolinguistics to legal issues. This rubberstamped the further usage of the term 'forensic linguistics'.

MacLeod and Wright (2020: 360) define forensic linguistics as an application of linguistic theory and method to any point at which there is an interface between language and the law. That is to say, forensic linguistics establishes an intersection between language and law. In forensic linguistics, both legal and linguistic experts are brought together to address various aspects of the law. The field is popularly viewed as comprising three main elements, namely the (written) language of the law, the (spoken) language of legal processes, and language analysis as evidence or as an investigative tool (MacLeod & Wright, 2020: 360). This means that, as long as analysis of language is applied in the legal field, forensic linguistics is at play and is relevant.

Ariani et al. (2014: 223) provide another interesting explanation by stating that forensic linguistics involves the application of scientific knowledge to language in the context of criminal and civil law. It means language applies to both civil and criminal law, with a focus on textual analysis and language use, both in and outside the courtroom. In this context, forensic linguists are interested in understanding the complexity and origin of the written law, as well as the use of language in forensic procedures. They also study the judicial process from the point of arrest, through the interview, charge, trial, and sentencing (Ariani et al., 2014: 223). In other words, forensic linguists are interested in almost every nook and cranny of the law.

The study of law has comfortably become interdisciplinary in the past years, where some linguists have made inroads into the legal world by addressing such issues as juror comprehension and competence to stand trial (Tiersma & Solan, 2012: 2). Such interest in the contributions of other fields to the study of law has made the legal field more receptive to cross-disciplinary thought in general, and open to linguistic research in particular. This warm reception has made it easy for forensic linguists to make tremendous contributions to the field of law. MacLeod and Wright (2020: 370) agree with this assertion, by arguing that as the value brought forth by forensic linguists to both criminal and civil investigations is clearer, those in law enforcement have enlisted their assistance in the gathering of evidence and, in some cases, have provided linguist-led courses to various stakeholders.

Forensic linguists

An expert in the field of forensic linguistics is called a forensic linguist. In other words, forensic linguists are also known as expert witnesses (Kondowe & Ngwira, 2023: 2) because they provide professional knowledge in disputes, and help answer questions that are centred on the language of both written and oral texts. According to MacLeod and Wright (2020: 360), forensic linguists often appear in court to provide their expert testimony as evidence for the side by which they were retained. The testimony of a forensic linguist is usually taken seriously or is admissible in court because the forensic linguist is regarded and respected as an expert linguist who has authority in their field.

Forensic linguists also find themselves confronted with a wide range of tasks, including settling matters of the disputed meaning of slang terms, commenting on the level of influence one speaker may have had over the contributions of another, determining the linguistic proficiency of an individual, or providing an opinion on whether or not an interviewee understood the content raised by an interviewer (MacLeod & Wright, 2020: 360). In other words, a forensic linguist is as important as any other expert witness in and outside the courtroom, but within the confines of the legal field. The forensic linguist is tasked with various roles, given that they are the focal point of any language-related question in court.

Knowledge and attitude towards forensic linguists

Kondowe and Ngwira (2023) carried out a study on the knowledge, attitudes and perceived importance of forensic linguists as expert witnesses in court. The study engaged legal professionals to determine how they perceive the importance of involving forensic linguists during case trials in Malawi. The study established that forensic linguists are rarely used in Malawian courts because most legal professionals are ignorant of the existence of these linguists (Kondowe & Ngwira, 2023). This shows that in most cases, forensic linguists are not engaged as expert witnesses in Malawian courts, a scenario the authors described as an undermining of the role of linguistics in the legal field.

Nonetheless, Kondowe and Ngwira (2023) established that legal professionals demonstrated high levels of knowledge and perception of the importance of forensic linguists, and a positive attitude towards the use of linguists as expert witnesses in Malawian courts. In other words, a majority of the legal professionals appreciated the importance of engaging linguist experts in both criminal and civil cases in Malawian courts. In addition, the study revealed that education and awareness had a bearing on legal professionals' understanding of the linguist experts' services in Malawian courts. This shows that prior knowledge influenced the legal professionals' perception of the role of the forensic linguist. Thus, those with prior knowledge of forensic linguistics and expert witnesses (forensic linguists) had positive attitudes and perceptions towards the role of forensic linguists.

The current study used this research as a stepping stone to its realisation. As a departure from the study by Kondowe and Ngwira (2023), which involved the attitude, knowledge, and perceptions of legal professionals towards the engagement of expert linguists in Malawian courts, this study focuses on the knowledge and perceptions of forensic linguistics by Malawian linguists. Since forensic linguistics is an amalgamation of language and law, the current study focuses more on the linguistic aspect of the concept, given that the study by Kondowe and Ngwira (2023) focused more on legal professionals.

Theoretical framework

The study adopted the Relevance Theory developed by D. Sperber and D. Wilson in 1986 and, later on, improved in 1995. The main assumption of the theory is that human beings are endowed with a biologically rooted ability to maximise the relevance of any incoming stimuli, which includes linguistic utterances and other communicative behaviour (Ramos, 1997; Yus, 2006). This is a post-Gricean theory that is based on the cognitive process of information presented to humans. According to Sperber and Wilson (1995), human cognition is relevance-oriented, where attention is given to information that seems relevant to us. Any information that does not seem relevant to people is usually disregarded. Thus, the Relevance Theory asserts that people's perception of concepts is based on how they find such issues relevant.

Wilson (2016) introduces the issue of context by citing that the Relevance Theory also considers context. Thus, relevance in a context and relevance to an individual. What can be relevant in one context can also be irrelevant in a different context. Hence, knowledge of a particular concept has to be relevant to both the individual and the context. Relevance should not only focus on utterances or other communicative acts, but also on any external stimulus or internal mental representation that can provide input to cognitive processes, so that not only utterances but sights, sounds, smells, thoughts, memories, or conclusions of inferences may all provide potentially relevant inputs for an individual at a time (Wilson, 2016: 22).

Cognitive effects are achieved when newly-presented information interacts with a context of existing assumptions by strengthening an existing assumption, by contradicting and eliminating an existing assumption, or by combining with an existing assumption to yield a contextual implication (Sperber & Wilson, 1995). In the context of the current study, either linguists can have prior knowledge of forensic linguistics, which then would prove that this information is relevant to them, or some linguists are not aware of such a subfield of linguistics. Such being the case, it is more likely that their perception of forensic linguistics would be a positive one. The new information and the existing knowledge and/or assumptions about forensic linguistics would have greater cognitive effects, hence greater relevance.

Methodology

Research design and participants

The current study adopted a mixed research design, combining qualitative and quantitative research designs. The target participants of the study were linguistics and/or language experts in tertiary institutions in Malawi. A total of eight tertiary institutions were involved in the study, and were both public and private tertiary institutions in Malawi. Since the study focused on linguists in Malawi, the participants were purposively selected, of which all qualified to be part of the study. The study also used the snowball sampling technique, where some respondents were asked to refer the researcher to other participants who fit in the category of participants for this study. In total, there were 26 participants.

Data collection

Data was collected through an online questionnaire that was generated using Google Forms. This data collection tool had a total of 17 questions, of which ten were close-ended and seven were open-ended. The instrument was divided into three parts; the first part solicited the socio-demographic characteristics of the participants, the second part dwelled on the participants' knowledge of forensic linguistics, and the last part solicited information on the participants' perceptions. After developing the online survey using Google Forms, the questionnaire was administered to a small sample as a pilot survey. This was done to determine and assess the feasibility and authenticity of the tool. The pilot survey showed that there was a need for some minimal improvements before the main administration. After improving and adjusting the tool accordingly, the online questionnaire was shared via email and WhatsApp, as the main conduits of administering the survey.

Data analysis

Data from the online questionnaire was downloaded in an Excel workbook format. The quantitative data was presented in the form of pie charts, tables, and bar graphs using SPSS. This was followed by an interpretation. Thus, below each thematic item, an interpretation was made. After the data presentation, a thematic discussion was done, to establish the knowledge and perceptions of forensic linguistics by linguists in Malawi.

Ethical considerations

Before administering the online questionnaire, the researcher made sure to seek consent from the participants. All respondents were assured that the information they would provide would be solely used for research purposes. To ensure that there was utmost confidentiality of the participants' information, the online questionnaire was designed to be anonymous. No name of any participant was ever recorded; only the data was recorded in a safe and secure place, after downloading it.

Findings

Socio-demography

Several socio-demographic characteristics were collected from the participants as part of the data. These ranged from age and years of experience to qualifications.

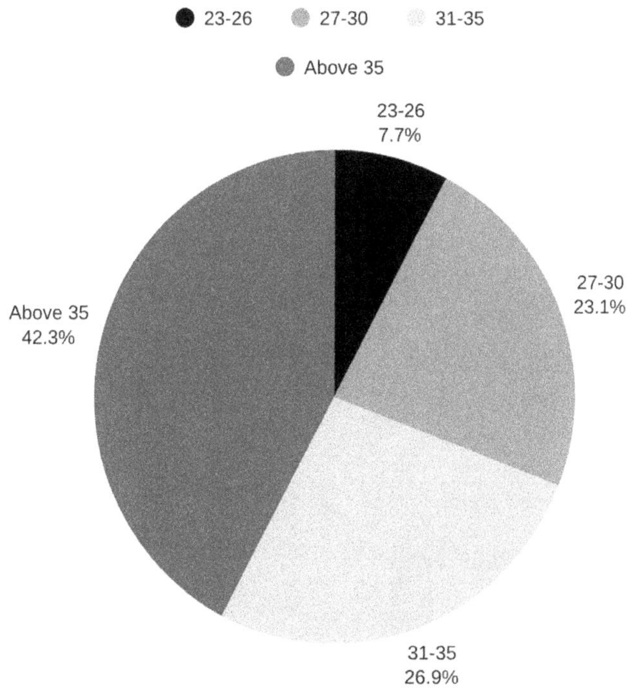

FIGURE 5.1: Age range of participants

The age range of the respondents was 23–35 years. According to the pie chart above, the majority of participants were above 35 years old (42.3%), seconded by those within the range of 31–35 years old (26.9%), and the youngest participants were within the range of 23–26 years old, with 7.7%. In terms of gender, there were 15 male participants and 11 female participants, making a total of 26 participants. The males represented 57.7% of the participants, while the females represented 42.3% of the total number of participants.

TABLE 1: Qualifications of Participants

Qualification	Frequency	Percentage (%)
PhD	6	23
Master's Degree	17	65.4
Bachelor's Degree	3	11.6
Total	**26**	**100**

In terms of qualifications, a total of six participants had PhD as their highest qualification, representing 23%; 17 participants had a Master's degree as their highest qualification, representing 65.4%; and three participants had a Bachelor's degree as their highest qualification, representing 11.6% of the total participants. The three Bachelor's degree holders were engaged as Staff Associates in linguistics in their respective institutions. As regards specialisation, 98% of the participants specialise in applied linguistics, with fields such as psycholinguistics, sociolinguistics, African languages and linguistics, translation and lexicography, ecolinguistics, and contact-induced language change. A minority of the participants (2%) specialised in pure linguistics.

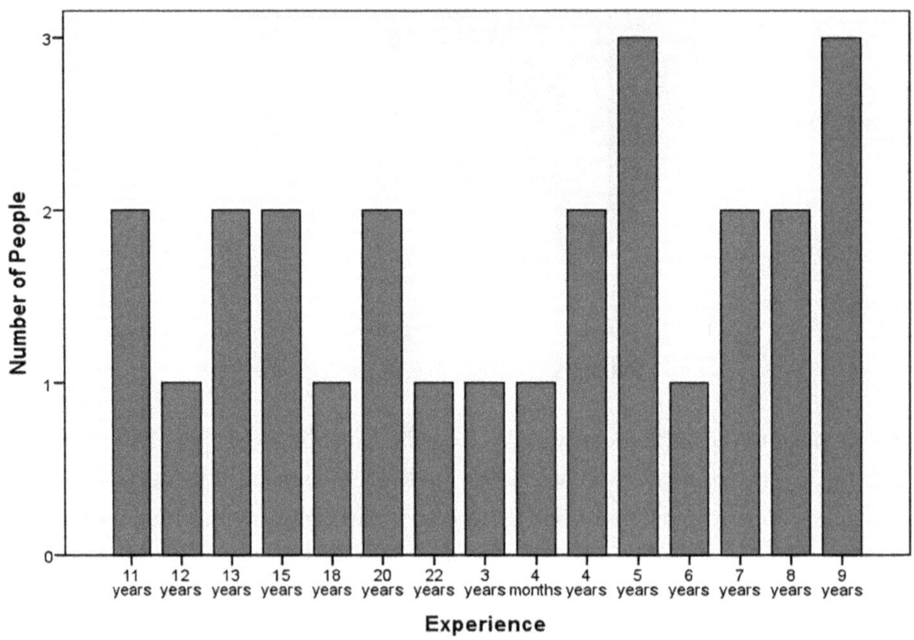

FIGURE 5.2: Years of teaching or working in the specialised field

The bar graph above shows the participants' years of experience in their respective fields of specialisation. The least years of experience was three and the highest number of years of experience was 22. Those within the range of 3–8 years of experience were 12, representing 46.2%; those within the range of 9–14 years were eight, representing 30.8%; those within the range of 15–20 years were five, representing 19.2%; and only one participant had 22 years of experience, representing 3.8%. Out of these participants, those with a PhD as their highest qualification had the most years of experience, between 18 and 22.

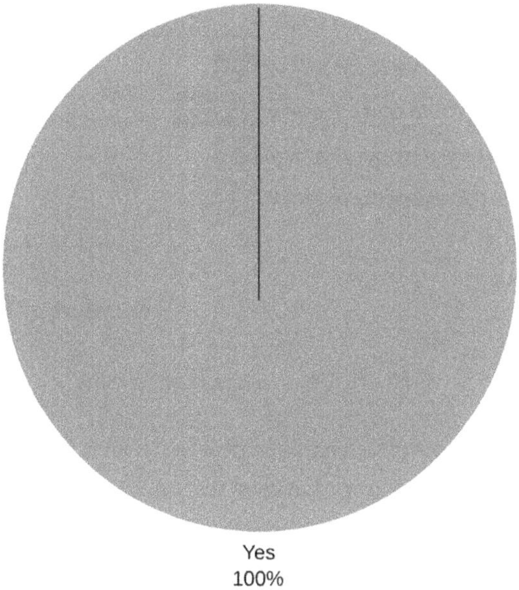

FIGURE 5.3: Knowledge of forensic linguistics

Figure 5.3 above shows that all the participants responded positively to whether they had ever heard of the concept of forensic linguistics. The study aimed at establishing if the respondents had ever come across the term 'forensic linguistics' in their field or in the course of their careers. To that effect, there was 100% indication that the linguists in Malawi had ever heard of forensic linguistics. Thus, all 26 participants indicated that they had ever come across the concept of forensic linguistics.

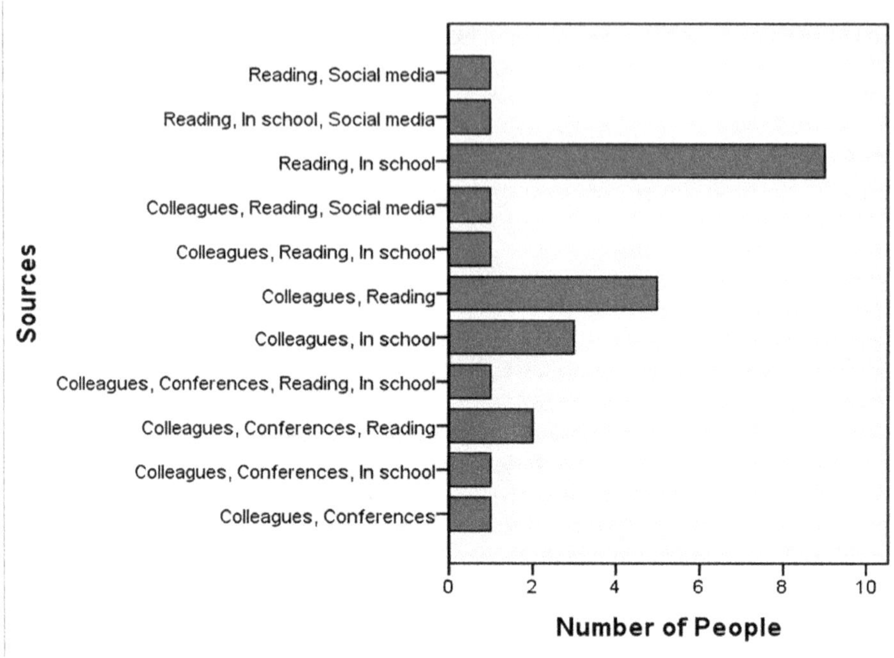

FIGURE 5.4: Source of knowledge

The bar graph above shows the channels through which linguists in Malawi knew forensic linguistics. The figure shows that most respondents came to know about forensic linguistics through reading various materials (80.8%). Others knew about forensic linguistics while in school (61.5%), which was slightly higher than knowing about it through their colleagues (57.7%). The least used channel for the knowledge of forensic linguistics were various social media platforms (11.5%). The study wanted to establish the channels through which the participants came to know about forensic linguistics. This means that a majority of linguists know about forensic linguistics through reading various materials such as books, journal articles, and other publications.

When asked to explain how they understood forensic linguistics, most participants indicated that it was a field of applied linguistics that involved the application of linguistic theories to the legal field. Others also said that it is a branch of linguistics that deals with using language to solve crimes. Yet, others explained that forensic linguistics is a merger or bridge between ordinary linguistics and law with a major focus on enforcing the law by looking at what the law says and the language used. These explanations provide a common denominator about the knowledge of forensic linguistics by the linguists, thus the intersection of language use and the law. When asked if their field of specialisation could incorporate forensic linguistics, all the participants indicated yes, meaning that they knew of and understood forensic linguistics, vis-à-vis their own specialisation.

Relevance and application of forensic linguistics in various fields

FIGURE 5.5: Relevance of forensic linguistics

When asked about the relevance of forensic linguistics in Malawi, all participants indicated that forensic linguistics is very relevant in Malawi. This is shown by the 100% score in Figure 5.5 above, which shows that the linguists are knowledgeable of forensic linguistics. This was coupled with the various fields in which forensic linguistics is relevant.

TABLE 2: Relevance of Forensic Linguistics in Various Fields

FIELD	RELEVANCE
Law Enforcement Institutions	• Analysing suicide and threat texts • Dealing with language crimes • Providing expert linguistic advice in relation to legal matters • Understanding language use in law settings
Health	• Awareness in relation to discourse and society
Education	• Dealing with plagiarism and threatening texts • Applying linguistic skills to resolve conflicts • Improving analytical skills in students
Business/Commerce	• Addressing issues of trademarks and contracts
Peace and Governance	• Applying linguistic skills to resolve conflicts • Understanding language use in law settings

Table 2 shows some of the areas where forensic linguistics is applicable/relevant. To that end, there were several fields that were highlighted to accommodate and make use of forensic linguistics in Malawi. These included law enforcement institutions, health, education, peace and governance, as well as business. Of all these fields, law enforcement institutions stood out as more pronounced, as it encompassed several areas and/or institutions such as the police, the army, the Anti-Corruption Bureau (ACB), the judiciary, the immigration department, prisons, and the Office of the Ombudsman.

Perceptions of forensic linguistics

The last part of the online questionnaire aimed at soliciting information on how linguists view forensic linguistics. One main question posed was if linguists think forensic linguistics can overshadow/replace mainstream linguistics in Malawi. The figure below shows the statistics of the responses.

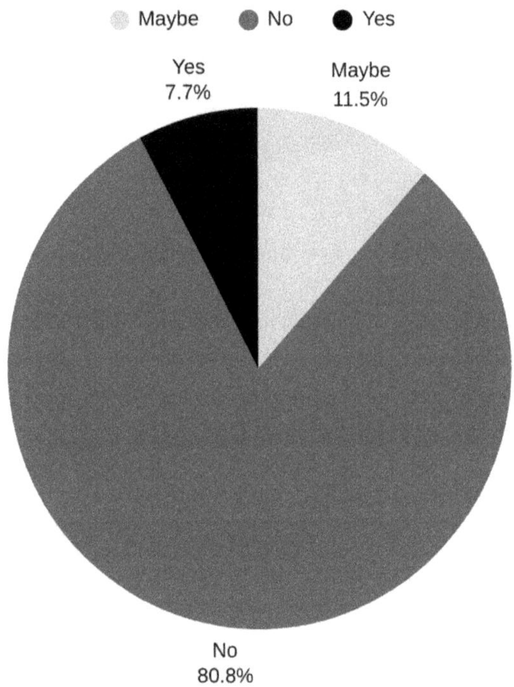

FIGURE 5.6: Is traditional linguistics replaceable by forensic linguistics?

The figure above shows that 80.8% (21 participants) of linguists think that forensic linguistics cannot overshadow or replace mainstream linguistics. 11.5% (three respondents) of the linguists were not really sure if forensic linguistics can replace mainstream linguistics or not. Then 7.7% (two respondents) of the participants think that forensic linguistics can overshadow or replace mainstream linguistics. These statistics show that the majority of linguists in Malawi do not think forensic linguistics can replace traditional linguistics in Malawi. When the majority was asked why forensic linguistics cannot overshadow mainstream linguistics, the common reason was that forensic linguistics is just a branch of linguistics. Others stated that it is a new field in Malawi, so currently it cannot overshadow mainstream linguistics. Those who responded 'yes' to this question stated that forensic linguistics focuses on emerging issues that are affecting the global village, hence people cannot stick to traditional linguistics any more. Those who indicated 'maybe' explained that if forensic linguistics can be developed as a fully-fledged programme at Bachelor's degree level, it can overshadow mainstream linguistics in the near future.

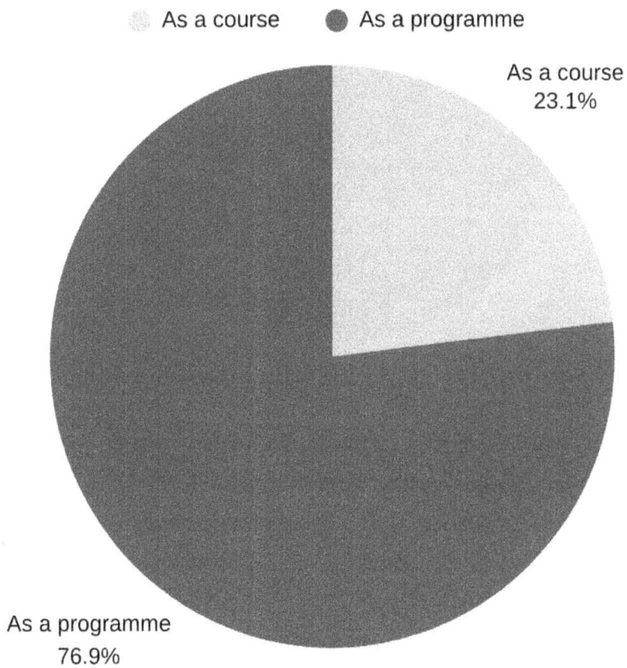

FIGURE 5.7: Forensic linguistics as a course or programme

The study also aimed at determining the linguists' perception by finding out their stand on whether forensic linguistics should be offered as a course within a programme or as a full programme on its own in Malawian universities. According to Figure 5.7 above, 20 participants stated that forensic linguistics should be offered as a full programme in Malawian tertiary institutions, representing 76.9%, while six participants said it should be offered as a course within a programme in various Malawian tertiary institutions, representing 23.1%. This shows that a majority of linguists would love to see forensic linguistics being offered as a full programme in Malawian universities/colleges.

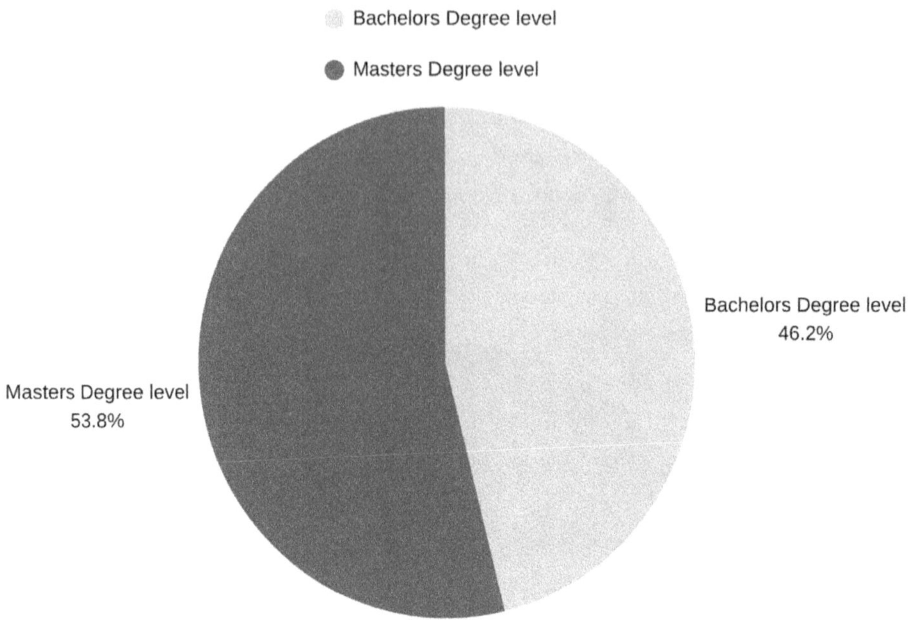

FIGURE 5.8: Level of offering forensic linguistics

Since the majority indicated that forensic linguistics should be offered as a full programme, there was a follow-up question as to what level should this be done. Based on Figure 5.8 above, 14 linguists (53.8%) proposed that forensic linguistics should be offered at Master's degree level, while 12 (46.2%) proposed that forensic linguistics should be offered at Bachelor's degree level. No participant indicated that forensic linguistics should be offered at PhD level in Malawian universities.

Discussion

The current study aimed to investigate the knowledge and perceptions that linguists in Malawi have about forensic linguistics. Based on the results, there was a 100% indication that the linguists who participated in this study have ever come across the concept of forensic linguistics. This is an indication that linguists in Malawi know the term forensic linguistics. Such knowledge was acquired through various means, of which reading was the most common way with a frequency of 21, representing 80.8%. This was seconded by school, with a frequency of 16, representing 61.5%. In other words, when most of these linguists were in school, probably pursuing postgraduate studies, they came to know of forensic linguistics. Others even studied and specialised in the same.

The knowledge of forensic linguistics by the linguists in Malawi was equally manifested in the explanation of how they understood the concept. Most participants indicated that forensic linguistics is an applied linguistics field that involves the application of linguistic theories to the legal field. This is in line with the definition provided by MacLeod and Wright (2020: 360), that forensic linguistics is an application of linguistic theory and method to any point at which there is an interface between language and the law. Other participants also said that it is a branch of linguistics that involves the use of language to solve crimes. In the same vein, other participants explained that forensic linguistics is a merger or bridge between ordinary linguistics and law, with a major focus on enforcing the law by looking at the dictates of the law and language application. Another interesting explanation of forensic linguistics by one participant was that forensic linguistics is the application of aspects of linguistics in situations that require analysis of writing styles to determine patterns or authorship. Such a statement shows that one is knowledgeable of what they are talking about. These explanations provide a common denominator about the knowledge of forensic linguistics by the linguists, thus the intersection of language use and the law.

The indication that forensic linguistics is 100% relevant in Malawi also shows how knowledgeable the linguists are. Being able to highlight the various fields or areas where forensic linguistics is relevant shows that linguists have some prior knowledge about this field. One cannot necessarily say in which field(s) forensic linguistics is relevant, unless they have prior knowledge and, as Sperber and Wilson (1995) put it, newly-presented information interacts with a context of existing assumptions and knowledge. In this case, linking the relevance of forensic linguistics in various fields bears witness to the assertion. Some of the proposed fields where forensic linguistics is relevant included the Malawi Police Service, the Malawi Defence Force (MDF), the Anti-Corruption Bureau (ACB), the judiciary, the immigration department, prisons, the Office of the Ombudsman, health, education, peace and governance, as well as business/commerce.

When asked if their field of specialisation could incorporate forensic linguistics, all the participants indicated 'yes', meaning that they knew and understood forensic linguistics, vis-à-vis their own specialisation. The prior knowledge in their various expertise made it easier to identify where forensic linguistics could fit in. Some participants indicated that in applied linguistics, you are able to differentiate speakers, you can trace speakers of certain conversations and through this, you can formulate conclusions about language crimes. A majority of the participants who specialise in applied linguistics also indicated that they may incorporate forensic linguistics in their fields, that forensic linguistics can be used to analyse texts in relation to discourse and society, and address cases of plagiarism and threatening notes. This shows the important overlapping essentials from the various fields (Kondowe & Ngwira, 2023: 18) in relation to forensic linguistics.

The study also sought to determine how linguists in Malawi look at forensic linguistics by asking the participants if forensic linguistics can overshadow or replace traditional linguistics on the market. 21 participants, representing 80.8%, indicated that forensic linguistics cannot overshadow mainstream/traditional linguistics. The main argument was that forensic linguistics is but a branch or subfield of mainstream linguistics. This means that although many linguists are accommodative of forensic linguistics, which is an emerging concept in Malawi, they cannot fathom that it can replace traditional linguistics. One would say forensic linguistics in Malawi is yet to find its feet, based on such statistics, where a majority of linguists are not ready to accept that forensic linguistics can overshadow traditional linguistics.

On the same issue of perception, three participants, representing 11.5%, were not sure if forensic linguistics could overshadow traditional linguistics in Malawi. The common denominator here was that if forensic linguistics can be accorded the support, promotion, and resources it deserves, then maybe it can become more pronounced than traditional linguistics. This is a bit similar to what the other two participants argued by responding with a resounding 'yes' to the question of forensic linguistics overshadowing traditional linguistics. These two participants, representing 7.7%, argued that forensic linguistics addresses contemporary and emerging issues in language and law, hence it can easily overshadow traditional linguistics. In other words, forensic linguistics seems to be more practice-based than being overly theoretical in nature. This shows that there are still some linguists who are positive that forensic linguistics could take centre stage in Malawi, replacing mainstream linguistics.

This feedback shows some internal representations of the thoughts (Yus, 2006) that linguists in Malawi have towards forensic linguistics. Some think that forensic linguistics is embedded in mainstream linguistics, while some opine that as an emerging field in Malawi, forensic linguistics will overshadow mainstream linguistics in the long run. Currently, a majority of linguists hold that forensic linguistics is still new to make echoes in the linguistics realms in Malawi.

This study has equally revealed that 20 of the linguists (76.9%) would love to see forensic linguistics being offered as a full programme in Malawian tertiary institutions. According to the study findings, a majority of the linguists (14 participants), representing 53.8%, would want to see forensic linguistics being offered at Master's degree level in Malawi. This is a clear indication that forensic linguistics is being welcomed in Malawi as an emerging field that has come to stay. The warm reception by the linguists shows that forensic linguistics is yet to make an impact that both the legal and linguistics fields would reckon with. The introduction of forensic linguistics as a full programme in Malawian colleges and/or universities would show that forensic linguistics is finding its feet and is being accommodated by both legal and language experts who would value the linguistic expertise (Kondowe & Ngwira, 2023) this introduction would bring.

Conclusion

Linguists in Malawi have demonstrated their knowledge and understanding of forensic linguistics by highlighting how their respective fields can incorporate forensic linguistics. Given that forensic linguistics is an emerging phenomenon in Malawi and indeed most parts of Southern Africa, it is imperative that key players such as linguists and legal experts are knowledgeable of the same. Almost every linguist in Malawian tertiary institutions has ever come across the term forensic linguistics. Most of these linguists know the fields where forensic linguistics is applicable and it is imperative that it be brought on board in such fields and/or institutions. It has equally been observed that forensic linguistics addresses contemporary and emerging issues with a practical approach, which is more of a departure from the traditional theoretical approach of linguistics.

It has also been revealed that the perception of forensic linguistics by linguists in Malawi is a positive one, despite many holding the notion that forensic linguistics cannot overshadow or replace mainstream linguistics in Malawi. The study has shown that forensic linguistics has a place in Malawi. This has been rubberstamped by the fact that most linguists suggest that forensic linguistics should be offered as a full programme at Master's degree level in Malawian universities. This is an assuring direction to be taken, especially since forensic linguistics has yet to find its feet in Malawi. The current study, hence, recommends that forensic linguistics be promoted in every way possible so that it gains ground and is embraced by not only linguists and legal professionals, but all interested individuals and institutions in Malawi as well as Southern Africa.

References

Ariani, MG., Sajedi, F. & Sajedi, M. (2014). Forensic linguistics: A brief overview of the key elements. *Procedi - Social and Behavioral Sciences*, vol. 158, pp. 222–225.

Coulthard, M. & Johnson, A. (2007). *An Introduction to Forensic Linguistics: Language as Evidence.* London: Routledge.

Kondowe, W. & Ngwira, FF. (2023). Linguist as an expert witness: Knowledge, attitude and perceived importance of legal professionals in Malawi. In Ralarala, MK., Kaschula, RH. &

MacLeod, N. & Wright, D. (2020). Forensic Linguistics. In Adolphs, S. & Knight, D. (ed.) *Routledge Handbook of English Language and Digital Humanities.* New York: Routledge.

Ramos, FY. (1997). A decade of relevance theory. *Journal of Pragmatics*, vol. 30, pp. 305–345.

Sperber, D. & Wilson, D. (1995). *Pragmatics and Time.* London: University College London Press.

Tiersma, PM. & Solan, LM. (ed.) (2012). *The Oxford Handbook of Language and Law.* Oxford: Oxford University Press.

Wilson, D. (2016). Relevance Theory. In Huang, Y. (ed.) *Oxford Handbook of Pragmatics,* Oxford: Oxford University Press.

Yus, F. (2006). Relevance Theory. In Brown, K. (ed.) *Encyclopaedia of Language and Linguistics* (Second edition.). Elsevier.

6 CULTURE AND LANGUAGE: DISCUSSING THE UNDER-USE OF INDIGENOUS LANGUAGES IN LEGAL EDUCATION AND LEGAL PRACTICE

Keneilwe Radebe

Introduction

Legal disputes concerning living customary law often involve using distinct indigenous law terms, which usually require a more technical translation, resulting in the translation of culture. Indigenous terms are frequently understood only by people practising and following customary law. Most prominent indigenous terms used in courts, among others, can include terms such as *lobolo, ukuthwala, magadi, induna, pula molomo, ukungena, ukukemeza, sego sa meetsi, gorosiwa, ubuntu,* and the translation of such terms often culminates into the translation of actual culture which frequently forms a significant part of the legal dispute before a court. The translation of such terms is not usually clear or straightforward and requires extensive knowledge of a particular cultural dispute before a court.

The translation of the abovementioned terms requires the expertise of a translator or legal practitioner who is also fully cognisant of living customary law to avoid the miscarriage of justice. The incorrect translation of these indigenous terms would often lead to inequitable outcomes for litigants. This crucial fact points to the critical link between language and culture and its effects on access to justice. The science of law requires language efficiency, which is essential in a trial and legal dispute. Ensuring that language barriers do not affect access to justice lies with court translators, legal scholars, and practitioners, necessitating the need to acknowledge the importance of indigenous language in litigation involving living customary law disputes. In that regard, teaching living customs should also emphasise the importance of indigenous languages.

This chapter argues that language is linked to culture and that some translations require specific cultural, technical expertise. The chapter is divided into subsections including legal education and indigenous languages, and courts and the use of indigenous languages. The chapter further recommends the creation of law glossaries, also referred to as lexicography, which is concerned with dictionaries that deal with languages of or knowledge of specialised disciplines. In that regard, the chapter references the University of KwaZulu-Natal's language policy as a model that could be used. Also, it focuses on the works of Khumalo and contributors from the University of KwaZulu-Natal to introduce and elaborate on this model. The use of lexicography also seeks to promote all South African official languages, and the author does not seek to propose a method that prefers specific languages per province. This feasible model is part of a project that legal scholars who speak various indigenous languages have embarked on, wherein key legal terms will be translated into multiple indigenous languages.

Legal education, language, and living customary law

Multilingual teaching and learning can promote transformation and cultural sensitivity in higher education (Maseko & Kaschula, 2009: 132). In that regard, students in some faculties are required to pass specific indigenous languages as part of their degrees, and this assists them in understanding and interpreting cultural issues embedded in cultural communities (Maseko & Kaschula, 2009: 139). For instance, the University of KwaZulu-Natal is forging ahead with a compulsory isiZulu language-learning policy (Kaschula, 2016: 201). Rhodes University has also introduced isiXhosa into its compulsory language policy, and this initiative has been described as a success (Kaschula, 2016: 201). These policies are in line with a recommendation made that future lawyers and prosecutors who cannot speak at least one indigenous African language should not be awarded their law degrees (Ndenze, 2017:4). This could assist in particular when dealing with customary law disputes where in some cases incorrect translations have resulted in the miscarriage of justice.

Kaschula makes an example of a matter dealing with a cultural Xhosa practice called '*unkondla*', which means nurturing and bringing someone up as your own (Maseko & Kaschula, 2009: 132). In the case, the term was described and misinterpreted as 'to feed', which unfortunately resulted in the defendant losing a claim for insurance benefits (Maseko & Kaschula, 2009: 133). The argument on the importance of indigenous language in studying customary law is also reiterated by Maimela and Maithufi (2020: 6), wherein they mention that both lecturers and students should be sufficiently conversant in indigenous languages so that they can understand customary law concepts, which may not be capable of being adequately translated into English or Afrikaans (Maithufi & Maimela, 2020: 6). Radebe and Maimela (2020: 2) argue in their contribution that the marginalisation of South African indigenous languages constitutes a barrier to justice and a miscarriage of justice. This necessitates the move by South African universities to prioritise the compulsory teaching of indigenous languages.

Introducing compulsory teaching of indigenous languages also emanates from calls for decolonising tertiary education, particularly in the law curriculum. The LLB programme or curriculum is dominated by English common law and Roman-Dutch law instead of living customary law. This explains the former requirement regarding the Advocates Act 74 of 1964, which requires all advocates and attorneys to study a one-year course in Latin (Geduld, 2019: 3). The importance of Latin as a compulsory subject emanates from South African common law, based on Roman-Dutch law, which consists of numerous Latin texts (Geduld, 2019: 3). This state of affairs is critiqued because it perpetuates the undermining of the importance of indigenous languages in the law curriculum (Radebe & Maimela, 2020). Fernandez also highlights that the language policy in the law curriculum has affected the South African legal system (Mphasha & Mutele, 2017: 387). The lack of knowledge and understanding of indigenous languages, perpetuated in the law curriculum, is argued to affect the development of living customary law. For instance, as mentioned by Mphasha and Mutele (2017: 387), sometimes an accused could be charged with a common crime in their culture. This indicates that cultural dependency and hegemony are intimately linked to language. This entails that language loss is a cultural loss (Mphasha & Mutele, 2017: 388). The argument made for the retention of Latin for purposes of a meaningful study in Roman law (Zimmerman, 1986: 605) can also be used in arguing for the introduction of compulsory courses in indigenous languages for purposes of a meaningful study in living customary law. Various scholars (Gwaravanda & Ndofirepi, 2020: 7) argued that indigenous African languages need to be developed to study African philosophy in African universities. In that regard, the non-use of indigenous African languages has retarded scholarship on African philosophy (Gwaravanda & Ndofirepi, 2020: 7). The continuous use of English as the language of instruction in expressing African concepts has made African concepts ambiguous, vague, and indeterminate (Gwaravanda & Ndofirepi, 2020: 8). Wiredu also advocates for studying African philosophy in the vernacular and argues for linguistic decolonisation as a way that could lead to cultural decolonisation (Fayemi, 2013: 4).

Since universities are centres of knowledge production, universities should be one of the starting points for implementing and revisiting knowledge about indigenous languages (Radebe, 2020: 14). The importance of indigenous languages in decolonisation should no longer be sidelined since there cannot be any successful decolonisation without emphasis on indigenous languages (Radebe, 2020: 13). The use of English promotes the embodiment of European culture, but this does not represent the cultures of indigenous people (Radebe, 2020: 13). In this regard, African indigenous languages are pivotal in decolonisation (Radebe, 2020: 13). Scholars such as Madadzhe (2019: 214) also believe that African languages should be used in universities if South African universities are to decolonise their curriculum.

However, South African universities have not fully embraced multilingualism and multiculturalism, which has been reflected by Harms (2012: 23) who mentions that universities South of the Sahara do not teach law in local languages. This has failed to develop African languages into a modern scientific legal vocabulary (Harms, 2012: 23). This emanates from the fact that someone who applied for admission into the legal profession was statutorily required to complete university courses in Afrikaans, English, and Latin (Harms, 2014: 25). Including the study of indigenous languages will promote the study of living customary law, which is a core module in the law curriculum.

Courts, language, and living customary law

The only language of record in the South African judicial system is English, which is a problem since no documents are written in indigenous languages (Kekana & Montle, 2022: 74). Hlophe (2004; 42) has argued that there is no legitimate reason why our courts should be exempted from embracing the new spirit of multilingualism. Hlophe (2004: 43) further cautions on the continued existence of linguistic and cultural barriers threatening our courts' effective dispensation of justice. There is a link between language and cultural issues, and an interpreter in court, in some cases, becomes a culture broker who must translate not only words but also ideas, laws, and customs (Hlophe, 2004: 46). Interpreters are, in that regard, faced with a very cumbersome task since they have to ensure that linguistic and cultural barriers do not threaten the effective dispensation of justice (Lebese, 2014: 193).

Furthermore, the ability of one to use their indigenous language in court or during a trial can also be viewed as an extension of the right to culture (Bambust et al., 2013: 217). This aspect places a cumbersome burden on interpreters as they are expected to convey more than just the literary meaning but also the context (Bambust et al., 2013: 217). The complex nature of translation and culture is illustrated by Ntlama-Makhanya (2021: 1090), wherein reference is made to the term '*indlovukazi yenkantolo*', which, when translated according to its literal terms in English, means 'the female elephant of the court'. However, this expression contextually and culturally means 'a lady or woman judge' or 'my ladyship', which affirms the richness and interconnectedness of indigenous languages and culture (Ntlama-Makhanya, 2021: 1090). This chapter argues for indigenous languages to be taken more seriously by our courts and for the gradual introduction of a system whereby indigenous languages will also be used as languages of record alongside English.

The following section of the chapter discusses various cases or practices dealt with in court where indigenous terms were used, thus highlighting the significance of using indigenous terms by litigating parties.

Ukuthwala

Ukuthwala, when translated, means 'to carry' or 'to abduct'. From a cultural perspective, however, *ukuthwala* has a far more extensive meaning. The term *ukuthwala* came into focus in the case of *Jezile v S (2015)*, which dealt with a matter of kidnapping, rape, and aggravated assault to which the accused in the case used the cultural practice of *ukuthwala* as a defence. In translating the term *ukuthwala,* the court required the expertise of cultural experts and *amicus curiae,* including the National Movement of Rural Women. An academic specialising in living customary law defined *ukuthwala* as an irregular method of securing a customary marriage (*Jezile v S,* 2015: para 72). A mock abduction would take place as agreed upon by the couple, where such abduction serves as an indication to the bride's family of the groom's intention to commence *lobola* negotiations. From a cultural perspective, *ukuthwala* means more than the words 'carry' or 'abduction'.

Furthermore, some requirements must be complied with for *ukuthwala* to occur as per culture. Mwambene and Sloth-Nielsen (2011: 4) describe the cultural practice as having the main aim of forcing the girl's family to enter into negotiations for the conclusion of a customary marriage. Moore and Himonga (2017: 63) describe *ukuthwala* as a culturally legitimised abduction of a woman whereby, before a customary marriage, a young man will forcibly take a girl to his home to probe *lobola* negotiations between the two families. Bennet (2004: 212) describes the cultural practice as one of the unconventional methods of opening marriage negotiations. The requirements are namely that:

1) There must be consent from both parties, and

2) The parties must be of marriageable age (*Jezile v S* ,2015: para 83).

The critical aspect that stood out in the judgment of Jezile v S is that the court focused on *ukuthwala* as it is traditionally practised and in its aberrant form (*Jezile v S,* 2015: para 95). The report of the South African Law Reform Commission 138 of 2014 on *ukuthwala* also emphasised the distortion of the cultural practice and criminalising such behaviour, which does not reflect *ukuthwala* as culturally practised.

It is worth noting and emphasising understanding the correct cultural meaning of *ukuthwala,* and that if the process is not followed correctly, it can result in a distorted version where women are abducted, raped, and in some cases killed (Manthwa, 2023: 9). In that regard, Mwambene and Sloth-Nielsen (2011:3) advocate against blanket criminalisation and recommend recognising its positive attributes. The practice can thus not be categorised as a forced marriage (Moore & Himoga, 2017: 63). This section points out the importance of understanding indigenous terms to avoid the misinterpretation of culture, which could result in the legal banning and discontinuation of essential cultural practices.

*The conclusion of customary marriage and **inhlawulo** (damages)*

- *Indigenous words used during **Lobola** negotiations*

Ukumekeza (Swati)

Utsiki (isiXhosa)

Ukuthwala (isiZulu)

Ukugqiba amasondo (isiZulu)

Uganile (isiZulu)

Ga batla sego sa metsi (Setswana)

Go bula molomo (Setswana)

Go kokota (Setswana)

Tibovu (Tshivenda)

Go kgopela ngwetsi (Setswana)

Go laiwa (Setswana)

Isiphanga (isiZulu/Xhosa)

Umembeso (isiZulu)

Makoti (Setswana)

Umkhwenyana (isiZulu)

Imvulamlomo (isiZulu)

Ubusobentombi (isiZulu)

Ingqibamasondo (isiZulu)

Ukuhambisa kwezibizo (isiZulu)

Ukulethwa kwezibizo (isiZulu)

Ubuso bentombi (isiZulu)

Uphidindlela (isiZulu)

Amaqwabati (isiXhosa)

Ukwenda (Tshivenda)

Mohlabiso (Setswana)

Go laya (Sepedi)

Lumalo (Tshivenda)

Lobola (Sepedi)

Thode/a ngeno (Tshivenda)

Cala (isXhosa)

Imbeleko (isiXhosa)

Umtsakazi (isiXhosa)

Ixakatho (isiXhosa)

Ukunxibisa (isiXhosa)

Ukuyalwa (isiXhosa)

Ukuhlonipha (isiXhosa)

Ukukho (isiXhosa)

Libovu (isiXhosa)

Lugege (isiXhosa)

Umtsimba (isiXhosa)

Imvume (isiXhosa)

Insulamyambeti (isiXhosa)

Umendiso uikutyiswa amasi (isiXhosa)

Thondo (isiXhosa)

Dombo (isiXhosa)

Abatshakazi (isiXhosa)

Ibhayi (isiXhosa)

Isikhakha/umbhaco (isiXhosa)

Discussion

Courts often grapple with whether a customary marriage has been validly concluded in terms of African custom or tradition. One of the essential requirements for the conclusion of a valid customary marriage is the integration of the bride into the groom's family, also known as the handing over of the bride to the groom's family. This signifies the introduction of the bride to the groom's family (Manthwa, 2023: 4). To understand whether this integration has occurred, thus confirming the conclusion of a valid customary marriage, courts must be conversant with the applicable terms used to signify certain rituals performed during the integration phase. The rituals or ceremonies which take place during the integration are as follows: *ukumekeza* (Siswati), *utsiki* (Xhosa), and ukugqiba amasondo (Zulu) (Sibisi, 2021: 370). *Ukumekeza,* as described in the case of *Mabuza v Mbatha* (2003: para 34), occurs when the bride cries to indicate that she is leaving her past family and joining the groom's family. *Utsiki* is observed in the Xhosa tradition, where an animal is slaughtered after the arrival of the bride to the groom's family as part of integrating her into the family (Manthwa, 2023: 4). In the ceremony, a large chunk of meat is given to the bride, who is instructed to finish it independently (Mtshiselwa, 2011: 291). This signifies that the bride will attend to her problems as a wife and should not share such issues with anyone (Mtshiselwa, 2011: 291). This ceremony is also a form of introduction of the bride as their now-new daughter to the ancestors so that she can be accepted as a member of the new family (Mtshiselwa, 2011: 291). Accordingly, the approval of the bride by the ancestors serves as a form of approval for the bride to go into the groom's family. The bride's approval by the ancestors takes place by the howl of the cow when it is slaughtered (Mtshiselwa, 2011). Another ritual which forms part of the integration process followed in the Venda tradition is known as the smearing of *libovu* (smearing of red ochre on the bride's face), and a beast is slaughtered as part of the integration process (Manthwa, 2023: 5). In some instances, *imvume* (Swati) is part of the integration process where the wife is introduced to the ancestors. This takes place when the groom pours cow bile on the head of the *makoti* (bride) when he introduces (*ukubikwa*) the bride to the ancestors (*Muvhali v Lukhele*, 2022: para 35). Courts must understand more than the literal explanation of the words and know that, in some instances, some rituals can be waived. However, the integration must still occur (Manthwa, 2023: 4). In some Batswana communities, the integration of the bride is known as *gorosiwa* whereby a lamb or goat is slaughtered, and bile is used to cleanse the bride and groom (*Tsambo v Sengadi*, 2020: para 10).

The matter of *MCM v T* (2019) also demonstrates the complexities of establishing whether a valid customary marriage has been concluded and also brings into sharp focus the use of African indigenous terms by litigants. Legal practitioners must be cognizant of these terms since they form part of the crucial legal issues in the matter. The litigant in the case of *MCM v T* used numerous African indigenous terms, specifically in isiXhosa, when providing evidence to the court, which was crucial in establishing whether a customary marriage had been concluded. The terms used were the following:

- *amadhaki*: traditional clothes in which a bride is dressed at her reception in the groom's home, signifying the transition from being a single woman to a married woman;
- *igama lomzi*: the new name given to a bride by the groom's paternal aunt, the eldest sister, mother, delegated family member, or blood relative as part of the customary marriage rituals;
- *inhlawulo*: an amount paid in money or kind to a woman's family after a man has impregnated her, which is sometimes referred to as damages;
- *imbheleko*: a ceremony and ritual performed for a child to introduce the child to the ancestors of a parent;
- *unmqomboti*: a traditional beer brewed for family rituals, ceremonies and festivities;
- *ukwamekela*: a ceremony held after successful *lobola* negotiations to receive the bride by her in-laws or the groom by his in-laws;
- *uduli*: the bride's family and the relatives accompanying the bride when she is taken to the groom's family home. They can also be used as a reference to gifts which the accompanying person carries to be given to the bride and groom's family;
- *ikukho*: a traditional mat or similar furniture which may include a bed, presented to the bride and on which she is placed during a ritual and ceremony where she is inducted into the new family as a wife;
- *makoti*: a wife as referred to after what needs to be done for the completion of a customary marriage;
- *unozakuzaku*: a delegation of elders sent to negotiate both the damages and marriage on behalf of the parties (*MCM v T*, 2019: para 2).

In the above case of *MCB v T*, the groom (appellant) appealed the decision of the magistrate's court, which contained an order that he and the bride (respondent) had concluded a valid customary marriage. The appellant provided evidence that the respondent fell pregnant, and at his request, the *unozakuzaku* approached the respondent's family for the payment of *inhlawulo* (*MCM v T*, 2019: para 3). The appellant disputes the existence of a customary marriage between himself and the respondent because the respondent was not clothed in *amadhaki* as was required by custom (*MCM v T*, 2019: para 17). The appellant also disputed that the respondent was given *igama lomzi* and that the Amabhele ancestors did not accept the appellant as *makoti* (*MCM v T*, 2019: para 18). Accordingly, the appellant argued that although he intended to marry the respondent, such marriage would not be concluded as a customary marriage because customary marriages are automatically deemed as a community of property (*MCM v T*, 2019: para 18). The court eventually came to a decision that, based on the respondent's information, a customary marriage had indeed been concluded, and that in some instances, ceremonies can be abbreviated for a variety of reasons due to the dynamic and changing nature of living customary law (*MCM v T*, 2019: para 39). In this instance the court relied on the authority found in the judgment in the case *of Mabuza v Mbatha* (2003; para 26).

In some instances, a marriage is not concluded; however, *inhlawulo* is paid when a woman is impregnated before marriage (Sikhosana, 2002: 16). In terms of the *inhlawulo* practice, for some families, a man must send a cow and a goat to the girl's family (Sikhosana, 2002, 16). The cow is meant to pacify the mother whose daughter has been made a woman without their concern (Sikhosana, 2002: 16). The goat is used to cleanse any misfortune that may befall the girl's home. The cleansing ritual will also include a mixture of *umswani* (salt) and *ingongoni* (grass) (Sikhosana, 2002:16).

On the other hand, Moore and Himonga mention that the payment of *inhlawulo* can also be in the form of only cattle or money, which is referred to as the 'payment of damages' (Moore & Himonga, 2017: 62). The issue of *inhlawulo* usually comes into play in cases involving child maintenance, child custody, and child visitation rights since the payment of *inhlawulo* acknowledges paternity (Moore & Himonga, 2017: 62). Accordingly, until the child's father pays *inhlawulo,* he may not be recognised as the child's legitimate father (Moore & Himonga 2017: 62). This means that the alleged father might be denied visitation rights at the child's family homestead (Moore & Himonga, 2017: 62). Although customary marriages are not only centred on the handing over requirement, courts often grapple with terms used to describe the process. In that regard, courts need to understand these indigenous terms to avoid confusion that could lead to a diversion from living customary law. In terms of living customary law, there need not be any stringent compliance with rituals involving the handing over of the bride; some rituals may be abbreviated and agreed upon by the two families. Courts need to be aware that litigants may sometimes use indigenous terms to confuse the courts, thus diverting the courts from focusing on living customary law that is not stagnant and overly stringent.

Various other terminology used in the negotiation of marriages

There are various terminologies used during *lobola* and marriage negotiations. For instance, the bride's payment price has been referred to as *lobola*, *bogadi*, *lumalo*, or *ikhazi* in *M.M v R.A.N* (2023: para 7). At the same time, the case of *Nemavunde v*

Mavhungu refers to the terms *thode/a ngeno,* which refers to the amount of money paid for staying with a bride without consent (*Nemavunde v Mavhungu,* 2015: para 24). In some traditional cultures, a bride must be dressed by her mother-in-law or *ukunxibisa.* Such attire in the Xhosa community is called *amadaki,* and the blanket used to cover the bride or *makoti* is called *ixakatho* (*Diba v Miselo,* 2021: para 8). The case of *Diba v Misela* (2021: para 8) also mentions a process where female senior members would advise the new bride on how to conduct herself as a bride and as a married woman, and this process is known as *ukuyalwa* for the Xhosa traditional communities. In Sepedi communities, the term *pula molomo* refers to money paid as a token for opening up negotiations, while the term *laya* refers to the counselling of the new bride (*S.M.S v V. R.S,* 2019: para 6 & 9).

In some cases, courts would focus on the compliance of certain rituals during death to establish whether a litigating party was indeed married to the deceased in terms of customary law. In *Diba v Miselo,* the court observed *Ukukho*'s practice. *Ukukho* is described as the place where a widowed wife must sit, and this is often a point which the litigants argue in court on whether the alleged wife sat on *Ukukho* thus signifying that she was the deceased's customary law wife (*Diba v Miselo,* 2021: para 8). The case of *Nduli v Minister of Home Affairs* refers to the term *ukulethwa kwezibizo* translated as the delivery of gifts (2023: para 36). In some Zulu communities, the term umembeso refers to giving gifts (*Mlamla v Rubushe,* 2019: para 13). The case of *Tshongweni v Kwankwa* (2021: para 9) called for the bride to pay the price to see the bride's face, which was referred to in the case as *ubuso bentombi.* Elders, in that case, were referred to as *amaqwabati* and the ceremony signifying the acceptance of the bride was referred to as *ukwenda.* In the case of *D. R. M v D. M. K* (2018: para 32), the used terms were: *go kgopela ngwetsi,* which means asking for the bride; *go kokota, pula molomo, go batla sego sa metsi,* or *imvulamlomo,* which refers to a token paid for the opening of *lobola* negotiations; and *go laiwa,* which refers to the counselling of the bride. *Tibovu* is also used to refer to the smearing of red ochre on the bride's face during the integration rituals (Bakker, 2018: 9). The above cases and Indigenous terms prove the need to fully incorporate Indigenous languages in teaching living customary law since understanding these terms is crucial for one to understand living customary law.

Oe gapa le namane

The traditional or cultural adoption is known as *oe gape le namane,* which, when translated, means 'you lead it with its calf' (*M.L. v K.G.,* 2013: para 11). A *namane* in Setswana means 'calf' and is translated to mean a child in African terms (*M.L. v K.G.,* 2013: para 11). This concept describes or relates to children under fourteen (*M.L. v K.G.,* 2013: para 16). The terms come into play in cases of claims made on behalf of children against their adopted parents. Usually, a man and a woman would marry each other while having children from previous relationships (*Modisane v Road Accident Fund*, 2013: para 13). The term used for such marriages is *go nyala mosadi ka ngwana yo o sa mo tsaleng ka madi,* which translates means 'to take a child born of another man into marriage with his mother' (*Modisane v Road Accident Fund*, 2013: para 14). The adoption in terms of *oe gapa le namane* has, in most cases, been developed by courts in terms of the Constitution of the Republic of South Africa (1996) as it falls under living customary law, which is recognised in South Africa (Monye, 2017: 1). The adopted children are brought into their new families (not biological fathers) through what is referred to as *go nyala mpha,* translated as 'to marry the womb' (Monye, 2017: 9). In some cases, the children can be brought into the family through *go nyala ngwana,* meaning 'to marry the child', or *go nyala lebitla,* meaning 'to marry the grave' in cases where the parent of the child is deceased (Monye, 2017: 9). This terminology emanates from idioms and proverbs, which are necessary cornerstones of culture in African communities (Monye, 2017: 10).

Cultural adoption occurs in the Setwana/Sesotho and Sepedi communities, as well as in other tribes and communities. Each African nation has its own phrase that is used for cultural adoption. For in Zulu/Xhosa/Swati communities, the term *ukuthatha inkomo nekonyana* is used while the term *u tshi kokodza luranga na mafhuri a a tevhela* is used in Venda communities (Mokotong, 2015: 344). Tsonga communities use the term *ku koka rhanga na vana va rona* and the Ndebele use the term *ikomo iragwa nekonyana* (Mokotong, 2015: 344). The child can be adopted by any family member, relative or friend through *go nyala ngwaga,* 'to marry the child', or *ukubogadi ingani* in Zulu, Xhosa, and Swati, or *nwana ukhou leliwa nga khotsi* in Tshivenda (Mokotong 2015: 347).

Thibela v Minister van Wet Orde also dealt with the legal issue of customary law adoption in the form *oe gapa le namane* (Maphalle, 2020). In this case, the plaintiff was suing for damages for loss of support resulting from the death of her husband. The claim also concerned the plaintiff's son, who was not her husband's biological child (Maphalle ,2020). Expert evidence was given in the trial proceedings on the relationship between marriage and customary law adoption (Maphalle, 2020). According to this evidence, the relationship between marriage and the son's adoption from the previous relationship occurred through the delivery of *Magadi/lobola* (Maphalle, 2020). It was held that it was Magadi's payment that transferred parental responsibilities to the plaintiff's husband and that the plaintiff could claim loss of support on behalf of her son. Maphalle mentions, notably, that according to the Lobedu provision, *ngwana ke wa dikgomo* translated into English means 'a child belongs to he who paid the bride price' (Maphalle, 2020). This discussion demonstrates how litigating parties have used indigenous terms to describe their cause of action. This proves the importance of understanding indigenous languages to understand living customary law.

Kingship/chieftainship rituals

- *Indigenous words used during kingship rituals*

Bayede (isiZulu)

Ndlovu (isiZulu)

Ibambambukhosi (isiZulu)

Inkosi (isiZulu)

Ukubekwa (isiZulu)

Ukuphendula ibantshi (isiZulu)

Ihashilenkosi (isiZulu)

Undlunkulu (isiZulu)

Ukungenisa isisu (isiZulu)

Ukuvusa indlu (isiZulu)

Umdeni we Nkosi (isiZulu)

Umakoti wendlunkulu (isiZulu)

Ukweshwama (isiZulu)

Umkhosi ukwesh (isiZulu)

Amabutho (isiZulu)

Inyanga (isiZulu)

Muti (isiZulu)

Discussion

South African courts are seen to be embracing the use of indigenous language expressions, such as in the matter of *Prince Mbonisi Bekithemba Ka Bhekuzulu and Others v President of the Republic of South Africa* (2023: para 1), wherein the judgment begins with the following salutations: *Wena we Zulu Bayede*! This matter concerned the legal question of whether the incumbent King Misizulu Ka Zwelithini had been correctly appointed King regarding Zulu customs (2023: para 2). Furthermore, in the judgment, the term *isilo,* signifying the King, was used (2023: para 9). The terms *imbamabukhosi* (successor), *umdeni we silo* (Kings relatives), and *Ibambabukhosi* (the monarch) were used in the matter of *Zulu v Mathe* (2022: para 2, 4 & 14). This matter dealt with the will of the late King Zwelithini and the alleged civil marriage between the late King Zwelithini and his first wife. In the case of *Executive Council of the Province of KwaZulu-Natal and Others v Luthuli* (2023), indigenous language words such as *inkosi* (King), the term *ukuphendula ibantshi* and *ukubekwa* (fee for allocation of sites/land), *ihashi lenkosi* (paying bride price for the *inkosi*), and *izinduna* were used (2023: para 19). Another matter which dealt with issues of chieftainship is the matter of *Dlomo v Premier of KwaZulu-Natal* (2023), wherein terms such as *undlunkulu* (great wife) and *indlunkulu* (main house or the great house) (2023: para 8 & 9) were used. Furthermore, terms such as *ibambabukhosi* (2023: para 13), and acting chief were referred to. The case concerned an application described in the judgment for *ukungenisa isisu* (2023: para 34). Reference was also made to the terms *ukuvusa indlu, umdeni we nkosi,* and *umakoti wendlukulu* (which means a newly wedded or married wife helping in the great house) (2023: para 34, 73 & 91).

The matter of *Smit NO and Others v King Goodwill Zwelithini Kabhekuzulu* (2009) is also a critical case that deals with a festival known as the *Ukweshwama* festival (2009: para 1). This matter concerned an application to interdict the slaughtering of a bull at the *Ukweshwama* festival. Animal activists applied this against the later King Zwelithini Kabhezulu (2009: para 4). The applicants in the matter argued that the practice was callous to animals (Cordeiro-Rodrigues, 2018: 188). The *Ukweshwama,* translated as the 'First Fruits' festival, is a ritual that celebrates the ripening of the season's crops (Cordeiro- Rodrigues, 2018: 188). This old tradition was revived by King Zwelithini Khabezulu (Rautenbach, 2011: 2). Under Zulu culture, no individual could taste new corn or fruit of the new year until sanctioned by the King (*Smit NO and Others v King Goodwill Zwelithini Kabhekuzulu,* 2009: para 4). This ritual is a means to thank the ancestors for protecting the Zulu nation and the Zulu King's leadership (Cordeiro-Rodrigues, 2018: 188). The ritual starts with a call from an *induna* (warrior chief) and also involves an inyanga (traditional herbal healer) who uses certain *muti* (Zulu medication) (Cordeiro-Rodrigues, 2018: 189). It is believed that if this blessing does not occur, the mystic powers of the ancestors may negatively interfere with the harvest and cause bad fortune (Cordeiro-Rodrigues, 2018: 189). In terms of this ritual, young men, known or referred to as *Amabutho* in Zulu culture, kill a bull with bare hands (Cordeiro-Rodrigues, 2018: 189).

Apart from the practice of *Ukweshwama,* there is a dance called *Indlamu,* performed by upper-class people in the Zulu nation, such as kings (Yenda & Ngema, 2023: 301). *Indlamu* is described as a well-practised dance performed before a king and requires careful dedication from the dancers and a strong sense of purpose (Yende & Ngema, 2023: 301). It is performed with drums, wearing traditional attire, usually during Zulu rites of passage and when cultural occasions are celebrated (Yende & Ngema, 2023: 305).

Another crucial matter that dealt with kingship was the *Law of Swaziland v Simelane.* This matter concerned a dispute centred around exercising the King's public powers and constitutionality, particularly the powers to appoint judges (Dube & Nhlabatsi, 2016: 265). In the matter, the King relied on the Swati idiom *umlomo longacali manga* (the mouth that does not lie), which, for purposes of the case, means that any exercise of public power by the King cannot be challenged based on constitutionality (Dube & Nhlabatsi, 2016: 265). It was argued in the case that *inkhosi yinkosi ngebantfu* (a king is a king through the people) and this principle in that regard was described as representing a form of checks and balances; thus, in that regard, there can be no place for dictatorship (Dube & Nhlabatsi, 2016: 274). This means the King's rule flows from the people (Dube & Nhlabatsi, 2016). The court, however, held that the idiom *umlomo longacali manga* had to be practised alongside the value of *ubuntu,* according to which philosophy advocates that everyone must be respected and accorded dignity by their mere status as human beings and common humanity, the court thus held that the King cannot be exempted from the African value of *ubuntu* (Dube & Nhlabathi 2016: 275). This discussion demonstrates how litigating parties have used indigenous terms to describe their cause of action. This proves the importance of understanding indigenous languages to understand living customary law.

Constitutional implications

Section 6 of the Constitution of the Republic of South Africa entrenches all 12 languages, including Sepedi, Sesotho, Setswana, Siswati, Tshivenda, Xitshonga, Afrikaans, English, isiNdebele, isiXhosa, isizulu and South African Sign Language as official languages (Namakula, 2019: 219). Section 35 of the Constitution of the Republic of South Africa guarantees the right to a fair trial, including the right to an interpreter if the accused does not understand the language used in court (Ngubeni, 2023). However, in 2017, the heads of the court adopted English as the official language of record in all South African high courts (Docrat & Kaschula, 2023: 2). Thus, a monolingual language of record is in place in South African courts (Docrat & Kaschula, 2023: 3). In that regard, the language of record policy is argued to unfairly affect section 35 of the Constitution of the Republic of South Africa, which provides for the right to a fair trial. Furthermore, section 30 of the Constitution of the Republic of South Africa provides the right to use the language of your choice in government communications, subject to reasonable limitations (Namakula, 2019: 221). This entails a link between the right to exercise one's right to culture through the use of indigenous languages and the right to a fair trial. This fact is often demonstrated when interpreters fail to interpret cultural expressions adequately. The argument is that there is no right to a fair trial if parties in a case lack understanding of the language used or if such parties cannot correctly express themselves due to linguistic challenges. The policy of monolingual language of record undermines multilingualism and multiculturalism. The effect is often the distortion of evidence during interpretation, ultimately derailing the course of justice (Namakula, 2019: 233). Language is thus the means of a trial. Although South African courts have a constitutional duty to ensure a fair trial, they remain hesitant to embrace the equal and fair use of our twelve official languages, resulting in some instances of an infringement of the right to a fair trial and the right to one's culture. Scholars Docrat and Kaschula (2023: 7) refer to the Senzo Meyiwa trial in demonstrating how the court's use of English only as the language of record caused a great impediment to both legal practitioners in the trial and witnesses who often failed to express themselves in English. Ngubeni (2023) also highlights how the issue of incorrect interpretation has ultimately resulted in the miscarriage of justice and, in this regard, refers to the case of *S v Maqubela,* 2017, where incorrect interpretation resulted in a retrial and ultimately an acquittal. Ralarala (2012: 56) makes an example of the Eugene Terre'Blanche trial where the language was a barrier; in that case, the actual translations of the police sworn statement contradicted the complainants' oral narratives. Ralarala (2012: 56) also cautioned that language barriers affect the complainants and alleged perpetrators, and challenge gathering evidence. Docrat and Kaschula (2023: 5) also mention that the linguistic challenges faced by the witness and other parties in the case are compounded by cultural taboos and the use of geographically determined terminology. In that regard, section 6, section 30, and section 35 of the Constitution of the Republic of South Africa, which are critical provisions related to language and cultural rights, are adversely affected by the monolingual language of record principle. This is a form of injustice since law is made possible by language and communication. The realisation is that sections 6, 30, and 35 rights can only be achieved when courts embrace the spirit of multilingualism and multiculturalism, such as in the cases of *S v Damani* and *S v Gordon*. In these cases, the courts proceeded in indigenous languages due to the non-availability of interpreters. The magistrates continued with the cases to avoid undue delays, in which isiXhosa was used, while in the other matter, the trial took place in Afrikaans (Docrat & Kaschula (2023: 5).Ensuring that courts embrace multilingualism rests with interpreters, the Department of Justice, and academia. In that regard, Docrat and Kaschula (2023:13) recommend maximising law students' linguistic competencies and capabilities to achieve linguistic inclusion and equality. The Legal Practice Council, through its education programme, must work in partnership with universities to linguistically transform the curriculum through providing legal training (Docrat and Kaschula, 2023:13). In that regard, it should be mandatory for all students to pass a vocation-specific legal course in any African language, and oral and written literacy and proficiency will be encouraged in African indigenous languages. Furthermore, Docrat and Kaschula (2023: 8) argue that a purposive interpretation and implementation of rights as contained in section 6 and section 35 of the Constitution of the Republic of South Africa for African indigenous languages to be used equally alongside English. In that regard, the use African indigenous languages should be equated to other important human rights. This aligns with Hlophe's (2004: 46) argument that the continued existence of linguistic and cultural barriers represents a genuine threat to our courts' effective dispensation of justice. This creates a very cumbersome burden on translators, and they do not have any legal expertise in most cases, as is required when translations could result in legal technicality issues, and eventually have an adverse effect on the procedural aspects of the trial. Universities should encourage the scientific development of African indigenous languages as was required and legislated previously for Latin to be a compulsory course within the law curriculum due to its link with Roman law. Since African indigenous languages are linked to living customary law, it would be equally important for law students dealing with customary law to be well acquainted with an African indigenous language.

This discussion points out that unless indigenous languages are placed on the same pedestal as English by legal education and by our courts, the right to a fair trial cannot be said to be fully realised by our courts. This discussion demonstrates how litigating parties have used indigenous terms to describe their course of action. This proves the importance of understanding indigenous languages to understand living customary law.

Proposed model for the incorporation of indigenous languages in legal education – University of KwaZulu-Natal model

This chapter refers to the University of KwaZulu-Natal's language policy as a proposed model to incorporate the teaching of indigenous languages. The university has boldly introduced a compulsory isiZulu module for all undergraduate students (Khumalo, 2014: ii). Furthermore, the university has a University Language Board set up through a committee charter in 2006 (Khumalo, 2017: 255. This board is in charge of the mandate of reviewing the university's Language Policy and Plan (Khumalo, 2017: 255). Part of the board's strategy is to institutionalise language planning, which encompasses language activities, which includes training workshops, translation and interpreting services, and the advocacy of sign language (Khumalo, 2017: 256).

The crucial projects emanating from the Language Policy and Plan is the publication of two books; among these is a glossary compiled by a lecturer from the university of KwaZulu-Natal, Khulekani Zondi. The book is titled *A Glossary of Law Terms* (Khumalo, 2019). This glossary was compiled to assist students doing legal studies and ordinary South Africans with a limited understanding of the law by providing them with essential explanations of legal terms in both isiZulu and English (Khumalo, 2019). The glossary also greatly assists magistrates and legal practitioners who encounter litigants who only have a command of indigenous languages (Khumalo, 2019). Accordingly, the glossary will assist in isiZulu legal discourse and allow students access to legal knowledge in a familiar language (Khumalo, 2019). Another book to emerge from the University of KwaZulu-Natal is titled *Illustrated Glossary of Southern African Architectural Terms* and was edited by Frescura and Myeza (Khumalo, 2019). This is part of an initiative called 'lexicography', concerned with dictionaries that deal with language or knowledge of specialised disciplines (Khumalo & Nkomo, 2022: 135). This demonstrates that it is possible to promote the use of indigenous languages through initiatives such as translations and the creation of glossaries.

The above development has led to a collaboration among academics who form part of various indigenous communities to create a glossary of legal terms for students in South Africa. This glossary will contain important legal terminology in all eleven languages. The model used would be that of the existing glossary compiled containing a glossary in English/isiZulu. Such projects require further collaborations with legal or law scholars and practitioners to ensure correct interpretation, which could not be misinterpreted, as mentioned in the chapter. A project of this magnitude requires a team of dedicated scholars. However, this promising initiative will add significant value to our law and retain indigenous heritage.

Conclusion

The South African Constitution articulates the imperative to develop indigenous languages, to treat all official languages equally, and to achieve a parity of esteem between English and indigenous languages. This is crucial to reverse the legacy of colonialism and Apartheid, which had less regard for African indigenous languages. The transition to a democratic society would not be complete without the revival of African heritage, language, and identity. This study shows that the use of African indigenous languages has been proscribed within the academy for a very long time. This chapter demonstrated the critical link between indigenous languages and living customary law. Our universities are good starting points where the use of indigenous languages in teaching living customary law can be gradually introduced. Litigating parties should not avoid using indigenous terms to describe their causes of action before a court of law since our Constitution guarantees us linguistic rights, the right to culture, and the right to a fair trial.

Courts and relevant stakeholders should move towards using indigenous languages as languages of record. As mentioned in this chapter, the language policy and initiatives progressing at the University of KwaZulu-Natal can be a great starting point and benchmark. Through this language policy, the University of KwaZulu-Natal has taken the initiative to cultivate, modernise, and elaborate on isiZulu so that it becomes a vehicle for knowledge production and knowledge dissemination. We also have witnessed significant progress in our courts where presiding officers, in some cases, prefer to write the judgments in indigenous African languages, such as the examples of Chief Justice Maya (*AfriForum NPC v Chairperson of the Council of the University of South Africa and Others,* 2020) and Justice Mabindla-Boqwana, who have both produced judgments in isiXhosa. This demonstrates excellent potential for incorporating such a project involving intellectualising African languages. The strong support for African languages in South African courts is a project that academics and legal practitioners can embark on, as the advantages of such a project will benefit South African litigants. The use of lexicography also seeks to promote all South African official languages, and the author does not seek to propose a method that prefers specific languages per province. This feasible model is part of a project that legal scholars who speak various indigenous languages embark on, wherein key legal terms will be translated into multiple indigenous languages.

References

AfriForum NPC v Chairperson of the Council of the University of South Africa and Others (2020)

Bambast, I., Kruger, A & Kruger, T. (2013). Constitutional and judicial language protection in multilingual states: a brief overview of South Africa and Belgium. *Erasmus Law Review,* 5 (3): 211–232.

Bakker, P. (2022). Integration of the Bride and the Courts: Is Integration as a Living Customary Law Requirement Still Required? *PER*, 25 (2): 1–21.

Bennett, TW. 2004. *Customary Law in South Africa* Cape Town: Juta and Company Ltd.

Bongela, KS. (2001). Isihloniphoamong Amaxhosa accessed @https://core.ac.uk/download/pdf/43164433.pdf [Date accessed: 03 February 2023].

Cordeiro-Rodrigues, L. (2018). Killing a bull with bare hands: Ukweshwama and Zulu cultural accommodation. *ANTHROPOZOOLOGICA* 53 (16): 187–194.

Diba v Miselo and Another (2021)

Dlomo v Premier of KwaZulu-Natal and Others (2023)

Docrat, Z. & Kaschula , RH. (2023). Cultural and Linguistic Prejudices Experienced by African Language Speaking Witnesses and Legal Practitioners at the Hands of Judicial Officers in South African Courtroom Discourse: The Senzo Meyiwa Murder Trial. *International Journal for the Semiotics of Law.* Accessed @file:///C:/Users/u25081978/Downloads/s11196-023-10071-6%20(1).pdf [Date accessed: 03 February 2023].

DRM v DMK (2018)

Dube, A. & Nhlabatsi, S. (2016). The King can do no wrong: The impact of The Law Society of Swaziland v Simelane NO & Others on constitutionalism. *African Human Rights Law Journal* 16 (1): 265–282.

Executive Council of the Province of KwaZulu-Natal and Others v Luthuli and Others (2023)

Fayemi, KA. (2013). The problem of language in contemporary African philosophy: some comments. *Inkanyiso, Journal of Humanities & Social Sciences* , 5 (1): 1–11.

FM v NR and Others (2020)

Geduld, AJN. (2019). Teaching Latin to law students in the midst of the decolonisation of the university curriculum. *In die Skriflig/In Luce Verbi*, 53 (2): 1–7.

Gwaravanda, E. & Ndofirepi, A. (2020). Eurocentric Pitfalls in the Practice of African Philosophy: Reflections on African Universities. *Phronimon*, 21: 1–21.

Harms, LTC. (2012). Law and Language in a Multilingual Society. *Potchefstroom Electronic Law Journal*, 15 (2): 21–31.

Hlophe, JM. (2004). Receiving justice in your own language is the need for effective court interpreting in our multilingual society. *Advocate Journal:* 42–47.

Jezile v S and Others (2015)

Kaschula, RH. (2016). In search of the African voice in higher education: The language question. *Stellenbosch Papers in Linguistics Plus*, 49: 199–214.

Kekana, TJ. & Montle, ME. (2022). The use of the official Indigenous languages in the South African judcial system reimagined, poignant and tacit issues explored. *ScienceRise*, 80(3): 73–82.

Khumalo, L. (2014). Language Matters@UKZN: University Language Planning and Development Office Final Quarterly Report. Accessed @https://ulpdo.ukzn.ac.za/wp-content/uploads/2022/08/2014-Q4.pdf. [Date accessed: 11 February 2025].

Khumalo, L. (2017). Intellectualisation through terminology development. *Lexikos*, 47: 252–264.

Khumalo, L. & Nkomo, D. (2022). The intellectualisation of African languages through terminology and lexicography: methodological reflections with specific reference to lexicographic products of the University of Kwazulu Natal. *Lexikos,* 32(2): 133–157.

Lebese, SJ. (2014). Do Justice To Court Interpreters In South Africa. *Stellenbosch Papers in Linguistics Plus*, 43: 183–208.

Mabuza v Mbatha (2003)

Madadzhe, RN. (2019). Using African languages at universities in South Africa: The struggle continues. *Stellenbosch Papers in Linguistics Plus*. 58: 205–218.

Maithufi, M. & Maimela, CA. (2020). Teaching the 'other law' in a South African university: some problems encountered and possible solutions. *Obiter*, 41 (1): 1–9.

Manthwa, TA. (2023). An Analysis of the Significance of Integration of the Bride in Customary Marriages and its Potential Constitutionality. *Potchefstroom Electronic Law Journal,* 26 (1): 1–22.

Maseko, P. & Kaschula, R. (2009). Vocational language learning and teaching at a South African university: Preparing professionals for multilingual contexts. *Stellenbosch Papers in Linguistics Plus*, 38: 130–142.

MCB v T.N.M (2019)

MCM v T (2019)

Mlamla v Rubushe and Others (2019)

ML v KG (2013)

MM. v RAN. (2023)

Modisane v Road Accident Fund (2013)

Mphalle, KA. (2020). A child belongs to (s)he who has paid the bride price. Accessed @https://www.taylorfrancis.com/chapters/edit/10.4324/9781315407104-5/child-belongs-paid-bride-price-kagiso-maphalle. [Date accessed: 03 February 2023].

Mphasha, LE. & Mutele, TC. 2017. Challenges Facing the Accused in the Use of English Only in Criminal Court Proceedings: Experiences from the Vhembe District, Limpopo Province, South Africa. *Journal of Social Sciences*, 41 (3): 385–394.

Mokotong, M. (2015). Oe Gapa Le Namane Customary Law Parenting (Step-Parent Adoption from an African Perspective). *Journal of Contemporary Roman-Dutch Law,* 78: 344–355.

Monye, S. (2017). Customary law and adoption: the *'o e gapa le namane'* custom as a reflection of customary-law development in South Africa. *Journal of Law, Society and Development*, 4 (1): 1–19.

Moore, E. & Himonga C. (2019). Living Customary Law and Families in South Africa. Accessed @https://ci.uct.ac.za/sites/default/files/content_migration/health_uct_ac_za/533/files/living%2520customary%2520law%2520and%2520families%2520in%2520South%2520Africa.pdf [Date accessed: 03 February 2023].

Mtshiselwa, M. 2011. A biblical perspective and critique of homosexuality by the Xhosa culture. *Theologia Viatorum,* 35 (2): 273–301.

Muvhali v Lukhele (2022)

Mwambene, L & Sloth- Nielson, J. 2011. Benign Accommodation? Ukuthwala, 'forced.

Marriage' and the South African Children's Act. *African Human Rights Journal,* 11: 1-22.

Namakula, CS. (2019). When the tongue ties fair trial: the South African experience. *South African Journal on Human Rights*, 35 (2): 219–236.

Ndenze, B. (2017). A law degree without fluency in indigenous language is proposed. Port Elizabeth: *Herald Newspaper*, Tiso Blackstar 4.

Nduli v Minister of Home Affairs and Others (2023)

Nemavunde and Another v Mavhungu and Another (2015)

Ngubeni, B. (2023). Navigating multilingualism in the South African justice system: Challenges and solutions for accurate interpretation in South African courts. Accessed @https://www.derebus.org.za/navigating-multilingualism-in-the-south-african-justice-systemchallenges-and-solutions-for-accurate-interpretation-in-south-african courts/#:~:text=Section%2035%20of%20the%20Constitution,less%20 common%20languages%20or%20dialects.[retrieved 03 February 2023]

Ntlama-Makhanya, N. (2021). Revisiting the Debate on the Constitutionalised Status of Indigenous Languages as Language of Record in South African Judicial Proceedings. *Beijing Law Review,* 12 (4): 1077–1094.

Prince Mbonisi Bekithemba Ka Bhekuzulu and Others v President of the Republic of South Africa and Others (2023)

Radebe, IS. (2019). The importance of indigenous languages in the decolonisation of higher education in South Africa: a case study of the University of KwaZulu-Natal's language policy. Accessed @https://researchspace.ukzn.ac.za/items/dac7dac6-c507-41b0-b75e-706ef6f25e33 [Date accessed: 03 February 2023].

Radebe, MK. & Maimela, CA. (2020). The importance of considering African indigenous languages in the decolonisation of legal education and practice. *Journal of Decolonising Disciplines,* 2(1): 1–16.

Ralarala, M. (2013). A compromise of rights, rights of language and rights to a language in Eugene Terre'Blanche's (ET) trial within a trial: evidence lost in translation. *Stellenbosch Papers in Linguistics*, 41: 55–70.

Rautenbach, C. (2011). Umkhosi Ukweshwama: Revival of a Zulu Festival in Celebration of the Universe's Rites of Passage. In Bennett, TW (ed.) *Traditional African Religions in South Africa*. University of Cape Town Press.

Shabangu, S. (2019). UKZN Launches Books to Advance IsiZulu. Accessed @https://ndabaonline.ukzn.ac.za/UkzndabaStory/Vol7-Issue28/UKZN%20Launches%20Books%20to%20Advance%20isiZulu%20/ [Date accessed: 11 February 2025].

Sibisi, S. (2020). Is the requirement of integration of the bride optional in customary marriages? *De Jure Law Journal*, 53 (1): 90–95.

Sibisi, S. (2021). The Supreme Court of Appeal and the handing over of the bride in customary marriages. *De Jure Law Journal*, 54 (1): 370–386.

Sikhosana, ELZ. (2002). A critical study of contemporary practice of Ulululation (ukukikiza) and its current values among the Zulus. Accessed @https://uzspace.unizulu.ac.za/items/3802219d-1a96-4f34-a35f-a27b0e33d021/full. [Date accessed: 23 February 2023].

Smit NO and Others v King Goodwill Zwelithini Kabhekuzulu and Others (2009)

SMS. v VRS. (2019)

Tsambo v Sengadi (2020)

Tshongweni v Kwankwa (2021)

Yende, SJ. & Ngema V. (2023). Indlamu: An Image of Zulu Upper-Class Culture of the Past. *E-Journal of Humanities, Arts and Social Sciences.* 4 (3): 300–311.

Zimmerman, R. (1986). Latin for lawyers. *De Rebus*, 605–606.

Zulu v Mathe and Others (2022)

7

MANIFESTATION OF POWER IN THE DISCOURSE OF LAWYERS AND WITNESSES IN THE MALAWIAN COURTROOM

Precious Lungu

Introduction

The courtroom is one of the places where spoken language is unprecedented. The generic term that covers all aspects of written, spoken, and gestured language in court is called courtroom discourse. Courtroom discourse serves as an instrument of institutional empowerment and control (Wagner & Cheng, 2011: 2). Such discourse involves a large number of participants (judge, jury, clerk, recorder, lawyers and their teams, the accused, and witnesses), although the extent to which they speak and listen is different depending on their role and the stage of the trial (Coulthard & Johnson, 2007: 96). It is usually lawyers who talk the most during court proceedings unless otherwise determined. Apart from lawyers and the judge, both witnesses and accused/respondents also have time to speak in court, especially when they are asked questions.

According to Kondowe (2023: 1), questions are the most dominant form of speech that lawyers employ when interacting with witnesses in a court of law. The notable phases of lawyer-witness interaction are the examination-in-chief, cross-examination, and re-examination, where questions are asked and answers, both convincing and unconvincing, are given (Tudurachi, 2013: 954). To lawyers, questions constitute the most significant adversarial tool for extracting vital information that would sway the outcome of the trial in favour of the party they are representing (Kondowe, 2023: 1). This means that in posing and responding to the questions, there is a power (im)balance between the lawyer(s) and the one(s) answering, in this case, witnesses and/or accused persons.

In the same vein, language is regarded as one of the tools used in the courtroom to establish power in discourse. Language can thus be viewed as a manipulation tool for situating courtroom interactions (Uwen, 2023: 22), and such manipulation includes power yielded in the discourse. As Wettergren and Blix (2015) put it, apart from power being directly connected to action, it is also an asymmetrical relation; a position that grants a person an upper hand to command others. Thus, whoever yields power in the courtroom, is able to control what and how much the other parties say. In discourse, such power is yielded through the language that one uses. For example, if a prosecutor asks an accused a yes/no question, it means the prosecutor has power (through the language in the question) to determine to what extent the accused can respond to such a question; whose answer will be either a 'yes' or a 'no'. Ramadhani et al. (2019: 2002) agrees with this, by asserting that the use of language in the courtroom may determine the power that shows the asymmetrical relationship between the companions. In legal settings, language plays an important role in daily operations as most events take place either in the form of spoken (lawyer-client interviews, hearings, and trials) or written (creation of legal texts and written laws) discourse (Boginskaya, 2022: 1).

In the Malawian context, the court is not spared of the same power dynamics that oscillate between the lawyer/prosecutor(s), the accused/respondent(s) and the witness(es). As Kondowe et al. (2022: 3) note, most witnesses who appear in criminal courts in Malawi are laypersons and illiterate, who rely on the prosecution to guide them. The mere fact that some players in the court proceedings in Malawi rely on lawyers/prosecutors for guidance, is a sign that power cannot be balanced between these two parties. This lies in the discourse that is used to establish such power in the courtroom.

Statement of the problem

Recent studies have investigated language in the courtroom from several angles (Liu, 2021). One of the angles is language used in the courtroom. Various players in the courtroom yield various levels of power through the language that they use. According to Fairclough (2003: 24), language is considered a medium that can be used to create and perpetuate the unequal distribution of power in the courtroom. Such inequality of power can be between lawyers, witnesses, and/or the accused, depending on the language that they use during court proceedings. The one with power controls how the exchange goes with the other party. This then warrants an analysis of how such power dynamics manifest. Hence, it is the goal of this study to analyse how power manifests in the discourse of lawyers/prosecutors and witnesses in Malawian courts.

Research objectives

The general objective of the study is to analyse how power manifests in the discourse of both lawyers and/or prosecutors, and witnesses during court proceedings.

Specifically, the study has the following objectives:

1) To analyse how power manifests in the lawyers'/prosecutors' discourse during examination in court.

2) To determine who yields more power between lawyers/prosecutors and witnesses during examination in the courtroom.

Research questions

In conducting the study, the following research questions will be pivotal:

1) How does power manifest in the discourse of lawyers/prosecutors during examination?
2) Who yields more power between lawyers/prosecutors and witnesses during examination in the courtroom?

Significance of the study

The study benefits forensic linguists as they gain a deeper understanding and insight into how counsels yield power through language use in courtroom discourse. The layman can also benefit from having access to this study, by realising that whatever linguistic approach lawyers adopt during court proceedings, the ultimate goal is to have the power to control how their questions are answered in a bid to downplay the witnesses' testimonies and win the case.

Limitations of the study

The main limitation of this study was time constraints, which resulted in failure to collect data from more court cases. This is because there were not many cases represented at the Mzuzu Courthouse every day. Such being the case, the researcher managed to collect data from two cases only.

Literature Review

Power

Power is one of the aspects that obtains in a court of law. Various players in the courtroom yield power depending on their roles. For example, judges and prosecutors belong to an elite group of professionals invested with both power and high social status (Wettergren & Blix, 2015: 2). In court, these players hold power that is vested in them by either law, statutes, or legislation. However, even amongst those elites who hold power in the court, there is no equality and/or power balance. Thus, judges tend to hold more power in the courtroom, as they can freely interrupt either witnesses or lawyers (Kondowe & Mtanga, 2023: 34). However, it should be noted that as much as the judges hold such power, they speak the least during proceedings. Nevertheless, Kondowe and Mtanga (2023: 34) argue that it is a mistake to conclude that judges interrupt lawyers and/or witnesses as a way of showing power, dominance, and control, as they speak less than lawyers in the Malawi legal system. This shows that it is not how much or how long one speaks that determines one's power, but rather on whom has such power been vested.

In the present context, the concept of power is two-fold; 'power over' and 'power to'. On one hand, according to Wettergren and Blix (2015: 5), 'power to' requires access to resources such as information, and is motivated by self-feelings such as self-confidence and self-esteem, as well as feelings about the context of action. The power lies within the confines of oneself as regards what and when to do something. One has the willpower to make or do something, and it is proportional to action. On the other hand, 'power over' is asymmetrical in nature, where a person has resources to command others to do something (Wettergren & Blix, 2015: 5). This means that the one who holds power is able to command and determine the course of action to be taken by the other party. When power (over) is abused or wrongfully used, it results in the feeling of guilt.

Power is also witnessed in how language is used. Supardi (2010: 69) asserts that language is spoken by such people as judges, prosecutors, attorneys, lawyers, jurors, and witnesses in the courtroom. Uwen (2023: 22) adds that language can be regarded as a manipulation tool for situating courtroom interactions, and is sometimes used as an ideological aspect of the legal genre. As these people use language, power can be gauged based on how they are using language. According to Supardi (2010), 'Language can become a powerful tool for communication because of its power. With the power of language, people have performed various purposes, such as communicating their thoughts and ideas, sharing information, expressing their feelings, influencing others and building relationships. In legal settings language is used in statutory regulations, ordinances, and other legal documents' (Supardi, 2010: 70).

Power is wielded through the use of language where various players hold different levels of power in the courtroom. Thus, the power in and behind language is transferred from the extralinguistic power represented by the wielder to language to catapult this power (Uwen, 2023: 23). Hence, the current study seeks to analyse how such power manifests and who holds more power between lawyers/prosecutors and witnesses during examination in the courtroom.

Examination

Examination takes place in the courtroom during proceedings, where questions and arguments are advanced. Examination takes place in three phases during an adversarial court sitting, thus: examination-in-chief, cross-examination, and re-examination. According to Ramadhani et al. (2019: 2003), cross-examination is a legal process that consists of an oral presentation of evidence whose purpose is to examine the witness, which is done by the counsel or attorney to elicit or confirm the facts of the case, thus determining whether the testimony of the witness is admissible or not, depending on how the questions are crafted and how the responses are given. Examination-in-chief is the initial solicitation of evidence; either the defence counsel or the prosecution asks their witnesses and clients questions (Boginskaya, 2022: 2). Each party is given a chance to examine their clients and/or witnesses as well as cross-examine their counterparts' clients and/or witnesses during a court trial.

Questioning techniques

During court trials, a lot of interaction takes place between lawyers and witnesses. It is usually the lawyers who pose questions and the respondents are such people as witnesses, accused, plaintiffs, and defendants. In all three stages of examination (examination-in-chief, cross-examination, and re-examination), questions are asked and responded to. What is interesting is how language is crafted by the lawyers in the course of asking the questions. Kondowe (2023: 6) argues that productive questions are those that convey less insincerity and are probing in nature, as they provide clarifications on the details of the case. Such questions usually carry a Wh-element (who, what, why, where, when, which, or how). Kondowe (2023: 10) further states that generally, prosecution counsels prefer to broadly use Wh- questions when questioning their witnesses, while defence counsels usually ask their witnesses yes/no questions. Questions and answers permeate the whole process of courtroom interaction, and guilt is determined and judgments are formulated largely based on the outcome of question-answer sequences. Hence, both the questioner and the respondent always choose their language strategically according to the constantly changing context (Haijuan, 2019: 7).

Theoretical framework

The study is guided by the Critical Discourse Analysis approach, as described by Van Djik (1995), as its theoretical framework. Critical Discourse Analysis (CDA) encompasses various aspects such as critical linguistics, critical semiotics, discourse, and communication. According to Machin and Mayr (2015), all levels and aspects of discourse may be examined in CDA studies. These include grammar (syntax and semantics), style, rhetoric, and speech acts. Critical Discourse Analysis focuses on group power, dominance, and inequality, as well as how these are perpetuated or contested by members of social groups through text and speech. This is in line with the current study, which focuses on power relations and/or dynamics between lawyers/prosecutors and witnesses.

Much of CDA's work centres on the underlying ideas that contribute to the reproduction of, or opposition to, dominance and inequality. Regarding discursively enacted dominance or its underlying ideologies, CDA aims to discover, unveil, or disclose what is implicit, hidden, or otherwise not readily apparent. Bringing the current study into this perspective, CDA will help in establishing the linguistic stance that players during examination take, to wield power in their discourse in the courtroom. The goal of CDA, as Machin and Mayr (2015) put it, is to examine how and why linguistic features are formed, as well as what possible ideological aims they may fulfil. Eventually, power dynamics between the aforementioned players that are buried in their use of discourse are brought to light.

Research methodology

Research design and approach

This study adopted the qualitative research design. According to Palmer and Bolderston (2006), the qualitative research method studies human experiences and realities through descriptions and words from the subject's point of view. Thus, human interactions (in the current setup, discourse) that occur in real life and time are best described using qualitative research. In terms of approach, the study equally employed the qualitative research approach. This was adopted during the thematic analysis of the collected data.

Data collection and sampling techniques

Data was collected through non-participatory observation of both criminal and civil cases in the courtroom. While observing the proceedings, the researcher noted down pertinent aspects of the discourse during examination. The questions and answers were recorded verbatim, to capture as much information as possible. In terms of sampling, the study used purposive sampling, whose target were both civil and criminal cases. The study also used the random sampling technique, where the cases were randomly selected, based on availability of represented cases at the Mzuzu Magistrates Court. The study used a total of two cases, where one was a civil case and the other one was a criminal case. When collecting the data, the main focus was on the three phases of examination: examination-in-chief, cross-examination, and re-examination. This is because, during these three stages, there is a lot of interaction between defence lawyers, prosecutors, witnesses, accused, and respondents. All data was collected from the Mzuzu Magistrates Court.

Data analysis

In terms of data analysis, the data collected was analysed qualitatively, especially textual analysis of the discourse between lawyers/prosecutors and witnesses/accused/respondents. The data was analysed thematically in line with the specific objectives of the study, and the theoretical framework. This was more of a content analysis of the data collected. The two cases analysed are: the civil case between Mr M.P., who was the petitioner wanting the court to equally distribute property between himself and his ex-wife, Miss E.N; the criminal case between the Republic and Mr A.M., in a case of theft by servant, where Mr A.M. was accused of selling a protected species of trees without permission.

Ethical implications of the study

Before collecting data, permission was obtained from the Senior Resident Magistrate in the Mzuzu Registry. To uphold utmost confidentiality, all persons in this study were anonymised; only initials were used as codes for proper data presentation and analysis. The data was solely used for research and academic purposes, without further sharing it with any other individual, institution, or third party. As pointed out earlier on, data was collected from two cases. For the sake of anonymity, the civil case, which was not concluded by the time data was collected, was coded 'Civil Case Number X of 2023', presided over by the Chief Resident Magistrate of Mzuzu Magistrates Court. The petitioner was coded 'P', the respondent was coded 'R' and the defence lawyer was coded 'DL1'. The criminal case, which had also not been concluded by then, was given the code 'Criminal Case Number Y of 2023', which was presided over by the Principal Resident Magistrate of Mzuzu Magistrates Court. In this case, the prosecutor was given the code 'P', the accused was coded 'A', and the witnesses were given codes 'W1', 'W2', 'W3, and 'W4'.

Findings and analysis

As intimated earlier on, this study uses data from two cases, one civil case and one criminal case. The analysis adopts a thematic approach, being guided by the study's specific objectives and the theoretical framework.

How power manifests in lawyers'/prosecutors' discourse during examination

Based on the data collected, there is an indication that power manifests in various ways during examination. There were two phases of examination where power manifested in the lawyers' discourse. These were examination-in-chief and cross-examination. There were three main conduits through which power manifested and was used during the court trials. Firstly, power manifested through the questions, thus, questioning techniques that lawyers and persecutors used during examination. Secondly, through interrupting the witnesses and/or accused while they were still speaking. The third was by controlling how the discourse or exchange was done between the lawyers/prosecutors themselves and the witnesses.

- *Questions and questioning techniques*

In both Criminal Case Number Y and Civil Case Number X, there was a total of 53 questions asked by lawyers, and nine questions asked by the accused, making a total of 62 questions. Out of the 53 questions, 13 were asked by the Prosecutor in Criminal Case Number Y (theft by servant) during examination-in-chief, while 40 were asked by the Defence Lawyer (DL_1) in Civil Case Number X during examination-in-chief as well. The accused in Criminal Case Number Y was not represented by any lawyer, hence he ended up asking the nine questions by himself, which led to him cross-examining the state witnesses. In summary, Table 7.1 below shows the statistics of the questions asked:

TABLE 7.1: Summary of questions asked

S/N	Civil Case X	Criminal Case Y	Total
Defence Lawyer	40		40
Prosecutor		13	13
Accused		9	9
			62

The table above shows that most questions were asked by the Defence Lawyer during Civil Case Number X proceedings. This is so because, as Kondowe (2023: 12) argues, the defence asked questions to properly guide his client, which in this case was the respondent. On the other hand, the prosecutor asked a few questions to the witnesses during examination-in-chief, probably to minimise antagonising the arguments put forth by the prosecution team. However, if the accused was well-versed with questioning techniques or if he was represented by a lawyer, it was more likely that the lawyer could have asked a lot of pressing questions during cross-examination to defeat the prosecution's arguments. This is in line with Kondowe's (2023: 13) argument, that if the prosecution asks their witnesses few questions during examination-in-chief, defence counsels make use of such an advantage during cross-examination to ask two or three times the number of questions.

In addition, there were 25 Wh- questions that were asked by the Defence Lawyer in Civil Case Number X; four Wh- questions were asked by the prosecutor in Criminal Case Number Y; and only one Wh- question was asked by the accused. This is almost half of the total number of questions asked. On the contrary, there was a total of 19 yes/no questions in both cases.

- *Use of interruptions*

During the court proceedings, it was also observed that power manifested through interruptions, where both the defence lawyer in the civil case, the prosecutor, and the accused in the criminal case interrupted the witnesses while they still held the floor. Interruption refers to a deep intrusion into the utterance of the one holding the floor (Kondowe & Mtanga, 2023: 34). In Civil Case Number X, there were six instances where the defence lawyer interrupted his witness. In Criminal Case Number Y, the prosecutor only interrupted her witnesses three times, while the accused only interrupted the witnesses two times. As much as there were not as many interruptions during court proceedings of the two cases, it still shows that those who interrupted tended to hold some power at the time of interruption, and that power in their discourse manifested by their interruptions.

- *Controlling the direction of the discourse/exchange*

Another way in which power was manifested in the court trials was through the lawyers' control of how and when the respondents answered their questions. This was observed when the lawyers/prosecutors asked the yes/no questions, where the witnesses were obliged to choose only one option and add nothing. This is also one of the techniques that lawyers use in a way to either clarify the information given or to leave no room for explanation on a particular argument advanced by their counterparts (Ramadhani et al., 2019: 2004).

Who wields more power

Apart from manifestation of power in the discourse of lawyers/prosecutors and witnesses/accused, the study also aimed at discussing who wields more power and at what level is such power wielded. Based on the findings, it showed that the Defence Lawyer in Civil Case Number X had more power than the respondent, who happened to be his client. This was observed during examination-in-chief, while he asked her questions. It was also observed that the prosecutor in Criminal Case Number Y had more power than all the four witnesses she examined. This was observed through the way the questions were being asked and the lack of confidence in most of the witnesses as they responded.

Discussion

Employing Wh- questions

The use of Wh- questions was observed to be prominent during examination-in-chief in the two cases, as a way of manifesting power in the discourse of the one(s) asking the questions. Most of the Wh- questions that were asked by the defence lawyer in the civil case sought to establish facts. For example, the excerpt below shows the kind of Wh- questions asked and the information provided in responding to the questions:

DL1: **What** are your names madam?

R: Esther.

DL1: **What**'s your home village?

R: Mzimba.

DL1: **Who** is the petitioner to you?

R: My ex-husband.

DL1: **How** did you meet him?

R: (hesitates to respond)

DL1: **Where** does the petitioner stay?

R: Akukhalanga kwa Sonda (He stays at Sonda).

From the discourse above, it is evident that the defence lawyer is in total control of the flow and he is the one who determines what kind of information should be given. This shows that in his discourse, the defence lawyer holds the power to determine what is said and what is not said by the respondent. This was done by asking narrow Wh- questions to the respondent. Another instance of employing Wh- questions to solicit facts, as a way of holding linguistic power was observed in the criminal case. The excerpt below sheds more light:

P: What happened for you two to meet?

W1: *Eeehh...tikaba kuti tikugwira kumoza* (We were working at the same place).

P: **How** do you know the accused?

W3: *Tinamulemba ntchito ku munda wa mwana wanga* (He was employed to work at my son's farm).

P: **What** do you do for a living?

W4: I am a pastor, but I also do business.

The discourse above also shows that the prosecutor holds power by determining what facts the witnesses provide in court. Such techniques show that the prosecutor and the defence lawyer make use of the linguistic power they have to solicit the information they need to build their cases and advance their arguments. Not only do lawyers use narrow Wh- questions, but they also use broad Wh- questions, which, according to Kondowe (2023: 10), give the respondents the opportunity to express themselves. The two excerpts below from the two cases show the same:

DL1: **How** come the petitioner stays at Sonda and you at Luwinga?

R: *Chifukwa cha nkhaza mbwenu ine nkhafumapo nakukasanga nyumba ku Luwinga* (Because of his cruelty, I left and found a house in Luwinga).

DL1: **Why** did he come there then?

R: *Iwo awa wakapukwa ine, kuti wazapoke katundu wane* (He was looking for me and also to grab my property).

P: **What** can you say about this document?

W2: This is an assessment report.

P: It is in evidence in this court that you gave the orders that the accused should sell the trees. **What** do you say about that?

W3: *Ayi, limenero ndi bodza, sindinamutumeko kuti agulitse mitengoine* (No, that is a lie, I never sent him to sell the trees).

Power here is manifested through the use of probing Wh- questions that aim at soliciting as much information as possible. Based on these excerpts, this study argues that power manifests in the discourse of lawyers/prosecutors through asking questions that solicit only the information they are looking for.

Asking yes/no questions

Lawyers also yield power by asking yes/no questions to the respondents. This technique, according to Haijuan (2019), leaves the respondents with only one option, with no room for clarifications. Thus, yes/no questions aim at cornering the respondents so much so that they do not have a chance to express themselves freely. For instance, the excerpt below shows how power manifests through yes/no questions posed by the accused when he was cross-examining the witnesses:

A: *Simunanditume kugulitsa mitengo?* (Did you not send me to sell the trees?)

W3: *Ayi* (No)

A: *Sindinabwere ndi nkhani kuti munthu akufuna kugula mitengo ya matabwa?* (Did I not come to tell you that someone wanted to buy trees for timber?)

W3: *Ayi* (No).

A: *Ku mundako, munandiwona kapena ayi?* (Did or did you not see me at the farm?)

W2: *Ayi* (No)

This is a rare situation where the accused yields more power than the state witness in the course of cross-examining the witness. The exchange above shows that the accused determined how the state witnesses should respond to his questions, with either 'yes' or 'no'. In this case, one can argue that the one who poses such kinds of questions yields more power than the one responding to the questions. In the courtroom, it is possible to have an accused person yielding more power than state witnesses, based on how the accused asks questions that aim at discrediting the witness's testimony (Boginskaya, 2022: 9; Ramadhani et al., 2019: 2005).

Using interruptions to wield linguistic power

Another way of yielding more power in one's discourse is through interrupting someone. As indicated in the findings, the lawyer and the prosecutor, as well as the accused interrupted their interlocutors in the course of the proceedings. The instances are provided in the excerpts from the two cases below.

> Excerpt from Criminal Case Number Y:
>
> P: Did you visit the crime scene?
>
> W1: *Apo pakawa kuti...* (What happened was...)
>
> P: Did you really visit the crime scene?
>
> W1: Yes.
>
> P: Do you have anything to add?
>
> W2: Yes I...
>
> P: That's all, you may sit.
>
> P: Tell us what happened next
>
> W3: *Kuchokera nthawi imeneyo...* (From that time...)
>
> P: Wait! Which time are you referring to?

> Excerpt from Civil Case Number X
>
> DL1: Yes, tell us what happened
>
> R: *Sono iwo akati...*
>
> DL1: No no no! We want to hear what happened at first
>
> R: *Nkhani ikachitika adjourn, mbwe...*

DL1: So, what did the petitioner say after the adjourn?

Such interruptions are proof enough that the prosecutor and the defence lawyer hold power in these conversations. When the respondents have not even completed their sentences, the prosecutor cut them off and either asked another question or closed the questioning. Likewise, the defence lawyer interrupted his client in the course of answering his questions. The interruptions in these two cases are also proof that linguistic power is usually wielded by lawyers/prosecutors more than witnesses. This is so because it is the lawyers/prosecutors who interrupt the respondents, not the other way round. This only shows that the lawyers/prosectuors were at liberty to interrupt the witnesses at any point, whether necessitated or not. Such interruptions, as Kondowe and Mtanga (2023: 41) put it, seek more information and clarification on what has been earlier said. As per the data above, most of the interruptions came about as a way of soliciting further information and clarification on what the respondents had said. This usually only goes one-way, where the prosecutor/lawyer interrupts the witnesses.

Controlling the direction of the examination

Another way in which the defence lawyer and the prosecutor wielded more power than the witnesses was through controlling how and when the respondents answered their questions. This was observed when the lawyers asked the yes/no questions, where the witnesses were obliged to choose only one option and add nothing. This is also one of the techniques that lawyers use to either clarify the information given or to leave no room for explanation on a particular argument advanced by the lawyer (Ramadhani et al., 2019: 2004). Both the criminal and the civil cases show that it was in the lawyer's/prosecutor's hands to determine how the examination-in-chief goes. Another technique used to control the discourse is using leading questions that are accompanied by the conjunction 'so' and question tags. For example, the excerpt below demonstrates this strategy:

DL1: **So**, how did the petitioner know?

R: *Kwali* (I do not know).

DL1: In other words, he was just profiting from you, not so?

R: Yes.

DL1: So, you say he was not coming to your bedroom?

R: *Enya* (Yes).

DL1: Last time the petitioner said you carried everything when leaving the house, **right**?

Using such techniques helps the lawyer to be in control of the conversation and dictate how the respondent answers his questions. Employing 'so' and question tags is one of the linguistic strategies used by an individual to control the intention or topic of discussion during an interaction (Ramadhani et al., 2019: 2004), in this case during examination of witnesses. Hence, this paper argues that due to the power that the lawyer/prosecutor holds during the examination-in-chief, they controlled and swayed the witnesses' discourse so that what was uttered was exactly what they (legal counsels) were looking for. The wielding of power is observed in the kind of questions asked, the interruptions made, and the direction in which the lawyer/prosecutor took the discourse in the courtroom, which are all indications that indeed, the lawyer/prosecutor holds power over the witnesses through discourse.

Institutional authority

Lawyers also wield power in their interactions with witnesses by taking advantage of their institutional authority. From the interactions in the data, it was observed that lawyers have an upper hand when speaking with witnesses. This is because the judiciary, as an institution, vests some powers in the lawyers, unlike the witnesses. The study argues that lawyers use such power to downplay the witnesses' testimonies. This is in line with what Wettergren and Blix (2015: 2) argue, that legal professionals belong to an elite group of professionals that are endowed with both power and high status in society. Devoid of such institutional power, both defence lawyers and prosecutors would not yield the same level of power as they do with the institutional authority they have. This power is manifested through the discourse that lawyers employ as they interact with witnesses in Malawian courtrooms. Nonetheless, this chapter still argues that some lawyers tend to misuse such institutional power to block witnesses from expressing themselves freely. This also reverberates with what Wettergren and Blix (2015: 2 & 3) propagate, that legal professionals are equally susceptible to critique of misusing their institutional authority.

As lawyers/prosecutors elicit information from witnesses, they also make use of the institutional power they have. The researcher observed that both defence lawyers and prosecutors determined how much information the witnesses should provide, by using their authority to limit the witnesses' discourse. This agrees with what Uwen (2023: 34) found in his study on language dynamics and power relations in courtroom interactions. He argues that the power that lawyers wield helps them dictate how long a witness' or defendant's testimony should be, and also control their answers using various interrogative patterns. This shows that lawyers and prosecutors use their institutional power to control not only the witnesses' discourse, but also the witnesses themselves. Given that witnesses do not have the privilege of institutional power, it is almost impossible for them to counterargue what lawyers and prosecutors say in the courtroom. Hence, the lawyers and prosecutors make use of the institutional power in their discourse.

Conclusion

The current study has analysed how power manifests through lawyers' discourse in the Malawian courtroom. The study has shown that legal counsels wield more power than witnesses during examination in court proceedings. One of the ways in which power manifests in their discourse is through the questions they ask the witnesses. The study has shown that lawyers/prosecutors mostly use Wh- questions, both broad and narrow, to solicit information from witnesses. They also use yes/no questions, in a way not giving the respondents room for clarification or counterarguments. Another way through which power manifests is the use of interruptions. It has been observed that lawyers interrupt the witnesses more often as a way of having linguistic power and control of the discourse at hand. The study has equally observed that legal counsels also determine how a conversation goes by using the conjunction 'so' and some question tags. This also shows that most of the time, it is the lawyer/prosecutor who has power through the discourse they use in the courtroom when examining witnesses. The study argues that power manifests in the lawyers'/prosecutors' discourse through various techniques employed during examination. The witnesses do not yield such power in their discourse, as they are limited in most of their discourse when answering questions.

References

Boginskaya, O. (2022). Adversarial, ludic and ritual nature of discursive interactions in a trial. *Journal of Language Studies*, vol. 22(1), pp. 1–15.

Coulthard, M. & Johnson, A. (2007). *An Introduction to Forensic Linguistics: Language in Evidence*. New York: Routledge.

Dewi, RF., Suharsono, S & Munir, A. (2018). Turn taking strategies and its relations to EFL learners' personality and power in the interaction of English conversation class. *English Teaching, Learning and Research Journal,* vol. 4(2), pp. 288–305.

Fairclough, N. (2003). *Analysing Discourse: Textual Analysis for Social Research.* London: Routledge.

Ghilzai, SA. & Baloch, M. (2016). Conversational analysis of turn-taking behaviour and gender differences in multimodal conversation. *Perspectives in Language, Linguistics and Media*, vol. 1, pp. 1–13.

Haijuan, H. (2019). Courtroom questioning adapted to institutional power. International Journal of Contemporary Education, 2(1), 26-32.

Kato, F. (2000). *Discourse approach to turn-taking from the perspective of tone choice between speakers*. [Unpublished Master's Thesis]. University of Birmingham.

Kondowe, W. & Mtanga, G. (2023). Interruptions as linguistic whistles: An examination of judges' language in Malawi courtroom discourse. In Kaschula, RH., Ralarala, MK. & Heydon, G. (ed.) *Language, Crime and Courts in Contemporary Africa and Beyond*. Stellenbosch: African Sun Media.

Kondowe, W. (2023). Insincerity in lawyers' questioning strategies in Malawian criminal courtroom discourse. *Text & Talk: An Interdisciplinary Journal of Language, Discourse & Communication Studies*. https://doi.org/10.1515/text-2022-0083

Kondowe, W., Liao, M. & Ngwira, FF. (2022). A study of intentional insincerity in Malawian Criminal Justice: Witnesses' discursive strategies. In Ralarala, MK., Kaschula, RH. & Heydon, G. (ed.) *Language and the Law: Perspectives in Forensic Linguistics from Africa and Beyond*. Stellenbosch: African Sun Media.

Liu, M. (2021). A Transitivity Analysis of the Courtroom Discourse: A Case Study of Jodi Arias Trial. *International Journal of Linguistics, Literature and Translation*, vol. 4(5), pp. 253–262. https://doi.org/10.32996/ijllt.2021.4.5.28.

Machin, D. & Mayr, A. (2015). *How to do Critical Discourse Analysis: A Multimodal Introduction*. London: Sage Publications.

Mugari, V., Mukaro, L., Mutonga, L., Samasuwo, NW. & Kadenge, M. (2015). Code-switching among chiShona-English bilinguals in courtroom discourse: Rape cases in Zimbabwe. *South African Journal of African Languages*, vol. 35(2), pp. 207–214.

Palmer, C. & Bolderston, A. (2006). A brief introduction to qualitative research. *Canadian Journal of Medical Radiation Technology*, vol. 37(1), pp. 16–19. https://doi.org/10.1016/S0820-5930(09)60112-2

Ramadhani, R., Indrayani, LM. & Mahdi, S. (2019). Language power in attorney's leading questions to discredit witness's testimonies during court trial: A forensic linguistic study. *International Journal of English Literature and Social Sciences*, vol. 4(6), pp. 2002–2009.

Supardi, A. (2010). A critical discourse analysis on language power and strategy used by jurists. *US-China Foreign Language Journal,* vol. 8(7), pp. 13–25.

Tudurachi, E. (2013). The impossibility of the lawyer-defendant to provide legal assistance to other defendants in the same cause. *Procedia: Social and Behavioral Sciences*, vol. 92, pp. 953-959.

Uwen, G. (2023). Objection overruled: Language dynamics and power relations in courtroom interactions. *Language Matters*, vol. 54(2), pp. 21–41. https://doi.org/10.1080/10228195.2023.2229533

Van Dijk, TA. (1995). Aims of critical discourse analysis. *Japanese Discourse*, vol. 1, pp. 17–27.

Wagner, A. & Cheng, L (eds.). (2011). *Language, Power and Control in Courtroom Discourse: Exploring Courtroom Discourse*. Burlington: Ashgate.

Wettergren, A. & Blix, SB. (2015). *Power, status, and emotion management in professional court work - the case of judges and prosecutors.* [Working Paper No. 23] Stockholm. www.sociology.su.se

PART III

Court Interpreting and Police Statement Taking

8 AN EXPLORATION OF RESEARCHERS' VIEWS REGARDING DIFFICULTIES FACED BY COURT INTERPRETERS AND HOW THEY AFFECT THE DELIVERY OF JUSTICE

Paul Svongoro

Introduction

This chapter explores key issues in court interpreting discourse globally, focusing on the difficulties interpreters face and their potential impact on justice delivery. It also discusses the skills and strategies needed to address these challenges, based on a comprehensive literature review, and the recurring themes in the discourse.

Interpreting scholars generally agree that court interpreting is a complex task that requires concentration, cognitive abilities, linguistic skills, and a clear understanding of courtroom procedures (e.g., Berk-Seligson, 2002; De Jongh, 1992; Docrat, 2022; Hale, 2004 & 2007; Mikkelson, 2000; Miyanda, 2009; Moeketsi, 1999a & b; Ngarambe & Ruvebana, 2023; Svongoro, 2015 & 2017; Wallmach, 2004). However, while scholars agree that interpreters are generally bilingual, they dispel the misconception that any bilingual person can interpret, as inaccuracies in interpretation can have serious consequences.

In light of the critical issues mentioned above, this chapter reviews literature on court interpreting difficulties, skills training, and their impact on justice delivery. It aims to explain major difficulties faced by interpreters, their effects on trial processes, and interpreting-related strategies to enhance service quality and improve justice delivery. The literature also identifies the effects of these difficulties on the trial process and suggests strategies interpreters can adopt to improve their service and client justice delivery.

Research questions

The chapter sought to answer the following research questions:

a) Does the literature identify any prerequisite skills for court interpreters?
b) Does the literature on court interpreting identify any difficulties faced by court interpreters during trials?
c) If the literature available identifies difficulties faced by court interpreters, how can they be categorised and explained?
d) In what ways can the identified difficulties affect the delivery of justice for the court and the persons for whom court interpreters mediate?
e) What kind of skills and strategies do court interpreters need to ameliorate some of the difficulties?

The literature on skills for court interpreters, court interpreter difficulties, and delivery of justice

The researcher reviewed the literature on court interpreters' skills, challenges, and clients' access to justice in order to contextualize the chapter (e.g., Berk-Seligson, 2002; De Jongh, 1992; Docrat, 2022; Gile, 1995; Lebese, 2013;; Hale, 2004 &2007; Mikkelson, 2000; Miyanda, 2009; Moeketsi, 1999a & b; Ngarambe & Ruvebana, 2023; Svongoro, 2015 & 2017). The literature was reviewed under the following subheadings.

Skills for court interpreters: An overview

Researchers generally agree that, interpreting in court is a complex task requiring concentration, cognitive abilities, and essential linguistic skills. Interpreters are typically bilingual, but this does not guarantee adequate interpretation (e.g., Berk-Seligson, 2002; De Jongh, 1992; Docrat, 2022; Hale, 2004 & 2007; Mikkelson, 2000; Miyanda, 2009; Moeketsi, 1999a &, b; Ngarambe & Ruvebana, 2023; Svongoro, 2015 & 2017). These studies challenge the misconception that any bilingual person can interpret (Moeketsi, 1999a).

An interpreter must be a language expert, not just bilingual, capable of processing two languages to reconstruct the same message in the target language. They must understand the linguistic, lexical, syntactic, pragmatic, and stylistic properties of languages, including standard and non-standard forms, regional dialects, formal and informal registers, jargons, argots, slang, and prison language (Hale, 1999; Jacobsen, 2009; Moeketsi, 1999a & b).

Apart from the above, the court interpreter must also master legal language, also known as legalese, which is distinct from everyday English. Legal professionals use a unique jargon, characterized by lengthy sentences, complex syntactic structures, subclauses, and complex numbering. Codeswitching into French and Latin is common in legalese. This makes it difficult for ordinary people to understand, making it precise yet ambiguous, wordy, unclear, pompous, and dull (Gonzalez et al, 1991).

In addition, court interpreters must be culturally proficient, recognizing cultural nuances like honorific terms, kinship terms, idioms, proverbs, taboo expressions, and euphemisms (De Jongh, 1992; Hale, 2004 & 2007; Mikkelson, 2000; Miyanda, 2009; Moeketsi, 1999a). They must also understand paralinguistic codes to discern expressions like anger and happiness from tone of voice, intonation, emphasis, stress, and hesitation. They must also be knowledgeable about non-verbal communication, such as kinesics, facial expressions, and gestures.

How well court interpreters give their renditions also depends on their prior background knowledge of the case before the court (De Jongh, 1992; Hale, 2004 & 2007; Mikkelson, 2000; Moeketsi, 1999a). This means that the more information a court interpreter has about a case, the better placed he/she is to interpret accurately. Apart from this, the court interpreter also needs to know the workings of the legal system in which he/she interprets.

Interpreting researchers agree good interpreters must be good speakers, demonstrating clear, steady voices, with articulate and eloquent speech at an appropriate pace (De Jongh, 1992; Hale, 2007; Mikkelson, 2000). They must also be confident, assertive, humble, and courteous, making them professional speakers (Gile, 1995; Hale, 1999).

Court interpreters must be familiar with general rules of conduct, court procedures, etiquette, and trial stages for the courts they interpret (De Jongh, 1992; Gile, 1995; Lebese, 2013; Miyanda, 2009; Moeketsi, 1999b; Moeketsi & Wallmach, 2005; Ngarambe & Ruvebana, 2023). Interpreters should dress appropriately for the formal environment and swear to interpret well and truly, placing a legal and ethical burden on them (Gonzalez et al, 1991). In Zimbabwe, Hoffman explains the 23 rules guiding court interpreting, which are fundamental principles of the system and any breach of them constitutes an irregularity. Scholars emphasize the importance of interpreters' attire and conduct in courtrooms, as well as their oath to interpret faithfully and truthfully (Hoffman, 1994; 28–38).

Finally, because court interpreting is viewed as a complex process, interpreting scholars agree that interpreters need to demonstrate an understanding of the different skills required for interpreting (De Jongh, 1992; Gile, 1995; Lebese, 2013). These include listening, comprehension, analysis, memory, production, and skills. Moeketsi (1999a) explains that court interpreting is therefore considered a complex process involving human information perception, storage, retrieval, transformation, and transmission. It is not mechanical or automatic, but requires interpreters to be analysts and mind readers, as scholars note that ordinary people often underestimate the complexities of cognitive, linguistic, and interpreting interplay (Gile, 1995).

In short, court interpreting is often misunderstood to be a task that can easily be performed by any bilingual person. Thus, bilingualism is but one of the many requirements for court interpreters. Court interpreting is a profession that is very demanding and reserved for those gifted (Gile, 1995; Moeketsi, 1999a & b; Jacobsen, 2009).

Literature on the relationship between court interpreters' skills, difficulties, and the effect on the delivery of justice

One key issue studied in court interpreting studies relates to the training of interpreters in different countries (e.g., De Jongh, 1992; Hale & Gibbons, 1999; Hale, 2001 & 2004; Moeketsi & Wallmach, 2005; Nord, 2003; Van Grieken, 2001; Svongoro & Kadenge, 2015). Central in this category are comparative studies on the performance of trained and untrained interpreters.

Hale and Gibbons (1999) and Hale (2001 & 2004) for example, focus on interpreter training issues in Australia. De Jongh (1992) focuses on the American situation. Lebese (2013), Docrat (2022) and Moeketsi and Wallmach (2005) examine the South African scenario, while Miyanda (2009) examines the court interpreting practice in Botswana. Nord (2003) investigates Germany. Van Grieken (2001) and Svongoro and Kadenge (2015), focus on the Zimbabwean situation, while Ngarambe and Ruvebana (2023) research the practice of court interpreting in Rwanda. All these studies on court interpreter training issues suggest a pressing need for a thorough re-evaluation of training, certification, and recruitment to ensure world-class interpreting services and improve justice in legal courts across all countries (see, for example, De Jongh, 1992; Hale, 2004; Hale & Gibbons, 1999; Nord, 2003; Van Grieken, 2001).

Hale's research on court interpreter training and the profession highlights the impact of misunderstood identity, mixed loyalties, and misunderstood roles on interpretation accuracy and justice delivery (Hale, 2004, 2007 & 2008). Interpreters face temptations to deviate from their roles due to poor or inadequate training, which can be influenced by pressures from institutional, professional, and interpersonal spheres. Hale (2004) for example, emphasizes the importance of proper training and a clear professional, institutional, and interpersonal environment for interpreters to confidently perform their duties. This highlights the need for a clear and supportive environment for interpreters.

Hale's research, therefore, offers valuable insights into court interpreting in Australia, tracing the development of practices and research. It focuses on the microlinguistic analysis of Spanish interpreters' courtroom performances, incorporating social and professional issues to understand their performance (Hale, 2004, 2007 & 2008).

Drawing insights from Hale's (2004) study, Svongoro and Kadenge (2015) investigate the intricate process of interpreting in Zimbabwean courtrooms, focusing on the discourse practices of interpreters and lawyers in a triadic interaction. Their findings have been incorporated into the development of curriculum and training programmes for court interpreters in Zimbabwe, enhancing their understanding of the legal system.

Miyanda's study in Botswana (2009) aimed to identify challenges faced by court interpreters, their training, familiarity with court procedures, etiquette, and legal terminology, and the interpretation and translation techniques they use. The study also aimed to identify potential issues that may hinder justice dispensing in Botswana's courts. Corroborating prior studies in other contexts (e.g., De Jongh, 1992; Hale, 2004; Hale & Gibbons, 1999; Nord, 2003), the findings reported by Miyanda (2009) confirm the link between training for court interpreters and their preparedness and performance during trials.

Still on the African continent, Ngarambe and Ruvebana (2023) studied court interpreting in Rwanda, focusing on the legal framework, challenges faced by interpreters, and strategies for improvement. They identified challenges such as training and employment, equipment, language proficiency, public misconceptions, and lengthy court proceedings. These issues highlight the need for better training, resources, and performance of interpreters worldwide, which can lead to injustice due to inaccurate interpretation or delayed proceedings.

Finally, using case law from South African courtrooms, Docrat (2022) criticizes the 2017 English language of record policy in South African courts, arguing poor interpretation services negatively impact access to justice. They call for linguistic training programmes for judicial officers and legal practitioners, highlighting the complex relationship between training for court interpreters and those working with interpreters to improve interpretation quality and access to justice (Docrat, 2022).

In short, this chapter reviewed scholarly works that emphasize the importance of court interpreter training in enhancing their performance during trials (Hale, 2005; Svongoro & Kadenge, 2015). It suggests that well-trained interpreters, who receive regular refresher courses and are supported by a conducive working environment, are more likely to interpret accurately than untrained interpreters, who are often accused of altering witness testimonies, potentially influencing trial outcomes (Hale, 2005).

Methodology

The systematic approach to literature review was chosen for its comprehensive, structured, and unbiased examination of current knowledge on court interpreter skills, challenges they face during trials, and their impact on the trial process and justice delivery. This method allowed for extensive evaluation, analysis, and condensation of available literature into manageable insights.

Search process and keywords

The chapter utilizes various search engines and databases – JSTOR, Scopus, Web of Science, EconLit, and ProQuest – to thoroughly explore literature on court interpreters' skills and challenges, providing insights from both the Global North and South, allowing for comparison of state-of-affairs in different worlds. The researcher used the following keywords to search for relevant literature:

a) Court interpreting;

b) Court interpreting skills;

c) Court interpreters' role;

d) Court interpreting difficulties/challenges/predicaments;

e) Court interpreting difficulties and the trial process; and

f) Court interpreting difficulties and the delivery/administration of justice.

The researcher utilized keyword combinations to explore court interpreter skills, challenges they encounter during trials, and their impact on justice delivery, assessing eligibility using peer-reviewed journal articles and official reports, with inclusion and exclusion criteria explained.

Inclusion/exclusion criteria

The literature review established clear guidelines for selecting relevant studies on the skills required for court interpreters, the challenges they face during trials, and how these difficulties affect the trial process and the delivery of justice.

- *Inclusion criteria*

On the exclusion criteria, the researcher considered the following:

a) Studies that directly address or significantly contribute to the understanding of the skills essential for court interpreters, the difficulties they face in executing their role during trials, and how these difficulties affect the trial process and hence the delivery of justice;

b) Prioritise studies conducted in different parts of the world (the Global North and South) to facilitate comparison on situations in different words regarding the subject being explored;

c) Include empirical studies, such as case studies and surveys, that provide concrete data and insights into the skills required for court interpreters, the difficulties they face in executing their role during trials ,and how these difficulties affect the trial process and hence the delivery of justice;

d) Include peer-reviewed journal articles, conference papers, and reputable reports to ensure the reliability and credibility of the sources;

e) Prioritise recent publications to capture the latest issues, trends, developments, and practices in court interpreting; and

f) Consider studies that discuss the policy and practical implications on court interpreting and access to justice.

- *Exclusion criteria*

On the exclusion criteria, the researcher considered the following:

a) Exclude studies that do not directly address skills required for court interpreters, the difficulties they face in executing their role during trials, and how these difficulties affect the trial process and hence the delivery of justice;

b) Exclude purely theoretical papers or literature reviews that do not present empirical evidence or contribute substantively to the empirical understanding of the topic;

c) Exclude sources that are not peer-reviewed or lack credibility, such as blog posts or non-academic publications; and

d) Exclude significantly outdated studies to ensure the review reflects the most recent research and developments.

These criteria aim to ensure the literature review encompasses relevant and robust studies that directly contribute to the exploration of court interpreting, specifically in the context of skills required for court interpreters, the difficulties they face in executing their role during trials, and how these difficulties affect the trial process and hence the delivery of justice.

Data analysis procedure

This chapter examines 59 scholarly papers on court interpreter training, interpreting abilities, and challenges, as was previously indicated in the chapter. The data collected includes books, chapters, journal articles, conference proceedings, dissertations, theses, and reports. Thematic analysis is used to identify and report patterns within qualitative data. The themes emerged from prior studies on court interpreting skills, training, and difficulties faced in real court situations. Themes also emerged concerning the effects of interpreting difficulties on access to justice for those court interpreters. Thematic analysis is particularly useful for research projects aiming to discover themes and concepts embedded within qualitative data.

Findings and discussion

Difficulties faced by court interpreters during trials and their effect on the trial process

The literature review showed that researchers generally concur that court interpreters potentially faced procedural, language, environmental, and ethical difficulties during the interpreting process (e.g. Anderson, 2002; Angermeyer, 2009; Berk-Seligson, 2002; Crawford, 2012; Hale, 2003, 2004, 2007 & 2008; Moeketsi, 1999a & b; Svongoro, 2016; Wallmach, 2004). In the following sections, I explore the difficulties within these four broad categories. A few examples from the literature are used where relevant to illustrate these difficulties.

Procedural difficulties

The literature reviewed seems to confirm that procedural difficulties are by far the most common challenge faced by court interpreters during their work. These difficulties are explained below in detail.

- *Controlling the flow of the testimony*

In her study, Berk-Seligson (2002) observed that court interpreters do not play a passive, invisible role in the courtroom. Interpreters manage the flow of testimony by directing or silencing the speech of witnesses or defendants, both verbally and non-verbally. They may assume this helps make the proceeding more effective, but it is not their intended role. Interpreters may err on the side of making the proceedings smoother (Berk-Seligson, 2002).

- *Prompting witnesses or defendants to speak*

Interpreters use prompting mechanisms to expedite a witness's response to attorney questions or routine 'Do you understand?' questions used by judges to address defendants (Berk-Seligson, 2002: 87). An example from Berk-Seligson's study shows that when a witness answers a question with affirmative 'Mhm', the interpreter urges them to answer yes or no, but only the judge requests such answers. In addition, prompting witnesses to answer is crucial in court proceedings, especially when multiple witnesses or defendants are present, as defendants may become reticent when asked the same question simultaneously (Berk-Seligson, 2002).

Importantly, Berk-Seligson (2002: 89) raises the question about the effect of such behavior of interpreters, which is a factor not to be underestimated. 'In reality, if a witness or defendant does not answer a question quickly, such hesitancy can often be a symptom of failure to comprehend the question. A frightened witness or defendant may not feel confident enough to say, "I don't understand."" She goes on to speculates whether the pressure put on them pushes them into answering prematurely, even without being sure about the meaning of the question.

Silencing witnesses or defendants

Berk-Seligson (2002) identifies two types of situations where interpreters can silence witnesses or defendants. First, interpreters may be instructed by judges to stop them from speaking before they can incriminate themselves, often when defendants begin explaining why they are wrongfully accused of a specific crime. Second, interpreters may need to silence witnesses or defendants when objections are raised, either through interjections like 'Sir, sir' or direct commands like 'Don't answer!', or a brief explanation of the situation.

Nevertheless, interpreters in court have authority to interpret objections to witnesses, but they are expected to stop interpreting when an attorney makes an objection. If the objection is sustained, interpreters should not interpret the witness' answer. If the objection is overruled, interpreters can either interpret the answer or request a repetition of both questions and answers by the court reporter or counsel.

Scholars like Zahler (1985) advocate for simultaneous interpretation of objections and judge rulings, as non-English speaking witnesses should be in the same situation as English-speaking witnesses. However, Berk-Seligson's findings show that some interpreters stop interpreting immediately when an objection is uttered, while others continue to provide interpretation of the question and answer (Berk-Seligson, 2002). Even if the answer is not interpreted, some words in the source language expressing yes or no might be understandable, potentially damaging the testimony. Berk-Seligson's study exemplifies how interpreters might deal with objections (Berk-Seligson, 2002).

However, Berk-Seligson (2002) explains that during interpreter proceedings, a lag time occurs when the interpreter begins speaking in the target language after the attorney finishes their question. This delay allows the judge to make a ruling on the objection raised, preventing the witness from answering the question. Simultaneous mode increases the risk of a witness answering the objectionable question (Berk-Seligson, 2002).

Scholars also agree that non-verbal cues can be used to silence witnesses or defendants in court, such as raising hand motions or placing one's arm in front of the witness's face (e.g., Berk-Seligson, 2002; Hale, 2008; Hale & Napier, 2016). These methods can stop or prevent a witness's speech. However, the situation differs for monolingual speakers and official language monolingual speakers in the same position. Verbal and non-verbal means can sometimes be used to prevent a monolingual speaker from speaking, but only if verbal means are sufficient (Berk-Seligson, 2002).

- *Requests for clarification*

Zambrano-Paff (2011) and Berk-Seligson (2002) argue that interruptions in the interpreting process are problematic, as interpreters can usurp power without permission from the interrogating attorney. They illustrate this by a Colombian defendant using a specialised political term, *quinto renglón,* to clarify its meaning (Zambrano-Paff, 2011).

- *Altering the wording of an utterance*

In a slightly different way, interruptions are used to correct or alter the wording of an attorney's question due to cultural implications or different linguistic behavior of the nations in question. This is often done with negatively worded questions, as a Spanish speaker can answer either *Sí* or No, prompting the interpreter to interrupt the flow of questioning and highlight the linguistic issue.

> Defence attorney: So, you are saying that you wouldn't have told the border patrol officer...
>
> Interpreter: Excuse m,e sir. I have to tell you that you're using the negative all the time and his answer really doesn't mean much when you're using the negative form of questioning because when he answers 'no' it actually comes out 'yes'. If you say, 'Wouldn't do this', or 'Wouldn't do that', 'yes, I wouldn't.' You see what I mean? You're using the negative and it's confusing him tremendously.

Svongoro (2017) used Berk-Seligson's (1990) and Hale's (2001) work to identify interpreter-initiated turns in Zimbabwean courtrooms. These turns include seeking information, confirmation, clarification, prompting witnesses, identifying speaker mistakes, instructing witnesses/accused, and intervening in conflicts. Svongoro (2017) found that these turns can alter the wording of a source language utterance.

- *Provision of clarification*

From the literature, scholars agree that interpreters may interject themselves into the record when they ask the judge for permission to explain the source of a witness/defendant's conclusion (Berk-Seligson, 2002; Jacobsen, 2009; Valero-Garcés, 2005). Berk-Seligson (2002) suggests that interpreters may clarify questions due to linguistic difficulties, sometimes without permission. They may suggest replacing *'entervista'* with another verb to address confusion. Interpreters make the examination process easier and faster, but they are not expected to fulfil this role. However, there are exceptions where interpreters intervene when a correct interpretation is made and they feel the message was not understood (Berk-Seligson, 2002).

▪ *Repetition of utterances that were not heard or noted down*

In other situations, interpreters may ask attorneys to clarify their utterances due to unclear or incomplete hearing of a question (Berk-Seligson, 1990; Jacobsen, 2009). This can occur in various forms, such as 'I didn't hear you', 'Please, repeat', 'Speak more slowly', or 'Pardon me?' (Berk-Seligson, 2002: 66). These requests can be made without a judge's permission. In one example, the interpreter asked the attorney to repeat a word in question, without requesting permission, as they did not hear it clearly.

Berk-Seligson (2002: 90) illustrates a scenario where a detailed utterance was produced in the target language, but the interpreter failed to note it down. She then requested the witness to repeat it.

> Prosecuting attorney: Where in Guatemala were you born?
>
> Interpreter: *¿En dónde en Guatemala nació Ud.?*
>
> Witness: *Santa Cruz de Solalá de Quetzaltenango.*
>
> Interpreter (addressing witness): *Por favor, repita.* (Please, repeat.)
>
> Interpreter (addressing attorney): I'm asking her to repeat. It's quite long, sir.

▪ *Referring to one's own interpretation*

Interpreters sometimes interrupt the testimony to inform the attorney about the wording of the interpreted utterance they have just produced. The reason for this seems to be the interpreter's need for its approval, since the interpreter feels it 'may be somewhat off the mark in its wording' (Berk-Seligson, 2002: 70).

> Prosecuting attorney: Do you feel that you could follow the path if you would go through it during the day? Is that the problem that it was dark and you could not pick out landmarks?
>
> Interpreter (addressing the attorney): Sir, the way I put the question is, 'It is your answer, then, that if it were during the day you could follow the road. But it was because it was at night that you cannot follow the road.' And his answer was, 'Yes.'

▪ *Lengthening the testimony*

According to interpreting scholars, interpreters tend to lengthen testimonies in their target language versions in various ways (Berk-Seligson, 2002; Gibbons, 2003; Záňová, 2013). Situations in which testimonies are lengthened are further explained below.

▪ *Converting fragmented speech style into a narrative one*

The literature reviewed also confirmed that interpreters often convert fragmented speech into a narrative style of testimony, which can negatively impact witnesses' credibility (Berk-Seligson, 2002; Gibbons, 2003; & Záňová, 2013). The main difference between narrative and fragmented speech is the length of answers given, which is largely controlled by the examining attorney. If a witness's answers are lengthened by another participant, such as a court interpreter, the attorney loses control, potentially affecting their credibility. Understanding this difference is crucial in court proceedings (Berk-Seligson, 2002).

Furthermore, according to some scholars, multilingual processes can take up to twice as long as those handled without an interpreter, contributing to the perception of interpreters as slowing down the process (Gibbons, 2003). However, some academics attribute some utterance lengthening to the 'great economy of English language', which refers to amplification during translation or interpretation due to the presence of more lexemes or morphemes in the target language (TL) than in the source language (SL) (Berk-Seligson, 2002).

- *Highlighting*

Berk-Seligson (2002) mentions another frequent mechanism that makes the interpreted utterance longer and Zambrano (2005) refers to it as highlighting. Jacobsen (2009) generally defines this phenomenon as additions in court interpreting. Highlighting is a process 'in which the interpreter adds material that is understood but not explicitly stated in the source language' (Zambrano, 2005: 173).

Reporting about Zimbabwean courtrooms, Svongoro (2017) following Jacobsen (2009), used the term 'emphasizing additions' to refer to highlighting. Emphasizing additions serve to emphasise or increase the force of the utterance, or part of the utterance, in the source text. The interpreter emphasizes certain items in the target language discourse that were not present in the source language text, either explicitly or implicitly, or by including items not stressed in the source language discourse.

Emphasizing additions reflect what Jacobsen (2009) terms *interpretese.* Research (e.g., Jacobsen, 2009; Svongoro, 2017) has shown that such interpretations *(interpretese)* differ significantly from the source language utterances. The differences between source and target language utterances were initially seen as errors in court interpreting, but are now seen as tactical manoeuvers to optimize information retrieval and delivery. These shifts are viewed as deliberate decisions to overcome interpretation difficulties, rather than errors in the process, and are observed at phonological, lexical, morphosyntactic, and discourse levels.

However, Morris (1995) found that court interpreters often treat speakers' hesitations, unfinished sentences, grammatical mistakes, and slips of the tongue as speech defects, contrary to Hoffman's (1994) rules that require utterances to be reproduced, even at the risk of sounding incompetent. This highlights the importance of personal and speaker-status when interpreting witness testimonies.

Svongoro (2017) also discusses down-toning additions (the opposite of emphasizing additions), which act as modal verbs or hedges to express uncertainty, thereby reducing the impact of the source language utterance. For Gibbons (1994: 100), modality can be understood either in terms of directness/indirectness (for example 'Take a seat' is more direct than 'You may take a seat'), or in terms of embedding information in a modal verb frame ('Could you tell us what the colour of the car was?' is more polite than 'What was the colour of the car?') (See also Gibbons, 2003). In courtroom questioning, modality is used to establish pre-conditions for more specific questions as modality decreases coerciveness (Rigney, 1999: 87).

Different types of down-toning additions (e.g., through the addition of verbal and non-verbal elements) can have the effect of threatening the defendant and, as a result, their credibility and rights in the trial process.

Zambrano gives a few examples of highlighting (2005: 172):

> Defendant: ...que está dedicado a atacar la guerrilla...
>
> Interpreter: ...that is dedicated to attack the guerrilla, **the Colombian guerrillas**...

Here, the interpreter adds information to the testimony, specifically stating that the guerrillas in question were the Colombian ones. However, the defendant uttered nothing of that sort. In a similar vein, in the next example the interpreter adds 'that's correct' to the one-word answer of the defendant, which in fact implies certainty of the speaker that was not present in the SL.

> Defendant: Sí.
>
> Interpreter: **That's correct**, yes.

- *Rephrasing and repeating interpretations*

In this process, interpreters reword their own interpretations and backtrack, in order to be more precise:

> Prosecuting attorney: Where were you at when you first saw Mr Hawkins?
>
> Interpreter: *¿Dónde estaba usted la primera vez que usted vio al señor* Hawkins?
>
> Witness: *La primera vez, la primera vez estaba en la camioneta.*
>
> Interpreter: The first time was at the **station wagon or small truck**.

The interpreter in the excerpt fails to properly repeat the expression *'la primera vez, la primera vez'* and instead interprets it as a station wagon or small truck, making the testimony and proceeding longer (Berk-Seligson, 2002: 130). Backtracking and rephrasing can negatively impact a witness's conclusiveness and make their speech sound powerless, similar to hedging. Rephrasing also allows for time gain during the interpreting process.

- *Using definitions instead of equivalent words and phrases*

Furthermore, Gibbons (2003), Záňová (2013), and Zambrano-Paff (2011) suggest that using definitions in testimonies can lengthen them, but it can also diminish the defendant's assertiveness and make them appear indirect, potentially hiding something (Zambrano-Paff, 2011).

> Defence attorney: How did you receive it?
>
> Interpreter: *¿Cómo lo recibió?*
>
> Defendant: *Lo recibió la empleada que nosotros teníamos.*
>
> Interpreter: The person that we had working for us received it.

In general, Spanish *empleada* means employee. In this particular context it would mean maid, but clearly, the interpreter used a long definition of that word – the person that we had working for us – and made the interpretation unnecessarily long.

- *Insertion of hedges, particles and hesitation forms*

A hedge is a word or phrase that weakens the certainty of a statement, making an interpreted testimony less affirmative and creating a vague impression of the person who testifies. It can also create a more colloquial speech style and give the answer a more logical connection to the witness's most recent utterance. Berk-Seligson (2002: 132) illustrates the archetypal hedge in a case of an undocumented noncitizen who answers with certainty about the appearance of a plane, which is not reflected in the interpretation.

> Witness: *Una avioneta pequeña blanca con rayitos azules.* (It was a small white airplane with blue stripes.)
>
> Interpreter: It was a small airplane, white, with a sort of, a sort of blue lines, blue stripes.

Importantly, Berk-Seligson adds that hesitation forms like 'uh' and 'well' are frequently the interpreter's own product, inserted into their speech when they concentrate mentally on the process of interpreting and are under pressure. All these insertions are to be found in the example from Berk-Seligson (2002: 141):

Attorney: Who else was with you?

Interpreter: *¿Quién más estaba con usted cuando usted cruzó?*

Witness: *Varios hondureños.* (Several Hondurans.)

Interpreter: Uh, uh, several other Hondurans.

Attorney: Approximately how many?

Interpreter: *¿Aproximadamente cuántos en total?*

Witness: *Un promedio de veintiuno.* (An average of 21.)

Interpreter: Uh, probably an average of 21 people.

In the above example, highlighting ('an average of 21 people'), hedging (probably), and hesitation form ('uh') work together but not in favour of the witness. He was asked who else was present at the fence where he illegally entered the USA. Although his replies are confident in Spanish, the rendition does not produce the same impression and it lacks the certainty of the SL message. Consequently, the witness and his testimony might be viewed as untrustworthy.

- *Shortening the testimony*

Various elements of speech style, such as hedges, are inserted by the interpreter into the rendition, many times only unconsciously (Berk-Seligson, 2002; Hale, 1999). On the other hand, these very elements are often systematically omitted as 'not salient enough for court interpreters to include them' (Berk-Seligson, 2002: 142). Hale (1999: 57) adds that discourse markers (words such as 'well', 'now', and 'see' that are common in everyday oral communication) get omitted as well. She adds that omissions or misinterpretations of these expressions can influence the illocutionary force of an utterance.

For example, an interpreter can improve a witness's testimony by making it more coherent and precise, omitting deictic expressions like repeating phrases and kinesics, which can diminish the urgency and forcefulness of the witness's testimony (Berk-Seligson, 2002).

- *Making side comments of the witness*

A court interpreter may face procedural challenges when a witness speaks on their side or addresses the interpreter personally during the examination process, stopping the attorney from directing answers. 'It is the interpreter's obligation to inform the judge of any such comments when they occur. She must also account for any remarks that she herself may be making to the witness in return' (Berk-Seligson, 2002: 84).This is illustrated by a Spanish-English example by Berk-Seligson (2005: 85):

Prosecuting attorney: Did you know you were entering the country illegally?

Interpreter: *Cuando Ud. entró a este país, señora,¿sabía Ud. que estaba entrando ilegalmente?*

Witness: *Sí, señorita.*

Interpreter: Yes, sir.

Interpreter (addressing attorney): Excuse me. I'm advising her not to answer 'Yes, ma'am' or 'No, ma'am' because I'm just the interpreter. Excuse me.

- *Changing the register*

Interpreters are expected to have a thorough understanding of various working languages, including legal arguments, technical registers, technical registers of expert witnesses, unique speaking styles of law enforcement personnel, street slang, and children's language, to accurately and faithfully convey information (Hale, 1997 & 1999; Mikkelson, 2012). Hale demonstrates a scenario where the register was not maintained in the target language, resulting in an informal yet factual answer from a witness, and the question tag at the end of the sentence represented a challenge to the attorney (Hale, 2004: 110):

Witness: *Pues sí, aquí están tengo escrito los da os que tiene, ¿no? Yo no los puedo descifrar porque no soy chapista ¿no?* (Well yes, here it is, I have the damages written down, see? I can't decipher them because I'm not a panel beater, am I?)

Interpreter: I have them written down here I can't decipher them because I'm not a panel beater.

Berk-Seligson (2002) also suggests that if there's a significant discrepancy between the speaker's social class and the interpreter's language, it could potentially resemble hypercorrect speech by a monolingual, English-speaking witness, leading to negative evaluations of the witness.

In an earlier study, Berk-Seligson's study on hyperformal interpretation, which lacks ellipses and syntactic deletions, found that it enhances a witness's image, making them appear more competent, intelligent, and trustworthy (Berk-Seligson, 1989). The findings by Berk-Seligson confirmed O'Barr's (1982) study, which showed that narrative-like testimonies are more positively evaluated than fragmented ones. The study also found that hyperformal interpretation can enhance a witness's credibility, even if it contrasts with their low socioeconomic status (Berk-Seligson, 1989).

Interpreting politeness

The literature reviewed also highlights the concept of powerless speech, which includes hesitation forms, hedges, and politeness, as a sign of a speaker's low social status (Berk-Seligson, 2002; Hale, 1997 & 1999; Mikkelson, 2012). Berk-Seligson (2002), for example, suggests that even in monolingual settings, speakers often incorporate powerless speech features into their testimonies, with experts or professionals with experience in public speaking often having speech without these features.

However, politeness alone is not a guarantee for a negative evaluation of a speaker, as other characteristics of powerless speech may also contribute to this evaluation (Berk-Seligson, 2002). Some scholars acknowledge that defendants speaking in a polite and narrative manner are more likely to be discharged (Záňová, 2013). However, the difference in linguistic habits between countries is also important. For example, Slovak people use less politeness markers in speech than British people.

In Latin America for example, politeness is a norm in court interactions, especially with working-class Latin Americans. Interpreters often initiate this practice with witnesses, leading to a reciprocal cycle of polite address usage (Berk-Seligson, 2002). However, this can be problematic if the attorney is male and the interpreter is female, or vice versa. If the witness or defendant addresses the interpreter, the interpreter can either omit all politeness markers or change address forms based on the attorney's sex, as this would be insulting to the attorney and make participants aware of the speaker's intentions. An example from Berk-Seligson's (2002: 139) study exemplifies such an accommodation:

> Attorney (male): Prior to boarding the aircraft, did you have to pay the pilot any more money?
>
> Interpreter (female): *Antes de abordar usted esa avioneta, de subirse, de montar en esa avioneta, ¿tuvo usted que pagarle al piloto alguna cantidad de dinero?*
>
> Witness: *Sí, señorita.*
>
> Interpreter: Yes, **sir**.

Finally, Berk-Seligson (2002) explains that interpreters may intentionally insert polite address forms even when not in the source language, especially when a witness or defendant answers a judge's question. This highlights the additional stress interpreters may face in courtrooms, beyond linguistic juggling, and demonstrates how far they may be from a neutral mechanical conduit (Morris, 1999).

Language difficulties

Apart from procedural difficulties, court interpreters also face grammatical, pragmatic, semantic, and sociolinguistic challenges during interpretation due to the adversarial system of justice (e.g. Berk-Seligson, 2002; Brown and Levinson, 1987; Hale, 1999, 2004, 2007; Quirk et al., 1985). Parties in courtrooms manipulate speech features, consciously and unconsciously (Berk-Seligson, 2002). This suggests that judges and attorneys have control over the production of responses to questions, which is crucial for questioning. Language difficulties such as passive and active voice, direct and indirect speech, and lexical choices made by interpreters also pose challenges. Understanding the dynamics of courtroom interaction is crucial for interpreters to navigate these challenges effectively.

One difficulty reported by scholars in the reviewed literature relates be the choice between interpreting in first or third person, the former standing for direct speech, the latter for indirect speech (Angermeyer, 2009; Berk-Seligson, 2002; Goffman, 1981; Waldensjö, 1998; Zetterstrand, 2004). Although most countries recommend that court interpreters stick to direct speech when interpreting, in reality, not all interpreters do so.

- *Direct speech*

The literature reviewed provided a clear distinction between direct and indirect speech (Angermeyer, 2009; Berk-Seligson, 2002; Goffman, 1981; Hale, 2007 & 2008; Waldensjö, 1998; Zetterstrand, 2004). Goffman (1981) explains that when interpreting in the first person, interpreters act as animators, not authors or principals, and are not responsible for the speaker's content or stance. Court interpreters display professional neutrality by acting as if they were not true participants in the interaction (Angermeyer, 2009). Even when using indirect speech, interpreters are aware of their performance evaluation and design their talk accordingly (Angermeyer, 2009).

The problem is when interpreters use direct speech, other participants of the court proceedings – be it the court personnel, witnesses, or defendants – may not understand this principle of direct speech use. Berk-Seligson (2002: 66) notes that standard language phrases like 'I don't understand' might create confusion. As a result, attorneys and judges at times are not certain if the interpreter is speaking for herself, or interpreting for the witness or defendant (Berk-Seligson, 2002).

On the other hand, a court participant may misunderstand a sentence, as it was in the case of a visa-applicant, when being told 'We have decided not to give you permission to stay in Sweden' (Waldensjö, 1998: 239). The assumption made was that the interpreter is a co-author of that utterance.

In brief, the literature suggests that interpreters' training and professionalism are crucial for effective interpreting in direct speech (e.g., Angermeyer, 2009; Berk-Seligson, 2002; Goffman, 1981; Hale, 2007, 2008; Waldensjö, 1998; Zetterstrand, 2004). Zetterstrand (2004) asserts that direct speech is the most effective way to work across language barriers in courtroom settings. Therefore, the researcher recommends that interpreters and court participants should primarily use direct speech in courtroom settings.

- *Indirect speech*

The reviewed literature concurs that indirect speech works against all the good positive communicative aspects of direct speech (see for instance, Angermeyer, 2009; Berk-Seligson, 2002; Goffman, 1981; Hale, 2007 & 2008; Waldensjö, 1998; Zetterstrand, 2004). Direct speech prevents miscommunication, delays, confusion, minimizes interpreter impact, promotes quality interpretation, and maintains record integrity, while indirect speech is often perceived as unprofessional (Zetterstrand, 2004).

Zetterstrand (2004) suggests that court participants, including judges and attorneys, should use direct speech for interpreting, ensuring clear communication and avoidance of confusion. This is especially important when using third-person pronouns. Failure to follow direct speech can lead to muddy records and miscommunication, affecting the trial process and justice administration. Therefore, direct speech is crucial for interpreters to avoid such issues.

Apart from the above, the use of third-person pronouns can delay communication, as speakers often interrupt for clarification. Zetterstrand (2004) suggests parties focus on the interpreter's indirect speech, and the interpreter must modify the utterance's style to make it more narrative. One example given by Zetterstrand (2004) is 'I regret what I did' compared to 'She regrets what she did.'

Similarly, some messages, especially those with emotive content, lose their force: 'I didn't do it. I swear to God, I didn't. Please, believe me' compared to 'He says he didn't do it. He swears to God, he didn't. Please, believe him.' (Zetterstrand, 2004: 2)

However, some scholars argue that indirect speech can be used in court interpretation to emphasize personal uninvolvement in the other's words. Waldensjö (1998) for example, suggests that interpreters present the other's words in third person, emphasizing uninvolvement. However, Goffman (1981) opposes this view, and Angermeyer (2009) supports Goffman's view. Berk-Seligson (2002) notes that interpreters often use indirect speech during decision-making situations, such as avoiding subject pronouns during sentencing and using passive voice or indirect speech.

Morris (2010) supports Berk-Seligson's argument by mentioning that interpreters may use indirect speech, often due to comments about their work product, and may request corrections. Proper third-person self-reference is crucial for removing ambiguities and maintaining record clarity when speaking on behalf of the interpreter (e.g., 'Your honour, the interpreter requests permission to correct an error') (Morris, 2010). This approach is essential for maintaining the accuracy and clarity of interpretations in court proceedings.

▪ *Passive and active voice*

The study of voice in court interpreting literature highlights its importance in courtroom settings (e.g. Berk-Seligson, 2002; Brown and Levinson, 1987; Quirk et al., 1985). Voice is a grammatical category that allows two ways to view a sentence's action without altering the facts reported (Quirk et al., 1985). Berk-Seligson (2002) explains that verb constructions can influence blame attribution or avoidance. When interpreting passive forms of a verb, they are often rendered active in the TL, sometimes naming the agent. The shift in grammatical case is a discourse strategy to place actors in the background of an activity, emphasising certain participants' responsibility and diminishing others' (Hale, 1999). Brown and Levinson (1987) view the passive voice as similar to impersonalization, shifting responsibility from a subject.

Court interpreters can create a pragmatic problem by making participants appear more blameless or blameworthy in court proceedings, which is not only true for English but also for languages like Spanish, Japanese, and Italian. Berk-Seligson (2002) highlights that the choice of voice in American courtrooms is often used in order to express the distance between agents and their actions.

On the other hand, Zimányi (2009) found a significant difference in passive-voice usage in English compared to Slovak and Czech. Interpreters in these languages may not maintain passive constructions as in the Czech language, risking expressing agency, appointing responsibility, or making personal statements, or vice versa. Compared to Berk-Seligson's results (2002: 118) which state that 'there is no doubt that interpreters make use of the passive to distance agents from actions and use the active case to link the two', it may be expected that Slovak and Czech interpreters do the latter more often.

▪ *Inaccurate lexical choice*

Court interpreters must use accurate lexical choices to avoid discomfort and unpleasant interpretations (Hale, 1999; Jacobsen, 2009; Wallmach, 2004). However, errors can be overlooked or objected to, as seen in Zambrano-Paff's study on immigration hearings (Zambrano-Paff, 2011). In a case involving a defendant's mother testifying on behalf of her daughter, the interpreter failed to accurately represent the term *misceláneas* in

Colombian culture, which typically refers to a store similar to a *bodega*. Additionally, the interpreter failed to consider the cultural difference in the meaning of the phrase *fuente de sodas*, which in Latin America typically signifies a café selling ice cream and soft drinks. The witness's interpretation of 'It had a soda' was not what the witness wanted to hear.

The mother's failure to mention the *miscelánea's* restaurant could have contradicted her daughter's testimony, damaged the defendant's credibility, or caused confusion. Interpreters can bridge linguistic gaps but not cultural ones, or be unaware of such gaps (Zambrano-Paff, 2011: 195). Sometimes, they choose not to address the cultural aspect of a message, even if the parties assume the interpreter is a cultural ambassador. Berk-Seligson emphasizes that a professional interpreter should ask for clarification if needed (Berk-Seligson, 2002: 4):

> Prosecuting attorney: Okay, now after he tried to hit you with a gun, what happened after that?
>
> Interpreter (addressing the attorney): Excuse me, I have to clarify something. When you say 'hit with a gun', do you mean 'shoot with a gun', or actually 'hit him with a gun'?
>
> Prosecuting attorney (addressing the interpreter): No, I mean, strike with a gun, not shoot.
>
> Interpreter (addressing the attorney): Okay, I'm sorry, I, that wasn't clear.
>
> Prosecuting attorney (addressing the interpreter): Okay.

- *Polysemy*

The literature reviewed also shows that polysemy (and ambiguity often associated with it) is a significant source of linguistic difficulties (e.g. Berk-Seligson, 2002; Brown & Levinson, 1987; Zambrano-Paff, 2011; Hale, 2004 & 2007; Quirk et al., 1985). Polysemy refers to the multiple meanings in a single word, which can lead to incorrect interpretations (Berk-Seligson, 2002). Interpreters often fail to ask for clarification when interpreting questions or utterances, as seen in a Spanish case where the word '*equipo*' was interpreted as a group, not as equipment (Zambrano-Paff, 2011). This incorrect interpretation took the immigration judge's interrogation in an unnecessary direction. The bilingual attorney noticed this and interrupted the judge's question without objecting properly, which irritated the judge (Zambrano-Paff, 2011).

Environmental difficulties

Research indicates that despite the training, remuneration, and professional association support provided to court interpreters, their work environment can still lead to interpreting difficulties. (Hale & Napier, 2016; - Matende et al, 2022; Miyanda, 2009; Ngarambe & Ruvebana, 2023; Svongoro, 2017; Svongoro & Kadenge, 2015; Wallmach, 2004).

Scholars agree that an interpreter's work environment, characterized by insufficient resources, poor working conditions, long hours, lack of preparation time, and lack of understanding by other court officers, leads to difficulties and stress for interpreters due to various issues (Matende et al, 2022; Miyanda, 2009; Ngarambe & Ruvebana, 2023; Svongoro, 2017; Svongoro & Kadenge, 2015; Wallmach, 2004). Stress consequently causes interpreting difficulties (Hale & Napier 2016; Svongoro, 2017; Svongoro & Kadenge, 2015). Misunderstandings about court interpreters' roles can lead to them being asked to perform duties beyond their language mediation role, potentially causing burnout. Stress factors identified include autonomy, workload, insufficient resources, poor work organisation, and working hours. (Matende et al., 2022; Miyanda, 2009). Court interpreters face fatigue, back pain, headaches, and throat irritation, which negatively impact their performance (Hale & Napier, 2016; Matende et al., 2022; Svongoro, 2017).

Reporting about court interpreters' work environment, Matende et al. (2022), reported that court interpreters face numerous environmental challenges, including long interpretations without breaks, working with court officials who publicly ridicule interpreters for mistakes, interpreting for difficult witnesses, accused persons using difficult words and multiple languages, and poor organisation and scheduling of work. These obstacles are increased by court authorities who do not respect the work of interpreters, notably when they interpret for difficult witnesses and accused persons who often employ difficult vocabulary and numerous languages (Matende et al, 2022). Miyanda (2009) also reports about challenges interpreters face in Botswana ranging from lack of resources (e.g., microphones) and lack of training to intimidation and abuse suffered at the hands of senior court personnel including magistrates, defence counsel, and judges. Wallmach (2004) regards these challenges as pressure when she explores court interpreting in legislative contexts in South Africa.

The conclusions Matende et al. (2022) and Miyanda (2009) make highlight the connection between court interpreters' work environment and their performance. Overwork, fatigue, and stress can negatively impact interpreters' performance, leading to decreased quality of work and ultimately, the delivery of justice. The nature of the working environment can negatively affect interpreters' performance during trials, highlighting the importance of addressing stress levels (Matende et al., 2022; Miyanda, 2009).

However, to deal with environmental difficulties, scholars suggest that court interpreters should be properly trained to handle difficult witnesses and accused persons, as impudent clients require strict handling. Hoffman (1994) argues that a court interpreter's training and skills improve their understanding of their job, environment, interpreting challenges, and the chance of accurate translation. Hale (2004) also emphasizes the importance of training, stating that higher levels of training lead to better understanding of the interpreter's role and the environment.

Ethical difficulties

Morris (1995) extensively covers ethical difficulties in court interpreting, but refers to them as moral dilemmas of court interpreting. In the section below, the researcher further explains some of the ethical difficulties court interpreters face.

- *Prejudice against the interpreter*

Interpreters often represent the same ethnic or national group as their witness or defendant (Morris, 1995 & 1999; Angermeyer, 2009). Despite a decrease in prejudice against ethnic groups, maintaining impartiality remains challenging when judges or court participants do not act in such a manner. In a case involving a nine-year-old boy, an interpreter faced an ethical dilemma when the father took legal action against the mother, who took the boy without his consent and lived with him for over a year:

> 'By law, the child should have been returned to the country of origin, but mother and son pleaded that they were afraid the father would be abusive on their return. The court wanted to substantiate their argument and asked an independent forensic psychologist to provide an expert opinion of the child's plea' (Zimányi, 2009: 56).

Before the actual proceeding, the boy privately informed an interpreter he wanted to return to his homeland, despite his mother's approval and despite their fear of the father. This situation put the interpreter in a difficult position. Hale (2007) suggests two solutions: avoiding such situations by not being left alone with witnesses or defendants, and adhering to the Code of Ethics.

- *Conflict of interest*

From the literature reviewed, scholars remind interpreters of The Code of Ethics which emphasizes the importance of interpreters staying impartial and avoiding conflicts of interest, including personal interests in case outcomes or being close to litigants (Angermeyer, 2009; Hale, 2004 & 2007; Mikkelson, 2012; Morris, 1995 & 1999). Interpreters should not accept jobs with personal interests, as it can harm their reputation and the entire court interpreter community. If a conflict arises, interpreters should inform the court immediately to ensure impartiality and respect for the court's decision-making process.

- *Dress code*

Generally, an appropriate outfit is a part of the court interpreter's profession that is usually self-evident. For instance, the Court Interpreter Code of Ethics refers to this aspect, too:

> 'To dignified appearance and decency, when interpreting, belongs suitable outfit and good looks. Any peculiarities in speech, as well as in external adjustment, and dress are inadmissible.'

Despite this fact, there are interpreters who need to be reminded of that, as the article from the *The Irish Times* (2006) confirms. It dealt with the case of a young Polish interpreter 'who was wearing tight, low cut jeans and a skimpy top, which left her midriff exposed.' Consequently, the judge had to address her:

> 'At the risk of sounding prudish, I think you are inappropriately dressed for this court, bearing in mind you are here in a professional capacity' (*The Irish Times*, 2006)

Conclusion

The chapter explores the challenges faced by court interpreters, including linguistic, environmental, procedural, and ethical issues, based on 59 academic publications. It highlights the impact of these difficulties on court processes and justice delivery. The literature reveals that while interpreting in the first person allows interpreters to maintain professional neutrality, other participants may not understand this principle. Additionally, when interpreters interpret in the third person, miscommunication can occur, potentially affecting the court's record. The chapter emphasizes the need for interpreters to be aware of these challenges to ensure effective court processes and justice delivery. Furthermore, interpreting in the third person can cause delays in court processes and lose the force of emotive messages, as speakers often interrupt for clarification. These language difficulties faced by court interpreters were discussed in this chapter.

The chapter discusses the challenges faced by court interpreters, including procedural difficulties, language, environmental, and ethical issues, which impact trial processes. It highlights the need for future legal interpreters to adapt their services to changing legal, social, and economic conditions, including globalization and law reforms. The chapter emphasises the importance of interpreter trainers being aware of the changing nature of the profession to adapt their roles and set learning outcomes for various contexts. The chapter also highlights the need for interpreters to possess the necessary skills to deal with these challenges, ensuring they can thrive in rapidly changing legal contexts.

References

Anderson, RBW. (2002). Perspectives on the role of interpreter. In Pöchhacker, F. & Shlesinger, M. (ed.) *The Interpreting Studies Reader* (pp. 208–217). London/New York: Routledge.

Angelelli, C. (2004). *Revisiting the interpreter's role: A study of conference, court, and medical interpreters in Canada, Mexico, and the United States.* Amsterdam: John Benjamins.

Angermeyer, PS. (2009). Translation style and participant roles in court interpreting. *Journal of Sociolinguistics,* 13(1), 3–28.

Berk-Seligson, S. (1989). The role of register in the bilingual courtroom: Evaluative reactions to interpreted testimony. *International Journal of the Sociology of Language,* 79, 79–91.

Berk-Seligson, S. (1990). *The Bilingual Courtroom: Court interpreters in the Judicial Process.* Chicago and London: University of Chicago Press.

Berk-Seligson, S. (2002). *The Bilingual Courtroom: Court interpreters in the Judicial Process.* O'Barr, WM. & Conley, JM. (ed.). Chicago, IL: University of Chicago Press.

Brown, P. & Levinson, S. (1987). *Politeness: Some Universals in Language Use.* Cambridge: Cambridge University Press.

Crawford, A. (2012). Court interpreter checks non-existent'. BBC News. Accessed @ http://www.bbc.co.uk/news/uk-19186942

De Jongh, E. (1992). *An Introduction to Court Interpreting: Theory and Practice.* Lanham: University Press of America.

Docrat, Z. (2022). A Review of Linguistic Qualifications and Training for Legal Professionals and Judicial Officers: A Call for Linguistic Equality in South Africa's Legal Profession. *International Journal of Semiotics and Law,* 35:1711–1731

Gonzalez, RD., Vasquez, VE. & Mikkelson, H. (1991). *Fundamentals of Court Interpretation: Theory, Policy and Practice.* Carolina: Carolina Academic Press.

Gibbons, J. (1994). Introduction: Language and disadvantage before the law. In Gibbons, J. (ed.) *Language and the Law* (pp. 195–198). London: Longman.

Gibbons, J. (2003). *Forensic Linguistics: An introduction to Language in the Justice System.* Oxford: Blackwell Publishing.

Gile, D. (1995). *Basic Concepts and Models for Interpreter and Translator Training.* Amsterdam: John Benjamins.

Goffman, E. (1981). *Forms of Talk.* Philadelphia, Pennsylvania: University of Pennsylvania Press.

Hale, S. & Gibbons, J. (1999). Varying Realities: Patterned changes in the interpreter's of courtroom and external realities. *Applied Linguistics*, 20 (2).

Hale, S. (1997). The treatment of register in court interpreting. *The Translator: Studies in Intercultural Communication,* 3(1), 39–54.

Hale, S. (1999). Interpreters' treatment of discourse markers in courtroom questions. *International Journal of Speech, Language and the Law,* 6(1), 57–82.

Hale, S. (2001). *The Discourse of Court Interpreting: Discourse practices of the law, the witness and the interpreter.* John Benjamins.

Hale, S. (2003). *'Excuse me, the interpreter wants to speak' – Interpreter interruptions in the courtroom: Why do interpreters interrupt and what are the consequences?* Proceedings of the Critical Link 3 Conference, Montreal.

Hale, S. (2004). *The Discourse of Court Interpreting: Discourse practices of the law, the witness and the interpreter.* Philadelphia: John Benjamins.

Hale, S. (2005). How faithfully do court interpreters render style of non-English speaking witnesses' testimonies? A data-based study of Spanish-English bilingual proceedings. *Discourse Studies,* 4 (1): 25–47.

Hale, S. (2007). *Community Interpreting.* New York: Palgrave Macmillan.

Hale, S. (2008). Working with interpreters effectively in the courtroom. Paper presented at the AIJA conference: 12-14 March 2008, Freemantle, WA. Accessed at: https://aija.org.au/wp-content/uploads/2017/10/Hale.pdf

Hale, S & Napier, J. (2016). 'We're just kind of there': Working conditions and perceptions of appreciation and status in court interpreting. *Target International Journal of Translation Studies,* 28(3): 351–371. https://doi. org/10.1075/target.28.3.01hal

Hoffman, J. (1994). *A Guide to Interpreting in Judicial Proceedings.* Government Printer: Harare.

Jacobsen, B. (2009). Additions in court interpreting: A PhD project investigating the language of court interpreting in Danish courtrooms. Aarhus School of Business. Accessed at: https://criticallink.org/wp-content/uploads/2020/04/CL2_Jacobsen.pdf

Lebese, SJ. (2013). The undefined role of Court interpreters in South Africa. [Unpublished Master's Thesis] University of South Africa.

Matende, T., Svongoro, P & Munyaka, T. (2022). How the work environment affects court interpreters working in Zimbabwe's Magistrates' Courts? *Journal for Translation Studies in Africa,* 3: 1–21.

Mikkelson, H. (2000). *Introduction to Court Interpreting.* Manchester and Northampton: St Jerome.

Mikkelson, H. (2010). Interpreting is interpreting – Or is it? Paper originally presented at the GSTI 30th Anniversary Conference, January 1999. Accessed at: https://acebo.myshopify.com/pages/interpreting-is-interpreting-or-is-it

Mikkelson, H. (2012). Garbage In, Garbage Out: The court interpreter's lament. Accessed @http://www.openstarts.units.it/dspace/bitstream/10077/7380/1/Mikkelson.pdf

Miyanda, F. (2009). Problems faced by court interpreters in Botswana. *Marang: Journal of Language and Literature,* 19: 43–58.

Moeketsi, R. (1999a). *Discourse in a Multilingual and Multicultural Courtroom: A Court Interpreters' Guide.* Pretoria: Van Schaik.

Moeketsi, R. (1999b). The do's and don'ts in court interpreting: A functional approach to a professional code. *Language Matters* 31 (1): 222–242.

Moeketsi, R. & Wallmach, K. (2005). From sphaza to makoya! A BA degree for court interpreters in South Africa. *The International Journal of Speech, Language and the Law,* 12(1): 77–108. https://doi.org/10.1558/sll.2005.12.1.77

Morris, R. (1995). The Moral Dilemma of Court Interpreting. *The Translator*, 5 (1), 25–46.

Morris, R. (1999). The gum syndrome: Predicaments in court. *Forensic Linguistics,* 6(1), 6–29.

Morris, R. (2010). Images of the court interpreter. *Translation and Interpreting Studies* 5 (1): 20–40.

Ngarambe, T. & Ruvebana, E. (2023). Court interpreting practice in Rwanda: Challenges and strategies for fair justice. *The International Journal for Translation & Interpreting Research,* 15 (2): 108–124.

Nord, C. (2003). 'Persons shall not be discriminated on account of Language': Training Interpreters for the Community and the Courtroom. *Across Languages and Cultures,* 4 (2): 253–264.

O'Barr, WM. (1982). *Linguistic Evidence: Language, Power and Strategy in the Courtroom.* New York: Academic Press.

Quirk, R., Greenbaum, S., Leech, G. & Svartvik, J. (1985). *A Comprehensive Grammar of the English Language.* New York: Longman.

Rigney, AC. (1999). Questioning in interpreted testimony. *Forensic Linguistics* 6 (1): 83–108.

Svongoro, P. (2015). The impact of additions in Shona and English consecutively-interpreted rape trials in Zimbabwean courtrooms. *Per Linguam*, 31 (1): 105–120.

Svongoro, P. (2016). Court Interpreter Training at the Crossroads: Challenges and Future Prospects for Zimbabwe. *Mediterranean Journal of Social Sciences,* 5 (23): 69–81.

Svongoro, P. & Kadenge, M. (2015). From language to society: An analysis of interpreting quality and the rights of the accused in selected Zimbabwean courtrooms. *Southern African Journal of African Languages,* 33(1): 47–62. https://doi.org/10.2989/16073614.2015.1023501

Svongoro, P 2017, Court interpreting in Zimbabwe: a descriptive study of consecutively interpreted trials in regional magistrates' courts. [Unpublished Doctoral Dissertation] University of the Witwatersrand, South Africa.

The Irish Times (2006, July 19). In short.

Valero-Garcés, C. (2005). Emotional and Psychological Effects on Interpreters in Public Service. *The Translation Journal* 5 (3): 106–119.

Van Grieken, AM. (2001). An investigation into the role and effectiveness of court interpreting. [Unpublished MLSP Thesis] University of Zimbabwe.

Waldensjö, C. (1998). *Interpreting as interaction.* London/New York: Longman.

Wallmach, K. (2004). 'Pressure Players' or 'Choke Artists'? How do Zulu simultaneous interpreters handle the pressure of interpreting in a legislative context? *Language Matters*, 34: 179–200.

Zahler, S. (1985). Simultaneous...? Preferences vary. *Polyglot,* 15(7): 5.

Zambrano, MJ. (2005). The interpreter's linguistic power: A new courtroom reality in immigration hearings. [Doctoral Dissertation] University of Pittsburgh.

Zambrano-Paff, M. (2011). The impact of interpreters' linguistic choices in bilingual hearings. In Ortiz-López, LA. (ed.) *Selected Proceedings of the 13th Hispanic Linguistics Symposium* (pp. 190–202). Somerville, MA: Cascadilla Proceedings Project.

Záňová, S. (2013). The Court Interpreters' Role and the Predicaments They Might Face. [Master's Diploma Thesis] Masaryk University.

Zetterstrand, S. (2004). NAJIT position paper: Direct speech in legal settings. Accessed at: https://courts.delaware.gov/forms/download.aspx?id=134458

Zimányi, K. (2009). On impartiality and neutrality: A diagrammatic tool as a visual aid. *Interpreting & Translation*, 1(2): 55–70.

9 LANGUAGE USAGE IN THE SAPS IN RELATION TO LANGUAGE RIGHT, THE LANGUAGE OF RECORD POLICY, AND CRIMINAL INVESTIGATIONS: LINGUISTIC CHALLENGES REGARDING A1 STATEMENTS, AND THE IMPLICATIONS OF POORLY CONSTRUCTED STATEMENTS

Natasha Venter

Introduction

Language rights in South Africa are a contentious issue. In a country with 11 official spoken languages, and a Constitution that guarantees the language rights of each person, the practice throughout the entire criminal justice system does not always reflect the prescribed equal rights of all language users. This position has become especially evident since former Chief Justice Mogoeng Mogoeng declared English to be the only language of record in South African courts in 2017 (South African Judiciary, 2017; *News24*, 2017). This directive entails that all sworn statements need to be made in English in a country where this language is the home language of only about 8% of the population (Statistics South Africa, 2018).

The rights of language users can, therefore, arguably be infringed upon from the very outset of criminal proceedings, i.e., when criminal charges are laid with the police. To expound upon this substantial threat to justice, and to suggest solutions thereto, the course of criminal proceedings is explained, and various language issues throughout the process are pointed out. Subsequently, this chapter will attempt to provide workable solutions to the various challenges facing both law enforcement officials and, specifically, victims of crime.

Linguistic challenges in criminal proceedings

Laying criminal charges

When a victim of crime wants to lay criminal charges against an alleged perpetrator, they must approach a police station where they will need to, with the assistance of a police official, make a written statement of what occurred during the incident in which the alleged crime was committed (Republic of South Africa, 2023). This statement (known as an A1 statement) is supposed to be taken down by a police official who presumably understands which elements of a crime need to be alleged to ensure that an offence had indeed been committed (*Basic Police Development Learning Programme*, 2016). Furthermore, victims (or any other deponent) are entitled to make statements in the language they prefer (*Standing Orders 322, 327 and Standing Order General 18*, 1990). Especially in metropolitan areas where victims and police officials hail from a wide array of language backgrounds, this could be problematic. Therefore, what often happens in practice is that police officials either try to persuade deponents to render their versions of incidents in English or (if the police official is not proficient in English) request that victims write the statements in English themselves (Kekana & Montle, 2022). The complainant's version is therefore restated by a so-called 'transpreter' (a combination of the roles of 'translator' and 'interpreter' according to Ralarala, 2014). According to (Lesch, 2025) this elevates the role of the transpreter who, by interpreting, translating, and writing down the spoken words of the complainant, provides for a version of the events that carry more power than that of the complainant's version.

What should happen, according to the National Instruction 10 of 2020 Attestation of Statements and Authentification [sic] of Reproductions or Copies for SAPS trainees, if none of the police officials speak any language of the deponent, an interpreter should be appointed to translate the deponent's statement into English. The police official is then required to write the statement in the English used by the interpreter. This translation will need to be certified by a commissioner of oaths.

These linguistic challenges are, however, not necessarily the fault of police officials because these ill-considered policies are often forced onto ground-level officials. However, it could pose serious detrimental consequences to a victim's case. Firstly, police officials are trained to ask certain questions in a manner so as to ensure that statements provide sufficient details (such as a description of the victim, the vicinity in which the crime was committed, the weapon that was used, etc.), and to ensure that all the elements of a crime (from the victim's point of view) are contained in the statement (National Instruction 10, 2020). If lay-deponents are forced to write their own statements, they are not necessarily aware of what content is essential to ensure that their statement will eventually hold up in court. Secondly, victims who approach police stations are often severely traumatised by the events they have suffered leading to the criminal charge. This places additional cognitive constraints on such victims who are frequently expected to provide a statement of a traumatic incident in English, which is most likely not their home language. The police official is required to read the statement back to the victim or witness after taking it down, whereafter the victim is expected to sign the statement to verify the veracity of its contents. (However, oftentimes police officials do not even read the statements back to victims, they simply ask them to sign it and swear that the content thereof is true and correct – which is often very far removed from the truth). The recent minority judgment of the Constitutional Court in *Kapa v S* (2023) (hereafter 'the Kapa-case') regarding the importance of linguistically sound A1 statements, as well as the issue of police officials acting as translators, is discussed in more detail below.

Another difficulty that arises from linguistic constraints between victims and police officials is that assigned investigating officers do not necessarily understand the home language of victims, which could lead to certain important facts of the case literally being 'lost in translation'. It is one of the reasons why cases ought rather be assigned to investigating officers who are at least fluent in the home language of the victim. Such a practice would allow investigating officers to effectively investigate cases, while also allowing victims to express themselves in their home language. However, the official who takes down a victim's A1 statement is very rarely also assigned to the case as the investigating officer. This is because any police official at a police station can take a victim's statement. This usually means that A1 statements are taken by low-ranking police officials who, in all probability, have not had the requisite training to ensure that statements are linguistically sound.

Therefore, the conundrum remains that police officials are expected, though not adequately trained, to act as both interpreters and translators when taking the statements of victims and witnesses. This is because the only language of record is English. A possible solution to this linguistic barrier is that the South African Police Service (hereafter 'SAPS') should deploy investigating officers who are proficient in the language of a region to such regions. A possible solution is presented by a recent review judgment rendered by the high court in Mbombela (S v Ndlangamandla, 2022). This solution is expounded on below.

Another solution is that linguistic training should be provided to all police officials, or designated roles should be assigned to language-competent officials who are then tasked with taking statements from victims and translating them to English. If this is not feasible, all police stations ought to have an official who is a trained translator for the predominant language spoken in the region and English. This official will then be tasked with translating all the statements into English, which will allow other officials in the field to take down statements in the language the victims prefer. This will allow the officials taking down the statements to focus on doing so word for word from the victim, without having to translate certain concepts into English, which may result in certain information getting 'lost'.

The evidentiary importance of A1 statements

Linguistic difficulties experienced when generating police reports is not a phenomenon unique to South Africa. In the multilinguistic country of the Philippines for example, Sumaljag (2018) states that 'the quality of police reports needs improvements' because these statements are often badly written. The question may arise as to what the importance of A1 statements are and why it is so crucial that these documents are drafted correctly. Language is the vehicle of the law, and as such, the cornerstone on which justice is founded. An A1 statement is the first statement victims make to police officials and as such, the catalyst of the resulting criminal proceedings. According to the rules that govern evidence in South African courts, previous statements that are inconsistent are admissible in court if an accusation of a recent deliberate false fabrication is made, and if it is alleged that the witness (without conscious dishonesty) recently imagined or reconstructed an event (*S v Chembe*, 2021).[1]

However, if such an A1 statement is in any way deficient or contradicts a victim's version in court, it could be (and usually is) argued by defence teams that the victim's versions of events contradict each other and, therefore, the victim's version of the incident is not credible. Furthermore, the A1 statements that have been translated by a police official into English are retranslated by the court translator to the victim or witness during court proceedings. This would be required by the majority of South Africans (De Vries & Docrat, 2022). If the witness should contradict the contents of the statement or the translation thereof by the court interpreter in court, this could influence the credibility of the witness, and even undermine the case.

The recent Kapa-case in the Constitutional Court illustrates the immense importance of well-drafted and linguistically sound A1 statements. In this case, the accused (Mr Makhi

1 In this matter an A1 statement of the victim (taken down by a police officer at the Krugersdorp Police Station) states the accused is a white man, but he is black – this fact was caught on CCTV-footage and also reported by the victim to investigators (*S v Chembe*, 2021).

Kapa) was convicted of murder and various other crimes during acts of vigilantism in Khayelitsha. He was sentenced to 15 years imprisonment by the Western Cape Division of the High Court. Mr. Kapa appealed against the conviction and the sentence to the Constitutional Court. The only eyewitness, Ms. Bomikazi Dasi, gave an A1 statement to the police about the incident. She, however, passed away before the commencement of the trial and therefore could not testify, nor could her testimony (including the content of her statement) be tested under cross-examination.

The A1 statement is cited in the case, and the linguistic defects contained therein are blatant:

> 'On Sunday 21 August 2016, at about plus/minus 16h00, I did arrive at home, coming from Gugulethu. I did heard from my mother that there were guys looking for me, driving a white Tazz. At that moment I did see this Tazz passing on my street. I decided to follow it. I did saw this Tazz parked on Makhi's house. I did also go there. I did saw Makhuze desisting [sitting]. Both hands were tied up with a rope. Also his legs were tied up with yellow-and-black rope. They did took off his trouser. Bongane was carrying a plank hockey stick, busy beating Makhuze on his hands. Azizo was carrying a silver golf stick, hitting Makhuze over his head. Makhi did pull Makhuze to other room as he was bleeding over his hedge [head] and mouth. Bongane said to Monwabisi, Nono, the deceased, nicknaming Nono, the deceased, he must stand up. And he said he can't stand. Nono did ask me to pick him up to those people in dining room. He did crawl to dining room. Anele did kicked him over his chest, and he fell down. Anele took out a knife and stabbed Monwabisi on his hips and left side and on right side. He also stabbed him twice on lower abdomen. Svegi did call Bulelwa as [she] was on that room. Sakumzi did hit Bulelwa with a plank over her head. Xolani was having a sjambok. He assaulted Bulelwa with it over her body. Anele did hit her with a chisel over her head on the back and she fainted. They did call Zukisani. His hands were both tied up with yellow-and-black rope and his both legs. I did assisted him to stand up. They informed him to clean blood on dining room. He was using a mop. Vubela Viwe, he did hit Zukisani under his feet and also hit him over his hands, saying he will hit [him] 20 times. Big [Mr Makoma] also did came inside the room and hit Makhuze with sjambok over his face. Makhi also hit Makhuze with golf stick over his body. Bongane also hit Makhuze with empty bottle over his head. Anele did stepped Makhuze on other leg twice and Anele did hit Makhuze with chisel on other leg four times. Big did put up Monwabisi on a mat and pulled him outside. Bongane did hit Monwabisi with a hockey stick of plank on the back of his neck. Big did put Makhuze over his shoulders and took him back home. I was with Big to Makhuze's place. Bulelwa and [her] brother, I did left them there. Monwabisi was already outside. Lazaro was also there but I didn't see him beating anyone. Anele did also hit me with chisel while I was trying to block him not to assault Makhuze. He hit me over the head. By the time I arrived, Monwabisi was already being assaulted as he was bleeding. Siyabulela did slap Monwabisi over his face several times. Mara did kick Makhuze on his groin several times. The role players on this matter who assaulted both deceased and victims are Makhi, Azizo, Andile, Anele, Svitch,

> Sakumsa, Vubela, Xolani, Siyabulela and Mara. All of them, they suspect that deceased and victim has stolen music of Makhi.' (Kapa v S, 2023)

Sentences such as 'Anele did kicked him over his chest', and '[a]ll of them, they suspect that deceased and victim has stolen music of Makhi', would be statements that need to be clarified in court by way of examination-in-chief and cross-examination. In other words, what did the deceased steal, CDs perhaps? Furthermore, the mistakes regarding 'head' being written down as 'hedge', and 'plank' instead of 'wooden' to describe the hockey stick could also have far-reaching implications in court if the statement contradicts any post-mortem reports of the deceased's injuries. This could create confusion about what weapon was used to attack the deceased, a plank or a hockey stick? In this case the obscure statements could not be clarified, because of the tragic passing of the witness. If the statement had been drafted by an official who received the proper linguistic training or if it had been drafted in the home language of the witness, it would arguably have carried more evidentiary weight.

In the minority judgment, the statement was rejected – one of the reasons provided by Mbatha JA is 'the language issue'. The defence on behalf of Mr. Kapa argued that:

> 'Ms Dasi's statement did not comply with regulation 2(1)(a) of the Regulations19 promulgated in terms of section 10 of the Justices of the Peace and Commissioners of Oaths Act. 20. This regulation states that a deponent must be able to confirm that she "knows and understands the content of the declaration". The contention here is that, because there was no qualified interpreter when the statement was taken, it is unclear that the English recordal is an accurate statement of what Ms Dasi said in isiXhosa or of what Sergeant Msolo translated back to her in isiXhosa.' (*Kapa v S,* 2023)

In this case, as would transpire in most instances of officials taking down A1 statements, Ms. Dasi's statement was taken down by Sergeant Msolo. Ms. Dasi gave her version of events in isiXhosa and Sergeant Msolo reduced the statement to writing in English (*Kapa v S,* 2023). Sergeant Msolo then read an isiXhosa translation of the statement back to Ms. Dasi, whereafter she confirmed the correctness thereof and signed the statement. In this case, there was therefore no less than three translations done by the police official. This highlights the absurdity of the current language dispensation in which English is the sole court language. (Furthermore, had Ms. Dasi been able to testify in court, her already translated statement would probably have had to be retranslated to her from English into isiXhosa once again.) If the statement had simply been written down by Sergeant Msolo in isiXhosa (a language which both parties clearly understood from the facts), it could have been translated by a sworn translator at a later stage (if necessary).

Furthermore, this once again underlines the fact that officials should receive the necessary linguistic training, or at least that each police station should have the proportional number of officials available who are adequately trained to translate statements.

As Mbatha JA states in para 53:

> 'It is unsettling that Ms Dasi's statement was recorded in a language that she did not understand. Her signing of the statement was not, in the circumstances, a satisfactory guarantee of her adoption of the English version recorded by Sergeant Msolo.' (*Kapa v S*, 2023)

The majority judgment, however, held that Ms. Dasi's statement should be admitted into evidence because it was corroborated by circumstantial and medical evidence (*Kapa v S*, 2023). The appeal was therefore dismissed, and Mr Kapa must serve out the sentence imposed by the High Court.

S v Ndlangamandla – presenting a viable solution

In an appeal matter in the High Court in Mbombela, the question of a record that was not in English came to the fore in *S v Ndlangamandla* (2022) (hereafter 'Ndlangamandla'). In this matter the presiding officer, Ratshibvumo J, held on appeal that the trial record was 'conspicuously incomplete' (*S v Ndlangamandla*, 2022: para 2). The reason for the missing parts of the record was ascribed to the interpreter's failure to interpret parts of the trial in the magistrates' court. The magistrate stated the reasons for this as follows:

> 'The court on the day in question had only one interpreter who was also not regularly interpreting the proceedings accordingly in court. Mr. Ndlangamandla had the rights to follow and understand all the proceedings in court, hence the court had to use both language that is vernacular (isiZulu) and translate such in English immediately after such communication.' (*S v Ndlangamandla*, 2022)

It is clear from the High Court judgment that the trial in the magistrates' court was 'fully conducted in one or two of the official languages except that sometimes the Magistrate would communicate with either the witnesses and/or the accused in isiZulu and that part of the trial was not interpreted into English' (*S v Ndlangamandla*, 2022: para 3).

From a linguistic perspective, the most important obiter dictum in this matter is the following: 'There is nothing wrong in having a trial conducted in any of the official languages as all of them are equal and need to be given equal treatment' (*S v Ndlangamandla*, 2022: para 3). The learned judge then continues and states that it is the duty of the presiding officer to ensure that the record of the proceedings is translated into English if it needs to be submitted to the High Court (this is usually only if the matter is taken on appeal or review to a higher court) (*S v Ndlangamandla*, 2022: paras 3 & 4).

Furthermore, the court held in Ndlangamandla that the onus is on the judicial official who makes a ruling on the trial language – if it is an official language other than English – to ensure that there are resources available to translate the record to ensure that there is no undue delay, which would prejudice any of the parties (*S v Ndlangamandla*, 2022).

It is understandable that the record should be translated if the trial proceedings are conducted in an official language that is not English because the presiding officer in the appeal or review will not necessarily understand the language used in the trial court. The translation of the record by a qualified translator, however, negates this problem. If such an approach could be followed, even if it is only applied in the magistrates' courts, it would arguably serve to alleviate, if not dispel, many of the language barriers faced by victims, witnesses, and accused persons in court. Especially magistrates' courts located in rural areas would benefit from such an arrangement because presiding officers and court officials in such courts are often fluent in the dominant language in the area as well. It has even been suggested by other authors that the language proficiency of judges should also feature when the criteria for the appointment of judges in terms of section 174 of the Constitution are considered (Docrat, 2022). This should entail that judges should be proficient in the language spoken by most persons in the province in which they preside. Docrat argues that this is neither a foreign, nor an impractical proposal as similar models exist in Belgium and Canada (Docrat et al., 2021).

It is however essential that records should be translated by accredited translators to ensure that the translation of the record for the appeal or review court is correct and to ensure that the presiding officer in the appeal or review matter has everything that was said in the trial court at their disposal.

What about open justice?

According to the Heads of Court Resolution on the Language of Record in South African Courts (South African Judiciary, 2017) one of the reasons for adopting English as the only language of record is to ensure fair trials and hearings to 'make sure justice is served and access to justice is promoted'. Promoting access to justice also entails that anyone who enters a court should be able to understand the proceedings. This is because justice must not only be done but must be seen to be done (*S v Jaipal*, 2005). The principle of open justice entails that court proceedings should be understandable to the public. This could be hampered if the suggestion above is followed in which court proceedings are conducted in a language other than English.

However, if the parties to the proceedings and the presiding officer are more proficient in another official language than English, this should take precedence over the ability of those people in the gallery to understand the proceedings. Here there will need to be a weighing up of the right of an accused to a fair trial (contained in section 35(3) of the Constitution of the Republic of South Africa, 1996) and the right of the public to understand what is being said in court. This means that someone's rights will need to be limited to ensure that the right that is considered the most important will prevail. In any case in which rights need to be limited, section 36 of the Constitution (the so-called 'limitation clause') comes into play. This section determines that:

> '(1) The rights in the Bill of Rights may be limited only in terms of law of general application to the extent that the limitation is reasonable and justifiable in an open and democratic society based on human dignity, equality and freedom, taking into account all relevant factors, including –
>
> (a) the nature of the right;
>
> (b) the importance of the purpose of the limitation;
>
> (c) the nature and extent of the limitation;
>
> (d) the relation between the limitation and its purpose; and
>
> (e) less restrictive means to achieve the purpose.
>
> (2) Except as provided in subsection (1) or in any other provision of the Constitution, no law may limit any right entrenched in the Bill of Rights.' (Republic of South Africa, 1996)

In all cases it is the rights of the parties to the case whose rights should foremost be considered. It is clear that these parties (especially in criminal matters) are the people who need to understand what is being said in court proceedings as the impact of the outcome of the case will be on them. Therefore, the limitation of the public's right to understand what is being said in proceedings, should be considered fair.

The courts have, however, in recent times emphasised the importance of open access to justice, and the right of the media to report on cases. If proceedings are conducted in a language other than English, this could mean that a reporter would not necessarily be able to follow proceedings to report thereon. A possible solution to this problem could be to have the court proceedings translated into English to the gallery if necessary. Furthermore, technology to automatically generate subtitles is advancing at a rapid rate. This technology could also be used if proceedings in which the trial language is not English are broadcasted. Some of these platforms can generate subtitles in all the languages available on Google Translate (including Afrikaans, isiZulu, isiXhosa, Sepedi, Sesotho, and Swahili). Granted, the translations may not be perfect at first (it will improve as the technology improves), but viewers will be able to understand what is happening in court.

Another factor that needs to be considered is the access to court documents, which are public documents in terms of Promotion of Access to Information Act 3 of 2000. In

Sanral v City of Cape Town (2016) (hereafter 'SCA') held that once a court document has been filed, it is a public document, which can be accessed by the public. This could create problems, because if A1 statements (that form part of the record) are recorded in a language other than English, and the media want to report on the matter, they would need to translate it at their own costs.

Conclusion

Former Chief Justice Mogoeng Mogoeng, when explaining the decision to opt for English as the only language of record, said that:

> 'Nobody is saying South Africans are not permitted to speak in their mother-tongue in a court of law. We are just saying, to facilitate efficiency and a smooth running of the court system ... We (should) have everything that is said in a particular case captured in one language that is understood by all the judges – and that language is English.' (*News24*, 2017)

He further stated that:

> 'We are alive to the reality that language is a very emotive issue. When you don't allow people to communicate in their mother-tongue, they feel disempowered. We are here to ensure that there is access to justice for all South Africans... If you are going to insist on changes that require additional resources, we will be more than happy to embrace that.' (*News24*, 2017)

The Heads of Court Resolution on the Language of Record in South African Courts also states that:

> 'An appropriate balance must be struck among the various cultural interests by addressing the need for factors such as the following: ... Developing and advancing the official indigenous languages, with particular regard for the development of legal terminology in all official languages.' (South African Judiciary, 2017)

From these statements and the discussion above, a few things should be noted. Firstly, pertaining to the statement that English as the only language of record will facilitate the smooth running of the court system, it is clear that this has not been the case. While there are many brilliant court translators, sadly, in many cases, one only needs to attend a court sitting to experience that court translations are often fraught with mistakes, and, in many cases, rather hampers proceedings instead of improving efficacy. Secondly, there are many viable options that could be implemented to enable a multilingual model in courts, which would not require too many resources – the judiciary should be 'more than happy to embrace that'. Lastly, designating English as the only language of record does not advance nor develop other official indigenous languages; in fact, quite the opposite has occurred (Docrat & Kaschula, 2019).

References

Basic Police Development Learning Programme (2016)

De Vries, A & Docrat, Z. (2022). Judges and court interpreters' experiences on multilingualism in South African courts. In Ralarala, MK, Kaschula, RH & Heydon, G. *Language and Law: Global Perspectives in Forensic Linguistics from Africa and beyond.* Stellenbosch: African Sun Media.

Docrat, Z. (2022). A Review of Linguistic Qualifications and Training for Legal Professionals and Judicial Officers: A Call for Linguistic Equality in South Africa's Legal Profession. *International Journal for the Semiotics of Law.* https://doi.org/10.1007/s11196-022-09902-9.

Docrat, Z., Kaschula, RH. & Ralarala, MK. (2021). *A Handbook on Legal Languages and the quest for linguistic equality in South Africa and beyond.* Stellenbosch: African Sun Media. https://doi.org/ 10.2307/j.ctv1qgnkb7.

Docrat, Z. & Kaschula, RH. (2019). Monolingual language of record: a critique of South Africa's new policy directive. In Ralarala, MK., Kaschula, RH. and Heydon, G. *New Frontiers in Forensic Linguistics: Themes and Perspectives in Language and Law in Africa and beyond.* 71–88. Stellenbosch: African Sun Media.

Kapa v S (2023)

Kekana, JT. & Montle, ME. (2022). English linguistic knowledge of police trainees in SAPS training academies. *EduLite, Journal of English Education, Literature and Culture,* 7(2), August: 279–295. https://www.academia.edu/89242161/English_linguistic_knowledge_of_police_trainees_in_SAPS_training_academies.

Lesch, LT. (2025). Inter- and intralingual translations of complainants' police sworn statements: A co-construction of a legal text in a South African context. [Doctoral Dissertation] University of the Western Cape.

Multichoice (Proprietary) Limited v National Prosecuting Authority (2014)

National Instruction 10, 2020 issued in terms of the South African Police Services Act 68 of 1995.

News24. (2017). English will be only language of record in courts – Mogoeng. 29 September.

Oosthuizen, Z. (2021). Interview. Personal correspondence. 10 September, Pretoria.

Ralarala, MK. (2014). Transpreters' translations of complainants' narratives as evidence: whose version goes to court? *The Translator*, 20(3), 377–395. https://doi.org/10.1080/13556509.2014.934002.

Republic of South Africa (RSA). (1996). *Constitution of the Republic of South Africa*. Pretoria: Government Printer.

Republic of South Africa (RSA). *How to report a crime*. https://www.gov.za/services/report-crime/how-report-crime [Date accessed: 1 February 2023].

Sanral v City of Cape Town (2016)

S v Chembe (2021, in the Roodepoort Regional Court, unreported)

S v Jaipal (2005)

S v Ndlangamandla (2022)

South African Judiciary. (2017). *Heads of Court Resolution on the Language of Record in South African Courts*. https://www.judiciary.org.za/images/news/2019/Heads_of_Court_resolution_on_the_language_of_record.pdf [Date accessed: 4 March 2023].

Standing Orders 322, 327 and Standing Order General 18 (1990).

Statistics South Africa. (2018). *General Household Survey*. P03182018.pdf [Date accessed: 20 February 2023].

Sumaljag, MVO. (2018). A Forensic Linguistic Analysis of Police Reports. *IOSR Journal of Humanities and Social Science (IOSR-JHSS)*, 23(1), pp.80–102. https://doi.org/10.9790/0837-23010480102.

The NDPP v Media 24 Limited & others and HC Van Breda v Media 24 Limited & others (2017)

10 PRESIDING OFFICERS AND COURTROOM INTERPRETERS' EXPERIENCES ON MULTILINGUALISM WITHIN SOUTH AFRICAN COURTROOMS

Mabilo T. Jonas, Josephat Mutangadura, Tebogo J. Rakgogo & Corle Smith

Introduction

Language plays a fundamental role in legal proceedings, as it is the primary medium through which justice is administered. In multilingual societies like South Africa, courtroom discourse is shaped by the linguistic diversity of its population, often requiring the use of interpreters to facilitate communication between legal professionals, the accused, and witnesses. This study was carried out in the Limpopo Province, which is home to a wide range of indigenous languages, including Sepedi, Tshivenda, Xitsonga, isiNdebele, Setswana, isiZulu, English, and Afrikaans, alongside languages spoken by immigrant communities such as Shona, Chichewa, Portuguese, and Swahili. This linguistic diversity presents opportunities and challenges in ensuring fair and equitable legal proceedings. Miscommunication, interpreter errors, and linguistic power imbalances may significantly impact the administration of justice, raising concerns about the effectiveness of courtroom discourse in a multilingual setting.

This study aims to investigate the effects of multilingualism in courtroom discourse in Limpopo Province by addressing three key objectives. First, it seeks to establish the linguistic landscape of the region, identifying both indigenous and immigrant languages present in the courtroom. Second, it examines how multilingualism influences courtroom interactions, focusing on the roles of interpreters and the experiences of the accused. Finally, it explores the impact of multilingualism on case outcomes, assessing whether language barriers contribute to misunderstandings, unfair trials, or delays in justice. By analysing these aspects, this chapter contributes to ongoing discussions on linguistic rights, legal fairness, and the need for improved interpretation services in South African courtrooms.

Background and the context of the study

South Africa is a highly multilingual country, with 12 official languages and numerous immigrant languages spoken across different regions. The Limpopo Province in South Africa is characterised by significant linguistic diversity, with multiple official languages, including Northern Sotho, Afrikaans, English, Tshivenda, Xitsonga, and isiNdebele (Madima et al., 2024), alongside languages brought in by immigrant communities, including Shona, Chichewa, Portuguese, and Swahili. This linguistic diversity extends to the courtroom, where legal proceedings often involve individuals who speak different first languages. While interpreters play a crucial role in bridging communication gaps, the accuracy of interpretation, language biases, and misunderstandings can significantly impact the fairness of trials. The legal system relies on precise language use, and any misinterpretation may lead to wrongful convictions, delayed justice, or unfair trial proceedings. Understanding the effects of multilingualism in courtroom discourse is essential for ensuring linguistic rights, equitable access to justice, and the overall effectiveness of South Africa's legal system.

Indigenous languages of Limpopo

The Limpopo Province of South Africa is characterised by its rich linguistic diversity, reflecting its historical, cultural, and socio-economic dynamics. The province is home to a variety of languages, primarily influenced by indigenous groups and immigrant populations from neighbouring countries such as Zimbabwe, Malawi, and Mozambique. This multilingual landscape poses both opportunities and challenges, particularly in contexts such as the courtroom, where effective communication is crucial for justice and equity. The South African Constitution recognises 11 official spoken languages, with Sepedi, Tshivenḓa, and Xitsonga being predominant in Limpopo, alongside other languages from neighbouring regions, such as isiNdebele, Setswana, and isiZulu, which further enrich the linguistic outlook of the area (Madima et al., 2024; Jordaan & Ngwanduli, 2020; Rakgogo & Zungu, 2022).

The indigenous languages of Limpopo, particularly Sepedi, Tshivenḓa, and Xitsonga, play a critical role in the cultural identity of the province's inhabitants. Sepedi, a standardised dialect of Northern Sotho, is spoken by a significant portion of the population, with estimates suggesting that it is the first language of approximately 4.6 million people (Jordaan & Ngwanduli, 2020; Tönsing et al., 2023). Tshivenḓa and Xitsonga are also widely spoken, contributing to the province's multilingual character. The presence of these languages in educational settings and public life is supported by the South African Constitution, which mandates the promotion of multilingualism and the use of indigenous languages in official contexts (Madima et al., 2024; Mkhize & Balfour, 2017).

Influence of immigrant languages

The influx of immigrants from neighbouring countries has introduced additional languages into the Limpopo linguistic landscape. Zimbabweans often bring Shona and isiNdebele, while Malawians contribute Chichewa, and Mozambicans introduce languages such as Xitsonga and Emakhuwa. These immigrant languages have diversified the linguistic environment and led to the emergence of new language dynamics, including code-switching and translanguaging practices among speakers (Mashwele et al., 2024; Makalela, 2015). The interaction between these immigrant languages and indigenous languages creates a complex sociolinguistic environment that can impact communication in various domains, including legal settings (Svongoro & Kadenge, 2015).

Similar issues exist in neighbouring Zimbabwe, where the right to an interpreter is guaranteed but not fully implemented, particularly for deaf and hearing-impaired individuals (Ndlovu, 2023). These challenges highlight the ongoing struggle to balance linguistic diversity with practical considerations in legal and educational settings. Multilingualism in courtrooms and legal settings poses significant challenges in Zimbabwe, Mozambique, and South Africa. In Zimbabwe, interpreting quality affects the linguistic rights of the accused (Svongoro & Kadenge, 2015). Mozambique faces challenges when citizens report domestic violence due to language barriers (Heydon & Mabasso, 2018). South Africa struggles with language policy implementation in the Limpopo Provincial Legislature (Madima et al., 2024). These countries share a common colonial legacy that has entrenched English as the dominant language in legal contexts (Stroud & Guissemo, 2017; Ngunga, 2011). This creates a monolingual bias in multilingual courtrooms, disadvantaging minority language speakers (Angermeyer, 2021). Cultural factors, such as the use of *Hlonipha* in Southern African courts, further complicate communication (Thetela, 2003). Efforts to address these issues include developing tools for explaining legal terminology in local languages (Heydon & Mabasso, 2018) and advocating for linguistic transformation in legal and educational systems (Docrat et al., 2021).

Influences of regional languages

Limpopo's geographical location adjacent to other provinces such as Gauteng and Mpumalanga means that languages from these regions also influence local linguistic practices. For instance, isiNdebele, Setswana, and isiZulu speakers frequently interact with Sepedi speakers, leading to a blending of linguistic features and vocabulary. This cross-pollination can enhance communication but may also complicate language use in formal settings, such as courts, where precise language is essential for legal clarity (Madima et al., 2024; Jordaan & Ngwanduli, 2020; Mashwele et al., 2024). The presence of these languages necessitates effective interpreting services to ensure that all parties can engage meaningfully in legal proceedings (Svongoro & Kadenge, 2015).

Despite constitutional provisions for language equality, multilingualism presents challenges for mother-tongue education implementation, particularly in areas with more than two languages (Singh, 2014). Despite constitutional provisions for language equality, English remains dominant in official settings (Madima et al., 2024; Kretzer & Kaschula, 2020). The implementation of language policies faces obstacles due to complex sociolinguistic settings (Motaung, 2021). While indigenous languages are valued for cultural heritage, English is perceived as having a higher functional value (Verhoef, 2023). Some institutions are exploring innovative approaches to promote multilingualism, such as dual-medium education (Joseph & Ramani, 2012). This reflects broader issues in South Africa, where a monolingual English language of record policy conflicts with constitutional multilingualism (Docrat et al., 2021; Docrat & Kaschula, 2023). The situation creates linguistic prejudice and barriers to justice for African language speakers (Mokoena, 2018).

The role of language in courtroom discourse

In South Africa, the subject of multilingualism has been in a debate for some time. Scholars such as Docrat et al. (2021), Chochi (2016) and Mafunyeka (2019). Confronted this subject in many ways. The argument starts from linguistic imbalance to its complexity from the societal point of view. Interpreters have played an important role in South African courtrooms for a long time, as evidenced by the Magistrates' Courts Act 32 (1944) requiring magistrates to find competent interpreters for accused persons who do not understand the language of the court. Therefore, this role has been the subject of study and some criticism by researchers and court officers. The interpreter often finds the position as a communicator between the two contesting parties who, by duty, must serve the two impartially, compromised as such by their position in the court hierarchy as their position as the cultural link between speakers of African indigenous languages. Interpreters are employed by the Department of Justice and Constitutional Development on a full-time or part-time basis and on average speak seven languages, including the two de facto languages of record: English and Afrikaans.

In the context of courtroom discourse, multilingualism presents both challenges and opportunities. The need for interpreters who are proficient in both the source and target languages is paramount to prevent miscommunication and ensure that the rights of the accused and witnesses are upheld (Svongoro & Kadenge, 2015). The linguistic diversity in Limpopo means that legal practitioners must navigate a complex web of languages, which can lead to misunderstandings if not managed effectively. The South African legal system recognises the importance of language rights, yet the implementation of these rights often faces practical challenges, particularly in rural areas where access to qualified interpreters may be limited (Madima et al., 2024; Mkhize & Balfour, 2017).

The impact of language on court cases is a point that is hardly looked at in most cases during court proceedings; it is only when the accused or lawyer becomes aware that the interpreter might misinterpret some of the words. Therefore, it is when they try to take the case to review or to launch an appeal to say that the interpreter misinterpreted words. There are a few judgments which attracted the attention of media and legal experts on the issue of language globally, and in South Africa in particular, which was the focus of this study. This subsection will touch on some judgments that affected language disputes, dating back from 1998 to date. This is to get an idea of whether such cases are continuously happening or if the past literature managed to address the issue. However, this tries to address how indigenous languages are treated in courtrooms, and how many cases were addressed using those languages. In addition, the impact will be shown by referring to literature by other authors in relation to cases which have been affected due to language-related issues. The impact of this tends to be neglected by the judiciary, just because most of them did not identify the mistakes that have been committed linguistically, which could result in wrongfully sending the accused to jail.

These impracticalities have led courts in two judgments, Matomela and Damoyi, to suggest to the Department of Justice and Constitutional Development that to aid in the administration of justice, one language of record should be adopted for the entire country. According to Davis et al. (2004) quoted Yekiso, in Damoyi, 'sanity' would point to the English language for such a role. This proposal has been approved by the Department; however, a judgment against this policy may have delayed its implementation. But is it inevitable?

Influence on court case outcome

Multilingualism in legal contexts presents both challenges and opportunities. While it can enhance legal interpretation by promoting a hermeneutic approach (Łachacz & Mańko, 2013), it also creates difficulties in ensuring equal access to justice. Courts often maintain a monolingual bias, forcing bilingual participants to act as monolinguals (Angermeyer, 2021). This can disadvantage minority language speakers by limiting their communicative abilities (Wamuti, 2021; Mulwa, 2023). Language discrepancies between versions of legal texts are typically resolved by considering the purpose of the norm (Ćapeta, 2009). However, interpreter-mediated interactions differ significantly from same-language interactions, challenging the assumption that interpretation can fully equalise linguistic disparities (Angermeyer et al., 2013). Cross-linguistic differences can impact witness memory and jury judgment (Filipović, 2013). While legal multilingualism aims to ensure legal certainty, discrepancies between language versions remain inevitable (Doczekalska, 2019).

The constitutional language legislation in South Africa's courtrooms

Language legislation was described by Turi (1993: 5-6) as legislation that is '...generally aimed at legally determining and establishing the status and use of designated languages by means of legal obligations and rights; in other words, legal regulations concerning language'. Language legislation exists in two categories based on its application. There is language legislation that deals with official/public usage and unofficial/private usage (Turi, 2012: 73). Official language legislation is legislation which designates one or more language(s) as official in specific domains of legislation, justice, public administration, and education (Turi, 1993: 7). The application of official language legislation is dependent on the circumstances regarding one of two principles are to be applied. The first principle is linguistic territoriality, which prescribes the use of one or more languages in a specific territory. The second principle is linguistic personality, which amounts to the obligation or right to use one's own language or any other language of choice (Turi, 1993: 7).

According to Du Plessis (2012: 197), primary language legislation has the power to bring about a turning point in the language dispensation of a country. This, however, can only take place where a language act contains sanctions and penalisations which will ensure the implementation of the legislation (Shohamy, 2006). These sanctions and penalisations are important in ensuring that language rights are given meaning. A language act does not inhibit the enacting of further primary language legislation in other domains, for example in the legal system (Du Plessis, 2012). This language legislation cannot be in contradiction to the National Primary Language Act.

Language policy and implementation challenges

The South African Constitution (1996) emphasises the importance of language rights and the need for equitable access to justice in all official languages. South Africa's Constitution explicitly recognises linguistic rights as fundamental to justice and equality. Section 35(3)(k) of the Constitution guarantees every accused person the right to have a trial conducted in a language they understand or, if that is not possible, to have an interpreter provided at the state's expense. This provision ensures that language barriers do not hinder an individual's ability to defend themselves in legal proceedings. Additionally, Section 6(1) and (2) recognise the country's multilingual nature by granting official status to 12 languages and emphasising the need to promote indigenous languages that were historically marginalised. Despite these protections, challenges remain in courtroom settings where the availability and quality of interpretation services vary, and the legal system predominantly operates in English. The failure to provide accurate and culturally appropriate translations can undermine fair trial rights, making it essential to assess the effectiveness of multilingual communication in legal proceedings in Limpopo Province.

Language planning in the judicial system continues to be politicised, with courts entrenching a political, elitist, English-only goal (Docrat et al., 2021). The politicisation of language planning is not unique to South Africa but is recognised as a global trend in Australia as well. Language was utilised as a political instrument to marginalise people. This issue persists in South Africa, where residents are denied their language rights in courtrooms. Former Chief Justice Mogoeng Mogoeng's decision to continue to promote the imbalance affects 90% of South African languages. The decision was taken on the basis of transformation, according to the Heads of Court, which is inaccurate and violates citizens' constitutional rights. The implementation of language policies in Limpopo has encountered various challenges, including a lack of resources, insufficient training for legal practitioners in multilingual settings, and the dominance of English in legal discourse (Madima et al., 2024; Mkhize & Balfour, 2017). These challenges can result in systemic biases against speakers of indigenous languages, undermining their ability to participate fully in legal processes (Svongoro & Kadenge, 2015). Furthermore, the complexities of multilingual communication in court can lead to significant implications for the fairness of trials, as language barriers may hinder the ability of defendants to understand proceedings and present their cases effectively (Svongoro & Kadenge, 2015).

In conclusion, the multilingual landscape of the Limpopo Province is shaped by a combination of indigenous languages and those introduced by immigrant populations. This diversity enriches the cultural fabric of the region but also presents significant challenges, particularly in formal settings such as the courtroom. Effective communication in legal contexts is essential for ensuring justice and equity, necessitating ongoing efforts to improve language policy implementation and interpreter training. As South Africa continues to navigate its multilingual reality, the importance of recognising and addressing the linguistic needs of all citizens remains paramount.

Theoretical framework

The study of multilingualism in courtroom discourse is grounded in linguistic and sociolinguistic theories that explain the relationship between language, communication, and legal outcomes. The Sapir-Whorf Hypothesis, also called Linguistic Relativity

Theory, highlights how language influences thought and perception, which is crucial in understanding how courtroom participants interpret legal proceedings. On the other hand, the Communication Accommodation Theory (CAT) explains how linguistic adjustments by interpreters, judges, and legal professionals can impact case dynamics, shaping access to justice for multilingual individuals.

Sapir-Whorf Hypothesis

The Sapir-Whorf Hypothesis posits that the structure and vocabulary of a language significantly influences its speakers' cognition and worldview. This theory, attributed to linguists Edward Sapir and Benjamin Lee Whorf, suggests that language is not merely a tool for communication but also a framework through which individuals interpret their experiences and surroundings (Mei, 2024; Regier & Xu, 2018). In the context of multilingual courtroom discourse, the relevance of this hypothesis becomes particularly pronounced, as legal concepts are often encoded differently across languages. For instance, specific legal terminologies in English may lack direct equivalents in Sepedi, Tshivenḓa, or Xitsonga, necessitating interpreters to navigate these linguistic gaps carefully (Constable & Becker, 2017).

The implications of the Sapir-Whorf Hypothesis in courtroom settings are profound. When legal practitioners and interpreters work within a multilingual framework, they must be acutely aware of how linguistic structures can shape the understanding of legal concepts. For example, a term that conveys a specific legal nuance in English may not carry the same weight or meaning in another language, leading to potential misinterpretations during legal proceedings (Regier & Xu, 2018). This linguistic disparity can hinder the ability of accused individuals or witnesses who are not fluent in the language of the court to fully comprehend the proceedings, thereby affecting their capacity to provide accurate testimony or understand their rights (Mei, 2024). Moreover, the hypothesis underscores the necessity for culturally sensitive interpretation practices. In a multilingual courtroom, interpreters must translate words and convey the underlying legal concepts accurately, considering the cultural context of the languages involved (Constable & Becker, 2017). This aspect of the Sapir-Whorf Hypothesis highlights the critical role of language in shaping legal understanding and the importance of ensuring that all parties involved in legal proceedings can engage meaningfully, regardless of their linguistic background (Mei, 2024).

Communication Accommodation Theory (CAT)

Communication Accommodation Theory (CAT), developed by Howard Giles, explores how individuals adjust their speech patterns and communication styles based on their social and linguistic contexts (Constable & Becker, 2017; Chen & Reppen, 2020).

In courtroom settings, this theory is particularly relevant as it examines how legal professionals, including judges, lawyers, and interpreters, may unconsciously modify their language in response to the perceived linguistic proficiency of the accused or witnesses (Regier & Xu, 2018). For instance, interpreters might simplify complex legal terminology to enhance comprehension for non-native speakers. At the same time, judges may adjust their language use when addressing different linguistic groups, potentially leading to inconsistencies in courtroom discourse (Constable & Becker, 2017).

The adjustments made under CAT can have significant implications for the outcomes of legal cases. If a witness or accused individual does not receive information in a linguistically appropriate manner, their ability to defend themselves or provide accurate testimony may be compromised (Regier & Xu, 2018). This is particularly critical in multilingual settings like Limpopo, where the diversity of languages can lead to varying levels of understanding among participants in legal proceedings (Constable & Becker, 2017). The theory emphasises the need for structured and standardised legal interpretation practices to minimise linguistic disparities and ensure equitable access to justice for all individuals, regardless of their language proficiency (Regier & Xu, 2018; Chen & Reppen, 2020). Furthermore, CAT highlights the social dynamics at play in courtroom interactions. How language is accommodated can reflect power dynamics, with more dominant language speakers potentially overshadowing less proficient ones (Regier & Xu, 2018). This aspect of communication can lead to unequal participation in legal processes, further complicating the quest for fairness and justice in multilingual contexts (Constable & Becker, 2017).

Interrelation of theories in multilingual courtroom discourse

The Sapir-Whorf Hypothesis and the Communication Accommodation Theory provide valuable insights into the complexities of multilingual courtroom discourse. The Sapir-Whorf Hypothesis emphasises language differences' cognitive and perceptual implications, while CAT focuses on the social dynamics and adjustments made during communication. These theories underscore the necessity for a deeper understanding of language use in legal contexts, particularly in regions like the Limpopo Province, where multiple languages coexist and interact (Mei, 2024; Constable & Becker, 2017). The interplay between these theories suggests that effective communication in multilingual courtrooms requires linguistic proficiency, cultural competence, and awareness of the social dynamics at play. Legal practitioners must be trained to recognise the potential impacts of language on cognition and perception and to adapt their communication styles to accommodate the diverse linguistic backgrounds of all participants (Constable & Becker, 2017; Regier & Xu, 2018; Chen & Reppen, 2020). This comprehensive approach can help mitigate the risks of miscommunication and ensure that the rights of all individuals are upheld in legal proceedings.

In summary, the Sapir-Whorf Hypothesis and the Communication Accommodation Theory are both highly relevant to the study of multilingualism in courtroom discourse, particularly in the context of the Limpopo Province in South Africa. These theories highlight the intricate relationship between language, thought, and social interaction, emphasising the importance of accurate and culturally sensitive interpretation practices in legal settings. By understanding and applying these theoretical frameworks, legal practitioners can work towards more equitable and effective communication in multilingual courtrooms, ultimately contributing to a fairer justice system for all individuals involved.

Methodology

This study employed a qualitative research approach to explore the effects of multilingualism in courtroom discourse in the Limpopo Province of South Africa. The qualitative method was chosen because it allows for an in-depth understanding of courtroom interactions, interpreter experiences, and the impact of language barriers on legal outcomes. The study relied on semi-structured interviews with courtroom interpreters, magistrates, prosecutors, and court managers to gather first-hand insights into language use in legal proceedings. These interviews focused on the challenges interpreters face in translating indigenous and immigrant languages, the linguistic difficulties experienced by the accused, and the broader implications of multilingualism in the justice system. Additionally, courtroom observations were conducted to analyse real-time language interactions, interpreter accuracy, and the influence of language on trial outcomes. This methodological approach aimed to provide a holistic view of the role of language in the legal process, ensuring that the study captured both subjective experiences and observable courtroom dynamics.

The study further incorporated document analysis of legal policies, constitutional provisions, and relevant case laws concerning linguistic rights in South African courtrooms. Official reports and legislation, such as Section 35(3)(k) of the South African Constitution (1996), which guarantees the right to a trial in a language the accused understands, were examined to assess the legal framework governing courtroom language use. The study also analysed court transcripts and judicial rulings where language disputes had been central to the legal process, helping to contextualise the findings. Data from the interviews and observations were systematically coded and analysed using thematic analysis, identifying recurring themes such as language barriers, interpreter challenges, and the impact of multilingualism on case outcomes. By triangulating multiple data sources, interviews, observations, and legal documents, the study aimed to enhance the validity and reliability of its findings while offering practical recommendations to improve language accessibility in South African courts.

Presentation of findings

TABLE 10.1: Summary of respondent profiles

Category	Code	Qualification	Location	Experience	Gender	Home Language
Court Interpreters	CIM1	MA in Languages	High Court	27 years	Male	Xitsonga
	CIM2	Language Practice	High Court	15 years	Male	Setswana
	CIM3	BA Language Practice	High Court	6 years	Male	Sesotho
	CIF1	Communication	High Court	3 years	Female	Sepedi
	CIM5	Language Practice	High Court	5 years	Male	Tshivenda
	CIF2	BA African Languages	High Court	4 years	Female	Sepedi
	CIM4	Communication	Pretoria High Court	3 years	Male	Chichewa
	CIM6	Language & Communication	High Court	10 years	Male	Setswana
Prosecutors	CPM1	Advocate (LLM)	Practicing	20 years	Male	Venda
	CPM2	B. Proc, LLB	Practicing	20 years	Male	Sepedi
	CPF1	LLB	Practicing	5 years	Female	Sepedi
Magistrates & Court Managers	MGTF1	B Proc, LLM	Practicing	11 years	Female	Sepedi
	MGTF2	LLB	Mahwelereng	5 years	Female	Xitsonga
	MGTM1	LLB	Practicing	8 years	Male	Sepedi
	CMGR	Hon BA	Practicing	15 years	Male	Sepedi

This table concisely summarises the respondents' profiles, highlighting their qualifications, experience, and linguistic backgrounds, which are essential in assessing multilingualism's role in Limpopo courtrooms. The study engaged 15 respondents, including eight court interpreters, three prosecutors, and four magistrates/court managers. These participants were selected to provide insights from different roles within the courtroom, ensuring a comprehensive understanding of the impact of multilingualism on legal proceedings. Among the 15 respondents were ten males and five females, indicating a gender imbalance, particularly among interpreters and prosecutors. Male participants dominated both interpreter and prosecutor roles, whereas female respondents were more evenly distributed among interpreters and magistrates. This imbalance may reflect broader trends in the South African legal system regarding employment distribution in these professions.

Linguistic distribution

The respondents spoke a variety of languages, reflecting the multilingual nature of the Limpopo Province:

a) Sepedi (5 participants) - Most widely spoken, aligning with its prominence in Limpopo.
b) Xitsonga (3 participants) - Also widely represented among interpreters and magistrates.
c) Setswana (2 participants) - Present among interpreters.
d) Tshivenda (1 participant) - Spoken by one prosecutor.
e) Tshivenda (1 participant) - Spoken by one interpreter.
f) Sesotho (1 participant) - Represented among interpreters.
g) Chichewa (1 participant) - Spoken by a court interpreter, highlighting the presence of immigrant languages in courtrooms.

This linguistic diversity showcases the challenges and demands for multilingual courtroom interpretation, particularly given the presence of immigrant languages like Chichewa and Shona. While official South African languages are well represented, the need for interpreters in languages beyond the country's 12 official languages remains a pressing issue.

Multilingualism in Limpopo courtroom discourse

It has been established in the study background that Limpopo Province is one of South Africa's most linguistically diverse regions, with a rich tapestry of indigenous and immigrant languages spoken across its communities. The province officially recognises Sepedi, Xitsonga, and Tshivenda as its dominant indigenous languages, alongside Afrikaans and English, which are used in administrative and legal settings. However, due to increased migration and cross-border mobility, Limpopo has also seen the introduction of languages such as Shona, Chichewa, Portuguese, and Swahili, brought in by immigrant communities from Zimbabwe, Malawi, Mozambique, and other neighbouring countries. In South Africa, language is a right; all citizens can express themselves in a language they can comprehend. This section had questions and responses to the first major objective of the study, which was to establish the existence of multilingualism in the Limpopo provinces. Only four questions were given to the respondents, and the few summarised responses below confirm this linguistic picture that the study wanted to establish. Indeed, many languages exist in the Limpopo Province.

- *What are the dominant languages spoken in Limpopo Province?*

This question was asked to the court officials, who confirmed that more than six languages were spoken in the province and that they experienced them within the courtroom as well. Sepedi, Xitsonga, Tshivenda, isiNdebele, Setswana, isiZulu, English, Afrikaans, Shona, Chichewa, and Portuguese.

> 'Limpopo Province is predominantly multilingual, with Sepedi, Xitsonga, and Tshivenda being the most widely spoken indigenous languages. Additionally, Afrikaans and English are commonly used in business, education, and legal settings.'

- *Are there any immigrant languages present in Limpopo Province?*

This question became relevant because, during the pilot study, the researcher had already established the existence of foreign languages and, therefore, used the study to confirm with respondents. The summarised response below confirmed the existence of immigrant languages and their identities.

> 'Yes, due to cross-border migration, Limpopo hosts a growing number of immigrant languages, including Shona (Zimbabwe), Chichewa (Malawi), Portuguese (Mozambique), and Swahili (East Africa). Migrant communities speak these languages and are increasingly encountered in social and institutional settings, including courtrooms.'

- *How does multilingualism manifest in everyday interactions within Limpopo Province?*

This question was asked to help understand and analyse the perceived influence of multilingualism in different spheres of the South African provinces. This response would further justify the objectives of this study, which focused on multilingualism in courtroom discourse.

> 'Multilingualism is evident in community interactions, businesses, schools, and government institutions, where individuals often switch between languages depending on the context. Code-switching is common, especially in urban areas where diverse linguistic groups interact frequently.'

Under this first objective, the last question was about the official language status in the Limpopo Province. This question was important to help understand how language use and control was applied at the High Court in Limpopo Province.

- *Is there an official language policy in Limpopo province that promotes multilingualism?*

> 'Yes, the South African Constitution (Section 6) recognises multiple official languages, and Limpopo's language policies promote the use of Sepedi, Xitsonga, and Tshivenda. However, in practice, English remains dominant in formal and legal settings, sometimes at the expense of indigenous languages.'

The response above shows that courts respect and abide by the laws of the country when it comes to the linguistic application of the law.

Multilingualism in courtroom discourse at the Limpopo High Court

This forms the second research objective and second major theme of this study. The linguistic diversity of the province shapes the practice of multilingualism in the Limpopo High Court, yet its implementation remains inconsistent. While interpreters are crucial in bridging language gaps, English remains the dominant language of record, often sidelining indigenous languages such as Sepedi, Xitsonga, and Tshivenda. Interviews with court interpreters, magistrates, and prosecutors reveal that, despite the constitutional right of accused persons to be tried in a language they understand, resource constraints, lack of qualified interpreters, and the dominance of English create significant challenges. The presence of immigrant languages like Shona and Chichewa further complicates legal proceedings, as interpreters for these languages are often unavailable, leading to trial delays or misinterpretations. This section presents the findings on how multilingualism is practised in the Limpopo High Court, focusing on the role of interpreters, the experiences of the accused, and the institutional challenges in ensuring language inclusivity.

The average response from the interpreter shows that there is a solution if the court had to consider multilingualism. They went on to say that for the court to run a fair trial, a competent person should be appointed to speed up the process. However, if the court has interpreters who are able to speak at least more than two languages, it impacts the proceeding positively, as one CPF1 attested by saying:

> 'Yes, because we have one witness speaking Xitsonga or Tshivenda and the accused speaking Sepedi. When we have an interpreter who can speak all these languages, it becomes more advantageous for the court to run smoothly because the accused will be able to understand, and the witness can also follow.'

Another attestation revealed by magistrate CMGRTF1 is that multilingualism's could reduce workload, meaning no more case postponement because there will be no delays because of the shortage of interpreters. Magistrate CMGRTF2 also agrees, as they add that having interpreters who speak many languages, especially foreign languages, assists them in dealing with minor cases quickly. For example, CPM1 stated:

> 'I don't think so because, as I am saying, we have some avenues, we have some database; if a certain language is required, we send the memo for them to assist us with an interpreter. At least we must know all the African languages, such as the Chichewa, who come daily from Malawi. Just now, when I left you here, I had somebody who was speaking Shona there. We are still waiting for Miss Thema, who can speak both Chichewa and Shona there.'

This implies that foreign languages, mainly from Zimbabwe and Malawi, are problematic to interpret in the courtroom because those languages do not have many interpreters represented within the courtroom in Limpopo. According to criminal procedure acts, an accused should appear in court within 72 hours; failure to do so may result in uncontested arrest. However, it is the duty of the court to do so. Moreover, if the court fails to produce an interpreter to the court for the accused, the accused could be excused and released. As the court manager emphasised:

> '... department of seeing the importance of multilingualism 'multi' yes, they have made provision to us hiring people with different languages.'

Lastly, another solution to multilingualism is that the court will comply with the constitutional Bill of Rights because it will be fit for all accused to be represented in the language that they understand better. Multilingualism could result in a solution that will be utilised to cap social status in court. It will further blend the richest and poorest in representation during court proceedings because most of the time, legal practitioners are obliged to use English between each other, meaning at some point, the witness of the accused is left out because the interpreter does not render interpreting between them.

Rights of the arrested or detained persons

Section 35 of the Constitution provides for the rights of arrested or detained persons and states that an arrested or detained person has:

a) The right to remain silent.

b) The right to be promptly informed of the right to remain silent and the consequences should you elect not to remain silent.

c) The right not to be compelled to make any submission or adduce evidence that can be used as evidence against that person.

d) The right to be brought before a court of law within 48 hours of being arrested.

e) The right to seek legal counsel, which can be exercised before making any statement to the police.
f) The right to be held in conditions consistent with the right of human dignity; and
g) The right to a fair public trial.

From the overall perspective of the interpreters, it shows that language can influence the decision that the presiding officer could make; they say if the court appoints incompetent interpreters, it will affect the entire outcomes of the proceeding. They further argue that lack of linguistic knowledge by some of the interpreters, whereby an interpreter does not know the regional dialect of a particular region, causes linguistic challenges, and the accused could dispute what the interpreter says. This will delay the proceedings of the case. Lack of representation of African languages in court also impacts the running of cases, especially for legal practitioners, because some lawyers criticise interpreters because of misinterpretation of some words, as attested by CTMNR who said:

> 'I can't say that because there are cases where an attorney is not prepared or did not prepare his/her case. He will complain and say the interpreter is not interpreting what his clients are saying so this one I can't answer, because the attorney is dodging it. He may claim that he said the correct thing. It means the interpreter needs to be changed, and when it is outside, the same attorney will go to the interpreter saying, "I am sorry, man, I did that, and you did not do anything wrong".'

In most cases, when the court does not have an interpreter for a particular language, the matter is postponed until the court manages to acquire an interpreter who will be able to assist the accused in receiving the trial with fairness. This challenge, in most cases, arises when the matter involves more than one accused person. Therefore, the court needs to acquire interpreters for everybody. Nonetheless, the case got delayed, as mentioned by CPM3 below.

He further stated that another impact is that the court lacks interpreters who speak the languages that the court requires. However, those who are available are those who do not have qualifications for these positions, so the court relies on casual interpreters, who are a handful, to satisfy the entire department. In addition, the courtroom needs an interpreter for the accused, who does not understand English. An interpreter functions as a bridge of communication for the court. That is why CIM5 attested that:

> 'The impact is that the interpreter is like the engine of the process; if the accused does not understand English and the trial runs in English, it will not be fair. For the trial to support the accused, it must be conducted in the language that the accused is conversant with.'

In addition, CIF1 viewed the impact as positive because she found education during the process to help her understand the law better.

> 'For me, one learns a lot. It helps to understand how the law works because one understands and knows if there are loopholes or things. It alerts one that one could also end up being in such a situation.'

CIM2 agreed with CIF1 in terms of the positive impact that was brought by the overall processes of courtroom interpreting. The participants agreed that it allowed the accused to express themselves using the best language they understood. Therefore, they will not go to jail to account for something that they have not committed. CIF1 said:

> 'The knowledge of languages could help the accused to express themselves in their mother-tongue easily and to give evidence on how one sees how things transpired in one's language. It is advantageous to express oneself in one's mother-tongue.'

Since the matter of multilingualism is a constitutional provision, it is an area of study that has not been explored that much in terms of the South African context since one magistrate concurred that if multilingualism is practised in courtrooms, most cases will not be delayed anymore because they will have multiple languages that will enable them to run the cases without delay. CPM1 emphasised that they do have them, as explained:

> 'Yes, we do. As you said, according to the Constitution, every person has the right to express *ka mkgo*, and the accused person should be interpreted in the language that the accused person understands.'

The matter of multilingualism, thus, is a constitutional provision. It is an aspect that has not been explored that much in terms of the South African context since one magistrate concurred that if multilingualism is practised in courtrooms, most cases will not be delayed anymore because they will have multiple languages that will enable them to run the cases without any delay. CPM1 emphasised that they do not have them as explained:

> 'Yes, we need more multilingual speakers in court because court cases are delayed. After all, we do not have them.'

The effect of multilingualism on the outcome of court cases

Language plays a critical role in courtroom proceedings, as it directly affects how evidence is presented, interpreted, and understood by all parties involved. In a multilingual setting such as the Limpopo High Court, where accused persons, witnesses, and legal practitioners often speak different languages, the accuracy of interpretation can significantly influence case outcomes. Misinterpretations, linguistic biases, and the lack of qualified interpreters can lead to miscommunication, unfair trials, wrongful convictions, or cause delays. Additionally, the dominance of English as the language of record, despite constitutional provisions for linguistic inclusivity, creates further challenges for those who are not proficient in it. This section explores how multilingualism impacts courtroom discourse, examining cases where language barriers have influenced trial proceedings, legal decision-making, and overall access to justice.

An agreement among the judiciary, the NPA, and interpreters is that they do recommend multilingualism in the courtroom because it will assist the court in speeding up the cases. In addition, the court's ability to be multilingual is one of the requirements that the Constitution proposes so that every linguistic right will not be violated. The response from prosecutors and presiding officers is that they recommend multilingualism in the courtroom because it aligns with the Constitution, which states that the accused has the right to receive a trial in his or her home language. The findings reveal responses to questions on how multilingualism may have an effect on case outcomes.

- *How does multilingualism affect the fairness of court trials?*

The court officials all agreed that since section 35(3)(k) ensures the right to a free trial in one's preferred language, there is bound to be challenges to case outcomes. The Magistrate, thus, stated:

> 'Multilingualism can enhance fairness by allowing the accused and witnesses to express themselves in a language they fully understand. However, when interpreters are unavailable or provide inaccurate translations, miscommunication may lead to wrongful convictions, unfair sentencing, or case delays. In such cases, language barriers can undermine the right to a fair trial as guaranteed by Section 35(3)(k) of the South African Constitution.'

- *Can interpreter errors impact the final judgment of a case?*

All the court interpreters agreed that misinterpretations will always happen when too many languages are involved in a court case. Fairness in court proceedings cannot be guaranteed in these situations. One interpreter said the following:

> 'Yes, misinterpretations or omissions can lead to significant judicial errors. If evidence is inaccurately translated, a witness's testimony may be misrepresented, potentially affecting the credibility of statements. Cases have been overturned on appeal due to poor interpretation, highlighting the critical role of interpreters in case outcomes.'

- *What challenges do courts face in ensuring accurate multilingual interpretation?*

This question drew decisive responses from all the respondents, all of whom acknowledged that courts in Limpopo have struggled to get sufficiently trained interpreters in all the languages that the courts have to deal with on a daily basis. The

Magistrate, therefore, strongly articulated the challenges that multilingualism brings to the courts every day in the following response:

> 'Courts struggle with a shortage of trained interpreters, inconsistent quality of interpretation, and a lack of legal terminology in indigenous and immigrant languages. These challenges often lead to case postponements or reliance on informal interpreters, such as police officers or family members, which can compromise the neutrality and accuracy of court proceedings.'

- *Does the dominance of English in courtrooms disadvantage non-English speakers?*

The magistrates and interpreters all agreed that the use of English and Afrikaans disadvantages almost 90% of the accused that come to their courts every day. Most accused are not first-language speakers of these languages, yet court records are given and stored in the two languages. Translation and interpretation always have their challenges, especially if the translator is also not a first-language speaker of English or Afrikaans. The prosecutor felt this situation disadvantaged a lot of the accused persons and resulted in unfair outcomes.

> 'Yes, because legal arguments, case documents, and judgments are primarily in English, non-English speaking accused persons may struggle to understand the proceedings, even with an interpreter fully. This language barrier may limit their ability to defend themselves effectively, thereby impacting trial outcomes and access to justice.'

- *What measures can improve the influence of multilingualism on case outcomes?*

All the respondents agreed that more needs to be done to ensure the availability of trained professional interpreters in all the available languages when court cases are heard. A senior court interpreter made elaborate and ambitious recommendations on how the challenge can be handled and solved, as shown in the response below.

> 'Courts can improve multilingual inclusivity by hiring more qualified interpreters, developing legal terminology in indigenous languages, and implementing technology-assisted interpretation services. Training legal professionals in basic multilingual communication can also enhance understanding and fairness in court proceedings.'

One interpreter, CIM5, also concurred with the prosecutor and the Magistrate that no more cases will be delayed in courtrooms.

> 'Yeah, which means when one is multilingual, one no longer sends down the case; one just interprets just like one has seen. They come in different languages, and the meeting is not adjourned so that we can get another interpreter, one just continues...'

Discussion of the findings

The investigation into multilingualism within the Limpopo High Court unveiled several critical insights that underscore the complexities and challenges inherent in a linguistically diverse legal system.

Dominance of English in legal proceedings

Despite South Africa's constitutional recognition of 12 official languages, English remains the predominant language in legal settings, including the Limpopo High Court. This prevalence often marginalises speakers of indigenous languages such as Sepedi, Xitsonga, and Tshivenda, potentially impeding their full comprehension and participation in legal proceedings. The reliance on English can lead to misunderstandings and a sense of alienation among non-English speaking participants, thereby affecting the fairness of trials. This observation aligns with Van Niekerk's (2015) analysis of the historical entrenchment of English in South African courts, which continues to influence contemporary legal practices.

Research on multilingualism in courtrooms reveals a complex interplay of linguistic, cultural, and legal factors. Despite constitutional provisions for multilingualism in countries like South Africa, there is a persistent bias towards monolingualism in legal settings (Angermeyer, 2021; Łachacz and Mańko, 2013)2013. This bias can disadvantage minority language speakers and impact the delivery of justice (Thetela, 2003; Docrat & Kaschula, 2023). Historical factors have contributed to the dominance of English and Afrikaans in South African courts (Van Niekerk, 2015; Mokoena, 2018). Challenges in implementing multilingual policies persist, as evidenced in the Limpopo Provincial Legislature (Madima et al., 2024). Scholars argue for linguistic transformation and decolonisation of legal systems to ensure equal access to justice for all language groups (Docrat et al., 2021). The tension between pragmatic monolingual approaches and constitutional imperatives for linguistic inclusivity remains a significant issue in multilingual courtrooms (Docrat et al., 2021).

Challenges faced by court interpreters

Court interpreters are pivotal in bridging language gaps; however, they encounter significant obstacles that can compromise the quality of their interpretation. The absence of standardised training and a clear legislative framework defining their roles often results in inconsistencies in interpretation. Interpreters may inadvertently omit, add, or alter information, which can lead to miscarriages of justice. Lebese (2013) highlights that the undefined role of court interpreters contributes to these challenges, emphasising the need for formal recognition and regulation of the profession to enhance the accuracy and reliability of court interpretations.

Impact of multilingualism on case outcomes

The interplay of multiple languages in courtrooms can significantly influence case outcomes. Misinterpretations or the lack of interpreters proficient in specific languages, including those of immigrant communities, can lead to delays, wrongful convictions, or dismissals. The case of *S v Maqubela* (2017) serves as a pertinent example, where interpreter errors necessitated a retrial, ultimately resulting in an acquittal. This case underscores the profound impact that linguistic inaccuracies can have on the administration of justice.

During courtroom discourse, there are several errors that may exist during the turns among the parties that are involved, and it has been established that those errors could have an impact during the proceedings. Ultimately such errors could be a danger in finalising the case judgment. Therefore, the accused could be wrongfully arrested due to such circumstances. It is also recommended to address the impact that multilingualism could have on courtroom interpreting. Lastly, the aim is to address the perspective emanating from the NPA and the Judiciary. Docrat (2019) is of the view that the multi-use of languages in the legal fraternity is not taken seriously; this is perpetuated by the decision that former Chief Justice Mogoeng Mogoeng made on 16 April 2017. It was reported that the languages of record, English and Afrikaans, had been changed to English only with immediate effect (Docrat et al., 2017: 1). The decision was reported to have been taken by the Heads of Court, comprising all Judge Presidents of all High Courts under the leadership of the Chief Justice of the Constitutional Court. This implies that other official languages, such as indigenous languages, which never enjoyed their status, were since declared as part of the official languages that comprise South Africa's accepted languages. Although the Use of Official Languages Act 12 (2012) merely scratches the surface, the point is that it creates a framework in which the concept of multilingualism and, specifically, all the official languages need to be looked at within each government department. The Use of Official Languages Act 12 (2012) compels the adoption of a language policy in each government department to ensure the practical use of the official languages.

Conclusions and recommendations

Conclusions

This study has demonstrated that multilingualism significantly impacts courtroom discourse and case outcomes in the Limpopo High Court. While the province is highly linguistically diverse, with indigenous languages such as Sepedi, Xitsonga, and Tshivenda, as well as immigrant languages like Shona and Chichewa, English remains the dominant language of legal proceedings. This creates barriers to justice for non-English speakers, leading to misinterpretations, case delays, and potential miscarriages of justice. The findings reveal that court interpreters play a crucial role. However, they face challenges such as inadequate training, lack of standardised legal terminology in African languages, and a shortage of qualified professionals, particularly for immigrant languages. Additionally, the constitutional right to a fair trial in one's preferred language (Section 35(3)(k)) is not fully realised due to systemic language policies favouring English.

The study also highlights that miscommunication in multilingual trials can directly influence case outcomes, sometimes leading to wrongful convictions or appeals based on linguistic errors. Furthermore, the absence of legal professionals fluent in indigenous languages exacerbates these challenges, as most lawyers and judges conduct proceedings in English. While multilingualism is recognised in theory, practical implementation remains weak, creating linguistic inequalities in South African courtrooms. Addressing these issues is essential for ensuring fair trials, equal access to justice, and compliance with constitutional language rights.

Recommendations

- *Training, standardisation, and recruitment of court interpreters*

To improve language inclusivity and ensure fair trials in South Africa's multilingual courtrooms, it is crucial to enhance the training, standardisation, and recruitment of court interpreters. The government, in collaboration with legal institutions, should develop comprehensive training programmes that equip interpreters with the necessary skills to translate legal terminology in indigenous and immigrant languages accurately. Additionally, the establishment of a national certification system for legal interpreters would help maintain high professional standards and ensure consistency in courtroom translations. A key priority should be the development of official legal glossaries in Sepedi, Xitsonga, Tshivenda, and other indigenous languages, along with commonly spoken immigrant languages such as Shona and Chichewa. This would ensure that interpreters have access to standardised legal terms, minimising misinterpretations that could lead to miscarriages of justice. Furthermore, interpreter recruitment should be expanded, particularly in rural areas, where the availability of multilingual professionals is limited. Courts should create regional interpreter databases to facilitate quick access to qualified professionals, reducing delays in cases requiring specific language expertise.

- *Integrating remote interpreting services and digital translation tools*

Technology should also be leveraged to support real-time translation and interpretation services in South African courtrooms. Integrating remote interpreting services and digital translation tools could assist in situations where in-person interpreters are unavailable. Additionally, courts could develop mobile applications and digital legal resources to provide interpreters and legal professionals with instant access to translated legal terminology. By implementing these technological solutions, courts can bridge language gaps more effectively, particularly for immigrant languages that lack an extensive interpreter network. However, technology should complement, not replace, human interpreters, as legal nuances and cultural contexts require skilled professionals to ensure accuracy. Law schools and judicial training programmes should also incorporate basic indigenous language training to encourage multilingualism among legal professionals. This ensures that judges, prosecutors, and defence attorneys are better equipped to communicate with non-English speaking accused persons and witnesses.

- *Enforcement of Section 35(3)(k) of the Constitution*

To strengthen the implementation of language policy in South African courts, there must be strict enforcement of Section 35(3)(k) of the Constitution, which guarantees every accused person the right to a trial in a language they understand. The judicial system should prioritise multilingual legal proceedings rather than relying solely on English as the language of record. This can be achieved by ensuring interpreters are present in all cases where language barriers exist, and allowing legal arguments and case documents to be presented in multiple languages when necessary. Additionally, further research should be conducted on the impact of linguistic barriers on legal outcomes, focusing on case studies where misinterpretations led to appeals or wrongful convictions. South Africa could also benefit from examining best practices from other multilingual legal systems, such as those in Canada or Switzerland, to develop a more inclusive and practical framework for courtroom language accessibility. By implementing these measures, South Africa's legal system can better uphold linguistic rights, promote fair trials, and ensure that language is not a barrier to justice.

Directions for future research

Addressing the linguistic challenges in South African courtroom discourse requires a broad-based research agenda.

Development of legal terminology in indigenous languages

Future studies can focus on creating comprehensive legal lexicons in indigenous languages. This development would aid interpreters in conveying complex legal concepts accurately, thereby enhancing the understanding of non-English speaking participants. Alberts and Mollema (2012) advocate for developing legal terminology in African languages to support court interpreters and ensure more precise communication in legal contexts.

Assessment of interpreter training programmes

Evaluating existing interpreter training programmes is crucial to identify gaps and areas for improvement. Research should explore the effectiveness of current curricula and advocate for standardised, accredited training that equips interpreters with the necessary skills to perform their duties competently. Such assessments can inform policy decisions and lead to the implementation of robust training frameworks.

Examination of technological interventions

Investigating the potential of technology, such as real-time translation tools and remote interpreting services, could offer innovative solutions to linguistic barriers in courtrooms. Research in this area should assess the feasibility, accuracy, and accessibility of such technologies within the South African legal context. Embracing technological advancements may provide cost-effective and efficient means to support interpreters and enhance multilingual communication in legal proceedings.

Exploration of policy implementation and its efficacy

Analysing the implementation of language policies within the judicial system can reveal discrepancies between legislative intent and practical application. Research should examine how policies are enacted at various judicial levels and their effectiveness in promoting linguistic inclusivity. Such studies can identify systemic barriers and recommend strategies to ensure that language rights are upheld in accordance with constitutional mandates.

References

Alberts, M. and Mollema, N., 2013. Developing legal terminology in African languages as aid to the court interpreter: A South African perspective. *Lexikos*, *23*(1), pp.29-58.

Angermeyer, MC., Matschinger, H. & Schomerus, G. (2013). Attitudes towards psychiatric treatment and people with mental illness: changes over two decades. *The British Journal of Psychiatry*, 203, 146–151.

Angermeyer, PS. (2021). Beyond translation equivalence: Advocating pragmatic equality before the law. *Journal of Pragmatics*, 174, 157–167.

´Capeta, T. (2009). Multilingual law and judicial interpretation in the EU. *Croatian Yearbook of European Law & Policy*, 5, 1-17.

Chen, M. & Reppen, R. (2020). A look at wh-questions in direct and cross-examinations: authentic vs. TV courtroom language. *Delta Documentação De Estudos Em Lingüística Teórica E Aplicada*, 36(3). https://doi.org/10.1590/1678-460x2020360310

Choshi, M.K., 2016. *Exploring the implications of the use of Official Languages Act 12 of 2012 on the establishment of the indigenous language courts in the Vhembe District, Limpopo Province, South Africa* (Doctoral dissertation).

Constable, M. & Becker, S. (2017). Right away: A late, right-lateralized category effect complements an early, left-lateralized category effect in visual search. *Psychonomic Bulletin & Review*, 24(5), 1611-1619. https://doi.org/10.3758/s13423-017-1246-3

Davies, A. and Elder, C. eds., 2004. *The handbook of applied linguistics* (p. 431). Oxford: Blackwell.

Docrat, Z., 2017. The Role of African Languages In the South African Legal System: Towards A Transformative Agenda. MA Thesis. Rhodes University: Grahamstown.

Docrat, Z., 2020. A critique of the language of record in South African courts in relation to selected university language policies. *Grahamstown: Rhodes University dissertation. DOI*, *10*(10962), p.141394.

Docrat, Z. & Kaschula, RH. (2023). Legal translation and court interpreting in Africa. *Research Handbook on Jurilinguistics*. Edward Elgar Publishing.

Docrat, Z., Kaschula, RH. & Ralarala, MK. (2021). *A Handbook on Legal Languages and the quest for linguistic equality in South Africa and beyond*. Stellenbosch: African Sun Media.

Doczekalska, A. (2019). *Hybrid and neutral language(s) in EU Multi-Level Legislative Drafting. Lawmaking in Multi-level Settings*. Nomos Verlagsgesellschaft mbH & Co. KG, 151-172.

Du Plessis, T. 2012. A language act for South Africa? The role of sociolinguistic principles in the analysis of language legislation. In Brohy, C., du Plessis, T., Turi, J.G and Woehrling, J (eds.). Law, Language and the Multilingual State. Proceedings from the 12th International Conference of the International Academy of Linguistic Law. Bloemfontein: SUN MeDIA. pp 195- 213.

Filipović, L. (2013). The role of language in legal contexts: A forensic cross-linguistic viewpoint. *Law and Language: Current Legal Issues*, 15, 328-343.

Heydon, G. and Mabasso, E., 2018. The impact of multilingualism on reporting domestic violence in Mozambique. *Language matters*, *49*(1), pp.84-106.

Jordaan, H. & Ngwanduli, M. (2020). Contextual influences on sentence repetition as a tool for the identification of language impairment in grade 3 Sepedi-English bilinguals: a case against bilingual norms. *South African Journal of Communication Disorders*, 67(1). https://doi.org/10.4102/sajcd.v67i1.762

Joseph, M. & Ramani, E. (2012). 'Glocalization': Going beyond the dichotomy of global versus local through additive multilingualism. *International Multilingual Research Journal*, 6, 22-34.

Kretzer, MM. & Kaschula, RH. (2020). (Unused) potentials of educators' covert language policies at public schools in Limpopo, South Africa. *Current Issues in Language Planning*, 21, 254-278.

Lachacz, O. & Mańko, R. (2013). Multilingualism at the Court of Justice of the European Union: theoretical and practical aspects. *Studies in Logic, Grammar and Rhetoric*, 34, 75-92.

Lebese, S.J., 2013. *The undefined role of court interpreters in South Africa* (Doctoral dissertation, University of South Africa).

Madima, S., Morris Thembani Babane, MT., & Klu, E. (2024). Language policy implementation challenges in postcolonial anglophone Africa: a case of Limpopo provincial legislature in South Africa. *Forum for Linguistic Studies*, 6(2). https://doi.org/10.59400/fls.v6i2.1164

Makalela, L. (2015). Translanguaging as a vehicle for epistemic access: cases for reading comprehension and multilingual interactions. *Per Linguam*, 31(1), 15. https://doi.org/10.5785/31-1-628

Mashwele, R., Mandende, I. & Sebola, M. (2024). Ethnolinguistic vitality in Thulamela Local Municipality: a case of Xitsonga. *Literator*, 45(1). https://doi.org/10.4102/lit.v45i1.1966

Mei, A. (2024). How does language influence our minds? From a linguistics perspective. *Lecture Notes in Education Psychology and Public Media*, 42(1), 205–209. https://doi.org/10.54254/2753-7048/42/20240840

Mkhize, D. & Balfour, R. (2017). Language rights in education in South Africa. *South African Journal of Higher Education,* 31(6). https://doi.org/10.20853/31-6-1633

Mokoena, DA. (2018). Black Panther and the Problem of the Black radical. *Africology: The Journal of Pan African Studies*, 11, 13–20.

Mooney, R. (2014). Auditory-vocal mirroring in songbirds. *Philosophical Transactions of the Royal Society B: Biological Sciences*, 369, 20130179.

Motaung, BL. (2021). *Translanguaging as a pedagogical strategy to implement multilingual language policy at a South African university*. University of the Free State.

Mulwa, A. (2023). *Technological strategies and performance of the judicial sector in Kenya: a case of Nairobi city county*. The Co-operative University of Kenya.

Ndlovu, E., 2023. The Right to an Interpreter in the Zimbabwean Justice System: The Missing Link. *Journal of African Languages & Literary Studies (JoALLS)*, *4*(1).

Ngunga, A., 2011. Monolingual education in a multilingual setting: The case of Mozambique. *Journal of Multicultural Discourses*, *6*(2), pp.177-196.

Rakgogo, T. and Zungu, E. (2022). The elevation of Sepedi from a dialect to an official standard language: Cultural and economic power and political influence matter. *Literator,* 43(1). https://doi.org/10.4102/lit.v43i1.1827

Regier, T. & Xu, Y. (2018). The Sapir Whorf hypothesis and inference under uncertainty. *Wiley Interdisciplinary Reviews Cognitive Science*, 9(3). https://doi.org/10.1002/wcs.1464

Republic of South Africa (RSA). (1944). *Magistrates' Courts Act 32 of 1944*. Pretoria: Government Printer.

Republic of South Africa (RSA). (2012). *Use of Official Languages Act of 2012*. Pretoria: Government Printer.

Shohamy, E. 2006. Language policy: Hidden agendas and new approaches. London: Routledge.

Singh, RJ. (2014). Is mother-tongue education possible in a language-diverse province? A case of Limpopo Province. *Mediterranean Journal of Social Sciences*, 5.

Stroud, C. and Guissemo, M., 2017. Linguistic Messianism: Multilingualism in Mozambique. *Sociolinguistics in African Contexts: Perspectives and Challenges*, pp.35-51.

Stygall, G. (1994). Resisting privilege: Basic writing and Foucault's author function. *College Composition & Communication*, 45, 320–341.

S v Maqubela (2017)

Svongoro, P. & Kadenge, M. (2015). From language to society: An analysis of interpreting quality and the linguistic rights of the accused in selected Zimbabwean courtrooms. *Southern African Linguistics and Applied Language Studies*, 33(1), 47–62. https://doi.org/10.2989/16073614.2015.1023501

Thetela, P. (2003). Discourse, culture and the law: The analysis of crosstalk in the Southern African bilingual courtroom. *AILA Review*, 16, 78–88.

Tönsing, K., Mothapo, N., Morwane, R. & Soto, G. (2023). Stakeholder validation of a Sepedi core vocabulary list as a resource for augmentative and alternative communication. *International Journal of Speech-Language Pathology*, 26(4), 566–577. https://doi.org/10.1080/17549507.2023.2241671

Turi, J.G. 2012. Law, Language and the Multilingual State. In Brohy, C., du Plessis, T., Turi, J.G and Woehrling, J. (eds.). Law, Language and the Multilingual State. Proceedings of the 12th International Conference of the International Academy of Linguistic Law. Bloemfontein: Sun MeDIA. pp 269-290.

Turi, J.G. 1993. The importance of the conference theme: "Language and equality". In Prinsloo, K., Peters, Y., Turi, J.G and Van Rensburg, C. (eds.). Language, Law and Equality. Pretoria: University of Pretoria. pp 5-24.

Van Niekerk, G. (2015). Multilingualism in South African courts: The legislative regulation of language in the Cape during the nineteenth century. *Fundamina*, 21, 372–391.

Verhoef, G. (2023). *The public domain and the legal protection of Indigenous Knowledge Systems*. North-West University (South Africa).

Wamuti, L. (2021). *Teaching of Japanese as a foreign language in tertiary institutions in Kenya: opportunities and challenges*. Kenyatta University.

11 LANGUAGE CHALLENGES IN COURTROOM INTERPRETING: A STUDY OF COURTROOM DISCOURSE IN THE LIMPOPO PROVINCE

Mabilo T. Jonas, Tebogo J. Rakgogo, Josephat Mutangadura & Corle Smith

Introduction

This study examines language challenges in courtroom translation and interpreting, which are integral to courtroom discourse. Courtroom interpreting in South Africa presents a unique set of challenges due to the country's diverse linguistic landscape. Ensuring accurate and effective interpretation is crucial for upholding the right to a fair trial, as enshrined in Section 35 of the Constitution.

Background and rationale

Historically, courtrooms were arenas where formalised language and rigid protocols dominated interactions. In ancient Greece, for instance, the emergence of rhetoric as a discipline was closely tied to legal discourse, with citizens required to represent themselves in court, leading to the development of persuasive speech techniques. This period marked the beginning of structured forensic rhetoric, emphasizing logical argumentation and eloquence (Aristotle, *trans.* 1991).

As legal systems matured, courtroom discourse became more specialised, with distinct roles for judges, attorneys, and witnesses. The language used in these settings often served to reinforce power dynamics, with legal professionals employing complex terminology that could be inaccessible to laypersons. This complexity sometimes led to challenges in ensuring that all participants fully understood the proceedings, potentially impacting the fairness of trials (Coulthard & Johnson, 2007). Moreover, historical analyses of courtroom interactions have revealed instances where linguistic strategies were used to marginalise certain groups, reflecting broader societal biases within the legal process (Kryk-Kastovsky, 2006).

An essential component of South African legislation, notably during court hearings, ensures an individual's right to speak and be talked to in a language they fully comprehend. Section 35(3)(k) of the Constitution, which guarantees the right to a fair trial, states that the court is compelled to employ a professional interpreter if the accused does not comprehend the language in which the proceedings are held. When the actions mentioned above are broken, many people might be unfairly prosecuted because of misinterpretation or improper portrayal by translators who do not speak the accused's mother-tongue. Furthermore, judges who do not speak the accused's language and rely on interpreters are more likely to make an incorrect conclusion in their final determination of case decisions.

The use of legal jargon, often referred to as 'legalese', can create barriers to comprehension for lay participants, including witnesses and defendants, potentially undermining the fairness of proceedings (Shaheen-ul-Zaman & Ali, 2023). The linguistic dynamics in courtrooms can lead to power imbalances, where legal professionals wield language as a means of control over witnesses and jurors (Farinde et al., 2015). This is particularly evident in cross-examination scenarios, where strategic questioning can manipulate the narrative and influence the jury's perception of credibility (Aldosari, 2024). Furthermore, the cultural and contextual variations in courtroom discourse, as explored by researchers like Doyiso, reveal that language-related issues are not confined to any single legal system but are prevalent across different jurisdictions, including those in Africa and Asia (Doyiso, 2022). The challenges posed by courtroom discourse are compounded by the necessity for interpreters in multilingual settings, where miscommunication can have dire consequences for justice (Du, 2015). Thus, the historical evolution of courtroom discourse and the language challenges it presents underscore the critical need for ongoing research and reform to ensure equitable access to justice for all participants in the legal process.

Courtroom discourse plays a crucial role in ensuring justice, yet language challenges often hinder effective communication and fair trial outcomes. In multilingual societies like South Africa, where 12 official languages and various dialects coexist, courtroom interpreting becomes a complex task. Misinterpretations, lack of word equivalence, and dialectal variations can distort meaning, affecting legal proceedings and the rights of the accused. The presence of foreign nationals further exacerbates linguistic barriers, necessitating skilled interpreters who understand both linguistic and cultural nuances. This study explores the language challenges faced in courtroom interpreting in Limpopo Province, examining their impact on trial fairness and proposing solutions to enhance legal communication.

Review of literature

As indicated in the introduction, the objective of this study is to explore the challenges of the intersection between language and law in a more practical sense. It is worth stating that the topic of 'court interpreting' falls under the jurisdiction of the Department of Justice and Constitutional Development. Thus, the relationship between language and law becomes a salient issue to be discussed.

The constitutional language legislation in courtrooms in South Africa

Even as the study focuses on language challenges, it is necessary to present a brief on the constitutional language legislation protecting citizens' linguistic identity. Language legislation was described by (Turi, 1992 & 1993: 5–6) as '... generally aimed at determining and establishing the status and use of designated languages by means of legal obligations and rights; in other words, legal regulations concerning language'. Language legislation exists in two categories based on its application. Language legislation deals with official/public usage and unofficial/private usage (Turi, 2012: 73). Official language legislation designates one or more language(s) as official in specific domains of legislation, justice, public administration, and education (Turi, 1993: 7). According to Wesson and Du Plessis (2012: 197), primary language legislation has the power to bring about a turning point in the language dispensation of a country. This, however, can only occur where a language act contains sanctions and penalisations which will ensure the implementation of the legislation (Shohamy, 2006). These sanctions and penalisations are important in ensuring that language rights are given meaning. A language act does not inhibit the enacting of further primary language legislation in other domains, for example, in the legal system (Wesson & Du Plessis, 2012: 198). This language legislation cannot contradict the National Primary Language Act.

Kaschula (2021) holds that languages are markers of identity and culture, and different languages' subtleties reveal much about their speakers. The loss of a language is thus not only an enormous cultural loss but also the eternal loss of a huge amount of indigenous knowledge. Any language professional knows that language is inextricably linked to culture. An interpreter needs to know and understand both to communicate across cultures. This includes knowledge of norms and idioms that can often be deeply culturally bound. Subsequently, citizens should be tried in their African languages so that they can wholly participate in the judicial proceedings.

Language-related challenges in courtroom interpreting

The history of courtroom discourse is deeply intertwined with the evolution of legal systems and the linguistic practices that emerge within them. Courtroom discourse serves as a critical site for the interplay of language, power, and ideology, where the language used by legal professionals, judges, and witnesses shapes the outcomes of legal proceedings. Historically, courtroom discourse has transitioned from formal, archaic language to more accessible forms, reflecting broader societal changes and the increasing importance of clarity and persuasion in legal contexts. The language of the courtroom is not merely a vehicle for communication; it is a strategic tool employed to influence perceptions and outcomes. For instance, Aldosari and Khafaga (2020) highlight the role of persuasive language strategies, such as questioning and emotive language, in shaping courtroom narratives and influencing judicial decisions. Similarly, the complexity of courtroom discourse is that it encompasses various goals, ideologies, and identities that interact dynamically within the social context of trials (Liu et al., 2021). This complexity necessitates understanding the linguistic features that characterise courtroom interactions, as they are pivotal in the construction of legal realities. Interpreters face more challenges every time they are on the job. Most of these challenges affect new interpreters and even highly seasoned professionals. Various circumstances could occur during a job, increasing the challenges interpreters face, where they find it difficult to hear the speaker. It could be traced to bad interpreting equipment, a deficient sound system, the ineptitude of the technician, or a bad location of the interpreters (Racoma, 2018). So, in this subsection, similar challenges are addressed based on theoretical and empirical literature, ranging from a South African perspective to an international one.

One of the most frequent challenges for court interpreters can be the terminological precision of legal language because legal terms differ from everyday English (Hale, 2007). Other than legal language, court interpreters must have a wide range of vocabulary from various domains, such as forensic pathology, chemistry, and narcotics, in case any relevant expert witnesses speak about these issues in the court (Pérez-González & Susam-Saraeva, 2012).

The South African legal system still operates in English, which poses difficulties to legal practitioners in understanding these African Languages because the method of teaching this profession in higher learning institutions does not offer African languages under the field of law. Cote (2014) mentions that the role of the interpreter varies from court to court and may lead to problems caused by the improper expectations of interpreters in the courtroom. He further emphasises the issues of practicability that determine whether a person will have a trial in a language that he or she understands or is allowed to have the proceedings interpreted in that language. He has alluded that it has been established that the only languages for which an interpreter would not necessarily be used are English and Afrikaans.

Frishberg (1990) moves further to explain how to deal with problems arising in the interpreting process. He believes the use of metaphorical language constitutes a problem for the interpreter, especially if the interpreter cannot think of a good equivalent in the target language. He suggests that since metaphors in one language may not work in the other, the interpreter needs to look for equivalent expressions rather than trying to hold tight to the image of the metaphor. In the case of literary allusion, interpreters should add the citation of an author or work, especially if it is not well known to speakers of another language.

Another challenge for the interpreter is when the speaker has made a visible error. Interpreters, at this point, can correct the errors in interpreting. In some situations, the interpreter might come across a vague or ambiguous message that he/she wants to change into a clear one in the target language. Mikkelson (2000) highlights the challenge imposed on court interpreters in criminal and penal cases where they are asked to accurately interpret the witnesses' testimony. She believes that interpreting on the witness stand is particularly stressful since court interpreters should be very careful to preserve the impact of the testimony in their interpretation to convey an accurate testimony.

Usadolo and Kotzé (2015) attest that court interpreters encounter a huge daily challenge when interpreting new words, terms, or concepts they are unfamiliar with. They give an example of an interpreter who stated that there had been a recurrence of such difficulties in courts, where an accused or witness used words that were unfamiliar, mixing with the standard language; moreover, South Africa's courts do have interpreters for some local languages, but there have been complaints about the quality of their training and work. So, this imposes a huge challenge in this field of courtroom interpreting because some cases will be delayed due to the unavailability of a relevant interpreter.

Furthermore, Docrat and Kaschula (2019) highlight that even though all languages are used in courtrooms, some legal practitioners, such as lawyers, are inclined to speak English. This is supported by the data, which was collected by Legal Aid South Africa. The function of Legal Aid South Africa is to provide legal aid to those who cannot afford their own legal representation. Their clients are already vulnerable economically; their inability to communicate fluently in English disadvantages them further. Subsequently, in their study conducted at Legal Aid, it was found that only 27% of state aid applicants in criminal cases speak, read, and write English at a satisfactory level. An average of 54.2% of applicants in criminal cases were found to have little or no knowledge of English as a medium of communication. In addition, they found that out of 100 legal practitioners, only 20.3% of South African citizens speak both Afrikaans and English at home, and 26.3% speak both at home. Legal Aid South Africa's study indicated that most clients spoke isiZulu, isiXhosa, or Afrikaans as their home languages.

According to Mikkelson (2016), court interpreters are required to enter an oath to interpret faithfully, and the system bestows significant weight to such oath swearing. However, 'no amount of oath swearing can guarantee high quality interpreting from an interpreter who does not have the necessary competency. From what the author states, it is a misconception that many people have about people who work with language; it could be the translator or interpreter. This study has put forward the competency issue because even mere communication officers claim to be interpreters in courtrooms.

Usadolo and Kotzé (2014) conducted further research on the issues of quality interpreting by examining the challenges posed by cross-border languages on foreign African court interpreting practices. Among the languages observed in the study are Chisena, spoken in Mozambique, Malawi, and Zambia, and Afrikaans, spoken widely in South Africa and Namibia. They further point out that the interpreters may not be adequately informed about the prevailing socio-cultural issues in the home country of the accused, especially when the accused is from a Lusophone country and the interpreter is from an Anglophone country. Another potential challenge identified in this regard is the different orthographies used for the Malawian and Mozambican varieties of Chisena. The two varieties have phonetically similar words but are spelt differently, which may challenge the interpreter. They emphasise that court interpreters should be well-informed about relevant circumstances in the countries in which the cross-border languages are spoken, and argue that the interpreter should conduct a pre-trial interview with the accused to be able to interpret from the source language (SL) into the target language (TL).

Cases in which language disputes emerged in the courtroom

These impracticalities have led courts in two judgments, Matomela and Damoyi, to suggest to the Department of Justice and Constitutional Development that one language of record should be adopted for the entire country to aid in administering justice. According to Davis et al. (2004), in Damoyi, 'sanity' would point to the English language for such a role. The Department has approved this proposal; however, a judgment against this policy may have delayed its implementation.

On the other hand, the problem of practicality was also examined by the court in *State v Pienaar* (2004). The judge found in that case that the State would not be able to meet the practicability test if it were to deny the use of Afrikaans in Northern Cape courts, where 72% of cases in those courts were conducted in Afrikaans. The costs involved, as well as the obligations of parity of languages in Section 6 of the Constitution, would make any practicality argument fall as a failure on the part of the Department of Justice to not correctly support the language needs of the Northern Cape as per their constitutional obligations. It has been argued that the judiciary cannot hide behind the facade of practicability to allow the continuation of the dominance of English and Afrikaans in the judiciary, forever leaving Africa.

As it stands now, South Africa's criminal justice system is still in a state of transition, and most of the actors in the legal system have little to no knowledge of the nine official indigenous languages spoken by most of their defendants. This is especially true of the high judiciary, i.e., the High Courts and above, where reviews and appeals of magistrate decisions are heard. Also, there are incredible cost burdens that all spheres of the public sector are currently facing. These costs may prohibit interpreting records and translating documents used in court.

There is an inaccuracy that the courtroom faces in terms of language, which has a negative effect on the court proceedings; this was demonstrated in the case of Paralympic Oscar Pistorius. Ms Michelle Burger, the state's first witness, requested to speak in Afrikaans. There appear to be differing explanations of why an interpreter was not easily accessible, but when one was obtained, the witness apparently had to revise the interpreter's translation. State prosecutor Gerrie Nel was accused of mouthing remarks to the translator to help her translate from Afrikaans to English.

Schafer (2012) in *News24* argues that it is just intolerable that trained interpreters for trials are not readily accessible. Witnesses giving testimony are painful enough; explaining their own evidence or using a language other than their own tongue is unforgivable. It may also be harmful to the witness, who may be mistakenly cited, and to the accused if the evidence incriminates him/her if it is incorrectly translated. It begs the question of whether the witness is unable to grasp the translation and, hence, is unaware that the testimony is being transmitted incorrectly.

The other point is that many police officers, who are not trained as interpreters/translators, wrongly interpret/translate the information of the accused from one language to another, which brings unfair judgment. Lastly, the language barrier really affects the effective delivery of justice because the courtroom language prevents the accused from fully understanding the legal proceedings. Scholars such as Moeketsi (2002) and Eades (2010), who have extensively investigated this problem, shed some important light on the issue. They all concur that suspects who are provided with non-partisan, unqualified, untrained interpreters/translators can bear serious implications for the practice. As such, this type of malpractice has the potential for miscarriage of justice. It is worth mentioning that this type of malpractice in the criminal justice system has a long history in South Africa, dating back as far as the Apartheid era.

Research methodology

This study is qualitative because it involves lived experiences in the context of courtroom discourse. It attempts to understand and thoroughly examine the thoughts or ideas of individuals or groups that are ascribed to a social or human problem (Creswell, 2014). This study used an ethnographic case study design.

Ethnography was the chosen research design for this study as it allowed for an in-depth examination of interpreters' roles, behaviours, and interactions within the complex social and institutional context of the courtroom. By engaging in participant observation, interviews, and analysis of relevant documents, the researchers gained nuanced insights into the communicative dynamics and cultural practices that shaped interpreting in legal settings. For instance, Tester (2021) conducted an ethnographic study exploring deaf interpreters' perceptions of their roles and positioning within the courtroom, highlighting the value of this approach in capturing the intricacies of interpreter-mediated interactions. Similarly, ethnographic methods were employed to study various aspects of courtroom interactions, providing rich, contextualised understandings that would have been unattainable through other research designs (Scheffer, 2001). Therefore, ethnography provided a comprehensive framework for investigating the multifaceted nature of courtroom interpreting.

Sample, and sampling procedure

The study employed a non-probability sampling approach, with two sampling techniques from which participants were chosen. Purposeful and convenient sampling were used. This study included 20 participants from the Polokwane High Court: ten courtroom interpreters, five presiding officers, four prosecutors, and one court manager.

Data collection

Semi-structured interviews were employed to collect data from the court personnel identified in the sample above. All the participants were asked pre-planned questions, the majority of which were open-ended. Direct observation was also used to gather necessary information for the study as the researchers took time to visit and observe court sessions at the Polokwane High Court. According to Lebese (2013), courtroom observation is used to assess whether what court interpreters consider to be translating is indeed what they do in practice. The observation involved systematically recording observed occurrences or behaviour in their natural setting. The researchers also gathered and analysed all necessary documents in courtroom discourse. Such documents included the Constitution of South Africa and interpreters' transcripts.

Data collection procedures were implemented to ensure accuracy and reliability in courtroom interpreting research. First, member checking was used, where participants were given the opportunity to review their interview transcripts to confirm that their responses had been accurately captured and interpreted (Creswell & Poth, 2018). Any discrepancies or misinterpretations were clarified and adjusted accordingly. Second, peer debriefing was conducted, where fellow researchers reviewed the data collection process, coding framework, and preliminary findings to identify potential biases or inconsistencies (Lincoln & Guba, 1985). Third, triangulation was employed by comparing data from multiple sources – semi-structured interviews, courtroom observations, and document analysis – to validate findings and ensure consistency across different data sets (Patton, 2002). Lastly, audit trails were maintained, documenting all data collection and analysis procedures to enhance transparency and allow for external verification of the research process.

Data analysis method

In this ethnographic study, informant selection was conducted through purposeful and convenient sampling, ensuring that key courtroom personnel, including interpreters, presiding officers, prosecutors, and the court manager, were included to provide diverse perspectives on language challenges. Before formal data collection, a pilot study was conducted to refine the semi-structured interview questions, ensuring clarity, relevance, and the ability to elicit in-depth responses (Creswell & Poth, 2018). The piloting process helped identify ambiguities and improve question-wording to enhance data reliability. During data analysis, thematic coding was used to categorise responses into key themes, such as challenges in meaning equivalence, dialectal variations, and strategies for mitigating interpretation difficulties. Codes were developed based on patterns emerging from participant responses and courtroom observations, allowing for a structured analysis of linguistic challenges in courtroom discourse (Braun & Clarke, 2006).

Presentation of results

The results below were obtained from the interview responses, and observations carried out at the site of the study. Language is a complicated subject, especially when it occurs in a diversified environment such as South Africa, which is multicultural and multilingual. In recent years, it received a magnitude of population from other countries, which increased the linguistic challenges, adding more to what already existed historically. So, the legal fraternity in South Africa has been operating in two languages, which are Afrikaans and English, which could be the language of records, until the former chief justice declared English as the only language of records.

The following questions were asked in that order, which in turn created the sub-themes upon which the results were presented, interpreted, and analysed.

1) What are the challenges of linguistic diversity in courtroom interpretation in South African courts?
2) To what extent does the existence of many languages in one province affect the quality of courtroom interpreting in the Limpopo High Court?
3) Do court interpreters experience challenges related to meaning of expressions due to closeness of source language messages to the isiNdebele Nguni language variety?
4) Does South Africa have international courtroom interpreters to cater for foreign nationals working and living in the country?
5) What is the influence of interprovincial linguistic migration in courtroom interpreting?
6) How do you mitigate the language challenges in your courtroom?

The respondents are summarised as follows: the Court Manager (**CRTMNR**), Court Magistrate (**CM**), Court Prosecutor (**CP**), and Court Interpreter (**CI**).

Exploring the challenge of linguistic diversity in courtroom interpreting

- Question 1. What are the challenges of linguistic diversity in courtroom interpreting in South African Courts?

South Africa has 12 official languages, with numerous dialects and variations within each. This creates a complex scenario where interpreters need to be proficient in multiple languages and understand the nuances of different dialects.

One court interpreter stated that our languages (referring to African languages) are not in-depth, so it becomes a challenge to some of the interpreters. Another point made is that these languages have many idioms. The interpreter (**CIF2**) contends that English is straightforward compared to these languages. African languages are full of figurative speech and are culturally influenced; therefore, as the principle of translation studies, one of the requirements needed from the translator/interpreter is to be competent in both the source text and target text.

Moreover, the findings revealed that native languages are tricky for people who are supposed to speak fluently. However, the challenges in the courtroom are that participants, particularly the accused or witnesses, use figurative language or idioms that most court interpreters find difficult to interpret from target text to source text. They further claimed that most interpreters find it more difficult to express themselves in their native language than in English; one interpreter, **CIM5**, posited that:

> 'Our native languages use more idioms than English because English is straight to the point; our languages use idioms to express something, but English is more straightforward; if one works in another language, one needs to explain more than in English.'

Furthermore, another interpreter concurred with the above participant on the issue of words, in that some of the challenges that arise are because of the diversity they find themselves in due to the culture and traditions found in South Africa. He attested to the issue of word equivalence and their semantic meaning. Then, alluded dialects in the same province are part of the cause of the challenges that are faced at their workstations. **CIM7** mentioned:

> '... of diverse as South African townships are, one will find that people will use one word, yet they mean different things or sense of proverbs the person from the Soshanguve township uses. The proverb is quoted as the same person from Mafikeng, yet the interpretation of that proverb is different; the language challenge in the courtroom around that circle whereby people are using one name means different things using the same word.'

The Bill of Rights (BOR) establishes specific language rights in Sections 9, 29(2), 30, and 35(3)(k) within disciplines to provide practical implementation and the realisation of Section 6. Section 35(3)(k) of the Constitution provides that the accused people have the right to be tried in a language that they understand, and where it is impractical to do so, proceedings are to be interpreted accordingly. **CIF1** added that in the courtroom, they are required to use English, especially between them and the presiding officers; however, the accused and witnesses are obliged to apply the abovementioned Act, which allows them to use the language they understand better.

> '... because normally, in court, we use English as the main language, but each accused has their own language, and they have the right to use their own home language. That's the reason we use various people speaking more than one language in court as interpreters.'

Language-related challenges in courtroom interpreting

- ### *Meaning and equivalence*
  - Question 2. Do court interpreters experience challenges of meaning variance due to language varieties?

The third major finding on languages revealed that terminologies and meanings of words are spoken by different people from the same area. This becomes a challenge to courtroom interpreters because one will battle to understand the accused, as the witnesses are from the region, but they speak the same words in a different way. It further indicates that dialects become a factor in terms of meaning and explanation.

If the interpreter is not aware of that, it becomes a challenge, and that could result in wrong messages to the court. Such challenges are specific to South African languages and particular words, which they find difficult to get meanings and equivalences for. In addition, one said that bombastic words are one of them, and another one alluded that some words do not exist in other languages, for example, as was shown by **CIM5:**

> 'There are some words that have so many meanings; I can even give an example. I can say "*serathane*" in Sepedi is a "bastard" or a "person who does not progress in life", and the other meaning is "the person who gives birth while still breastfeeding".'

Moreover, this implies that these challenges are concurrently appearing in every court due to the movement of people who travel from one province to another. This is according to one of the participants (**CIM1**) agreeing that every province experiences similar challenges due to geographical factors. He further said that the previous arrangement of black communities that created Bantustans contributed a lot. As a result, the country still experiences tribal and linguistic demarcations. Moreover, this further affects interpretation, especially in the lower courts, because it is where most of the people appear to address their wrongdoings.

Moreover, a court prosecutor (**CPF1**) concurred with a similar view on the challenges that the court faces regarding language, stating that regional dialects also complicate things further since an interpreter's vocabulary is limited to a specific jurisdiction. This implies that an interpreter lacks more words that are spoken in other districts, so if he/she misses that word, no one could be aware of whether the word is interpreted correctly or not.

> 'I say, if we have an interpretation that a certain word that is used regularly to a certain jurisdiction, for instance, here "*tubatse*", referring to the word "*bitch*" or someone who is more after men or "*kobane*" from where I come, it won't be familiar with myself, so it only affects those who are not within the jurisdiction who do not reside within the jurisdiction of that area (dialects), yes.'

Usadolo and Kotzé (2015) attest that court interpreters encounter a huge daily challenge when having to interpret new words, terms, or concepts they are unfamiliar with. They give an example of an interpreter who stated that such difficulties had recurred in courts, where a defendant or witness used unfamiliar words mixed with the standard language. The challenges revealed by this study indicate that interpreters who cannot interpret foreign languages face great challenges.

- *Interference with isiNdebele*
  - Question 3: Do court interpreters experience challenges of meaning due to closeness with the isiNdebele Nguni language variety?

The third finding revealed that Limpopo Province faces issues related to isiNdebele; this language is one of the minority languages that is spoken in eastern Mpumalanga. Representatives of this language in other provinces, like Limpopo, are scarce, where most people would claim to speak other Nguni languages to accommodate the minority group. When they are arrested, all participants struggle with their language, as concurred by **CIM1,** who claimed that:

> 'Locally, we have challenges with the isiNdebele and foreign languages because of the influx of people into the country; when one arrests those people, one does not even know which language they speak.'

A similar view from the other participants comes from the prosecutors and presiding officers, who concur with **CIM7** and **CIM5**, asserting that the culturally specific equivalence reveals that this issue does not affect only courtroom interpreters because other officials are affected. That is why the prosecutor (**CPM1**) claims that sentiments from interpreters and certain words become challenges to interpreters. This implies that some courtroom interpreters are not rich in language, specifically language which is utilised in the courtroom as shown below:

> 'Yeah, they have challenges with dialects and jargon as they use it in court. One finds that the interpreter cannot interpret fruitfully in Polokwane, where language is used in a unique way. This is not to say that the person is not competent, but it is because of the dialect. Yes, and again, the language commonly used in court refers to it as jargon and some interpreters do not all follow it.'

In addition, one presiding officer noted that when the language has few interpreters in the province, the courtroom interpreter for that variety is outsourced from Gauteng or Mpumalanga. As a result, court cases must be postponed until the court acquires that interpreter.

- *The inter-lingual challenges faced by foreign interpreters in South Africa*
    - Question 4. Does South Africa have international courtroom interpreters to cater for foreign nationals working and living in the country?

South African courtrooms do not exclude foreign languages, as foreign nationals flock to the country for greener pastures. So, some of them find themselves being on the other side of the law. There are many cases of foreign nationals who cannot speak the two main languages in South African courtrooms. Economically, South Africa is comparatively regarded as the powerhouse of Africa. This has lured foreign African migrant workers from other southern African countries, such as Zimbabwe, Botswana, Malawi, Lesotho, Zambia, and Mozambique, in search of better job opportunities. So, the presence of some of these immigrants in the country is not without linguistic-legal consequences. On a daily basis, news of the occurrence of crimes committed by foreign immigrants in South Africa is reported in the media.

The presiding officer (magistrate) and the court manager were of the view that foreign languages are a challenge in the courts that they are presiding over. All the prosecutors and magistrates agree that these languages, especially Shona and Chichewa, are the ones who appear the most in their cases. This is caused by the influx of foreign nationals into South Africa, especially undocumented ones, who find themselves behind bars for that reason, as they do not have papers.

From the researchers' observation, most foreign nationals claim to understand English, and some understand local languages; however, at some point, they get stuck. Therefore, the case must be postponed so that the court can get suitable interpreters for that language. Therefore, the South African government is forced to appoint court interpreters who speak these foreign languages to come and assist with the language issues so that they can speed up cases. **CIM2** acknowledged that it is a challenge to service a case involving foreign nationals since the law allows them to be tried in a language they understand. He said:

> 'Sometimes, I am forced to use two languages, more especially in my case; if one finds that the person is Malawian, then there are different languages in Malawi. I find that the accused comes from a certain region in Malawi, and then I fail to specifically accommodate the accused. So, I can speak Chichewa, but some will claim they speak Yahu and Tonga, some of the most popular languages in Malawi.'

- *Movement of South Africans across provinces*
    - Question 5. What is the influence of interprovincial linguistic migration in courtroom interpreting?

Whilst there are 12 official languages in South Africa, it does not mean they are all spoken with the same level of proficiency across the country. Limpopo is one of the provinces that is dominated by linguistic diversity, particularly the three official languages: Sepedi, Xitsonga, and Tshivenda. The contribution that is made by language, translation, and interpreting in the courtroom is a huge one, because the verdict of the case outcome relies on the words that are spoken during the proceedings.

Due to the movement of people in search of better living and exposure, all 12 official languages have a chance of being encountered in one province. Since Limpopo is further north, it is unlikely to find fluent speakers of isiZulu or Setswana, for example, among courtroom interpreters, yet native speakers of these languages are available and can commit crimes. Courtroom interpreters acknowledged that they had to bring assistance from Gauteng and other provinces to help with cases where language was a challenge.

In addition, according to the court manager, the issue of freedom of movement causes language to be complex within legal courts because, from the view of this court, they were formed under the influence of the Bantustan policy, so now everybody is everywhere with their own languages. therefore, when arriving in the courtrooms, it becomes complex because some should be strictly using English, as per language policy of their profession, and one should be the one who is facilitating all the languages in court. Therefore, **CIM1** asserted that the background given to this question explains that everybody has the right to move freely and speak whatever language they are comfortable with, so all provinces are experiencing similar challenges when it comes to courtroom interpreting,

> 'Yes, everywhere, today, as we speak, everybody has the right to speak whatever they want to, so in Limpopo, there are Xhosas, Swati, and all nationalities today. They are just like Gauteng did not like before when they were concentrating on one language during the Bantustan, one goes to Rustenburg and finds that there is Setswana. and isiZulu at the mines.'

The conclusion that the interpreter drew involves what the previous interpreter said; the assertion is that people are moving from one place to another, so these challenges will arise from time to time since the population is mixed, with different cultures, traditions, and languages. **CIF2** said:

> 'Yeah, they are because people immigrate all the time, and they are from different provinces; people from the Eastern Cape want to live in Limpopo, so challenges are there all over because immigration is all that is happening... Looking for green pastures, people who want to survive.'

The term 'courtroom discourse' encompasses many kinds of spoken and written language: the verbal interaction in a trial among all participants (judges, lawyers, witnesses, defendants, etc.), judges' instructions to juries, sentencing, lawyer talk, depositions, testimonies, and evidence. Whether the focus is on spoken language in the courtroom or on written documents, the idea of the courtroom assumes interaction among participants (S v Doty, 2010: 20).

- *Ways to address these language challenges in courtroom interpreting*
  - Question 6. How do you mitigate the language challenges you encounter in your work interpreting in court?

When an organisation or institution faces a challenge that could affect its operation from time to time, a turnaround strategy should mitigate the effects of such challenges. In legal institutions such as courtrooms, if there is no interpreter, it is the duty of that court to ensure that the accused is represented in the language of choice to avoid violating criminal procedure acts. So, this sub-theme is built on how challenges are managed by all parties involved if they do arise.

Prosecutor participants acknowledged that there are indeed challenges, and if they arise, there are processes to be followed so those challenges are resolved. One of the procedures that participants indicated is the postponement of the case and trying to seek a relevant interpreter from other courts. They go as far as out of the province to ensure that the rights of the accused are not violated. The response that **CPM1** made highlighted that in such instances, the court interpreters prepare ahead of the court cases. They are also given charge sheets so that they can see how they will execute the tasks. He has shown that based on his experience since he has been in court.

> 'How they do that, I think the experience *ya ka* court *ge ba etla* everyday *ba botšiša*, study most of them *o kraya motho wa gona a prepera* ahead , if you are going to have a trial, *o checka* charge sheet *go re* what is been charged with *go re ke tlo* interpreter *eng eng, go diregileng,* let's say for example accident *wa checka* what act yes charge *ya yona e tswa go yona* things like that (From the experience I have, I see most of them prepare ahead by studying, before the seating of the trial, with a hint of what will be happening, for example, accident case).'

To emphasise that, **CTMNR** added that to mitigate the challenge, they go to the database to search for registered casual interpreters who can interpret the language that the court requests.

> 'If we have a person like Shona, the department is paying money for those services for those casual interpreters who are being registered on our database so that they can come and assist in those different languages.'

In their responses, the presiding officers alluded that if the court does not have that interpreter, the case will be postponed, giving the court a chance to get an interpreter for the accused. However, this could violate criminal procedure acts because in case of failure by the court to provide an accused with an interpreter within 72 hours, the accused may be released. **CMGRTF1** attested to that by saying:

> 'The court requests that the state provide an interpreter so that the case can continue. Secondly, we put the case on hold until we arrange the interpreter. For instance, we outsource interpreters for foreign languages.'

Another presiding officer (**CNGTM1)** emphasised, echoing the participant above, that, indeed, something is done to manage the challenges that arise in courtrooms during proceedings regarding interpreting.

> 'We managed to deal with the language challenges as we normally do. In the first appearance, we try to get a date from the interpreter who speaks a certain

> language and gives us an available closer date, as we do not want our accused persons to stay in custody for more than seven days.'

However, it emerged from all the responses from the participants that the processes and procedures explained by courtroom interpreters that they mitigate these challenges differently. Interpreters always have principal and chief interpreters amongst them. They are those who oversee all the language-related issues with the court. So, interpreters, in their views, always stipulate that such matters are reported to their seniors. Moreover, **CITM1** reported one of the ways they manage these challenges as follows:

> 'Normally what we do, we consult other courts where those are in abundance to give us one of the people to come and help us here because those cases just come once, twice, like sign language, for example, I give sign language as much as they want to bring it to the fore but there is only on the rare occasion where one finds that there is sign accused or witness, so one has to put them on standby and put them on service level agreement, but I have encouraged the department to employ some of the people who speak sign language. Where the problem comes from cannot be able to be assessed by them because one does not know the language oneself. However, we rely much on DeafSA, which entered into a service agreement with the department; those must be employed via DeafSA. We do that, but what about the people who are arrested at the police station? Who will ask us to come and assist with the statement? At the end of the day, we should use one person in court. That creates a conflict of interest.'

In addition, **CIM5** states if such matters arise, an interpreter does not try to interpret something that he/she is not knowledgeable about because this process is not all about the interpreter, but all parties involved. He said:

> 'One sees when one interprets the most things that must not be done as a court interpreter; one must not try to interpret to the court or to the witness something one is not certain or understanding of what has been said. The only way to deal with that is to understand by asking for clarity from the speaker so that one can be on the same page with the speaker. The speaker gets clarification from the interpreter.'

The challenges identified and discussed above need to be addressed so that they do not result in negative consequences. The findings in this study revealed that these challenges are part of mitigation that is initiated by the court to ensure that the rights of the accused are not violated. It reveals that the court case cannot proceed if the relevant interpreter is not available. Michael (2016) asserts that in cases where an accused person does not understand the official language of the court, an interpreter must be provided for them without any expense. Goodrich (1987) states that the interpreter must interpret correctly to the accused person anything said in the language they do not understand. Simultaneously, there should be an adequate interpretation provided to the court, communicating anything said by the accused person. Another way to address these challenges is to give all languages equal opportunity to be presented in courtrooms; if the court continues to give English a higher status, there is no way that other languages will enjoy parity in the courtroom. It is the requirement of the Constitution that every language used in court should enjoy equal status.

Conclusions and recommendations

Language challenges can arise in any courtroom, and they may occur anywhere in the world. In South Africa, language is a right; all citizens can express themselves in a language they can comprehend. The average response from the interpreter shows that, indeed, there is a solution if the court had to consider multilingualism. The impacts of language use in the courtroom range from positive to negative. Subtle differences in dialects within the same language can pose challenges for interpreters. Accurately conveying the intended meaning and ensuring all parties understand the nuances of the spoken language is crucial. The contribution made by language, translation, and interpreting in the courtroom is huge because the verdicts of case outcomes rely on the words spoken during the proceedings. Nothing in the courtroom should be taken for granted because someone's freedom depends on that.

South African higher learning institutions, most of which still exclude African indigenous languages, still do not offer African languages as part of law programmes and courses, which is why we still have legal professionals who are unable to converse in these languages. However, in previous programmes, Latin was included, which every legal professional was required to know. That is one of the many factors that contribute to multilingualism; if these languages are treated similarly to Latin, multilingualism could be on the rise.

This research has illustrated that the issue of language in legal proceedings is either an afterthought or considered insignificant. Not all languages have readily available legal terminology, making it difficult for interpreters to convey the precise meaning of legal concepts and procedures. This can lead to confusion and misinterpretations, potentially impacting the outcome of a case. Expert evidence presented in court is confined to ballistics, entomology, and pathology, amongst others, with the exclusion of forensic linguists. There is a misconception when it comes to language analysis (the analysis of language through documents, text messages, language rights, and other forms of evidence) that all police officers, legal practitioners, and judicial officers are experts in the field and possess the necessary expertise to assume the role of a forensic linguist.

Prosecutors and magistrates lacked knowledge of the principle of culture and African languages; it is a risk to deploy a member of the NPA and/or the JSC who lacks knowledge of the cultural background of their jurisdiction. It will be risky when the interpreter is included. The tendency to circulate members of the court (prosecutors, magistrates, and interpreters) who lack knowledge about community members results in ramifications that could lead to an unsatisfying conclusion, and, potentially, wrongful arrest.

The challenges that arise mostly occur linguistically, unbeknownst of both courtroom interpreters and legal professionals. They can only be identified by a person who understands language practice and knows what multilingualism is. Court interpreters are often surprised when you, a researcher, speak about this subject; it is a clear indication that they lack knowledge of the language issues that could put an accused in jail. Misinterpreted evidence or statements can have grave consequences, potentially leading to wrongful convictions or acquittals.

Recommendations

The Department of Justice and Constitutional Development should provide extra training to interpreters so that they can learn other African languages, especially all South African ones, to address the shortage of interpreters in courtrooms. Equipping interpreters with specialised legal knowledge, cultural sensitivity, and ethical guidelines is crucial.

Having a bilingual language policy at universities, where that language is an African language, is possible, and the University of KwaZulu-Natal and some universities in Canada use models that can be emulated. Universities should teach law students and those studying safety and security in African languages, just as they do for language practice and linguistics, and must include a programme that involves African languages. Encouraging the development of legal terminology in various languages can bridge the gap in available resources. Ensuring interpreters possess the necessary skills and qualifications can enhance the quality of interpretation.

Furthermore, foreign languages must be taught in South African institutions since the country is struggling with immigration; newcomers keep coming, and some of them are engaged in criminal activity.

References

Aldosari, B. (2024). Questioning strategies in courtrooms. *World Journal of English Language*, 14(2), 376. https://doi.org/10.5430/wjel.v14n2p376

Aldosari, B. and Khafaga, A. (2020). The language of persuasion in courtroom discourse: a computer-aided text analysis. *International Journal of Advanced Computer Science and Applications*, 11(7). https://doi.org/10.14569/ijacsa.2020.0110744

Aristotle. (1991). *On rhetoric: A theory of civic discourse*. Kennedy, GA. (trans.). Oxford University Press.

Arzoz, X. (2012). Multilingualism in Legal Contexts. In Chapelle, CA. (ed.) *The Encyclopedia of Applied Linguistics.* Oxford: Wiley-Blackwell.

Arzoz, X. (2020). The Protection and Promotion of Language Equality in the EU: Gaps, Paradoxes, and Double Standards. *The European Union as Protector and Promoter of Equality*, 97–112.

Barasa, SN. (2005). Linguistic Internationalism: A Step towards Harmonious World Relations. *Proceedings of 17th-18th March on Across Borders: Benefiting from Cultural Differences, DAAD Regional Office in Africa, Nairobi*, 300–312.

Berk-Seligson, S. (2002). *The Bilingual Courtroom: Court interpreters in the Judicial Process.* University of Chicago Press.

Berk-seligson, S. (1990). Bilingual court proceedings: The role of the court interpreter. *Language in the Judicial Process*, 155–201.

Bless, C., Higson-Smith, C. & Kagee, A. (2006). *Fundamentals of Social Research Methods: An African Perspective.* Juta and Company Ltd.

Bless, C., Higson-Smith, C. & Sithole, S. (2013). Qualitative Analysis. In Bless, C., Higson-Smith, C. and Sithole, SL. (ed.) *Fundamentals of Social Research Methods: An African Perspective.* Juta & Company Ltd.

Blommaert, J. & Bulcaen, C. (2000). Critical discourse analysis. *Annual review of Anthropology,* 29(1): 447–466.

Bowen, GA. (2009). Document analysis as a qualitative research method. *Qualitative Research Journal,* 9(2): 27–40.

Braun, V. & Clarke, V. (2006). Using thematic analysis in psychology. *Qualitative Research in Psychology, 3*(2), 77–101.

Bujang, MA., Omar, ED. & Baharum, NA. (2018). A review on sample size determination for Cronbach's alpha test: a simple guide for researchers. *The Malaysian Journal of Medical Sciences: MJMS,* 25(6): 85.

Cameron, I. (2013). Procedural aspects. In Føllesdal, A., Peters, B. & Geir Ulfstein (ed.) *Constituting Europe: The European Court of Human Rights in a National, European and Global Context.* Cambridge University Press.

Chimhundu, H. (1992). Early missionaries and the ethnolinguistic factor during the 'invention of tribalism' in Zimbabwe. *The Journal of African History,* 33(1): 87–109.

Choshi, MK. (2009). Law and language: Solution for multilingual societies. *Direito, língua e cidadania global.*149–164.

Choshi, T. (2016). *The affordance of indigenous language parity in Limpopo and Mpumalanga magistrates' courts.* [Unpublished dissertation] University of Limpopo.

Cohen, D. & Crabtree, B. (2006). Qualitative Research Guidelines Project. Cape Town: Oxford University Press.

Cokely, DR. (1985). *Towards a sociolinguistic model of the interpreting process: Focus on ASL and English (Interpreting, sign language).* London: Georgetown University.

Conley, JM., Riner Conley, R. & O'Barr, WM. (1998). *Just words: Law, language, and power.* University of Chicago Press.

Cote, D. (2014). *The right to language use in South African criminal courts.* [Master's Thesis] Cape Town: University of Cape Town.

Coulthard, M. & Johnson, A. (2007). *An Introduction to Forensic Linguistics: Language in Evidence.* New York: Routledge.

Creswell, JW. (2014). *Research Design: Qualitative, Quantitative, and Mixed Methods Approaches* (fourth edition). SAGE Publications.

Creswell, JW. & Poth, CN. (2018). *Qualitative Inquiry and Research Design: Choosing Among Five Approaches* (fourth edition). SAGE Publications.

Creswell, JW. & Clark, VLP. (2017). *Designing and Conducting Mixed Methods Research.* Cape Town: SAGE publications.

Creswell, JW. & Poth, CN. (2016). *Qualitative Inquiry and Research Design: Choosing Among Five Approaches* (third edition). Cape Town: SAGE publications.

Culture & Language Press. (2014). *What is Interpreting?* Accessed @https://www.thecommunityinterpreter.com/what-is-interpreting. [Date accessed: 27 April 2022].

Davis, DM., Marcus, GJ. & Klaaren, JE. (2004). The administration of justice. *Annual Survey of South African Law,* 2004(1): 819–854.

De Vaus, D. (2001). *Research Design in Social Research.* Cape Town: SAGE Publications.

Derrett, JDM. (2021). Justice, equity and good conscience. In Anderson, JND. (ed.) *Changing Law in Developing Countries.* London: Routledge, 114–153.

Docrat, Z. & Kaschula, RH. (2019). Monolingual language of record: A critique of South Africa's policy directive. In Ralarala, M., Kaschula, R. and Heydon, G. eds., 2019. *New frontiers in forensic linguistics: themes and perspectives in language and law in Africa and beyond.* African Sun Media.

Doyiso, D. (2022). Endurence midinette koumassol dissake, language and legal proceedings: analyzing courtroom discourse in Cameroon. *Linguistique Et Langues Africaines*, (8(1)). https://doi.org/10.4000/lla.1040

Du Plessis, L. (2008). Affirmation and celebration of the 'religious Other' in South Africa's constitutional jurisprudence on religious and related rights: Memorial constitutionalism in action? *African Human Rights Law Journal,* 8(2): 376–408.

Du Plessis, T. (2008). The role of language legislation in national identity construction: A South African perspective. *Language Matters, 39*(2), 200–215.

Du, B. (2015). The silenced interpreter: a case study of language and ideology in the Chinese criminal court. *International Journal for the Semiotics of Law - Revue Internationale De Sémiotique Juridique*, 28(3), 507–524. https://doi.org/10.1007/s11196-015-9431-z

Duff, P. (2019). The prosecution service: Independence and accountability. In Duff, P. & Hutton, N (ed.) *Criminal justice in Scotland.* Routledge, 115–130.

Eades, D., 2010. *Sociolinguistics and the legal process.* Multilingual Matters.

Etikan, I. & Bala, K. (2017). Sampling and sampling methods. *Biometrics & Biostatistics International Journal,* 5(6): 00149.

Etikan, I., Musa, SA. & Alkassim, RS. (2016). Comparison of convenience sampling and purposive sampling. *American Journal of Theoretical and Applied Statistics,* 5(1): 1–4.

Farinde, R., Ojo, J. & Ogunsiji, Y. (2015). Declaratives and Control in Nigerian Courtroom Discourse. *English Language and Literature Studies*, 5(2). https://doi.org/10.5539/ells.v5n2p70

Frishberg, N. (1990). *Interpreting: An introduction.* RID Publications.

Fuller, WA. (2011). *Sampling Statistics.* London: John Wiley & Sons.

Gibbons, J. (2003). *Forensic Linguistics: An introduction to Language in the Justice System.* Oxford: Blackwell Publishing.

Goodrich, P. (1987). *Legal Discourse.* UK: Palgrave Macmillan.

Gorard, S. (2013). *Research Design: Creating Robust Approaches for the Social Sciences.* SAGE.

Gordon, A. & Bruce, D. (2016). *Transformation and the Independence of the Judiciary in South Africa.* The Centre for the Study of Violence and Reconciliation.

Gorman, GE., Clayton, PR., Shep, SJ. & Clayton, A. (2005). *Qualitative Research for the Information Professional: A Practical Handbook.* Facet Publishing.

Grutman, R. (2019). Multilingualism. In Baker, M. & Saldanha, G. (ed.) *Routledge Encyclopedia of Translation Studies.* Routledge: 341–346.

Gutt, E. (1998). Pragmatic aspects of translation: some Relevance-Theory Observations. *The pragmatics of translation,* 12:41.

Gutt, E. (1996). Implicit information in literary translation: A relevance-theoretic perspective. *Target. International Journal of Translation Studies,* 8(2): 239–256.

Hale, S. & Napier, J. (2013). *Research Methods in Interpreting: A Practical Resource.* London: A & C. Black.

Hale, S. (2007). *Community Interpreting.* Palgrave Macmillan.

Hale, S. (2004). *The Discourse of Court Interpreting: Discourse practices of the law, the witness and the interpreter.* Philadelphia: John Benjamins, 1-288.

Hale, S. (2008). Controversies over the role of the court interpreter. *Benjamins Translation Library,* 76: 99.

Hale, S. (2010). Court interpreting. In Coulthard, M. & Johnson, A. (ed.) *The Routledge handbook of forensic linguistics.* Routledge, 440.

Hanley, JA. (2016). Simple and multiple linear regression: sample size considerations. *Journal of Clinical Epidemiology,* 79:112–119.

Harling, K. (2012). An Overview of Case Study. *Available at* SSRN: https://ssrn.com/abstract=2141476 or http://dx.doi.org/10.2139/ssrn.2141476.

Heaton, DP., Schmidt-Wilk, J. & Travis, F. (2004). Constructs, methods, and measures for researching spirituality in organizations. *Journal of Organizational Change Management,* 17(1): 62 82.

Hlophe, JM. (2004). Receiving Justice in Your Own Language: the Need for Effective Court Interpreting in our Multilingual Society. *Advocate Journal,* 17(1): 42–47.

Igwenagu, C. (2016). *Fundamentals of research methodology and data collection.* London: LAP Lambert Academic Publishing.

Josselson, R. (1995). *Interpreting Experience.* Cape Town: SAGE.

Kajornboon, AB. (2004). Creating useful knowledge: A case study of policy development in e-learning at Chulalongkorn University Language Institute. [Dissertation] University of Melbourne, Faculty of Education.

Kaschula, RH. (2021). Languages as markers of identity in South Africa's multilingual legal landscape. *South African Journal of African Languages,* 41(1), 23–40.

Kaschula, RH. (2021). *Languages, Identities and Intercultural Communication in South Africa and Beyond.* Routledge.

Kruger, J. (2003). Book review: Research at Grass Roots: For the Social Sciences and Human Service Professions. AS de Vos (editor), H. Strydom, CB Fouché and CSL Delport. *Unisa*

Psychologia, 29(1):154–158.

Kryk-Kastovsky, B. (2006). Historical courtroom discourse: Introduction. *Journal of Historical Pragmatics, 7*(2), 163–179.

Kumar, R. (2014). *Research Methodology: A Step-by-Step Guide for Beginners* (fourth edition). SAGE Publications.

Ladzani, KY. (2014). Moral regeneration in the lives of Vhavenda youth through indigenous knowledge systems: applied ethnography of communication-based approaches with special reference to Tshivhenda. [Dissertation] University of South Africa.

Lakhotia, A. & Sterling, L. (1990). How to control unfolding when specializing interpreters. *New Generation Computing,* 8: 61–70.

Lebese, SJ. (2013). Courtroom interpreting and translation: A South African perspective. *Language Matters, 44*(2), 56–74.

Lebese, SJ. (2014). Do justice to court interpreters in South Africa. *Stellenbosch Papers in Linguistics Plus,* 43:183–206.

Lebese, SJ. (2013). The undefined role of court interpreters in South Africa. [Dissertation] University of South Africa.

Lebese, SJ. (2015). Formulation of court interpreting models: A South African perspective. *Stellenbosch Papers in Linguistics,* 44: 61–80.

Lincoln, YS. & Guba, EG. (1985). *Naturalistic Inquiry*. SAGE Publications.

Liu, K. & Guo, F. (2016). A review on critical discourse analysis. *Theory and Practice in Language Studies,* 6(5):1076.

Liu, W., Han, Z., Chen, H. & Ren, W. (2021). Discursive practice of Chinese criminal adjudication: a genre perspective. *Círculo De Lingüística Aplicada a La Comunicación*, 86, 69–80. https://doi.org/10.5209/clac.75496

Lyons, J. (1981). *Language and Linguistics.* Cambridge: Cambridge University Press.

Madiba, M. (1999). Multilingualism and Nation-building in the 'New' South Africa: problems and issues. *Language Matters*, Volume 30, Issue 1.

Mafuyeka, V. (2019). Language challenges in South African magistrates' courts: The role of courtroom interpreters. [Unpublished thesis] University of Pretoria.

Maree, J. (2020). An impact analysis of customs risk management processes in South Africa. [Dissertation] North-West University.

Maree, K. (2020). *First steps in research* (third edition). Van Schaik.

Maryns, K. (2012). Multilingualism in legal settings. In Martin-Jones, M, Blackledge, A. & Creese, A. (ed.) *The Routledge handbook of multilingualism.* Routledge: 313–329.

Mathers, NJ., Fox, NJ. & Hunn, A. (1998). *Surveys and questionnaires.* NHS Executive, Trent.

Matthews, I. (2009). The National Prosecuting Authority. *Criminal (in)justice in South Africa, Pretoria: ISS,* 99.

Matu, PM., Odhiambo, K., Adams, Y. & Ongarora, D. (2012). The court interpreters' role perception: The case of English-Dholuo interpreters in Subordinate Courts in Nyanza Province, Kenya. *Greener Journal of Social Sciences,* 2(4):121–126.

Maxfield, MG. & Babbie, ER. (2015). *Research Methods for Criminal Justice and Criminology.* Cengage Learning.

May, KA. (1991). Interview techniques in qualitative research: Concerns and challenges. In Morse, JM. (ed) *Qualitative nursing research: A contemporary dialogue*. SAGE:188–201.

Mbaabu, I. (1996). *Mother-tongue in education.* Cape Town: Lectern Publications.

Michael, CO. (2016). Communication of an interpreter and fair trial under Nigerian criminal justice system. *International Journal of Legal Discourse,* 1(1):213–233.

Michael, E. (2016). Language barriers in legal proceedings: The role of courtroom interpreters. *International Journal of Legal Studies, 8*(1), 45–60.

Mikkelson, H. (2000). *Introduction to Court Interpreting*. Manchester University Press.

Mikkelson, H. (1999). Court interpreting at a crossroads. *Proceedings of Annual Conference of the National Association of Judiciary Interpreters and Translators (NAJIT) – Washington.*

Mikkelson, H. (2016). *Introduction to Court Interpreting* (second edition). London: Taylor & Francis.

Moeketsi, R. & Wallmach, K. (2005). From Sphaza to Makoya!: A BA degree for court interpreters in South Africa. *International Journal of Speech, Language and the Law,* 12: 77–108.

Moeketsi, RH. (1999a). Discourse structure in a criminal trial of a magistrate's court. *South African Journal of African Languages,* 19(1): 30–38.

Moeketsi, R., 2002. Understanding the other: A case of mis-interpreting culture-specific utterances during alternative dispute resolution. In *Language in the Legal Process* (pp. 196-210). London: Palgrave Macmillan UK.

Mphasha, LE. & Mutele, TC. (2014). Challenges Facing the Accused in the Use of English Only in Criminal Court Proceedings: Experiences from the Vhembe District, Limpopo Province, South Africa. *Journal of Social Sciences,* 41(3): 385–394.

Mphasha, N. & Mutele, N. (2014). Courtroom interpreting in South Africa: Challenges and solutions. *South African Journal of Linguistics, 32*(3), 99–114.

Muhwasane, MM. (2020). Language flux: the decline in the use of taboos regarding pregnancy the birth among vhaVen a from a critical language awareness perspective. [Thesis] University of South Africa.

Natapoff, A. (2020). Criminal Municipal Courts. *Harvard Law Review,* 134:964.

Nieuwenhuis, J. (2007). Qualitative research designs and data gathering techniques. In Maree, K. (ed.) *First steps in Research.* Van Schaik: 70–97.

Ntlama, N. (2014). *The transformation of the South African judiciary: A measure to weaken its capacity?* Presentation at New York Law School's workshop Constitutional Rights.

Okal, BO. (2014). Benefits of Multilingualism in Education. *Universal Journal of Educational Research,* 2(3).

Ozolins, U. (2015). Ethics and the role of the interpreter. In Mikkelson, H. & Jourdenais, R (ed.) *The Routledge Handbook of Interpreting*. Routledge: 319–336.

Patrcik, A & Bhengu, C. (2023). Sign language officially becomes SA's 12th official language. Accessed @https://www.news24.com/news24/southafrica/news/sign-language-officially-becomes-sas-12th-official-language-20230719. [Date accessed: 02 August 2023.]

Patton, MQ. (2002). *Qualitative Research and Evaluation Methods* (third edition). SAGE Publications.

Pérez-González, L. & Susam-Saraeva, . (2012). Non-professionals translating and interpreting: Participatory and engaged perspectives. *The Translator,* 18(2):149–165.

Pérez-González, L. & Susam-Saraeva, . (2012). Non-professional interpreting and translation: State of the art and future avenues of research. *The Translator, 18*(2), 149–172.

Philister, YC. & Mwangi, PM. (2020) Linguistic challenges faced by the interpreter in presentation of litigants evidence in Kericho county, Kenya. *International Journal of Management Studies and Social Science Research*, Volume 2, Issue 2.

Piszcz, A. & Sierocka, H. (2020). The role of culture in legal languages, legal interpretation and legal translation. *International Journal for the Semiotics of Law – Revue internationale de Sémiotique juridique,* 33(3): 533–542.

Pöchhacker, F. (2010). Interpreting Studies. *Handbook of Translation Studies,* 1:158.

Pöchhacker, F. (2015). *Routledge Encyclopedia of Interpreting Studies.* Routledge.

Racoma, B. (2018). The challenges of courtroom interpretation: A global perspective. *Journal of Legal Linguistics, 10*(1), 67–85.

Racoma, B. (2018). Why Cultural Considerations Matter In Translating Content. *Day Translationsblog,* 20.

Ralarala, MK. (2012). A compromise of rights, rights of language and rights to a language in Eugene Terre'Blanche's (ET) trial within a trial: evidence lost in translation. *Stellenbosch Papers in Linguistics,* 41: 55–70.

Republic of South Africa (RSA). (2012). *Use of Official Languages Act 12 of 2012. Government Gazette,* 568(35742).

Republic of South Africa (RSA). (1995). *Pan South African Language Board Act 59 of 1995.* Pretoria: Government Printer.

Republic of South Africa (RSA). (2002). *National Language Policy Framework.* Pretoria: Government Printers.

Schafer, D. (2012). Criminal conviction rate: Lies, damned lies and statistics. *News24).*

Scheffer, T. (2001). *Exploring court hearings – Towards a research design for a comparative ethnography of criminal procedure*. Accessed @https://www.lancaster.ac.uk/fass/resources/sociology-online-papers/papers/scheffer-exploring-court-hearings.pdf

Seleskovitch, D. & Lederer, M. (1989). *Pédagogie raisonnée de l'interprétation.* Didier érudition Paris.

Shahbazi, M. & Rezaee, M. (2017). Reflection of ideology on translation: A critical discourse analysis perspective. *Journal of Applied Linguistics and Language Learning,* 3(4):97–101.

Shaheen-ul-Zaman, Khan, AU. & Ali, A. (2023). Play of Legalese in Witness Examination: A Forensic Perspective on Courtroom Discourse. *International Journal of Linguistics and Culture, 4*(2), 221–237. https://doi.org/10.52700/ijlc.v4i2.203

Shohamy, E. (2006). *Language Policy: Hidden Agendas and New Approaches*. Routledge.

Smith, K. (2002). Translation as secondary communication. The relevance theory perspective of Ernst-August Gutt. *Acta Theologica,* 2002(sup-2): 107–117.

Solan, LM. (2016). Interpreting Multilingual Laws: Some Costs and Benefits. *Brooklyn Law School, Legal Studies Paper* (443).

S v Doty (A143/2010) [2010] ZAWCHC 142 (19 August 2010)

State v Pienaar (2004)

Stern, L. (2011). Courtroom interpreting. In Malmkjær, K. & Windle, K. (ed.) *The Oxford handbook of translation studies.* Oxford Academic.

Struwig, FW. & Stead, GB. (2001). *Planning, Designing and Reporting Research.* Pearson Education.

Svongoro, PR. (2017). Court interpreting in Zimbabwe: a descriptive study of consecutively interpreted rape trials in regional magistrates' courts. [Unpublished Doctoral Dissertation] University of the Western Cape.

Tester, CA. (2021). Intralingual interpreting in the courtroom: An ethnographic study of Deaf interpreters' perceptions of their role and positioning. [Dissertation] Accessed @https://www.researchgate.net/publication/363518143_Intralingual_Interpreting_in_the_Courtroom_An_ethnographic_study_of_Deaf_interpreters%27_perceptions_of_their_role_and_positioning

Turi, J. (1992). *Language Policy and Linguistic Rights in the Legal System.* Cambridge University Press.

Turi, J. (1993). Legal language and linguistic diversity: Implications for justice. *International Journal of Legal Linguistics, 12*(2), 5–19.

Turi, J. (1992). *The Importance of the Conference Theme:'Language and Equality'.* Prinsloo, Karel. Proceedings of the Third International Conference of the International Academy of Language Law (IALL) held in South Africa.

Turi, J.G. 2012. Law, Language and the Multilingual State. In Brohy, C., du Plessis, T., Turi, J.G and Woehrling, J. (eds.). Law, Language and the Multilingual State. Proceedings of the 12th International Conference of the International Academy of Linguistic Law. Bloemfontein: Sun MeDIA. pp 269-290.

Usadolo, SE. & Kotzé, E. (2014). Cross-border languages and court interpreting in South Africa. *International Journal of Applied Linguistics, 24*(1), 88–103.

Usadolo, SE., & Kotzé, E. (2015). Challenges faced by court interpreters in South Africa: An applied linguistic perspective. *Southern African Linguistics and Applied Language Studies, 33*(1), 67–79.

Usadolo, SE. & Kotzé, E. (2014). Some interlingual communicative challenges for foreign African interpreters in South African courtrooms. *Stellenbosch Papers in Linguistics Plus,* 43(1): 345–357.

Usadolo, SE. & Kotzé, E. (2015). Communicative challenges of interpreting in cross-border languages in South African courtrooms. *South African Journal of African Languages,* 35(1): 57–65.

Usadolo, SE. (2010). Justice through language: A critical analysis of the use of foreign African interpreters in South African courtrooms. [Doctoral Dissertation] Cape Town: Nelson Mandela Metropolitan University.

Wesson, M. & Du Plessis, M. (2008). The transformation of the judiciary: Fifteen-year policy review. *Presidency of the Republic of South Africa.* Accessed @http://www.the presidency. gov. za/docs/reports/15year_review/jcps/transformation _judiciary.pdf. [Date accessed: 06 June 2022].

Williams, BA. (2002). Guilty Until Proven Innocent: The Tragedy of Habeas Capital Appeals. *JL & Pol.,* 18:773.

Xu, Z. & Zhou, Y. (2013). Relevance Theory and Its Application to Advertising Interpretation. *Theory & Practice in Language Studies,* 3(3); 1–15.

Yin, RK. (2003). Case study research design and methods third edition. *Applied social research methods series,* 5.

Zeisel, H., Kalven, H. & Buchholz, B. (1959). *Delay in the Court.* Little, Brown Boston.

12

'... TO HAVE THE PROCEEDINGS INTERPRETED IN THAT LANGUAGE': PROBING THE INCLUSION AND EXCLUSION OF INTERPRETING DURING COURT PROCEEDINGS, A CASE STUDY OF THE SENZO MEYIWA MURDER TRIAL

Nomfundo Mali

Introduction

The paper explores the inclusion and exclusion of interpreting during court proceedings about section 35(3)(k)'s reference to having the proceedings interpreted in the language of the accused. A specific focus is on the interpretation of the court proceedings. One is prompted to question if 'court proceedings' means the whole business of the court, or whether court proceedings are limited to cross-examination, including or excluding other conversations within the allocated space and time of the court proceedings. The time allocation for the interpreting practice during court proceedings in the posed question is of interest. The probing of the inclusion and/or exclusion and any other hindrances to the provision of interpreting within the allocated time and space is of importance.

The discussion is also founded on the observation that language rights are treated as synonymous with a privilege, and a lack of the observance of African languages' rights thereof:

> 'Language rights are enshrined in the South African Constitution of 1996 (Section 35 (3) (K)). However, this amounts to nothing more than a variety of rights, which resemble privileges rather than fundamental rights in the real sense of the word (Kaschula and Ralarala, 2004: 254–257). This allows leaders to negate the indigenous languages if they wish to do so, which further entrenches the hegemony of English, at least in the public domain.' (Kaschula et al., 2008)

The provision of interpreting in courts is among the rights afforded to the accused, a responsibility accounted for by the court interpreter. In the case of exclusion or inclusion by default, the fair practice of that right may be defined not as a right but a privilege.

Problem statement

A generic definition that captures the key aspects of interpreting is that it is essentially a multi-step process that includes receiving a message in one language, grasping its meaning and intent, and delivering it into another language. It is of essence, in other words, that the interpreter possesses technical, cognitive, and equivalence from the source language to the target language. Exclusion and (technical) inclusion of the interpreter can mean disabling the practice of those interpreting competencies and discriminating against the language right of the receiver or beneficiary.

All the South African courts are obligated by law to provide interpreting in the language of the accused during court proceedings. The service should be as efficient, accurate, and comprehensive as possible in order for the accused to fully participate and follow the proceedings. Usadolo and Kotze (2014: 346) affirm the central legislative role of interpreting in referring to Khoon (1990: 110) who:

> '… justifies why it is necessary to bridge communication barriers between diverse language groups in the courtroom. This is carried out by providing court interpreters to assist many South Africans and others who appear before the courts and who are not proficient in the main court languages (Afrikaans and English) used during the proceedings. This is clearly stipulated in the South African Constitution which states that "[e]very accused person has a right to a fair trial, which includes the right to be tried in a language that the accused person understands; or, if that is not practicable, to have proceedings interpreted in that language" (South African Constitution, 1996: section 35 [3(k)]).' (Usadolo & Kotze, 2014: 346)

The exclusion and inclusion of interpreting services in courts have been identified in most live-streamed court cases and even during physical visits in most South African courts. This somehow downplays the professional role of the interpreter. In some instances, such as in the Meyiwa Trial (CAS 2014 & 2019) there was an instance where the judge was reminded by the defense (Advocate Msholo) to allow the interpreter to interpret a witness statement (Zandile Kumalo) read in court without being interpreted. In this case, the judge even joked at the 'deliberate' exclusion that the interpreter must proceed to interpret so that he does not lose his job.

The right of the accused to have the proceedings interpreted in his/her language is violated in such occurrences where the inclusion of interpreting is considered an after-thought, not 'really' necessary, or only a job-saving mechanism. This study, therefore, concentrates on an analysis of the inclusion and exclusion of court interpreters during court proceedings and the impact of such irregularities with regard to a fair trial, using the Meyiwa Trial as a case study.

Objectives of the study

This chapter seeks to:

a) Investigate the timing of court proceedings if they begin when the judge enters the courtroom until he/she leaves the courtroom;
b) Explore the elements of court proceedings if they encompass all utterances, official or unofficial, by all formal court participants within the courtroom;
c) Examine whether the interpreter provides their services throughout the court proceedings in relation to the above two questions, including the number of interpreters per session or per day (e.g., with SASL it is two interpreters a day taking turns regularly);
d) Explore instances in the case where the interpreter does not adhere to interpreting throughout the court proceedings and the nature of the hindrances;
e) Investigate if the interpreting hindrances detected can be translated into a violation of the section under discussion, and ultimately to an unfair trial or limitation to access to justice for all.

Research questions

The article seeks to respond to the questions below:

a) Do court proceedings begin when the judge enters the courtroom and continue until he/she leaves the courtroom?
b) Do court proceedings encompass all utterances, official or unofficial, by all formal court participants within the courtroom?
c) Does the interpreter provide their services throughout the court proceedings in relation to the above two questions? (e.g., with SASL it is two interpreters a day taking turns regularly);
d) In the case where the interpreter does not adhere to interpreting throughout the court proceedings, what are the hindrances?
e) Can the interpreting hindrances be translated into a violation of the section under discussion, and ultimately to an unfair trial or limitation to access to justice for all?

The research design and methodology

The research paper follows the conversational methodological analysis approach, a type of qualitative research method and form of discourse analysis. The Authenticx (2023) describes conversation analysis as a methodological approach that studies communication through an analysis of the structure and organisation of conversation. It involves the systematic examination of verbal and nonverbal behaviours, such as turn-taking, pauses, and gestures, to understand how people communicate with each other. In line with the conversational analysis, the paper draws its data collection and analysis from secondary data collected from readily available online videos of the Meyiwa Trial. Also affirmed by Usadolo and Kotze's (2014) article of the methodology, they involved observations of proceedings in open courtroom sessions to establish the communicative roles of the main actors such as the magistrate, the prosecutor, the court interpreter, and the attorneys. Ahmad (2019) defines the qualitative research method as a process of naturalistic inquiry that seeks an in-depth understanding of social phenomena within their natural setting, focusing on the 'why' rather than the 'what' of social phenomena. The article examines the reasons or causes 'why' the interpreter is included and excluded during court proceeding contrary to section 35(6)(k) guiding inclusive provision for interpreting during court proceedings for a fair trial.

In the context of the Meyiwa Trial, the research focuses on the overall practice of interpreting in relation to interpreting covering all the communication in court. Observation of interpreting starts at the beginning of the court proceedings in the session conducted on each day selected for the purpose of analysis. Crossman (2021) refers to a systematic way of organising and conceptualising the research process, including the research question, data collection methods, analysis techniques, and interpretation of findings.

The article follows an exploratory research design described by universalteacher.com (2023) as aiming to find out ideas and insights, carried out to give a better understanding of a situation. Through exploratory research, researchers wish to generate hypotheses about what is happening in a situation. This method affirms the objective of exploring the intricacies of exclusion and inclusion of the interpreting process in the administration of justice with a specific interest in the Meyiwa Trial as a case study. The exploratory research design is further classified as case analyses, as it is a research method where researchers can understand a lot about a situation by exploring carefully chosen examples or cases of the phenomenon. In the case under review, the source language, also referred to as L1, is English. The target language, also referred to as L2, is isiZulu, and Sesotho is referred to as L2/3. During the Meyiwa Trial, there was an instance of two interpreters either taking turns to translate, or of one interpreter summarising the other interpreter's statements. For example, a court practitioner will ask a question in L1 to the accused followed by an interpretion in L2 (isiZulu), followed by Sesotho interpreting in L2/3. In some instances, it is just a summary after long back-to-back conversations, also called consecutive summary interpretation by Licoppe and Boéri (2021).

Literature review

The Constitution of the Republic of South Africa and the legislative framework on interpreting

By law, the provision of a court interpreter is a right according to section 35(5)(k)(3) of the Constitution, which states that 'every accused person has a right to a fair trial, which includes the right to be tried in a language that the accused person understands or, if that is not practicable, to have the proceedings interpreted in that language.' It is by means of this legislative intervention, where the language of the accused is not used to run the business of the court, that the role of the court interpreter emerges by constitutional default. Sections 6. (1) and (2) make provisions of such stating:

1) 'The official languages of the Republic are Sepedi, Sesotho, Setswana, siSwati, Tshivenda, Xitsonga, Afrikaans, English, isiNdebele, isiXhosa and isiZulu.
2) Recognising the historically diminished use and status of the indigenous languages of our people, the state must take practical and positive measures to elevate the status and advance the use of these languages.' (Republic of South Africa, 1996)

This affirms the official status of eleven spoken official languages in South Africa. Thus, these languages should all be afforded equal access in all spheres of government, which is not the case in the courts now. It is my view that the status of the fair trial is already impacted or affected by the failure or inability of the court to conduct the proceedings in the language of the accused despite the language being afforded the prestige of official status. Furthermore, section 6(2) affords mitigating provision and an alternative to ensure the elevation of the accused's language, in this instance that of the provision of interpreting in court. The central concern, then, is in the case where provisional mitigation is not fully adhered to due to the inclusion and exclusion of the interpreter during the proceedings. Thus, the aim of this article is to evaluate the impact on the status of a fair trial in relation to the provision of interpreting to the language of the accused.

Also contrary to sections 6(1) and (2) provisions is the former Chief Justice Mogoeng Mogoeng's prominent announcement in 2017 that English will be the only language of record in all South African courts. This has been debated by linguists, researchers, and on various platforms. The views expressed in the open letter by Bailey et al. (2017) posed an argument against the exclusion of African languages and Afrikaans in courts, including the implications to the litigants.

> 'Moreover, we question how this decision is constitutionally sound, with regards to an accused's S35(3)(k) constitutional language right. The alleged decision in our view negates the right to an interpretational right only, a decision we firmly believe discriminates unfairly against accused persons on grounds of language

> in terms of both Section 9(3) of the Constitution and the Promotion of Equality and Prevention of Unfair Discrimination Act with specific reference also to the requirement to promote diversity' (Bailey et al., 2017)

Despite the indictment of the exclusion of the indigenous languages in this announcement, for the purpose of this paper I will not dwell much on it.

The language policy of the Department of Justice and Constitutional Development on interpreting

Section 4 examines the role of the court interpreter and interpreting in relation to selected legislative obligations as it enables a fair trial. Section 4 on the objectives of the Department of Jutsice and Constitutional Development (DOJCD) language policy asserts the language rights of all South Africans in relation to access to justice. Subsection 4.1.2 refers to the promotion and equitable use of all 11 official spoken languages and further affirms its objectives in relation to the redress of the linguistic inequalities of the past in subsection 4.1.7. These provisions lay the foundation for a comprehensive and effective implementation of language rights within the justice system, including the right for efficient and comprehensive interpreting in the language of the accused throughout the proceedings. It is based on the above legislative prescripts that the role of interpreting in court is underscored in this article.

It is noted that despite the objectives setting instruction for equitable use of the official languages with African languages, it is not the case specifically with the provision of interpreting. Hence, the argument that in South Africa, there is no legislation defining the role of court interpreters. This has resulted in legal officials (magistrates and judges) forming their own opinions as to what the role of court interpreters is (Lebese, 2013). This is the case in the scenario where a court interpreter is excluded as seen in the Meyiwa Trial (Adv Msholold and Zandile Khumalo cross-examination reading of the sworn statement).

In section 14, I examine the application of 'language of court proceedings' in courts, wherein subsection 14.1 refers to,

> 'the use of official languages in court, including court interpretation services, court processes, court documents and recording of court proceedings, shall be regulated,
>
> consistent with section 171 of the Constitution, by the Rules of Court or any other
>
> applicable legislation.'

However, Section 171 of the Constitution does not provide a direct regulation or even an instruction for guidelines for court interpreting during court proceedings. It only states that 'Court procedures 171. All courts function in terms of national legislation, and their rules and procedures must be provided for in terms of national legislation' (Republic of South Africa, 1996). The fluid presentation of this provision further dilutes the role and the visibility of the interpreter in court. This invisible role is even more concerning in the Magistrates' Courts Act 32 of 1944 (1944) which provides the magistrate with a choice of whether to call upon an interpreter or not based on the opinion 'which not measurable nor can be quantified' that the accused is 'insufficient' in conversation:

> '... the onus on a magistrate to call a competent interpreter if he is of the opinion that the accused is not sufficiently conversant in the language in which the evidence is given, irrespective of whether it is one of the official languages (section 6(2)).' (*Migstrates' Courts Act 32,* 1944)

Exploring interpreting and the interpreter's time allocation: 'All Stand - Court Adjourns'

When foregrounding the interpreter's time for action, it is important to briefly outline the role of the interpreter. Agood court interpreter must have the ability to translate faithfully without adding to the questions asked or the answers given (Steytler, 1982). They must be completely impartial, take no personal interest in the outcome of the case, and remain unaffected by anything seen or heard. The phrase 'unaffected by anything' sums up the examination of the hindrances affecting the interpreter either by the act of exclusion or inclusion during the trial proceedings.

In seeking to investigate the alignment of interpreting with the timing of court proceedings, the chapter focuses on the time when the proceedings begin and the time when they end. Is it the time when the judge enters the courtroom until he/she leaves the courtroom? Most sources suggest that the pronouncement of the arrival/entrance of the judge or presiding officer signals that 'the court is in session'.

However, sections 4(2) and (3) of the practice guidelines and trial roll of the Johannesburg Civil Court 25 (2020) on court sittings states that the commencement of court proceedings or court sittings starts at the time of the roll call.

> 'Roll call of civil trials commences at 8h30.
>
> All other courts in the Civil Section will commence sitting at 9h00. The courts adjourn at 11h00 and resume sitting at 11h15. The courts adjourn at 13h00 and resume sitting at 14h00. The courts adjourn for the day at 15h30.'

This is the stage where the accused interacts with the court by confirming their presence in response to the call. At this stage, the visibility of the interpreter is blurred, or excluded. The practice guidelines in sections 12(1)(2) and (3) further state the allocation of interpreters and the prerequisites for allocation. What is positively noted, though it may also affect the accused, is the postponement of the case in the event of the non-availability of an interpreter and the exclusion of using one's own interpreter. Once the judge enters the courtroom, the role of the interpreter begins and communicative engagements will be undertaken, inclusiding of the following:

a) Exchange of documents that do not include/exclude the interpreter;
b) Conversation between the legal practitioners themselves;
c) Conversation between the legal practitioner/s with the witnesses.

Thus, the visibility of the interpreter in these circumstances is identified as non-existence. One would then think of the implications of the implementation of the interpretation in the language of the accused.

Exploring interpreting and court proceedings

This section explores the elements of court proceedings if they encompass all utterances, official or unofficial, by all formal court participants within the courtroom as well as how these proceedings are translated by an interpreter. Steytler's (1993) description of the roles of an interpreter emphasises the role of the interpreter to interpret all the communications in court. Steytler further defines each participant during the proceedings, where the main facilitator is the interpreter. These include:

The judge:

a) There is one judge, who listens to all the evidence. It is for the parties to present the evidence.
b) The judge does not investigate the case.
c) He/she listens to the evidence that is put up and may ask questions.

The counsel/advocates:

a) The case is usually presented orally at trial by an advocate (also referred to as 'counsel').
b) (Although some attorneys have the right to present cases in the high court).
c) In larger and more complex cases, one or more advocates are likely to be instructed at the beginning of a case.
d) They are/will be fully involved in drafting the pleadings and preparation of the case for trial.
e) The plaintiff advocate usually starts by presenting the plaintiffs' case.
f) The defendant's advocate then presents the defendant's case. This is called 'opening submissions'.
g) As is the practice in the context of South Africa, there is no jury.
h) The general rules are that, at trial, witnesses of fact give oral evidence and are cross-examined.
i) Expert witnesses are also cross-examined.

j) The parties then summarise their cases (called 'closing submissions').

Interpreter

Steytler (1993) notes that 'In South Africa most accused in court require interpreters, a practice which is likely to continue in the future. This is of particular significance for undefended accused, who constitute almost 90 percent of all accused today, a figure that may not change dramatically in the future. Because of the absence of a lawyer, the undefended accused who are not conversant with the court language are thus almost exclusively dependent on interpreters for their understanding of their rights and participation in the trial.'

The exclusion of the interpreter in this instance is very critical. It implies that the undefended accused, with no English capability/knowledge or understanding of his/her language rights, is totally disregarded and thus undergoes an unfair trial.

Data collection and data analysis

Data collection: Secondary Data Analysis (SDA)

In responding to the research questions of this paper, the existing data from the ongoing Meyiwa Trial is used. This means the online videos are employed as secondary data to explore the inclusion and exclusion of the interpreter during court proceedings. The author relies on secondary data in the form of free online YouTube videos of the Meyiwa Trial. This is in line with Chivaka's (2018) definition of secondary data as the reuse of other researchers' data, reanalysis of previous data, and using data gathered by other researchers usually for a different purpose. Punch (2005) defined it as the reanalysis of previously collected and analyzed data and as the analysis of data by researchers who were not involved when the data was collected (Ragin, 1999)). Therefore, secondary data analysis is used for the collection of data for the purpose of the analysis of the case study under review.

Data analysis: Conversational Data Analysis approach

The data analysis captures the content and context of the examination of whether the interpreter provides their services throughout the court proceedings in relation to the timeline of utterances or court discourse, including the number of interpreters per session or per day. It also explores instances in the case where the interpreter does not adhere to interpreting throughout the court proceedings and the nature of the hindrances. It further investigates if the interpreting hindrances detected can be translated into a violation of the section under discussion and ultimately to an unfair trial or limitation to access to justice for all. In line with the above exploratory inquiries, the data analysis of the Meyiwa Trial (CAS 2014 & 2019) employed the critical data analysis frameworks for data analysis for both the inclusion and exclusion of the interpreter.

Foregrounding data analysis in the selected videos is observing whether the interpreter is included or excluded from communicative engagements during the:

a) Roll call of civil trials commences at 08:30 hours;
b) Exchange of documents that do not include/exclude the interpreter;
c) Conversation between the legal practitioners themselves;
d) Conversation between the legal practitioner/s with the witnesses.

The second part of the data analysis is the examination of the content analysis presented by Authenticx (2023) which provides standard steps for conducting conversational analysis:

1) Select the conversation: Choose a conversation to analyse. It can be a recorded conversation, a transcript, or a live conversation that you record.
2) Transcribe the conversation: Transcribe the conversation word for word. Include pauses, overlapping speech, and nonverbal cues.
3) Identify the sequence of actions: Analyse the conversation to identify the sequence of actions that occur.
4) Identify patterns: Look for patterns in the conversation, such as the use of particular words or phrases.
5) Analyse the conversation: Apply the principles of conversation analysis to analyse the conversation.
6) Write a conversation analysis report: Write a report that summarises your analysis. Include a description of the conversation, your analysis of the conversation, and your conclusions about the conversation.

Along with the content analysis, standard steps presented by Authenticx (2023) are features of content analysis, presented as:

1) Turn-taking:
   a) refers to the process by which speakers exchange turns during a conversation;
   b) researchers analyse how participants signal their desire to speak, how they transition between turns, and;
   c) the use of nonverbal cues to signal turn-taking.
2) Adjacency pairs:
   a) refers to adjacency pairs or the pattern of organisation in a conversation where one turn is followed by a related turn;
   b) examples of adjacency pairs include question-answer pairs, greeting-response pairs, and invitation-acceptance pairs.
3) Repair sequences:
   a) refers to how participants repair communication breakdowns in conversation.
4) Sequence organisation:

a) refers to the structure and organization of conversation, including the opening, closing, and transitional phases of conversation;
b) researchers analyse how participants initiate, maintain, and end conversations.

5) Nonverbal cues:
   a) such as facial expressions, gestures, and intonation;
   b) researchers analyse how participants use nonverbal cues to convey meaning, signal turn-taking, and regulate conversation.

Each step aligned to the above-mentioned elements of content analysis is recorded in the analysis of interpreting the Meyiwa Trial in establishing both the inclusion and exclusion of the interpreter.

Analysis: Interpreting of court proceedings

Scenario 1 – Video 1: Senzo Meyiwa Murder Trial (YouTube ·SABC News·12 Jun 2023).

Background: 51,370 views, streamed live on Jun 12, 2023, accessed @ https://www.youtube.com/hashtag/sabcnews. The Senzo Meyiwa Murder Trial is set to continue with the testimony of state witness Zandile Khumalo. Khumalo previously spent a day and a half on the witness stand testifying against five men accused of murdering the Bafana Bafana captain in October of 2014. She was among those who were there when Meyiwa was killed.

A. Generic observation

Inclusion and exclusion of the interpreter in communicative engagements during the court proceedings:

1) Roll call of civil trials commences at 8h30.
   a) On this date, the roll call was not included in the video. Thus, the limitation is noted in the video, as the video starts when the judge has already assumed his position, his seat, and is perusing his papers/files.
2) Exchange of documents that do not include/exclude the interpreter.
   a) There is no projection of movement or document exchange shown in the video, which is another limitation of the video selected.
3) Conversation between the legal practitioners themselves.
   a) Exclusion of the interpreter: The judge (J) begins by instructing the clerk of the court (CoC) followed by the prosecutor (P), the defense lawyers (D), and no Interpreter (I), but only the legal practitioners:

      Judge (J): Call the matter!

      Interpreter (I): None.

      Clerk of the court (CoC) (Reads the case): S v... Sibiya and another four (and the CAS number).

Interpreter: None.

Prosecutor (B): As the court pleases My Lord...

Interpreter (I): None.

Defense 1 (S): As the court pleases My Lord, I am (...) representing accused number one and two. As the court pleases My Lord.

Interpreter (I): None.

Defense 2 (Ma): As the court pleases My Lord, I am advocate... Standing in for advocate Mn... representing accused number three. As the court pleases My Lord.

Interpreter (I): None.

Defense 3 (ZN): As the court pleases My Lord, I am advocate... representing accused number four. As the court pleases My Lord.

Interpreter (I): None.

Defense 4 (ZN): As the court pleases My Lord, advocate... representing accused number five. As the court pleases My Lord.

Judge (J): Firstly, I would like to apologise for this matter to start late (a glimpse at his watch). I want to apologise the matter should have started early... I had a meeting with... The reason (interpreter interjects).

Interpreter (I): (not an audible interjection and not shown in the video but noticed through the response by the judge).

Judge (J): Yes!

Interpreter: ***Manje...*** (The interpreter provides the summary of the judge's utterances in isiZulu beginning with/from the judge's apology).

1) Conversation between the legal practitioner/s with the witnesses (Senzo Meyiwa Murder Trial continues. 54,532 views, streamed live on Aug 2, 2023. Accessed @ https://www.youtube.com/hashtag/dstv403).

   a) In the case referred to above, the defense lawyer for accused number three (Adv. Mnisi) is cross-examining the expert with the exclusion of the interpreter. Below is the transcript:

      0:00

      Defense Lawyer: after information was downloaded into the X Roi file and you went through the

      0:05

      photos that you said to plus minus 700 Mr Gininda then approached you and

      0:10

      specifically identified the photos that you that you had to compile a photo album

      0:16

      Expert: on yes even if the figure I never said this

      0:22

      plus minus 700 but I did as you say

0:27

Interpreter: *Angizange ngisho...*

In the above conversation, the interpreter includes himself between the two speakers as he has already been left out by the defence lawyer to provide interpreting.

B. Authenticx (2023) standard step of conversational analysis

Scenario 1 – Video 1: Senzo Meyiwa Murder Trial (YouTube ·SABC News·12 Jun 2023)

Steps	Select the conversation	Transcribe the conversation	Identify the sequence of actions	Identify patterns	Analyze the conversation	Write a conversation analysis report
Turn-taking.	Exclusion of the interpreter: The judge (J) begins by instructing the clerk of the court (CoC) followed by the prosecutor (P), the defense lawyers (D), and no Interpreter (I) but only the legal practitioners.	**Judge**: Call the matter! **Interpreter: none** **CoC**: (Reads the case) S v ...Sibiya and another four (and the CAS number). **Interpreter: none** **Prosecutor (B)**: As the court pleases My Lord... **Interpreter: none** **Defense 1 (S):** As the court pleases My Lord, I am (...) representing accused number one and tow. As the court pleases My Lord.	1. the judge gives instruction to the clerk of the court. 2. The CoC reads the case number/Case identification. 3. The prosecutor introduces him/herself 4. The defense lawyers introduce themselves in order and the accused they are representing. 5. The judge assumes the leading conversation. 6. The interpreter interjects for his/her interpreting role (non-verbal cue/signalling) – not shown in the video.	Use of particular words or phrases: 1. The judge plays his leading role – gives instructions (CoC), signals direction – (prosecutor & defence introductory statements), and signals/gives way to the interpreter ('Yes!'). 2. All the legal practitioners follow a sequence of introducing themselves with the phrase 'As the court pleases... My Lord.' 3. The CoC and the interpreter are absolved from the repeated phrases.	1.Throughout the preliminary opening utterances the interpreter is excluded. 2. The interpreter pleads his case through interjecting the judge in order to interpret. 3. The response by the judge does not show acknowledgement of unintentional exclusion but rather a 'Yes!' as if it is not the time, or an afterthought. 4. One could classify this exclusion as either a systematic exclusion, with intent, or due to the interpreter's role being overshadowed.	-Speaker's exchange turns during a conversation: {Only the legal practitioners are given turns and the CoC by instruction) -Analyze how participants signal their desire to speak, how they transition between turns, the use of nonverbal cues to signal turn-taking. {The interpreter used either a non-verbal cue or a signal as it was not audible but only noticed through the response of the judge "Yes!".

Steps	Select the conversation	Transcribe the conversation	Identify the sequence of actions	Identify patterns	Analyze the conversation	Write a conversation analysis report
		Interpreter: none **Defense 2 (Ma)**: As the court pleases My Lord, I am advocate... Standing in for advocate Mn... representing accused number three. As the court pleases My Lord. **Interpreter: none** **Defense 3 (ZN)**: As the court pleases My Lord, I am advocate... representing accused number four. As the court pleases My Lord. **Interpreter: none** **Defense 4 (ZN)**: As the court pleases My Lord, advocate... representing accused number five. As the court pleases My Lord.				

Steps	Select the conversation	Transcribe the conversation	Identify the sequence of actions	Identify patterns	Analyze the conversation	Write a conversation analysis report
		Judge: Firstly, I would like to apologise for this matter to start late (a glimpse at his watch). I want to apologise the matter should have started early... I had a meeting with... The reason (interpreter interjects). **Interpreter:** (not an audible interjection and not shown in the video but noticed through the response by the judge). **Judge**: Yes! **Interpreter**: Manje... (The interpreter provides the summary of the judge's utterances in isiZulu beginning with/from the judge's apology)				

Steps	Select the conversation	Transcribe the conversation	Identify the sequence of actions	Identify patterns	Analyze the conversation	Write a conversation analysis report
Adjacency pairs	*(Senzo Meyiwa murder trial continues. 54,532 views Streamed live on Aug 2, 2023. Accessed @https://www.youtube.com/hashtag/dstv403)*	0:00 **Defense Lawyer:** After information was downloaded into the X Roi file and you went through the 0:05 photos that you said to plus minus 700 Mr Gininda then approached you and 0:10 specifically identified the photos that you that you had to compile a photo album 0:16 **Expert:** on yes even if the figure I never said this 0:22 plus minus 700 but I did as you say 0:27 **Interpreter:** Angizange ngisho...	The action follows this sequence in terms of people: the defense, the expert, the interpreter. Interpreter excluded by the defense, resorts to provide mitigation to the exclusion by summarising both speakers' utterances.	The following order should have been followed: the defense, the interpreter, the expert, the interpreter.	In the case of the Meyiwa Trial during some instances, the pattern of organised information has not been followed. The pattern would have been expected to be the speaker, followed by the interpreter, then the respondent. Thus the, for example, the judge, the interpreter, the respondent (legal practitioner, secretary of the court/witness/accused), the interpreter – in that order. However, in some cases as referred in the turn-taking above, there are notable errors in the application of this synectic standard feature.	-The pattern of organisation in a conversation where one turn is followed by a related turn. (Equal allocation v summary) -Examples of adjacency pairs include question-answer pairs, greeting-response pairs, and invitation-acceptance pairs. -In this scenario, it was not followed.

Steps	Select the conversation	Transcribe the conversation	Identify the sequence of actions	Identify patterns	Analyze the conversation	Write a conversation analysis report
		Defense Lawyer (Adv. Mnisi): 0:54 now you you (Music) 1:06 now you de-scribed you gave a description in photo 15 in photo 19 and 18. let's 1:17 go to photo 15, 18 and 19. 1:25 foreign (Music) 1:34 I think that is page 15. I'm sorry that's page 15. 1:39 so when you gave a description of what you saw in photo 15 you say I see a 1:46				

Steps	Select the conversation	Transcribe the conversation	Identify the sequence of actions	Identify patterns	Analyze the conversation	Write a conversation analysis report
		gentleman with dreadlocks not sure that's true 1:56 and in photo 18 you also say I see a gentleman with dreadlocks not so 2:11 and you say to the very same thing also about your description of what you see 2:17 in photo number 19 also this is 2:25 nice thank you **Expert**: that's true **Interpreter:** (Summarises both speakers' utter-ances)				

Steps	Select the conversation	Transcribe the conversation	Identify the sequence of actions	Identify patterns	Analyze the conversation	Write a conversation analysis report
Repair sequences					As identified above, the interpreter in all the conversations in court should be at the centre. There should be a systematic rule and penalty for any court participant who responds to the other speaker without the interpreter playing their role. This observation of sequence should be the order of the court proceeding from the presiding officer up to the witness in the witness box. The visibility and professional respect of interpreters rely on the acknowledgement of such in the courtroom.	-How participants repair communication breakdown. (Though in the case of the Meyiwa Trial there are other videos which were not included in the paper). The interpreter gets overshadowed by other participants, but the recommendations applied and regulated can repair the inefficiency in the sequence.

Steps	Select the conversation	Transcribe the conversation	Identify the sequence of actions	Identify patterns	Analyze the conversation	Write a conversation analysis report
Sequence organization					The regulation of the interpreting practice in the courtroom during court proceedings is crucial. The development of unambiguous guidelines on the inclusion of the interpreter as a professional participant in court will enable the organisation of court processes.	-The structure and organisation of conversation, including the opening, closing, and transitional phases of conversation. -Analyse how participants initiate, maintain, and end conversations.

Steps	Select the conversation	Transcribe the conversation	Identify the sequence of actions	Identify patterns	Analyze the conversation	Write a conversation analysis report
Nonverbal cues					In the training and practice of interpreters, it should be a norm that they do not only interpret verbal cues but non-verbal cues as well. For example in the case of the judge saying 'Yes!', the interpreter should have included the gesture. It should be the case with the interpreting of other speakers' utterances that if there is a gesture accompanying the utterance, the interpreter must be able to include that. This is part of the work done by forensic linguists, therefore it will either mean the interpreter is upskilled or each court has a forensic linguist during court proceedings, a very rare skill in the South African context.	-Such as facial expressions, gestures, and intonation. -Analyse how participants use non-verbal cues to convey meaning, signal turn-taking, and regulate conversation.

Recommendations

The findings in this research paper addressed the research questions of interest which included, firstly, the question of when court proceedings begin and if they begin when the judge enters the courtroom until he/she leaves the courtroom. The paper suggests that the role of the interpreter should be included from the start of court proceedings to protect the language rights of the accused. As Steytler (1993) puts it, the roll call for accused and witnesses involves language. This means that all the information is crucial, even directing and announcing information about the trial such as the venue and the confirmation of presence. It has equally been identified that the opening of the court proceedings and the instruction for the introduction of the case for adjudication by the secretary of the court may exclude the provision of the interpreter. This leaves the accused in limbo and in a state of uncertainty or loss of confidence as he/she is excluded right at the beginning of the court proceedings.

Secondly, the question of whether court proceedings encompass all utterances, official or unofficial, by all formal court participants within the courtroom has been addressed by the paper. The research has proven that the language rights of the accused are affirmed in the Constitution and that the proceedings should be conducted in the language the accused understands. It has been noted in this article in the case study that all the court proceedings should be interpreted in the language of the accused. This reinforces the professional role and expertise of the interpreter. It is a practical way of ensuring comprehensive language rights for the accused.

As noted in the analysis, legal practitioners tend to communicate between themselves without the inclusion of the interpreter, and there are instances where the interpreter must interject. It is recommended that a fair trial requires legislative intervention in the form of developing guidelines with a code of conduct for all court participants to alleviate the alienation of the role of the interpreter. It has been noted that in the case where an emotive or evidence-poking argument is pursued (for example, the cross-examination between the defense lawyer and the accused) the role of the interpreter is totally shut down. This technical or emotional exclusion of the interpreter has been evident in the cross-examination between Adv. Mshololo and Tumelo Madlala. In this instance, the argument was about qualifications 'passed matric' and the date of employment 'March – in March'. This became a toe-to-toe cross-examination with the exclusion of the interpreter. The interesting part was that the interpreter was also excluded by the witness himself as he also began to argue in English while all along, he was speaking isiZulu and the interpreter provided translation from English to isiZulu. A question of interest for another study is whether the court can have a measure of a client's efficiency in the languages used in court. In this case, the interpreter had to impose his role by interjecting, instructing the witness to speak isiZulu not English.

It is evident that an interpreter cannot be a Jack-of-all-trades or a terminology specialist for all fields such as a forensic expert, a ballistic expert, or a medical expert to mention a few. This has been evident in the analysis that specialised language experts (in this case, forensic linguists) should be part of court proceedings to close the competence and specialist gap left by court interpreters. This is also applicable to the question of whether the interpreter provides their services throughout the court proceedings. The role of the forensic linguist will complement the interpreter and serve as a substitute in regard to cross-examination on specialist or expert evidence, while at the same time avoiding misinterpretation, lagging, and non-interjection during exclusion, which may also be caused by fatigue due to the allocation of one interpreter for all proceedings with no extra interpreter to take turns.

Lastly, in cases where the interpreter does not adhere to interpreting throughout the court proceedings due to hindrances, those interpreting hindrances should be considered a violation of the section under discussion and ultimately to an unfair trial or limitation to access to justice for all. This paper proposes that any violation or non-application of a right affirmed by law is eligible to be tested by courts. This is the case with a lack of comprehensive interpreting and in this case, the interpreter is viewed to be the main witness for the accused whose right to the use of language through interpreting has been violated.

Conclusion

In conclusion, the absence of a code of conduct, guidelines, and a regulatory body for court interpreters or interpreting in courts hinders the effective provision of interpreting throughout court proceedings. Court interpreters have no ombudsman/watchdog to report to when their services are excluded or included by default during their allocated time of interpreting. In the absence of these structures, the implementation of a fair trial to the accused remains unsolved and open for litigation.

Secondly, the lack of specialisation in the field of interpreting means the quality and competence of the interpreter is often under-valued such that his/her role becomes invisible. At times, the interpreter must interject the proceedings to highlight his/her presence (exclusion). Lastly, the role of forensic linguists as language and law specialists in court leaves a huge burden for court interpreters to juggle all the factors in the air which results in their areas of expertise not being clearly defined and not respected and afforded their space during court proceedings.

References

Bailey, A., Docrat, Z., Kaschula, RH., Lourens, CJA., Ralarala, MK. & De Vries, A. (2017). Courts should promote all languages. *City Pres* via *News24*.

Chivaka, R. (2018). Secondary data analysis. *Coventry University UK*.

Crossman, A. (2021). An Overview of Qualitative Research Methods. *ThoughtCo*, Accessed @thoughtco.com/qualitative-research-methods-3026555.

Kaschula, RH., Mostert, A. & Ralarala, MK. (2008). Communicating across cultures in South African law courts: Towards an information technology solution*. *Stellenbosch Papers in Linguistics Plus*, Vol. 36, 89–104

Licoppe, C. & Boéri, J. (2021). Is there such a thing as summary interpreting? "Cross-linguistic formulation", facilitation and mediation in French asylum proceedings. *Language & Communication*, Volume 77, Pages 56–69 13. ISSN: 0271-5309.

Republic of South Africa (RSA). (2019). *Language Policy of The Department of Justice and Constitutional Development*. Accessed @https://www.gov.za/sites/default/files/gcis_document/201904/42422gon616.pdf

Republic of South Africa (RSA). (2020). *Practice Guidelines: Trial Roll*. Johannesburg Magistrate's Court Civil Section.

Republic of South Africa (RSA). (1944). *Magistrates' Court Act 32 of 1944*. Pretoria: Government Printer.

Republic of South Africa (RSA). 1996. *Constitution of the Republic of South Africa*. Pretoria: Government Printer.

Steytler, NC. (1993). Implementing language rights in court: the role of the court interpreter in South Africa. *South African Journal on Human Rights,* Volume 9, Issue 2.

The Senzo Meyiwa Trial, (Docket CAS number is 636/10/2014 and the Second Docket CAS number is 375/1/2019). https://universalteacher.com

Usadolo, SE., Kotzé, E. (2014). Some interlingual communicative challenges for foreign African interpreters in South African courtrooms. *Stellenbosch Papers in Linguistics Plus*, Vol. 43, 345–357 https://doi.org/10.5842/43-0-184

Annexure 1.1 Transcript 2

1.	2.	3.	4.	5.	6.
0:04 foreign 1:12 foreign 2:01 abandoned myself appear for the state 2:04 okay 2:06 this is 2:09 number one and two pharmaceutical 2:12 initial S is 2:17 um - isiZulu Interpreter 2:21 on behalf of accused number three mate 2:24 this is record My Lord for the record um 2:26 I appear for I choose number four thank 2:29 you 2:29 is it possess the court My Lord 2:31	Advocates that inshallah on behalf of 2:33 excuse number five 2:36 firstly I'd like to apologise for this 2:39 matter 2:40 to start late do you have anything to 2:43 okay 2:45 I want to apologise the matter should 2:47 have started early 2:49 but the period that we had earlier I had 2:52 a meeting with the legal representatives 2:55 of all the accused 2:57 who had to 2:59 consider what we discussed and to take 3:03	3:11 the reason 3:12 yes 3:30 um 3:39 foreign 3:52 is not available due to ill health and 3:56 may not be available for a long time 3:59 subject to what 4:01 his medical doctors may say 4:04 um 4:30 however because of the importance of 4:33 this matter and the publicity that it is 4:37 getting from the media we have made 4:39 arrangements 4:41	5:00 I know 5:07 uh 5:12 for that reason the matter is not going 5:15 to proceed today 5:17 it was scheduled to proceed from today I 5:21 think until about Thursday yeah the 5:23 resources are true 5:29 um 5:37 the witnesses will be excused the state 5:40 indicated that it's not necessary for me 5:42 to want those witnesses to appear 5:45 on the date on which this matter will be 5:48	6:16 that of the defense that you'd like me 6:19 to warn 6:21 ing 6:23 witnesses thank you 6:27 thank you very much 6:35 your meta is postponed to the 17th of 6:39 July 6:40 the trial will proceed from that date 6:43 it may proceed for for the whole term 6:47 for the whole of the third time 6:49 imagine 6:50 um 7:16 and the accused will remain in custody 7:23	7:27 and the legal representatives are making 7:30 arrangements so that this matter the 7:33 trial should proceed on the 17th of July 7:40 um 7:46 foreign 8:12 I confirm a lot the arrangement is in 8:14 order 8:15 thank you very much cottages English (auto-generated)

1.	2.	3.	4.	5.	6.
	instructions so that this matter 3:06 should proceed and be finalised as soon 3:10 as possible	that this matter should proceed in the 4:45 third term so that it can be finalised 4:47 as soon as possible	postponed to 5:49 imagine 5:55 um 6:12 and I think that same applies to the 6:15 defense witnesses is there any witness	and I can just add the leadership of 7:26 this court	

13

EXPLORING THE DEVELOPMENT OF LEGAL TERMINOLOGY IN INDIGENOUS LANGUAGES AS A TOOL TO JUSTICE FOR ALL IN SOUTH AFRICAN COURTS

Nomfundo Mali, Aliziwe Sidiki, Qhamani Masiki, Lindile Mali & Indiphiwe Mxakaza

Background

By law, South African courts should be operating within the parameters of South African legislative provisions, including the use of African languages in courts. The South African Constitution makes provision for the recognition, use, and elevation of previously marginalised languages. This chapter seeks to explore the availability of legal terminology in African languages for use by all court participants, specifically court interpreters as intermediaries of communication. It is the objective of the research to identify gaps and provide legal terminology in different fields of language use within the court. The paper, in its selection of the specific fields or legal classification of cases, will consider the areas that impact indigenous language speakers the most. Section 6(3) of the South African Constitution refers to the elevation of previously marginalised languages. This is also affirmed by a Parliamentary Monitoring Group article stating that:

> 'In accordance with subsection 6(2) the State is obliged to promote the status and use of the indigenous languages, in the context of the historical curtailment of their use and status, by means of practical and substantial measures. The use of the term 'State', which goes undefined in the Constitution, includes all levels of government and all three spheres of the State, while subsection 6(4) deals only with the national and provincial governments.'

The aim is to elevate the status of previously marginalised languages, developing them so that they can be used in a proper and effective manner in the justice system. As a way of exploring pioneering and utilising the terminology, the capturing of the terminology will cover the Nguni languages from which Sesotho will be added in future publications. Furthermore, to expand access to justice for other African languages beyond South

African borders, Chichewa and Shona will be part of the terminology collection which will all be based on already existing English legal terminology. The focus will be on the following subheadings but not limited to; generic court proceedings terminology, homicide, gender-based violence, theft and robbery, and family court proceedings.

Introduction

The South African legal system strives to uphold the principles of justice, fairness, and equality. However, the gaps in the justice system caused by language barriers within South African courts pose a significant challenge to achieving these goals. By predominantly using colonial languages, indigenous language speakers are often excluded or face difficulties in fully participating in legal proceedings in their own motherland. This research delves into the importance of developing legal terminology in indigenous languages to ensure justice and inclusivity for all individuals within the South African legal system. The chapter is grounded in forensic linguistics, a fairly new field of sociolinguistics, defined by Wikipedia as, 'legal linguistics, or language and the law, which is the application of linguistic knowledge, methods, and insights to the forensic context of law, language, crime investigation, trial, and judicial procedure. It is a branch of applied linguistics.'

Problem statement

The lack of standardised terminology for legal terms in indigenous languages can have far-reaching consequences for those who require legal interpretation services. Without standardised terminology, indigenous language speakers may be unable to access critical legal information or understand their rights. Misinterpretation of legal documents and proceedings may lead to unfair outcomes, and misunderstanding of legal concepts and terminology can result in a lack of legal knowledge and access to services. In the worst-case scenario, this may lead to discrimination and exclusion from the legal system, leaving individuals without recourse for legal issues. As noted by Hagan et al. (2013), current legal interpretation services often rely on ad-hoc translation of English legal terms into isiXhosa, which can result in ambiguity and misunderstandings. This lack of standardised terminology can also lead to a lack of legal knowledge among isiXhosa speakers and can contribute to inequalities in the legal system. Given the serious implications of the lack of standardised terminology for legal terms in indigenous languages, research is needed to develop and implement standardised terminology in this area. This will ensure that indigenous speakers can access and understand legal information and proceedings and will help to protect their rights and ensure fair legal outcomes.

Objectives

a) To identify and assess the current gaps in legal terminology in indigenous languages.

b) To develop standardised terminology for legal terms in isiXhosa while providing features of terminology development, classification, and exemples relating to available data of court cases found in the public domain.

c) To evaluate the potential benefits of standardised terminology for legal terms in isiXhosa.

Research questions

a) What are the current gaps in standardised terminology for legal terms in isiXhosa?

b) How can these gaps be addressed through the development of a standardised terminology?

c) What are the potential benefits of standardised terminology for legal terms in isiXhosa?

d) What are the challenges in implementing standardised terminology for legal terms in isiXhosa?

e) What are the implications of standardised terminology for legal terms in isiXhosa on access to justice and legal outcomes?

Research design and methodology

The chapter adopts the Conceptual Analysis Research Design which is a method within the qualitative research methodology. Furner (2004) affirms the definition by Pamplona (2022) who defines conceptual analysis as the examination of a concept into simpler elements to promote clarification while having a consistent understanding; analysis can include distinguishing, analysing, and representing the various aspects to which the concept refers. Myburgh and Tammaro (2013) further state that conceptual analysis in practice concerns distinguishing terms, analysing the understandings they refer to, and representing this.

In the context of legal terminology development, for this chapter, we adopt the Synectic Product Development's (https://synectic.net) concept development process. This online site provides the following features for concept development:

a) Define the problem: Clearly understand the problem before you begin, as it will help you focus your thoughts and help keep your ideas relevant and aligned with your goals.

b) Generate concepts: Encourage creative thinking and employ various techniques to generate diverse ideas and concepts. This includes brainstorming, mind mapping, reverse brainstorming, research, and benchmarking.

Key steps of concept development processes (Synectic)

a) Depict concepts: Consider different perspectives, including everyone who will use or handle the product. Accounting for various groups' needs and interests helps you generate well-rounded ideas.

b) Refine concepts: Gather information on consumers, market trends, and competitors, and use this information when brainstorming concepts.

c) Assess concepts: Always keep the customer in mind when conceptualising by considering their needs, preferences, and requests.

d) Select the winning concepts: Collaborate with others and seek feedback on your concepts from your target demographic.

e) Final term list: Refine and test your ideas and make necessary changes and adjustments based on the results.

Literature review

Legislative Framework

- *Description and definition of concept development*

A general definition of a concept or a term can be described as a process of developing ideas to solve specified design problems. This process often involves identifying the key characteristics of the concepts, outlining their scope and boundaries, and determining how they relate to other concepts. Sager et al. (1993: 3) refer to concept development as terminology concerned with concepts. They further describe terminology as the study of and the field of activity concerned with the collection, description, processing, and presentation of terms, i.e., lexical items belonging to specialised areas of usage of one or more languages.

The Synectic presents concept development as a means of defining and refining a specific idea or set of ideas to bring clarity, coherence, and structure.

Sloutsky and Deng (2020) postulate that concept development emanates from 'human intellectual activity'. This means that an action or an activity by a human within their surroundings leads to a concept symbolising that particular act. They further argue that the development and acquisition of a concept involves planning, thinking, reasoning, problem solving, and decision making. Our point of emphasis, therefore, is that a concept developed needs to be used for that concept to be normalised, domesticated, and adopted as a concept attached to an action or activity.

Furthermore, Stauffer (1965: 100) traces concept development as far back as a description presented by Aristotle, who referred to it as 'concept attainment'. His argument highlights that a concept exists due to people seeking meaning which can be attained through classification and generalisation of things. In other words, according to Stauffer, meaning takes precedence before a concept is given.

During concept development, you will take an abstract idea and turn that thought into a well-formed design using critical thinking skills, research, and analysis. This article has adopted the same framework in harvesting a set of terms used in the context of different court cases. The research about the selected concepts/terms was informed by the information recorded in online judgments such as in the Southern African Legal Information Institute (SAFLII) platforms. This is not only limited to judgments, but also includes some terms recorded in old cases available in publications.

Legislative framework on the provision of interpreting and legal terminology in indigenous languages

Access to justice by African language speakers in South African courts has been questionable for some time, and this is the case despite the constitutional declaration of this linguistic right to all South African official language speakers. The South African Constitution's section 6(1)(2) affirms that:

1) The official languages of the Republic are Sepedi, Sesotho, Setswana, Siswati, Tshivenda, Xitsonga, Afrikaans, English, isiNdebele, isiXhosa, and isiZulu.
2) Recognizing the historically diminished use and status of the indigenous languages of our people, the state must take practical and positive measures to elevate the status and advance the use of these languages.

Contrary to the constitutional linguistic rights for African language speakers was the pronouncement of 2017 by then-Chief Justice Mogoeng Mogoeng that English only shall be the language of record in South African courts. Staunch forensic linguists and language activists such as Kaschula, Ralarala, Docrat, Lourens, and Bailey questioned the decision as a reversal of language constitutional rights (Bailey, et al., 2017). The pronouncement is also endorsed in the Department of Justice and Constitutional Development (DOJCD)'s own language policy, contrary to the use and elevation of previously marginalised official languages. Section 7(8.2) on the Use of Official Languages for Government Purposes, states that 'it is determined that English is the language of record for the Department'. However, the department affords prestige to foreign language speakers for the provision of interpreters at the cost of the department itself.

Data collection

The first step in developing standardised legal terminology in indigenous languages is to gather data on the existing terminology used in legal contexts. This data can be collected through a variety of methods, including analysing existing legal documents and proceedings. Once this data is collected, it can be analysed to identify gaps and inconsistencies in the current terminology. The next step is to develop new terminology that is consistent, accurate, and comprehensive. This study analyses a secondary data analysis, which involves examining answers to research questions that are different to those modelled in the original study by using existing data (Hinds et al., 1997). This type of analysis can be useful in developing a terminology as it can provide insights into how the terminology is currently being used in practice. Secondary data analysis allows researchers to analyse data that has already been collected, often for a different purpose. This can be a cost-effective and time-efficient way to conduct research and can provide insights that would not be possible with primary data collection.

Data analysis

Conceptual analysis is the method of choice because it allows researchers to focus on concepts and ideas rather than on data itself. This type of method is often used in qualitative research, to explore ideas and concepts in depth. As Salkind (2018: 212) notes, 'Conceptual methods can be used to develop theories, analyse text and discourse, or to understand the relationship between different concepts.' Corbin and Strauss (2008: 149) support Salkind's argument that conceptual analysis can be used to understand the relationships between concepts and ideas; they state that 'Conceptual analysis provides a strategy for understanding people's experience and gaining insight into the social worlds they create and inhabit.' The findings in the investigated cases will be presented descriptively, identifying the main challenges faced by indigenous language speakers within South African courts. These challenges may include difficulties in understanding legal terminology, lack of effective communication in their case, be it with their defense lawyer or with the translator, or comprehending court proceedings.

Terminology lists on classified court cases

In line with Synectic analysis, concept development includes the following steps:

- *Define the problem*

Clearly understand the problem before you begin.

The focus and the objectives of the chapter included identifying the unavailability of standardised legal terminology in indigenous languages. This prompted a need to consolidate and harvest legal terminology in different court cases. The cases were classified as:

a) Gender-based violence (*Amatyala okuxhaphaza/oxhatshazo ngokwesini*);
b) Homicide (*Amatyala okubulala*);

c) Theft and robbery (*Amatyala obusela/obugewu/ubugulukudu*);

d) Generic court proceedings, terminology, and titles (*Isigama senkundla*);

e) Family court cases e.g. custody (*Amatyala angemiba yeentsapho. Umzekelo. isodlo*).

Furthermore, in relation to the Synectic analysis, concept development includes the following steps:

- *Generate concepts*

a) Encourage creative thinking and employ various techniques to generate diverse ideas and concepts.

b) Brainstorming, internet surfing, mind mapping, reverse brainstorming, research, benchmarking, and consultations on the production of the terms.

The following lists were generated based on the Synectic analysis:

- *Gender-based violence (Amatyala okuxhaphaza/oxhatshazo)*

English Term	IsiXhosa Term	Description	Cases
Femicide	*Ukubulala abasetyhini*	*Ukubulawa kwamabhinqa kuba engamabhinqa*	*S v Ntamehlo* (2023). In comparison, in 2017, 52% of women were killed by intimate partners. Intimate femicide is much more common in South Africa than in most ...
Intimate partner violence	*Ubundlobongela beqabane/ bomntu osondeleyo*	*(i-IPV) ligama elichaza ukuxhatshazwa okanye ukulimazwa liqabane langoku okanye langaphambili okanye iqabane kubudlelwane obusondeleyo. I-IPV inokubandakanya ubundlobongela bomzimba, ngokwesondo, ngokwengqondo, okanye ngokweemvakalelo, kunye nokulandela, ukunyanzela, okanye ukulawula ukuziphatha. I-IPV inokuchaphazela nasiphi na isini.*	Bester/Magudumana Case. Nosicelo Mtebeni. Thabani Mzolo's Case (2018). Namhla Mthwa (Mthatha Case).
Exploitation of minors	*Ukuxhatshazwa kwabantwana*	*Ukuxhatshazwa kwabantwana sisenzo sokusebenzisa umntwana omncinane ukufumana inzuzo, ukusebenza njenge sicaka, ukwanelisa ngokwezesondo, okanye ukuthengisa ngomntwana ukufumana inzuzo yemali*	*S v Osabiya* (2021) - He allegedly lived off the earnings of the sexual exploitation... South Africa with the promise of a job but forced into sex slavery.

Homicide (Amatyala okubulala)

It is essential to fully understand the legal concepts and terminology in homicide case law not only for legal professionals, but for litigants, and individuals interested in the criminal justice system. By examining legal language use in different forms of homicide, legal defences, degrees of culpability, and sentencing considerations, this indigenous legal terminology translation seeks to provide a comprehensive understanding of the intricacies involved in homicide cases. A clear understanding of these legal concepts in the South African official languages can contribute to fair and effective legal processes and decisions in cases of unlawful killings.

English Term	IsiXhosa Term	Description	Cases
Serial killer	*Isigwinta/ umbulali ogqugqisayo/ isihange/ isigebenga*	*Lo ngumbulali ophila ngokunukiselwa ligazi, uhleli nje urhawuzelelwa sisihlahla ufuna ukuqwenga umntu. Amaxesha amaninzi uba nesizathu sokubulala, alandele okanye azichongele uluhlu loluntu oluthile azakulibulala*	*S v Makhanda* (2022) – Eastern Cape High Court, Mthatha. This was on the basis that the murders were committed in execution of a common purpose.
Crime Scene	*Indawo yentlekele/ yesehlo/ yexhwayelo*	*Yindawo yesehlo solwaphulo-mthetho okanye indawo apho kwehle khona intlekele, indawo ebonakalayo, efumaneka naphi na apho kwenziwe/kwenzeke isenzo sobukrelemnqa okanye ulwaphulo-mthetho, indawo leyo ethi inike ubungqina obubambekayo kubacuphi okanye abaphandi betyala okanye intlekele leyo nengaxilongwa ziinkcubabungqina.*	Senzo Meyiwa Court Trial (Kelly Kumalo's Voslorus home)
Cold-blooded murderer	*Umbulali ongenalusini/ isigwinta*	*Lo ngumntu obulala uluntu ngokungenalusini, ukubulala sele iyinto esegazini nekwangumsebenzi kuye. Ubulala ngendlela emasikizi neshiya uluntu lukhwankqisekiwe bubundlobongela nobukrelemnqa besikhohlakali esi singenalo nosizi.*	South Africa's 'Monster of Tholeni' Bulelani Mabhayi Jailed for 625 Years for a rape and murder spree, 'Village of Death', where the serial killer raped neighbours, then hacked them and their children to death.

- *Generic court proceedings terminology (Isigama sasenkundleni)*

English Term	IsiXhosa Term	Description	Cases
Imprisonment	*Ukuvalelwa/ugwetyelwe ngaphakathi*	*Ukuvalelwa entolongweni, / Kuvalelwa lowo uthe wafunyaniswa enetyala.*	*S v Mogale* (2011)
Sentenced	*Indawo yentlekele/ yesehlo/ yexhwayelo*	*Isigwebo esiwiswa yinkundla ngokusesikweni emva kokufumana umangalelwa enetyala. Umangalelwa uthi anikwe yinkundla yamatyala imiminyaka azakuthi ayichithe entolongweni emva kokufunyaniswa enetyala.*	*De Lange v Smuts NO and Others* (1998)
Offender	*Umoni/ ibanjwa/ ibhantinti/ isibotshwa*	*Umntu obanjelwe ukwenza ulwaphulo-mthetho okanye ityala , ze wasiwa kwiinkundla zamatyala.*	*S v Coetzee and Others* (1997)

- *Theft and robbery (Amatyala obusela/obugewu/ubugulukudu)*

English Term	IsiXhosa Term	Description	Cases
Armed Robbery/ unarmed robbery	*Ukuxhonyiswa/ Ukuxhonyiswa ngesixhobo/ ngesikhali/ ngompu*	*Uhlobo olongezelelekileyo lobusela olubandakanya ukusetyenziswa kwesixhobo esibulalayo ukwenza ubundlobongela okanye isoyikiso sobundlobongela kwixhoba.*	*Tilayi v S* (2021)
Gangster	*Ilungu leqela loonqevu/ labophuli mthetho/ amaphara/ ilungu lemigewu*	*Eli lilungu lombutho wolwaphulo-mthetho owenza imali ngokucwangcisiweyo kwimisebenzi efana nokuqhekeza, ukugcakaza, ukurweba ngabantu ngokungekho mthethweni kunye nokubolekisa ngemali ngokungekho semthethweni*	*Adams and Another v S* (2022)
Burglary	*Ukuqhekeza/ukungenelwa ngootsotsi*	*ukungena kwisakhiwo ngokungekho semthethweni ngenjongo zokwaphula umthetho*	*Mahlahla v S* (2023) (1) The appellant was charged with robbery with aggravating circumstances read with the provisions of s51(2) ...

- *Family court case (Amatyala angemiba yeentsapho)*

English Term	IsiXhosa Term	Description	Cases
Maintenance	*Isondlo/ulondolozo*	*Luxanduva lokubonelela umntwana ngezinto azidingayo, umzekelo ikhaya, ukutya, impahla, imfundo kunye nonyango*	*CL v CJL* (2022)
Divorce	*Uqhawulo-mtshato*	*Uqhawulo-mtshato kukwahlula ngokusemthethweni isibini*	*CL v CJL* (2022)
Custody	*Ukugcinwa/ukukhulisa komntwaba/kwabantwana ngokusemthethweni*	*Ilungelo elisemthethweni okanye uxanduva lukuthatha kwaye unakekele umntwana, ngakumbi xa abazali bathe bohlukana okanye basweleke.*	*RMD v KD (2023)*

For this article, only three examples or scenarios per classification have been tabled to sample the work already covered in relation to the collection of legal terminology for courts and legal practitioners as well as for the general public to understand, access, and participate in the legal system.

Recommendations

This research recommends developing legal terminology for indigenous languages requires working with a team of experts that includes policymakers, legal professionals, native speakers of the languages, and language experts who believe in promoting linguistic inclusivity in legal processes. The linguists can help to ensure that the terminology is accurate and appropriate for the target language, while lawyers can provide insight into the specific legal concepts and terms that need to be translated. The native speakers can then review and provide feedback on the translations to ensure that they are accurate and appropriate for the intended audience. Additionally, it is important to consider the cultural context of the language and ensure that the translations are culturally appropriate.

Conclusion

The development of legal terminology in indigenous languages is critical for ensuring equal and fair access to justice for all within South African courts. By addressing the language barriers posed by legal and technical language, the legal system can become more inclusive, empowering indigenous language speakers to be active rather than passive participants in the legal proceedings. This research seeks to raise awareness and promote effective strategies to enhance linguistic diversity within the South African legal system, ultimately fostering a more just and equitable society. The time to influence and initiate the change within the dynamics of South African indigenous language injustices has arrived.

References

Adams and Another v S (2022)

Ahmad, S. et. al. 2019. Qualitative v/s Quantitative Research. Journal of Evidence Based Medicine and Healthcare 6(43):2828-2832. DOI:10.18410/jebmh/2019/587

Authenticx. 2023. Types Of Conversation Analysis. https://authenticx.com

Bailey, A., Docrat, Z., Kaschula, RH., Lourens, CJA., Ralarala, MK. & De Vries, A. (2017). Courts should promote all languages. *City Pres* via *News24*.

Campbell, JP., McCloy, RA., Oppler, SH. & Sager, CE. (1993). A theory of performance. In Schmitt, E., Borman, WC. & associates (ed.) *Personnel Selection in Organizations* (pp. 35-70). San Francisco: Jossey-Bass.

CL v CJL (2022)

Corbin, J. & Straus, A. (2008). *Basics of Qualitative Research.* (third edition) Thousand Oaks. CA: SAGE Publications.

De Lange v Smuts NO and Others (1998)

Furner, J. (2004). Conceptual Analysis: A Method for Understanding Information as Evidence, and Evidence as Information. *Archives and Museum Informatics* 4(3-4). University of California, Los Angeles.

Hagan, S., Swartz, L. Kilian, S., Chiliza, B., Bisogno, P. & Joska, J. (2013). The accuracy of interpreting key psychiatric terms by ad hoc interpreters at a South African psychiatric hospital. *Centre for Public Mental Health, Department of Psychology*, Stellenbosch University.

Hinds PS., Vogel RJ., & Clarke-Steffen, L. (1997). The possibilities and pitfalls of doing a secondary analysis of a qualitative dataset. *Qualitative Health Research* 7(3): 408-424.

Mahlahla v S (2023)

Myburgh, S. & Tammaro, AM. (2013). Constructing Theoretical Framework. *Exploring Education for Digital Librarians*. 133-172. https://doi.org/10.1016/B978-1-84334-659-3.50007-4

Pamplona, F. (2022). Understand how to conduct a more accurate and detailed conceptual analysis research to convert it into a more concrete concept. Accessed @ https://mindthegraph.com/blog/conceptual-analysis-research/

Parliamentary Monitoring Group publication: Language Rights in the Constitution: The Unborn Language Legislation of Subsection 6(4) and the Consequences of the Delayed Birth. https://static.pmg.org.za/docs/120118lourens_0.pdf

Punch. Keith F. 2005. Introduction to Social Research-Quantitative & Qualitative Approaches. London: Sage.

RMD v KD (2023)

Republic of South Africa (RSA). (1996). *Constitution of the Republic of South Africa.* Pretoria: Government Printer.

Salkind, NJ. (2018). *Exploring Research.* (eleventh edition). Thousand Oaks, CA: SAGE Publications.

Sloutsky, VM. & Deng, WS. (2020). Categories, Concepts, and Conceptual Development.. *Lang Cognitive Neuroscience*, (10):1284-1297.

Stauffer, RG. (1965). Concept Development and Reading. *The Reading Teacher*, Vol. 19, No. 2.

S v Makhanda (2022)

S v Coetzee and Others (1997)

S v Mogale (2011

S v Ntamehlo (2023)

S v Osabiya (2021)

*Synectic Product Development:*2023 *A subsidiary of Mack.* https://synectic.net/

The Southern African Legal Information Institute (SAFLII). (2016). LawCite Help/Guide Overview. https://www.google.co.za/url?sa=t&rct=j&q=&esrc=s&source=web&cd=&ved=2ahUKEwjPuM6RlKmEAxXTUEEAHevzD4YQFnoECBoQAQ&url=https%3A%2F%2Fwww.saflii.org%2Flawcitehelp.pdf&usg=AOvVaw1ec2ogC2OD7fmgxnVFie9o&opi=89978449

Tilayi v S (2021)

The Senzo Meyiwa Trial, (Docket CAS number is 636/10/2014 and the Second Docket CAS number is 375/1/2019) - Cas 375/1/2019. Cas 375/1/2014

PART IV

Customary Law, Legal Language Policies, and Legislation

14

THE IMPACT OF LANGUAGE POLICIES AND LEGISLATION IN THE SOUTH AFRICAN LEGAL SYSTEM REVIEWED

Donovan Pitt & Lloyd Matenga

Introduction

This chapter will unpack the impact of language policies and legislation in the South African legal system with the aid of a comparative analysis with the United States of America (USA), particularly the states of Arizona and Virginia. From the onset it is important to consider the theories of legal justice which have a direct bearing on the content of the language policies and legislation in any legal system (Cavanagh, 2014). It follows that Judge Moseneke succinctly remarks that 'a creative jurisprudence of equality coupled with a substantive interpretation of the content of "socio-economic" rights should restore social justice as premier foundational value of our Constitutional democracy side by side, if not interactively with, human dignity, equality, freedom, accountability, responsiveness and openness' (Moseneke, 2002: 309 & 314). Notably, for South Africa, after 1996, the post-Apartheid era, the current language policies and legislation derive their legitimacy from the Constitution certified by the courts in 1996. Put differently, any language and legislation validity are dependent on compliance with the Constitution of South Africa, 1996 (Republic of South Africa, 1996). Consequently, all the policies and legislation must be measured against the Constitution in assessing either the positive or negative implications.

Influence of language policy and legislation on jurisprudence

In the pre-Apartheid era, it is important to note that English and Afrikaans were the official dominant languages (Harms, 2012). It follows that even litigants would use either English or Afrikaans in presenting their cases before courts. The import of language policy pre-Apartheid is the attainment of justice between parties involved in a dispute. A classic relevant case is *University of Pretoria v Minister of Education* (1948) in which the University of Pretoria case was dismissed because Malan J arguably understood the arguments advanced in English more, as opposed to Afrikaans. It is therefore important to recognise that arguments for the University of Pretoria were advanced in Afrikaans whilst the legal representatives made their arguments in English. To further buttress the import of language and legislation on jurisprudence is the fact that Malan J delivered the judgment in English.

S39 (b) of the Constitution of the Republic of South Africa (Republic of South Africa, 1996) is a peremptory provision which bounds South Africa to enforce international law domestically. The peremptory provision of S39 (b) is significant due to the fact that South Africa is a signatory to the International Covenant on Economic, Social and Cultural Rights (ICESCR) as envisaged by General Comment 13 which inter alia entrenches the right to education, which is essentially intertwined to language rights (Brickhill et al., 2023: 42–4 & 42–5). The ICESCR, General Comment 13 read with S29 (2) of the Constitution arguably is at odds with 'reasonableness' standard to the realisation of the educational rights which are intertwined with linguistic rights to greater extent (Osode & Glover, 2010: 86–87). General Comment 13 to the ICESCR articulates that education is 'Both a human right and indispensable means of realising other human rights. As an empowerment right, education is the primary vehicle by which economically and socially marginalized adults and children can lift themselves out of poverty and obtain the means to participate fully in their communities... Increasingly, education is recognised as the best financial investments states can make. But the importance of education is not just practical: a well-educated, enlightened, and active mind, able to wander freely and widely, is one of the joys and rewards of human existence'. Therefore, linguistic rights entrenched in ICESCR read with S29 (2) strongly suggest that linguistic rights should be accorded the same strength as other constitutional rights such as human dignity and freedom.

The advent of constitutionalism in South Africa, post 1996 in terms of the 1996 Constitution ushered in a new dispensation of multilingualism (Currie & De Waal, 2013: 32–33). This is because the South African Constitution now recognises 11 official spoken languages. The indigenous languages are now recognised as official languages with the recent addition of South African Sign Language as the 12th official language (Republic of South Africa NA, 2023). However, to the extent that all the indigenous languages are recognised as official languages, English and Afrikaans remain dominant and therefore continue to shape, influence, and develop jurisprudence. Section 39 (2) of the South African Constitution requires the Courts to develop common law to the extent that is in compliant with the Bill of Rights (Republic of South Africa, 1996). Remarkably, the origin of common law is Roman-Dutch law and the official languages of choice in development of jurisprudence are most dominantly English and to a lesser extent Afrikaans as far as back as 1948 in which the judgment by Malan J was delivered in English in the *University of Pretoria v Minister of Education*.

The apex court, that is the Constitutional Court (hereinafter referred to as the ConCourt) has a language provision under Rule 25. Rule 25 provides for English as the medium of communication between litigants and the Court. Thus, post-Apartheid era, English arguably retains its super-dominant position over indigenous languages based on the proposition that English is the language understood by all. To the extent that the basis of the conclusion of English being understood by all, it is mandatory that any document submitted by litigants to the court must be translated into English. However, the provision of translation of indigenous languages to English arguably falls short to the extent that all official languages must be equal because the official medium of communication by the courts adopted by custom is English.

The right of litigants to use their own language is of importance in a multiracial and multicultural society such as South Africa. Critics of the super-dominant position of English as the official means of communication in the justice system argue that 'the right to use one's language of choice is also meaningless if the court cannot understand that language or if what is said or written therein is' (Harms, 2012). The significance of the argument is that in a multilingual society such as South Africa, the court and litigants should be in a position to conduct court proceedings and correspondence without heavily relying on interpreters to facilitate the communication. In so far as the litigants have the right to use any of the official 11 spoken languages, they must however be translated into English, which means indigenous languages are subservient to the English language. Hence, George Orwell stated 'all languages are equal, but English is more equal than others' (Harms, 2012).

Democratic governance

South Africa is also known as the 'rainbow nation' because of multiracialism being a cornerstone of the Constitution of South Africa (Republic of South Africa, 1996), inter alia, the document recognises the diversity of all people with regards to race. On the basis of multiracialism comes multilingualism and, therefore, language policies have a direct bearing on the exercise of rights, specifically in democratic governance. According to Du Plessis J in *Lourens v Die President* (2010) '... the state and local governments have an obligation to use indigenous language as an official language of communication to its constituents'. The legal requirement that local government use indigenous language in official communication is a ripple effect which empowers constituents to understand the law in their own language and meaningfully participate in various democratic activities. Thus, on this basis official communication of government policies using indigenous languages enables constituents to make submissions and voice objections where they deem necessary in the process, such as public consultations on bills before they are enacted into law. This was demonstrated by the ConCourt in the case of *Brummer v Minister of Social Development* (2009), where it was strongly remarked that 'access to information is crucial to the right of freedom of expression which includes freedom of the press and other media and freedom to receive and impart information or ideas'.

Notably, in the past few years, particularly in the Eastern Cape Province, cities and towns have been renamed to reflect local indigenous languages. With the renaming of some cities for example, Port Elizabeth renamed to Gqeberha, the same has also been applied to renaming of courts to customarily use the dominant indigenous language, which as isiXhosa in the Eastern Cape Province as per the Government Gazette (Republic of South Africa, 2021). The change of the names of cities, towns, and courts from the English to isiXhosa language is consistent with the goal towards elevating indigenous languages to the same level as English. The Minister of Arts and Culture, through public consultations, initiated the change of names through a legal process. The process followed by the Minister was exceptionally important in pursuit of democratic governance. This is because a proposal was made to Eastern Cape Province residents who were asked to submit comments or objections to the renaming of the cities and towns to the isiXhosa language from the English language. Thus, an essential component of public participation is evident as objections that were submitted were regarded as insufficient to overturn the process of name changes to indigenous names. It follows that the import of renaming of cities, towns, and courts is a positive step towards the actualisation of policy that local governments should communicate in indigenous languages as they are recognised official languages (Turi, 1993: 12).

The right to use any of the official languages and association with a linguistic group is a fundamental human right expressly guaranteed by the Bill of Rights under the South African Constitution under section 31 (a) and (b). It is thus an important qualification in as far as the right to use any of the official languages with specific reference to any linguistic group. This is because an obligation is imposed on public office bearers to promote and protect the Bill of Rights in language policies and legislation. The exercise of freedom of expression is encapsulated in section 16 of the Constitution, which is a fundamental human right directly linked to the right to use any of the official languages and association with a linguistic group. Therefore, the right to freedom of expression consequently demands that any language policy and legislation must not violate the right to use any of the official languages. Notably, freedom of speech has arguably become a point of contention in the 21st century and it follows that language rights under the Constitution are protected as envisaged in a rainbow nation.

Equality and prevention of unfair discrimination

Equality before the law pertaining to language rights and linguistic association is another fundamental human right guaranteed by the Bill of Rights in Chapter 2 of the Constitution. For instance, according to the Magistrates' Courts Act 32 of 1944, section 6(1) (2) provides that '... either of the official languages may be used at any stage of the proceedings in any court and evidence shall be recorded in the language so used'. Therefore, it means that all the eleven official spoken languages and the recent addition of South African Sign Language are on par with English and Afrikaans (Ramoupi, 2014). However, in as much as equality under the auspices of language rights and linguistic rights association are on principle equal, there remains a lacuna for indigenous languages to be fully operational (Maclennan, 2023).

The Constitution under section 9 expressly states that 'everyone is equal before the law and has the right to equal protection and benefit of the law, (3) stipulates that the state may not unfairly discriminate directly or indirectly against anyone on one or more grounds, including race, gender, sex, pregnancy, marital status, ethnic or social origin, color, sexual orientation, age, disability, religion, conscience, belief, culture, language, and birth'. Unequivocally, section 9 prohibits any form of unfair discrimination as envisaged by the Bill of Rights, and language rights are no exception. The importance of the law, as provided under section 6 of the Constitution, is to ensure that all persons are treated equally before the law in canvassing in any of the official languages is underscored as the 'symbolic power of language'. Flynn connotes that the 'symbolic power of language' is a key determinant of 'legal capacity and personhood under the law' (Cavanagh, 2014). Therefore, due to constitutional prescript of equality before the law in tandem with the 'symbolic power of language', it is ensured that individuals and diverse linguistic communities at large are empowered through recognition of indigenous languages to fully exercise their legal rights.

Decolonisation of education and language policy

As a norm in a constitutional democracy, legitimacy of policies and legislation is derived from the Constitution. Section 29 of the Constitution reads 'everyone has the right to receive education in the official language or languages of their choice in public educational institutions where that education is reasonably practicable... ' Section 29 is undeniably the bedrock for the promulgation of the Higher Education Act 101 of 1997 (HEA) which in turn gave birth to Language Policy of Higher Education. Notably, the HEA was promulgated in 1997, soon after the independence of South Africa in 1994. The adoption of the HEA and consequently the Language Policy of Higher Education is arguably driven by the fact that 'formal colonial education systems have remained culturally and linguistically alien to the majority of the population'. Hence, the promulgation of the HEA and adoption of the Language Policy for Higher Education is a significant and positive step in decolonising the education systems which were flawed in as far as recognition and use of indigenous languages is concerned (Ramoupi, 2014).

The state or the government, in terms of paragraph 3.1 of the Language Policy of Higher Education, read with S29 of the Constitution, confers a positive obligation to 'ensure the effective access to, and implementation of this right, the state has to consider all reasonable educational alternatives including single medium institutions, taking into account equity, practicability, and the need to redress the results of past racially discriminatory laws and practices'. This means, in as far as the language policy and legislation in a democratic and independent South Africa are concerned, the principles underscored in *Government of the Republic of South Africa and Others v Grootboom and Others* (2000) are applicable. The importance of the principles in the *Grootboom* case is the judicial precedent set for the enforcement of socio-economic rights. In enforcement of the social-economic rights as it relates to language rights is directly dependant on the available resources to the government to ensure that indigenous languages are officially adopted and used as a medium of learning and teaching. Put differently, undoing the discriminatory laws and practices pertaining to languages is a progressive realisation of the language rights as envisaged under the Constitution.

In so far as language policy and legislation pertaining to higher education is concerned, it is important to note the indispensable role of higher institutions of education, as 'multilingual proficiency is critical' for the students to fully participate in the nation. However, against the backdrop of the desire to achieve 'multilingual proficiency', the stumbling block arguably is the language policy at high school level where one either studies Afrikaans or English as their home language. Thus, at matric level it further buttresses the importance of English and Afrikaans despite the provision that 'everyone has the right to receive education in any of the official languages…' The contentious issue of the medium of instruction at public institutions is perhaps even clearer in higher institutions of education, with special reference to universities.

Comparative analysis using foreign jurisprudence case law

Cavanagh opines that 'the study of language can reveal how knowledge manifests itself in the creation of various institutions and other social phenomena that define a culture or subculture…' (Cavanagh, 2014). Court decisions are therefore important to examine the role and importance of language in shaping society (Cavanagh, 2014). The classic decision of *Ruiz v Hull* is a good example of the importance of language policies and the inherent power of language. *Ruiz v Hull* (1998) is a decision of the Arizona

Supreme Court in the USA, which is therefore binding on all lower courts. *Ruiz v Hull* is primarily a matter which dealt with a constitutional amendment to the Arizona State Constitution to the effect that 'all state and local government business in Arizona to be conducted only in English'.

It follows that the amendment of the Arizona State Constitution where English would be deemed to be the only means of communication was a direct violation of the USA Constitution's first amendment of the right which guarantees freedom of speech. The first amendment stipulates that '[c]ongress shall make no law respecting an establishment of religion or prohibiting the free exercise thereof; or abridging the freedom of speech, or of the press; or the right of the people peaceably to assemble, and to petition the Government for a redress of grievances'. Therefore, the Arizona Supreme Court struck down the amendment to be unconstitutional as it violated the first amendment rights. The import of the *Ruiz v Hull* judgment that struck down English to be the exclusive means of communication in the state of Arizona is that not all people speak or understand English. As a result, the promulgation of English-only language policy into the state Constitution failed to pass the constitutional safeguards of protecting fundamental human rights guaranteed under the first amendment.

Equal protection under the law is another major basis for the Arizona Supreme Court striking down the adopted amendment to the Arizona Constitution (Cavanagh, 2014). The violation of the first amendment rights consequently infringed the fourteenth amendment rights, specifically the equal protection clause with reference and agreement to the Ninth Circuit Court's decision in the matter of *Yniguez v. AOE* (1997). Therefore, the amendment to the effect that the medium of communication only be in English was untenable and justifiable because 'American tradition of tolerance recognises a critical difference between encouraging the use of English and repressing use of other languages'. Notably, the equal protection clause encapsulated in the fourteenth amendment is equally applicable and underwritten in Section 9 of the South African Constitution. Hence, the Arizona Supreme Court judgment is relevant under the South African context, particularly in the pre-Apartheid era dispensation.

Further, the role and import of language is at the core of the decision of the Supreme Court in the matter of *United States v Virginia* (1996). In *United States v Virginia*, Justice Ruth Ginsberg, through the use of language as a tool or aid of constitutional interpretation struck down the Virginia military policy, which included men only and excluded women. It is important to note that the men-only exclusive policy of enlisting in the military in the state of Virginia was primarily based on Justice Ruth Ginsberg's purposive approach in constitutional interpretation. '[A] framework of progress' language was employed in striking down the unconstitutional policy which excluded women from the state of Virginia from being enlisted in the army. The constitutional interpretation adopted by Justice Ruth Ginsberg is also reflected in the South African cases of *Ferreira v Levine NO and Others; Vryenhoek and Others v Powell NO and Others* (1996), in which the ConCourt asserted that '[t]he generous interpretation of a charter right would require a court to interpret the language in the widest possible manner. By contrast the purposive interpretation is predicated upon the purpose of the right, with the result being that the widest possible interpretation will not inevitably be the one which will be supported.' Therefore, the case of *United States v Virginia* extrapolates the indispensable positive impact of language in 'producing change for everyone not just for those in power.' Also, the positive impact of language in this matter is that constitutional rights are protected and enforced.

The case of *Brown v Board of Education* (1954) is also significant and important in unpacking the critical role and importance of language. The USA Supreme Court denoted that 'education is the very foundation of good citizenship', therefore, arguably the primary language and medium of instruction to learners demands all languages be on par to the extent that ensures that language policy does not become a barrier to equal access to education. The import of the judgment in *Brown v Board of Education* is the pronouncement of a new phase which began the process of outlawing racial segregation and strove towards creating equal opportunities for all. Thus, strengthening the position that language policy must promote equals access to education for all, as this is a fundamental human right of learners.

Discussion of SA case law

The pursuit of language rights is feasibly underpinned by the quest for equal educational opportunities and inevitably a better quality of life, particularly in a post-Apartheid South Africa. Malherbe, with reference to linguistic rights, thus opines: 'the right goes further than Article 2 of Protocol I of the European Convention on Human Rights and Fundamental Freedoms as it was interpreted and applied in the Belgian Linguistic cases, and that it indeed imposes a duty on the state to provide such education wherever reasonably practicable. The right is not confined to existing facilities either. The right applies to all education and is not restricted to basic education. Even institutions of higher education are therefore required to provide instruction in the languages preferred by students. However, the right extends only to the official languages and not to all languages used in South Africa.' (Malherbe, 2004)

Haysom (2005: 23–5), opines that 'the increasing tendency to recognise and protect language rights in more recent national constitutions reflects a concern with resisting the "globalisation" of dominant languages, and, much more specifically, with the recognition of the value of diversity as opposed to uniformity – an appreciation that equality does not imply sameness'. It is therefore indispensable in a post-Apartheid South Africa that all official languages are equally important, and learners should as reasonably as possible receive basic and higher education in their preferred language of instruction.

The ConCourt further asserted the importance of language rights in enjoyment and exercise of constitutional rights in the case of *EC for Education: KwaZulu-Natal and Others v Pillay* (2007), and remarked that 'At its core is the notion that sometimes the community, whether it is the state, an employer or a school, must take positive measures and possibly incur additional hardship or expense in order to allow all people to participate and enjoy all their rights equally. It ensures that we do not relegate people to the margins of society because they do not or cannot conform to certain social norms'.

S29 of the South African Constitution provides the express right to education which differs from that of the USA. Therefore, South Africa has a firmer foundation for creating equal educational opportunities with its diverse population, as similarly denoted in the case of *San Antonio Independent School District v Rodriguez* (1973). The express right to education is directly connected to language rights of learners to receive education in any of the official languages, thereby inevitably protecting numerous constitutional rights such as right to education, dignity, equality, and freedom of expression (Steinmann, 2016). Notably, it must be taken into account that 'the right to education is synonymously referred to as an empowerment right'. Coomans (2005: 56–7 & 57–8). Thus, the pursuit of linguistic rights in post-Apartheid South Africa has been a point of contention, especially in higher institutions of learning, with special reference to the adoption of a language policy applicable to an institution. Hence, South African case law shall be discussed to shed more light on the impact of language policies and legislation on the South African legal system.

In the case of *University of the Free State v Afriforum* (2017) (hereinafter referred to as the UFS case), the legality of the decision of the university to adopt English as the primary language of instruction was challenged in context of S27 of the Higher Education Act 101 of 1997. The UFS case brought to light the challenges and to some extent irreconcilable differences of the pursuit to place all official languages on par with one another. For instance, despite Afrikaans having historically been the primary language of instruction, it was inevitable that in a post-Apartheid South Africa the language policy had to be reviewed to ensure that it is compliant with the constitutional values of a democratic society. Because the UFS primary language of instruction was Afrikaans, it automatically meant that English was made the alternative language of instruction. Consequently, this gave birth to a parallel language medium policy.

Prior to the judgment of the Supreme Court of Appeal verdict in the UFS case, the acute overriding issue was the toxicity of escalated racial tensions and complaints between staff, extending even to students. This was despite the desirability of Afrikaans and English to arguably both be mediums of instruction, which was consistent with S27 of the Higher Education Act. Therefore, it can be concluded that in instances where the co-existence of official languages, which results in a parallel medium language policy with untenable consequences, it is justified to adopt a single language policy which is in the best interests of everyone in a free and democratic South Africa.

The case of *Gelyke Kanse and Others v Chairperson of the Senate of the University of Stellenbosch and Others* (2017) (or the Stellenbosch case) is also significant and relevant in unpacking linguistic rights pursuant to the impact of language policies and legislation in South Africa. Akin to the UFS case, the applicants in the Stellenbosch case launched a review application seeking to set aside the decisions of the senate and council to no longer have Afrikaans as the medium of instruction as illegal on the basis of S27(2) of the Higher Education Act. Stellenbosch University, in this matter, adopted English as the new medium of instruction to replace Afrikaans. Notably, the Stellenbosch case illuminates the dichotomy of the simultaneous development of a multilingual environment in higher education while at the same time ensuring the existing language of instruction is not an impediment to development and access to opportunities.

It is worth noting that the Constitutional Court held in the UFS case that 'University of the Free State was not under legal obligation to apply the Language Policy for Higher Education (LPHE) and was free to depart from it for good reason'. Thus, the same principle was applicable in the Stellenbosch case (Cele, 2021). This means institutions of higher learning are not compelled by law to comply with the LPHE pursuant to ensuring that all official languages are treated equally. However, it is only S29 (1) (2) of the Constitution which is binding in pursuance of linguistic rights. S29 (1)(2) is perhaps the best defence available for the protection and advancement of linguistic rights, according to the Stellenbosch case. From the Stellenbosch case, the benchmark to the realisation of linguistic rights is 'reasonableness'. It follows that the simultaneous development of languages together with a well-established language of instruction is debatably at its infant stages because the full-blown realisation of language rights is highly dependent on 'resource constraints and feasibility of adopting a particular language'.

Notably, the unanimous verdict of the ConCourt in *Chairperson of the Council of Unisa v AfriForum NPC* (2021) (or the Unisa case) is also of great importance in the analysis of the impact of language policies and legislation in South Africa. The ConCourt in its decision meticulously distinguished the Unisa case from the UFS and Stellenbosch cases, respectively. This is because in the Unisa matter, the ConCourt established that Unisa failed to discharge the onus of proof on a balance of probabilities of equity, practicability, and redress of the past in abandoning Afrikaans as a medium of instruction to the adoption of English. As a result, the Unisa long distance mode of learning was deemed not to perpetuate racial segregation based on the language of instruction. Unisa was therefore differentiated from prevailing factors in traditional in-class learning as depicted in the UFS and Stellenbosch cases. It follows that Unisa was not justified to arbitrarily cancel Afrikaans as a medium of instruction on the object to advance equity, practicability, and redress of the past, which is even acknowledged in the preamble of the Constitution.

Conclusion

To conclude, linguistic rights are socio-economic rights which are guaranteed by the International Covenant on Economic, Social and Economic Rights (ICESCR). South Africa is a signatory to the ICESCR and therefore, in terms of S39(2) of the Constitution, is bound to domesticate and implement international law. It follows that section 29 of the Constitution was adopted as the grand norm to give effect to the ICESCR with regards to linguistic rights. In as much as the linguistic rights are inherently constitutional rights, the enforcement is dependent on availability of resources.

Consequently, the realisation of linguistic rights, progress, and development is constrained by the availability of resources to ensure that all official languages are on par. Also, the English language has arguably consolidated its dominant role in day-to-day life in South Africa despite the availability of ten other official spoken languages. Notably, it can be argued that linguistic rights are indispensable and intrinsically linked to access to resources, development, and success of an individual and inevitably the society at large in the post-Apartheid South Africa.

References

Brickhill, J., Hassim, A., Bishop, M. & Ngcukaitobi, T. (2023). *South African Constitutional Law*. Cape Town: Juta.

Brown v Board of Education (1954).

Brummer v Minister of Social Development and Others (2009).

Cavanagh, MA. (2014). Ruiz v. Hull: A Legal and Rhetorical Examination of 'English-Only' Legislation. *First Amendment Studies,* 48(2) 81–96.

Cele, N. (2021). Understanding Language Policy As a Tool for Access and Social Inclusion in South African Higher Education: A Critical Policy Analysis Perspective. *South African Journal of Higher Education* 35 (6), 25–46. https://doi.org/10.20853/35-6-3730.

Certification of the Constitution of the Republic of South Africa, 1996 (CCT 23/96) [1996] ZACC 26; 1996 (4) SA 744 (CC); 1996 (10) BCLR 1253 (CC) (6 September 1996). https://www.saflii.org/za/cases/ZACC/1996/26.html

Cheadle, H. & Davis, D. (2002). *South African Constitutional Law: The Bill of Rights*. South Africa: LexisNexis.

Constitutional Court Rules. (2003). Juta's Statutes Editors. (2015). *Superior Courts Act & Magistrates' Courts Act and Rules*. Cape Town: Juta.

Coomans, APM. & Veriava, F. (2005). The Right to education. In Brand, D. & Heyns, C. (ed.) *Socio-Economic Rights in South Africa* (pp. 57–83). Pretoria University Law Press.

Chairperson of the Council of Unisa v AfriForum NPC (2021).

Currie, I. & De Waal, J. (2013). The *Bill of Rights Handbook*. (sixth edition). Cape Town: Juta.

Davis, D., Cheadle, H. & Haysom, N. (1997). *Fundamental Rights in the Constitution: Commentary and Cases.* Cape Town: Juta.

Du Plessis v De Klerk and Another (1996).

Ferreira v Levine NO and Others; *Vryenhoek and Others v Powell NO and Others* (1996).

Gelyke Kanse and Others v Chairperson of the Senate of the University of Stellenbosch and Others (2017).

Gelyke Kanse and Others v Chairman of the Senate of the Stellenbosch University and Others (2017).

Glover, G. & Osode, PC. (2010). *Law and Transformative Justice in Post-Apartheid South Africa*. Spekboom Publishers.

Government of the Republic of South Africa and Others v Grootboom and Others (2000).

Harksen v Lane (1998).

Harms, L. (2012). Law and Language in a Multilingual Society. *Potchefstroom Electronic Law Journal* 15(2) 23–25.

Haysom, N. (2005). South African Constitutional Law. In: Cheadle, H. & Davis, D (ed.) *South African Constitutional Law: The Bill of Rights*. South Africa: LexisNexis.

International Covenant on Economic, Social and Cultural Rights. https://www.ohchr.org/sites/default/files/cescr.pdf [Accessed 30 October 2023].

Language Policy Framework for Public Higher Education Institutions, Department of Higher Education and Training. Government Gazette. GN 1160 GG43860 [Date accessed: 30 October 2023].

Lourens v Die President (2010).

Maclennan, S. (2023). Teaching children how to read for meaning- a complex process. *Daily Dispatch.* Accessed @https://www.dispatchlive.co.za/news/2023-10-25-teaching-children-how-to-read-for-meaning-a-complex-process/ [Date accessed: 30 October 2023]

Magistrates Courts Act of 1944 as amended. Juta's Statutes Editors. (2015). *Superior Courts Act & Magistrates' Courts Act and Rules*. Cape Town: Juta.

Malherbe, R. (2004). The Constitutional Framework for Pursuing Equal Opportunities in Education. Perspectives in Education 22(3).

Maseko, P. (2014). Multilingualism at work in South African higher education: From policy to practice. In Hibbert, L. & Van der Walt, C. (ed.) *Multilingualism in South Africa: Reflecting society in higher education*. Bristol: Multilingual Matters. https://doi.org/10.21832/9781783091669-005

Moseneke, D. (2002). Fourth Bram Fischer Memorial Lecture: Transformative Adjudication. *South African Journal on Human Rights,* 18 (309).

Ramoupi, NLL. (2014). African Languages Policy in the Education of South Africa: 20 Years of Freedom or Subjugation. *Journal of Higher Education in Africa* 12(2).

Republic of South Africa (RSA). (1944). *Magistrates' Court Act 32 of 1944*. Pretoria: Government Printer.

Republic of South Africa (RSA). (1996). *The National Education Policy Act 27 of 1996.* Pretoria: Government Printer.

Republic of South Africa (RSA). 1996. *Constitution of the Republic of South Africa.* Pretoria: Government Printer.

Republic of South Africa (RSA). (1997). *Higher Education Act 101 of 1997*. Government Gazette, 390(18515):1–47.

Ruiz v Hull (1998)

San Antonio Independent School District v Rodriguez (1973).

Sheff v O'Neill (1996).

Steinmann, AC. (2016). The Core Meaning of Human Dignity. *Potchefstroom Electronic Law Journal* 19. https://doi.org/10.17159/1727-3781/2016/v19i0a1244.

Turi, JG. (1993). The importance of the conference theme: Language and equality. In Prinsloo, K., Peters, Y., Turi, JG. & Van Rensburg, C. (eds.) *Language, law and equality*. Proceedings of the Third International Conference of the International Academy of Language Law (IALL) held in South Africa, April 1992. Pretoria: University of South Africa (Unisa). 5–24. https://bit.ly/2QyA4Qw [Date accessed: 5 August 2023].

United Nations (UN). (1948). *Universal Declaration of Human Rights*. New York: United Nations. Accessed @https://bit.ly/3weMewX [Date accessed: 30 October 2023].

United States of America (USA). (2007). *The Constitution of the United States of America as Amended.* Washington, DC: Government Printing Office. Accessed @ https://www.govinfo.gov/content/pkg/CDOC-110hdoc50/pdf/CDOC-110hdoc50.pdf [Date accessed: 30 October 2023].

United States v Virginia (1996).

University of the Free State v Afriforum (2017).

University of Pretoria v Minister of Education (1948).

Vereinigung Bildender Künstler v Austria (2007).

Woolman, S. (1998-2003). Limitations. In M. Chaskalson, M. J. Kentridge, J., Klaaren, J., Marcus, G., Spitz, D. & Woolman, S. (ed.) *Constitutional Law of South Africa* (first edition). Cape Town: Juta Law. 12–1; 12–66.

Yniguez v AOE (1997).

15 ORAL LEGAL TRADITIONS AS AN INSTRUMENT OF PEACEBUILDING: ANALYSING THE CUSTOMARY COURT PROCEEDINGS OF BANEN COMMUNITY OF CAMEROON

Endurence K.M. Dissake

Introduction

To promote international cooperation and achieve peace and security, nations created two inter-governmental organisations; the League of Nations in 1919, and the United Nations (UN) in 1946. Despite their membership in the UN, many African nations have known bloody wars, for instance; the Somali Civil War in 1991; The Rwandan genocide in 1994; the Allied Democratic Forces insurgency in 1996; the Ituri conflict in 1999; the Insurgency in the Maghreb in 2002; the war in Darfur in 2003; the Sudanese nomadic conflicts in 2008; Boko Haram insurgency in Nigeria, Cameroon, Niger, and Chad in 2009, etc.

Indeed, excluding the conflicts of Vietnam, Cambodia, and Afghanistan, as well as the case of Palestine, Africa is the continent of the world where armed conflicts occur most frequently, and for thirty years has had the greatest number of war victims (Adam, 2002). Of the 45 African countries located south of the equator, about ten, at most, escaped an almost chronic situation of collective conflict, while nearly half of those countries experienced wars involving, directly or indirectly, the death of at least ten million people. The number of victims of African wars has greatly exceeded the figures of so-called 'natural' disasters. For instance, the war in Sudan has claimed more than two million lives, and recent conflicts in Liberia, Sierra Leone, the Democratic Republic of Congo and the Central African Republic, Uganda, and Côte d'Ivoire have claimed over one million lives (Gendreau, 1996).

As a matter of fact, western peacebuilding instruments (e.g. inter-governmental organisations, non-governmental organisations, international human rights legislation, liberal internationalism, etc.) imposed and implemented in Africa have not been able to respond, and even less to adapt, to African needs (Stiffman, 2015; Wegener & Otter,

2008). However, history suggests that before the arrival of settlers and their legal systems, African nations enjoyed long stretches of peace.

During the pre-colonial period, African communities arbitrated many disputes through customary laws. These laws were successful strategies of peacebuilding in Africa because they were made by Africans, in Africa, and for Africans (Owino, 2016). Customary laws are also called 'oral laws' or 'oral legal traditions' because they are transmitted orally. For centuries, communities depended upon oral communication to teach their members important traditional values on how to peacefully live in the community. Mbiti (1975) further asserted that 'most African people did not invent an alphabet for the art of reading and writing', hence, they could not keep written records of their history. Research on African oral or customary laws does not only implicate legal and anthropological studies, but also involves linguistics research (the theoretical and societal description of African languages in legal settings).

Using the case of the Banen community's customary law and native language (Tunen), this article outlines a relatively new method of peacebuilding (the communal peacebuilding strategy*)* to demonstrate the efficacy of oral legal traditions in rural areas of Africa. The article is divided into five sections; the first section serves as an introduction, with some background information, the research statement, and the aim of the work. The second section discusses the communal peacebuilding strategy. The third section describes the research methodology i.e. the data collection and data analysis frameworks (documentary linguistics, oblique translation, and ethnography of communication). The fourth section presents and analyses the customary court discourse collected during the Banen community's traditional legal proceedings. Finally, the fifth section concludes the work.

A communal peacebuilding strategy

The UN peacebuilding department defined peacebuilding as an activity that aims to resolve injustice in nonviolent ways, and to transform the cultural and structural conditions that generate deadly or destructive conflict. Peacebuilding also involves a range of measures targeted to reduce the risk of lapsing or relapsing into conflict by strengthening national capacities at all levels for conflict management and laying the foundations for sustainable peace and development (Peacebuilding & The United Nations, 2012). Many differentiate the term 'peacebuilding' from other related labels (e.g. peacemaking, peacekeeping, and conflict resolution) to specify the time and context of war. I used the term 'peacebuilding' more broadly to refer to any stage of conflict.

To manage conflicts, promote peace, and sustainable development in Africa, readymade western measures must be set aside to give more space to local solutions, those that conform to African traditions and beliefs. De Coning (2013) argued that peacebuilding is essentially local. This article thus suggests a local strategy for peacebuilding in Africa, a strategy I term a 'communal peacebuilding strategy'; 'communal', in the sense that native or traditional activities like customary court proceedings are instrumentalised to resolve conflicts and bring peace. But before scrutinising the concept of African customary laws, it is first necessary to define the terms that are dedicated to it.

In this article, terms like 'customary law', 'oral legal traditions', and 'customary court proceedings' are used to refer to laws in Africa. Nevertheless, each of these appellations has its specificity. First, the term 'customary law' can be defined as a set of customs, practices, and beliefs that are accepted as obligatory rules of conduct by indigenous peoples and local communities (WIPO Secretariat, 2013). Counter to codified laws, which emanate from a constituted political authority, customary laws consist of a group of customs that are recognised and shared collectively by a community, people, tribe, or ethnic group. The second appellation, 'oral legal tradition', outlines the grammatical status of customary laws i.e. the oral or spoken form. Customary laws are also termed 'oral laws' because they are handed down and perpetuated by word of mouth rather than by writing; in other words, they are not codified. The third appellation, 'customary court proceedings', refers to the process of application/implementation of customary law. Customary court proceedings consist of naturally occurring discussions between traditional legal authorities and litigants (i.e. plaintiffs, accused, and witnesses) in palaces or chiefdoms. The proceedings are usually divided into two contexts of discussions; 1) customary court debates, and 2) customary court deliberations. While customary court debates are interactions between traditional rulers and litigants, customary court deliberations are discussions among traditional rulers to decide whether or not an accused is guilty and in case he/she is declared guilty, they agree on the punishment to apply.

In the Republic of Cameroon, customary court proceedings are conducted in national languages in rural areas. Apart from English and French (the official languages) Cameroon counts more than 250 national languages distributed over its ten regions, namely Adamawa, Centre, East, Far North, Littoral, North, Northwest, South, Southwest, and West. The national language of the Banen natives is Tunen. Therefore, in the Banen community, all customary court proceedings are conducted in the Tunen language. Banen natives are located in the Centre and Littoral regions of Cameroon. In the Centre region, they are sited in the Mbam division, Ndikinimeki and Makenene Subdivisions. In the Littoral region, they are found in the Nkam division and Yingui Subdivision. Their native language, Tunen, is a narrow-Bantu language classified under the Bassa (A.44) subgroup. Tunen is spoken by approximately 40,000 people (Eberhard et al., 2022).

To use the customary court proceedings of the Banen community as a peacebuilding strategy, three main domains of research are taken into consideration: law, culture, and language. Thus, this work broadens the perspectives of peace and conflict studies by way of a multidisciplinary research approach. Actually, as an applied linguist, I suggest the application of linguistics knowledge (language description) to analyse oral law to demonstrate its efficacy in peacebuilding in Africa.

The research methodology

This research proceeds on both theoretical and empirical levels. At the empirical level, the data collection was carried out in 2020 during a documentary linguistic project where I was the principal investigator. The project, *Documenting communicative practices of customary court proceedings: The case of Tunen native-speakers of the Ndikbiakat Canton*, sponsored by the Endangered Languages Documentation Programme, aimed at audio- and video-recording customary court proceedings in the Ndikbiakat Canton, a village of the Littoral region of Cameroon inhabited mainly by Banen natives. The documentation followed a strict documentary linguistics methodology, i.e. field trips, recordings, metadata maintenance, transcription, annotation, translation into languages of wider communication, and archiving (Gippert et al., 2006). My team and I spend three months in Ndikbiakat. During the field trip, we audio- and video-recorded customary court hearings, traditional leaders' deliberations, chief verdicts, and traditional leaders' interviews. In sum, we video-recorded three hours of court hearings, 17 minutes of court verdicts, three hours of interviews, and audio-recorded 59 minutes of court deliberations. I later processed the recordings into ELAN, an annotation tool for audio and video recordings. By processing, I mean transcribing, annotating, and translating to English and French. Finally, I archived the data in ELAR, a digital repository for preserving multimedia collections of endangered languages. The data can be accessed through the link https://www.elararchive.org/dk0615 (Dissake, 2021).

The data analysis follows two theoretical frameworks; oblique translation and ethnography of communication. For data accessibility, I chose to translate the recorded discourse from Tunen to two languages of wider communication (English and French). Translation is an intercultural and intralingual activity that deals with (at least) two linguistic systems embedded in two different cultures. The difficulties inherent in the translation process vary proportionately with the degree of distance between the languages and the cultures involved (Bandia, 1993). Translation from African to European languages is an example of a translation between non-related languages and cultures. It is a translation of an oral 'text' into written form, on the one hand, and a translation from one language culture into an alien language culture, on the other (Snell-Hornby, 1988). To successfully translate distance languages Vinay & Darbelnet (1960) suggested the oblique translation strategy. Oblique translation is used when the structural or conceptual elements of the source language cannot be directly translated without altering the meaning or upsetting the grammatical and stylistic elements of the target language. Oblique translation involves five methods of translation: transposition, modulation, reformulation or equivalence, adaptation, and compensation. Three methods are used in this research, namely transposition, adaptation, and equivalence.

Transposition describes a word class shift without changing the texts' semantics. We can illustrate it with the Tunen noun *mɔndɔ̀* ('leg/foot') which changes its words class from noun to adjective in the translation below:

TU	**mɔkɔlɔ̀**	wɔ̀	**mɔndɔ̀**
GL	**foot**	1.AGR	man
OT	Man's **foot**		

The second method, adaptation, is used when the metalinguistic condition referred to in the original text does not exist in the target language. For instance, the concept of 'school' was unknown to the Banen people for many years. Consequently, the word school does not exist in the Tunen lexicon. Banen natives adapted the English word 'school' to the phonetic and morphological rules of Tunen as seen in the example below:

TU	Bá	lɛ̀	nduɔ	ákána	u	**isukùlu**
GL	they	NEG	PR	go	to	**school**
OT	They are going to **school**					

The third oblique method, equivalence, is often used when translating names of institutions, interjections, idioms, or proverbs. Translators used completely different lexes to transfer meanings of names and expressions. Equivalence is used for rendering more elaborate structures between source and target languages. For instance, the English word 'court' does not exist in many African languages' lexicons because it owes its existence to a codified legal system, hence, African natives are often compelled to find equivalence during legal discussions. In the example below, a Banen native uses the Tunen noun *nàkúm* (hall) to refer to 'court':

TU	**nàkúm**	nàm		àkúlúwóné
GL	**hall**	people	PR	greet
OT	I greet the **court**			

The illustrations given in the previous paragraphs allow me to suggest that translation from an African to a European language does not rely solely on the skills of the translators but also considers the language use, performance, and competence of native speakers. Indeed, the translations, *nàkúm* – 'court' and *isukùlu* – 'school', come from the linguistic intuition of Tunen speakers and not from the translator's lone competence. As a matter of fact, no translation is done without social consideration. Nevertheless, it is up to the translators to choose the best method of translation, the one that satisfies the targeted audience. After the oblique translation strategy, in the data processing, the ethnography of communication framework followed.

Ethnography of communication (EC) is a multidisciplinary approach that employs ethnographic accounts of actual communication events and occasions to understand distinct cultural and contextual dimensions of communication (Chaim, 2017). I chose to analyse the customary court discourse using the EC approach because EC pursues language as an important and integral part of social life and cultural activity; it focuses on events and rituals that are part of the culture that is studied. EC permitted me to outline the peacebuilding themes developed by court participants during the trial. Indeed, EC turned out to be an appropriate analytical tool for the collected data.

Aside from EC research skills, SPEAKING is a helpful tool for a holistic analysis of communication (Hymes, 1962). This acronym is a memory aid that includes eight letters: S – designates setting, including time, duration, and cultural definitions of the event; P – designates participants and participant identities, ranging from age, sex, and social status to relationships between participants; E – designates ends, seeking the goals and outcomes of communicative events; A – refers to act sequence and act topic, which concern communication structure and the topics and themes being communicated; K – refers to key or tone, which are the ways or manners that the communication is framed; I – represents instrumentalities or the linguistic code, referring to language and dialect; N – designates norms and refers to rules of interaction and G – refers to genre, which concerns the literary-stylistic type of communication. The table below contextualises the acronym SPEAKING to the customary court proceeding of the Banen community.

TABLE 15.1. SPEAKING in the customary court proceeding of the Banen

S	The Ndikbiakat village in the Littoral region of Cameroon in 2020
P	4 men and 1 woman (1 chief, 1 notable, 1 accused, 1 plaintiff, and 1 witness)
E	Judging a cassava theft case
A	Questions and answers
K	Formal conversation (customary court discourse)
I	The Tunen language
N	Chief examining the litigants (trials)
G	The narrative form of discourse

Customary court proceedings

The customary court discourse collected in the chiefdom of the Ndikbiakat village aimed to bring justice to a cassava field owner who was robbed of a large part of her cassava crop. After the keeper of the fields (the witness) informed Mrs Therese (the plaintiff) that the cassava thief was Mr Bienvue (the accused), the plaintiff went to file a complaint with the village chief. In the following paragraphs, I outline the peacebuilding themes developed during the court discourse to demonstrate the efficacy of oral legal traditions in conflict resolution.

Phonetic Transcription *PL: nàkúm nàmà kúlú wóné*

TC 00:00:13.140 – 00:00:14.940

English Translation PL : I greet the court

TC 00:00:13.140 – 00:00:14.940

French Translation PL: *Je salue la cour*

TC 00:00:13.140 – 00:00:14.940

Phonetic Transcription PL: *mìjɔ́ ŋmɛ́ná sáhá lj fɛ́m nà*

TC 00:00:22.790 – 00:00:25.800

English Translation PL : I came here today to

TC 00:00:22.796 – 00:00:25.806

French Translation PL: *Je suis arrivée ici aujourd'hui pour*

TC 00:00:22.790 – 00:00:25.790

Phonetic Transcription PL: *nà sólókó ndí ínà wɛ́ há nɛ́n ò wàmí tɛ́ní màkpàmbà ó*

TC 00:00:29.080 – 00:00:36.660

English Translation PL : For Mr Mbie whom I caught in my field stealing my cassava

TC 00:00:29.086 – 00:00:36.660

French Translation PL: *Pour monsieur Mbie que j'ai attrapée dans mon champ volant mon manioc*

TC 00:00:29.080 – 00:00:36.660

Phonetic Transcription PL: *ìmá nà bìsɛ́m hâá úbà búmó tʒɛ́p sí nà bú màkpàmbà*

TC 00:00:41.930 – 00:00:48.410

English Translation PL : I have a field here, I have been growing cassava there for a year

TC 00:00:41.930 – 00:00:48.410

French Translation PL: *J'ai un champs ici, ça fait un ans que j'y cultive le manioc*

TC 00:00:41.930 – 00:00:48.410

Phonetic Transcription PL: *ìkrísɛ́ mé kɔ̀mà nìsɛ màkpàmbà, ǎ màkpàmbà ó ndàmìsɔ́ kpámí màβùmà*

TC 00:00:49.834 – 00:00:55.450

English Translation PL : I had already noticed that my cassava was stolen, but I never knew who was doing that

TC 00:00:49.830 – 00:00:55.450

French Translation PL: *J'avais déjà constater qu'on a volé mon Manioc, mais je n'ai jamais su qui faisait ça*

TC 00:00:49.820 – 00:00:55.450

Phonetic Transcription PL: *nà mwɛ́jà nà bámí sɔ̄m*

TC 00:00:56.463 – 00:00:59.007

English Translation PL : When this one was doing his rounds

TC 00:00:56.460 – 00:00:59.000

French Translation PL: *Lorsque celui-ci fasait sa ronde*

TC 00:00:56.460 – 00:00:59.010

Phonetic Transcription PL: *ndʒánà wɛ́ kɔ̀mánɛ́*

TC 00:01:00.571 – 00:01:02.283

English Translation PL: he caught him

TC 00:01:00.570 – 00:01:02.280

French Translation PL: *il l'a attrapé*

TC 00:01:00.580 – 00:01:02.290

Phonetic Transcription PL: *we[l] nà mêlásὲ*

TC 00:01:02.506 – 00:01:04.495

English Translation PL: he came to tell me

TC 00:01:02.500 – 00:01:04.490

French Translation PL: *il est venu me dire*

TC 00:01:02.500 – 00:01:04.490

Phonetic Transcription PL: *ánú mɔ̀dùbànìmò ámù ámà á màkpàmbà ó kwísɛ́*

TC 00:01:04.680 – 00:01:08.813

English Translation PL: that he knows the one who steals my cassava every time

TC 00:01:04.680 – 00:01:08.810

French Translation PL: *qu'il connaît celui qui vole mon manioc chaque fois*

TC 00:01:04.680 – 00:01:08.810

Phonetic Transcription PL: *û sèkɔ́ sìmí náwɛ́ sɔ́mínâ há...kùtù ɛ́ bàtà ɛ̀mèné mámà kúmà búsí mbɔ́m*

TC 00:01:09.723 – 00:01:16.146

English Translation PL: That's why I came to complain, but before, I asked him why he finished my cassava in the field

TC 00:01:09.720 – 00:01:16.140

French Translation PL: *C'est pourquoi je suis venue me plaindre, mais avant, je lui est demande pourquoi il a fini mon manioc au champs*

TC 00:01:09.720 – 00:01:16.140

In this first extract, the plaintiff recounts the elements that led to the trial without using abusive language. One of the first objectives of traditional court proceedings is reconciliation, where debates must remain convivial. This conviviality continues even when the chief addresses the accused. The chief does not offend the accused in his remarks; he instead gives the benefit of the doubt to the latter by insinuating that the theft was done unconsciously.

Phonetic Transcription CH: *ɛ̀rìkwákwá jàté nǎ lɔ́ŋɔ́ sò kwákwáj nɔ̀kɔ́ sôbò*

TC 00:04:46.450 – 00:04:51.561

English Translation CH : what made you steal her cassava

TC 00:04:46.450 – 00:04:51.560

French Translation CH: *qu'est ce qui t'a envoyé volé son manioc*

TC 00:04:46.440 – 00:04:51.570

According to many African traditions, humans are never fully responsible for their bad deeds. Evil spirits often lead people to harm their fellow brothers. So, when the chief asked 'what made you steal her cassava?', he implies that the thievery was unconscious. This question allows me to underline the spiritual, or even mystical, side of traditional courts, where both humans and spirits are tried for crimes. Thus, the court indirectly blames the accused while directly condemning the evil spirit that sows discord. The spiritual feature of customary court proceedings often promotes peace in the sense that people are more likely to forgive those who hurt unintentionally.

A second feature or theme of customary court proceedings is brotherhood; no one should ever solve his/her problems alone. Generally, when families are called upon to solve a problem, they seek to find compromises to promote peace. It is for this reason that the accused implicated his uncle in his remarks. In the excerpt below, the accused suggests the plaintiff talk to his uncle.

Phonetic Transcription AC: *mɔ́mí ǎ βítjá nájá twá ʃìké káwɛ̀bǎ tɔ́ ʃɛ̀ íké ká sɔ̀mɛ̌n tɔ́ sɛ̀ ì májénán únâ ʃìkéjá díkí mbɛ́ wɛ́kù mjánɔ́ nàŋ hátí wáj bíké mínàbà hátâwà bíké*

TC 00:05:37.846 – 00:05:46.048

English Translation AC: that's why I asked him to go see my uncle after complaining to the chief. My uncle might have something to say too

TC 00:05:37.840 – 00:05:46.040

French Translation AC: *c'est pour cela que je lui est demande d'aller voir mon oncle après m'avoir porter plainte au chef. Mon oncle pourrait aussi avoir quelque chose à dire*

TC 00:05:37.840 – 00:05:46.040

Another feature of customary court discourse is acceptance. Accused persons often endorse the proceedings by recognising their crimes and taking responsibility for their actions. Although it was suggested that an evil spirit caused the accused to steal, he never denied he was the thief. The accused voluntarily presented himself to the court to solve the problem without any form of resistance.

Phonetic Transcription AC: *mjɔ̌ wàgbà gá ná númjɔ́ kúʃɔ̂ŋ bíná dè jâwà mbáŋ ábú míján bè bɛ́tá mɛ́ná túkísí bàlkɛ̀l mɔ̀n*

TC 00:07:06.174 – 00:07:11.874

English Translation AC : I learned that she has already filed a complaint against me at your place. I, therefore, agreed to present myself to the court

TC 00:07:06.170 – 00:07:11.870

French Translation AC: *j'ai donc appris qu'elle est déjà venue déposer une plainte contre moi chez toi, j'ai accepté de venir me présenter pour être juge*

TC 00:07:06.170 – 00:07:11.870

A fourth feature of customary court proceedings is conciliation. Traditional leaders seek to settle conflicts without resentment and hatred. This is the reason why, after the plaintiff has spoken, the chief turns to the accused not to ask him to defend himself but to suggest solutions. Fortunately, the accused seized this opportunity to apologise.

Phonetic Transcription CH: *tímé bìsɔ́ lɛ̀nû lá*

TC 00:07:22.174 – 00:07:24.695

English Translation CH: what are you saying now

TC 00:07:22.170 – 00:07:24.700

French Translation CH: *que dit tu donc maintenant*

TC 00:07:22.170 – 00:07:24.690

Phonetic Transcription AC: *gùlùzǔ mísâ bámá ìné bíjé súbà ísâ bámí númɛ̀n*

TC 00:07:49.684 – 00:07:54.387

English Translation AC : I didn't know, I'm sorry, I didn't know

TC 00:07:49.680 – 00:07:54.380

French Translation AC*: vraiment je ne savais pas, je m'excuse, je ne savais pas*

TC 00:07:49.690 – 00:07:54.390

The chief then encouraged the plaintiff to accept the accused's apology:

Phonetic Transcription CH*: ókó ɔ́kíjɛ̀ túwɛ̀ mí àkʁâŋ*

TC 00:08:07.430 – 00:08:10.360

English Translation CH : You heard what this gentleman said

TC 00:08:07.430 – 00:08:10.360

French Translation CH: *Tu as suivi ce que ce monsieur a parlé*

TC 00:08:07.420 – 00:08:10.360

Phonetic Transcription CH: *kèkà ʁíní húwà sɛ́ àʁán ʃìdɛ́ bìté*

TC 00:08:11.970 – 00:08:14.931

English Translation CH: He made a mistake, he didn't know it was your field

TC 00:08:11.970 – 00:08:14.930

French Translation CH: *Il s'est juste trompé il ne savais que c'était ton champs*

TC 00:08:11.970 – 00:08:14.930

Phonetic Transcription CH*: ɔ́sɔ́ símíjé mĕm bɛ̀fámá*

TC 00:08:15.443 – 00:08:22.139

English Translation CH: well now what do you think

TC 00:08:15.440 – 00:08:22.130

French Translation CH*: bon, la maintenant qu'est-ce que tu penses*

TC 00:08:15.450 – 00:08:22.140

It rarely happens in a traditional court that litigants do not comply with the chief's demands. Indeed, in traditional law, the chief has both legal and spiritual powers. It is believed that traditional chiefs are crowned by ancestors and by gods. To disobey the chief is to disobey the gods. It is, therefore, normal that litigants express their respect and follow the chief recommendations.

Phonetic Transcription AC: *tóká pàpà sóbá ìkíné jàm ndɛ̀m tóká tóká tòndòmò wàjìbúsímí má jèssàmè jé tòmàtá tómínál sánàjé tóné fə̀nà*

TC 00:07:43.642 – 00:07:49.684

English Translation AC : 'we don't despise the chief, let's just go in front of the chief, I'll ask for forgiveness'. That's what I came to do today

TC 00:07:43.640 – 00:07:49.680

French Translation AC: *'on ne méprise pas le chef, allons seulement devant le chef, j'irai te demander pardon'. C'est ce que je suis venue faire aujourd'hui*

TC 00:07:43.650 – 00:07:49.690

I have termed litigants' tendency to respect the power and legitimacy of traditional authorities 'deference'. Thus, deference is the fifth and last theme outlined in the customary court discourse analysis. The fact that the authority of the chief is recognised and respected by all facilitates peacebuilding in African rural areas. As a matter of fact, several centuries ago, Africans did not need to build prisons and courts to maintain peace. The only instructions of chiefs were solid enough to build and maintain peace.

In sum, five themes were pointed out from the customary court discourse of the Banen people: spirituality, brotherhood, endorse, conciliation, and deference. This work argues that those themes constitute a communal peacebuilding strategy, a model of peace which best matches African cultures and beliefs. Each theme corresponds to an African cultural reality: 1) spirituality accords with the mystical/religious beliefs in African cultures; 2) brotherhood accommodates the yearning for unity, living together, and communitarianism; 3) endorsement correlates with the feeling of pride and honour which, however, is much more prominant in men than in women; 4) conciliation coincides with the ability of chiefs to reconcile and bring together, in peace, all the members of a community; and 5) deference agrees that all authority is given by gods and ancestors. Besides, none of these beliefs is expressed in any language other than African languages; in this case, the Tunen language of the Banen people.

Conclusion

A retrospective analysis of the situation of peace and conflicts in Africa indicated that African communities experienced less social conflict when ruled by customary laws. To demonstrate the efficacy of a communal peacebuilding strategy in the African continent, I documented, transcribed, translated, and analysed the customary court proceeding of the Banen community of Cameroon using a multidisciplinary approach (legal, linguistics, and anthropological sciences). The five themes outlined in the analysis (spirituality, brotherhood, endorse, conciliation, and deference) attest that the success of customary law in Africa is not simply due to its judicial authority but also to its cultural character. People understand, accept, and apply laws that resemble their context and culture, and that are expressed in languages they understand.

The UN slogan 'United we stand and divided we fall' has no value if the said unity promotes only one cultural reality. There are many cultures in the world, but so far only one predominates; Western culture. If we observe the world with an African lens, we may all testify to the reality that is Western Ethnocentrism in Africa. The laws promoted by the UN reflect far more European than African realities. This could explain the failure of these laws in Africa. It is therefore necessary to go back to basics; to implement a communal peacebuilding strategy as do the Banen people of Cameroon.

References

Adam, M. (2002). Guerres africaines: De la compétition ethnique à l'anomie sociale. *Études rurales*, 167–186.

Bandia, FP. (1993). Translation as Culture Transfer: Evidence from African Creative Writing. *TTR, 6*(2), 55–78. https://doi.org/10.7202/037151ar

Chaim, N. (2017). Ethnography of Communication. *The International Encyclopedia of Communication Research Methods*, 1–12.

De Coning, C. (2013). Understanding Peacebuilding as Essentially Local. *Stability: International Journal of Security and Development, 2*(1), 1–6. https://doi.org/http://doi.org/10.5334/sta.as.

Dissake, KM. (2021). *Documenting communicative practices of customary court proceedings: The case of Tunen native-speakers of the Ndikbiakat Canton.* Retrieved from Endangered Languages Archive @http://hdl.handle.net/2196/55fb4774-dd53-47ae-bf2a-d211c7e65974.

Eberhard, DM., Simons, FG. & Fennig, DC. (2022). *Ethnologue: Languages of the World. Twenty-fifth edition.* Dallas, Texas: SIL International. Accessed @http://www.ethnologue.com

Gendreau, F. (1996). La dimension démogra-phique des conflits africains. *Afrique contemporaine*, 129–141.

Gippert, J., Himmelmann, NP. & Mosel, U. (2006). *Essentials of Language Documentation.* Berlin: Mouton de Gruyter.

Hymes, DH. (1962). The ethnography of speaking. In Gladwin, T. & Sturtevant, W. (ed.) *Anthropology and human behavior* (pp. 15–53). Washington, DC: Anthropological Society of Washington.

Mbiti, SJ. (1975). *Introduction to African Religion.* Oxford: Heinemann Educational Publishers.

Owino, L. (2016). Application of African Customary Law: Tracing its Degradation and Analysing the Challenges it Confronts. *Strathmore Law Review*, 143-164.

Peacebuilding & The United Nations. (2012). *United Nations Peacebuilding Support Office.* Accessed @https://www.un.org/en/peacebuilding/pbso/pbun.shtml

Snell-Hornby, M. (1988). *Translation Studies: An Integrated Approach.* Amsterdam/Philadelphia: John Benjamins.

Stiffman, E. (2015). Cultural Preservation in Disasters, War Zones: Presents Big Challenges. *The Chronicle Of Philanthropy.*

Vinay, JP. & Darbelnet, J. (1960). Stylistique comparée du français et de l'anglais. *Revue belge de philologie et d'histoire*, 451-452.

Wegener, C. & Otter, M. (2008). Cultural Property at War: Protecting Heritage during armed conflict. *The Getty Conservation Institute*, 1-23.

WIPO Secretariat, 2013. *Customary Law, Traditional Knowledge and intellectual property: An Outline of the Issues.* Accessed @https://www.wipo.int/export/sites/www/tk/en/resources/pdf/overview_customary_law.pdf

16

ITYALA NGUMPHIKWA: EVIDENCE LOST IN TRANSLATION AND INTERPRETATION. A CRITICAL ANALYSIS OF LANGUAGE IMPLICATIONS DURING COURT TRIALS. SITYODANA MSESWA'S CASE UNDER THE WITCHCRAFT SUPPRESSION ACT 3 OF 1957

Happyness Nokwatu Raselabe

Introduction

The need for an inclusive language policy and its application to the judiciary system in South Africa is magnified by numerous reports of evidence lost in translation and interpretation. There is a growing imperative to promote African indigenous languages as languages of record and this needs to be prioritised in the language transformation agenda within the justice system. The country's constitutional language rights are undermined by failure to do so.

Post Apartheid, South Africa had 11 official languages until September 2023 when President Cyril Ramaphosa officially announced South African Sign Language as the 12th official language. According to the Constitution of the Republic of South Africa Act 108 of 1996 (1996), all official languages must enjoy and be accorded equal respect and treatment. It follows that African languages need to be elevated and held in the same high esteem as English. This is to help promote language transformation in the South African judicial system and ensure the elevation of the status of African indigenous languages.

This chapter seeks to highlight the role of language during court proceedings. It argues that the monolingual language of record disadvantages court participants, and highlights the important role of comprehensibility and understanding of a language in court. A case under the Witchcraft Suppression Act 3 of 1957 (WSA) (1957) is used for this analysis. The case, which took place in 1959 at Caguba village in the former Transkei, was retrieved from the Western Cape Archives and Records Service. Utilising an archived case helps to highlight how little, if any, change has occurred in the justice system, compared to the justice system that existed before democracy and during the Apartheid era. The chapter further investigates the nature of the WSA, questioning its origin, validity, and relevance.

This study contributes to knowledge pertaining to language, culture, interpreting, and translation during court proceedings. It further interrogates the use of common law and Roman-Dutch law in a country where indigenous people previously had their own legal system, namely traditional law. Findings of this study will help us understand language gaps that might still exist during interpretation and translation, especially in cases that are embedded in language and cultural nuances, whilst interrogating the negative effects of law systems that do not reflect the indigenous people of South Africa. These language gaps might highlight a need for further research in this area. Lack of knowledge of African languages, of socio-cultural knowledge, and of local traditions negatively affects how non-English and Afrikaans speakers comprehend the languages and jargon used in court for record purposes.

Failure from judges, interpreter(s), and court personnel to make sense of cultural and traditional undertones proves to affect verdicts, rendering proceedings unjust. These factors compromise the accuracy and validity of the court proceedings and outcomes of the judgment.

The study highlights the role of language, questions the monolingual application in courts for records, looks at the impact of social and political influences in the judiciary system, and examines the Eurocentric impact on the culture and traditions of native South Africans during the 1950s. The analysis further highlights the lack of transformation in the legal and justice system of South Africa post Apartheid and colonialism.

This serves as a subtle reminder to dig deep into the history of our native land South Africa, to learn from and embrace this history, and lament the painful and inhumane experiences of the past. This will help to pave the way for working towards a country with more inclusive laws and for a justice system that reflects transformation. Digging in the archives becomes critical in finding artefacts and making sense of history. In the words of Marcus Garvey, 'A people without the knowledge of their past history, origin and culture is like a tree without roots' (Inko-Tariah, 2010).

Hence, to dig up the legal roots of the South African legal system, this chapter covers the following: 1) an analysis of Sityodana Mseswa's case in terms of; 2) the Witchcraft Suppression Act 3 of 1957 (WSA); 3) an examination of language limitations in Sityodana's court record; 4) a need for language transformation in the justice system; 5) a consideration of justice versus law; and 6) an analysis of the African proverb '*Ityala ngumphikwa*.' The chapter concludes with recommendations from different stakeholders regarding the need to repeal the WSA.

The Witchcraft Suppression Act 3 of 1957 (WSA)

The Witchcraft Suppression Act 3 of 1957 (WSA) is a parliamentary act of the Republic of South Africa. It is based on the repealed 1895 Witchcraft Suppression Act of the Cape Colony. This act originated from the Witchcraft Act of 1735 of the Kingdom of Great Britain (Grobler, 2014). The Witchcraft Act was repealed in 1951 and replaced by the Consumer Protection Regulations in the United Kingdom of Great Britain (Justice.gov.), yet it remains in the laws of the Republic of South Africa. The Witchcraft Suppression Act 3 of 1957 has seen two amendments since 1957, with the latest amendment being the Witchcraft Suppression Amendment Act 50 of 1970.

Even though this act is among the shortest acts – it has only four sections – it is an act emerging from a foreign culture, tradition, and language, which provides enough proof to question the legitimacy of its application in South Africa, a 'foreign land'.

This act was put in place to criminalise actions such as witchcraft, witch-hunts and witch-smelling. As with many laws that were imposed upon the indigenous people of South Africa during colonialism and Apartheid, the WSA was created to assist in 'civilising' the native people of South Africa from their 'backward' beliefs. The Suppression of Witchcraft Act may have shielded some innocent people from accusations of practising witchcraft, but it has failed to address the issue since those who truly do practice these deeds have been shielded from being fairly charged and put on trial (Hund, 2000: 386).

The legislative discussions held in the House of Assembly prior to the promulgation of the act demonstrate the lawmakers' lack of cultural awareness and their European focus. These legislators failed to distinguish meaningfully between *sangomas* and witches, because they were confused between witches and 'witch-doctors'. The legislators who enacted this act failed to address the issue of witch-hunts and the violence associated with them (Hund, 2000: 388).

According to Hund (2000), the discussion transcript states that the 1957 act was initiated by judges who desired the consolidation and unification of earlier colonial anti-witchcraft legislation across the several regions. There is some truth to this, but

I believe that cultural (and ontological) imperialism was the act's primary motivation. For instance, a legislator voiced concerns about African culture potentially overtaking European awareness. Hund (2000) quotes Mr DC. Barlow stating the following at one of the legislative discussions: 'witchcraft is getting stronger. There are witch-doctors all over the place, and white folks are visiting them rather than feeling concerned about murders committed for witchcraft'. It is abundantly evident that the 1957 act was white legislation intended to eradicate African culture.

These concerns and the nature of this act have led to the review of the WSA. This review is still underway, preceded by the South African Law Reform Commission. There has not been any feedback or publications regarding this matter since the last publication of the revised discussion paper on 24 June 2022, noting the closing date for comments dated 22 October 2022. Altogether, there has been effort in the right direction, namely towards meaningful reform of the WSA.

What the WSA means in South Africa

The separation brought about by foreign ideals during the Dutch and English colonial era in South Africa encouraged internal strife among the indigenous people. These were years when foreign laws were forcefully imposed on the native people, whilst the traditional legal system which they had been accustomed to for centuries was swiftly being dismissed and replaced by Western and common law.

Socio-political influences contributed towards dismantling the traditional justice system (Rakate, 1997). The implementation of the WSA was one of the tools that helped divest traditional leaders and chiefs of their power and relevance amongst the people they ruled. After witnessing the degree of obedience and confidence the native people had in their traditional leaders, chiefs, and laws, the settlers caused division amongst the native people in their pursuit of supremacy.

The Apartheid government used the colonial laws under the Suppression of Witchcraft Act to apply more severe penalties, and put pressure on traditional leaders to stop hearing witchcraft claims because they deemed them to be 'repugnant, unfounded, and even diabolic' (Ludsin, 2004).

Academics like Louw and Duvenhage (2016) argue that the existence and relevance of the WSA in a non-Western society is still unacceptable. It is unjust to suppress people's beliefs and impose common law on native people, especially in matters relating to culture and traditions distinct from those of the West. While there are common themes and principles found in African witchcraft, it is essential to recognize the diversity and complexity of beliefs and practices across the continent. It is crucial to acknowledge that 'witchcraft' in the African view differs from the Western understanding of witchcraft. The disobedience of basic and compulsory tradition and cultural practices may be deemed as witchcraft, as will be exemplified in the case study. Understanding and respecting these cultural nuances is crucial for anyone seeking to explore or discuss the topic. An understanding of how these cases were dealt with prior to the implementation of the WSA sheds more light on how the WSA conflicts with the beliefs and traditions of the indigenous people.

In the past, chiefs, traditional leaders, and diviners would oversee institutional responses that adhered to common African conceptions of reality. Multiple procedures were devised by traditional courts to deal with witchcraft manifestations (Ludsin, 2004). In contrast, state courts in South Africa lack the resources and have never been able to convict someone of a crime for which there is no tangible proof in a court of law.

Trials under the WSA took place in English and Afrikaans during the decade of Sityodana's trial. For decades these two languages were the only official languages in South Africa. This arrangement was a result of similar legislative procedures and practices. Some of the reasons for this practice were the fact that most presiding officers were adequately competent in both English and Afrikaans. English and Afrikaans enjoyed equal official status, thus translating to successive constitutional arrangements. Unfortunately, this placed African languages at a distinct disadvantage, leaving them without official status of language or record.

African languages were only used by witnesses, litigants, accused, and other court personnel and only to get evidence for the court (Malan, 2009: 144).

According to Malan (2009:145), judges of the high court usually delegated cases in accordance with the judges' language proficiency in the relevant court. The proceedings would be documented in the accused's native language, granted that the accused spoke either English or Afrikaans as their mother-tongue. Litigation involving Afrikaans was solely delegated to judges who were proficient in that language. This was because most judges understood English, whilst not all those who were proficient in English were highly skilled in Afrikaans. The language of record during a case of an accused African language speaker would be determined by the mother-tongue of the presiding judge or magistrate, either English or Afrikaans.

Furthermore, regional linguistic patterns existed and determined which language the presiding officer would use, regardless of their personal inclination. Cases held in the Eastern Cape and KwaZulu-Natal were conducted in English, as this was the predominant language. The same principle held for the Free State and the Western

Cape, where Afrikaans was the dominant language and the presiding officer conducted proceedings in Afrikaans (Malan, 2009: 145).

Nature of Sityodana Mseswa's trial

The case used in the analysis was retrieved from the Western Cape Archives and Records Service. The trial took place in 1959 under the Witchcraft Suppression Act 3 of 1957. The hearing was held on 13 March 1959 at the Port St Johns Magistrate's Court in the former Transkei region, now known as the Eastern Cape. The accused, Sityodana Mseswa, is described as a 41-year-old native male and peasant born in South Africa near Caguba village in the former Transkei, now the Eastern Cape.

Sityodana Mseswa was charged with the offence of imputing witchcraft in contravention of section 1 (a) of Act 3 1959. According to the court, this was because Sityodana Mseswa wrongfully and unlawfully imputed his brother's wife. The relevant section of the law reads as follows:

- Section 1 (a):
  Offences relating to the practice of witchcraft and similar practices.
- Any person who-
- (a) imputes to any other person the causing, by supernatural means, of any disease in or injury or damage to any person or thing, or who names or indicates any other person as a wizard.

Evidence adduced from the hearing

The evidence presented to the court was that Sityodana Mseswa had accused Magibisela Mseswa of using supernatural means in causing disease in or to another person or indicated Magibisela Mseswa as a wizard. Jack Mseswa, who was Sityodana's brother and Magibisela's husband, was part of the trial in defence of his wife. The accused also claimed to have warned Magibisela to stop walking through his land, but Magibisela continued doing so despite these warnings.

The court record reads as follows:

> 'By court: Sityodana Mseswa was charged with the offence of imputing witchcraft in contravention of section 1 (a) of Act 3 1957 at Port Saint Johns in the Eastern Cape. The court proceeding happened on the 13th of March 1959. The accused Sityodana Mseswa is described as a 41-year-old native male and peasant born in South Africa near Caguba village in the former Transkei. He wrongfully and unlawfully imputed his brother's wife Magibisela Mseswa described as a native female also from Caguba location in Port Saint John's district. Sityodana Msweswa [sic] accused Magibisela Mseswa of using supernatural means in causing disease in or to another person or did indicate Magibisela Mseswa as a wizard, which is to say that the said accused did say to Jack Mseswa, the husband of Magibisela

> Mseswa, in the presence his wife, "You must stop your wife from sending evil spirits (*Tokoloshe*) to my kraal. I am tired of curing my sick child who is being bewitched by your wife by means of evil spirits" or words to that effect. [The accused also claimed to have warned Magibisela to stop walking through his land, but Magibisela continued doing so despite these warnings.]
>
> By court: *Tokoloshe* is an evil spirit accompanying the lightening bird *Mpundulu* causing the death or illness of a person. That is what I understand it to be.'

Trial outcomes/verdict

Although the accused being arraigned pleaded not guilty, the judge found him guilty, and he was consequently sentenced to six months of hard compulsory labour.

Language limitations in Sityodana Mseswa's Trial

The interpreter(s) played a significant role in court and throughout the proceedings, especially for the participants who did not speak or understand the court's language, primarily English in this case.

Using Sityodana Mseswa's case as a point of reference, this chapter attempts to amplify the role played by language during the court proceedings. The analysis explores how inaccurate translation could lead to incorrect information being filtered down to both ends that the interpreter is assisting. The former Transkei region had a majority of isiXhosa mother-tongue speakers who barely understood or spoke English and Afrikaans (Van Niekerk, 2015). In Sityodana Mseswa's case, the accused and the plaintiff did not understand nor speak English. This reveals that they did not fully comprehend the jargon and language used during court proceedings, given that they were native isiXhosa mother-tongue speakers. Nevertheless, they were expected to participate in court trials undertaken in a language that they were unable to communicate in or understand.

According to Lubbe (2009), language can be viewed as an engine in the court of law. The use of speaking is the driving force towards ensuring that legal proceedings happen. In keeping with English as the lingua franca, we learn that there are two isiXhosa words that are used in the Sityodana Mseswa's case record; '*Tikoloshe*' and '*Mpundulu*'. We will also look at the usage and meanings of the words 'wizard' and 'kraal' in the context and nature of the case.

It is fair to argue that if one cannot find the equivalent term of a word in a particular language, the next best thing is to simply give a definition of that word. None of this was done in this case, considering that the two above-mentioned Nguni words were left as is. The word 'wizard' also seemed inappropriate for this record, and its usage makes one question whether the judge may have missed a clue that could have changed his understanding of the matter presented before him. The usage of the word 'kraal' is also problematic, in that the way it is used in this case does not fit the context. Given the cultural and traditional meaning and status of 'kraal', the second instance of the usage of the word 'kraal' could be indicative of where the judge could have missed another clue which may have led to a completely different verdict. Further engagement with and analysis of these words and terms will be covered in the next sub-section using a lexicographical approach to understanding the words and terms.

There have been many occasions where interpreters and/or translators were unable to fully relay statements accurately due to a lack of training or inability to read and express people's body language, understand socio-cultural nuances that contribute to the speaker's testimony, and often an inability to give accurate translations (Roberts, 1935). Given the richness and complexity of language, it is evident how a lack of training of both translators and interpreters could hinder translations during court hearings.

The Magistrates Court Act 32 of 1944 (1944) reveals the use of English and Afrikaans as lingua franca in all court proceedings, including cases under the WSA of 1957. According to several definitions, 'lingua franca' is generally understood to mean 'a common second language, shared by people who are unable to interact with one another in their native tongues' (Van Niekerk, 2015). Van Niekerk (2015) further explains that the phenomenon is linked to political supremacy and that the establishment of a lingua franca could be an outcome of empire. Additionally, throughout Sityodana's case and other court proceedings that took place during those decades of colonialism and Apartheid ruling, English served as the lingua franca along with Afrikaans, reflecting who had political leverage.

English gained the upper hand over Dutch/Afrikaans in the early 1900s due to an influx of British settlers, British teachers, and Scottish ministers relocating to South Africa in large numbers. The Dutch colonists' proficiency in speaking and comprehending English, compared to the British colonisers' lack of proficiency in Afrikaans, was one of the reasons, but not the chief reason why English dominated (Van Niekerk, 2015).

Afrikaans only achieved equal official status with English in 1925. These two languages continued being the official languages in South Africa. Unfortunately, not much change has happened since 1994 towards officially affording any of the indigenous languages the same prestige and esteem as English in law.

According to Malan (2009: 145), an interpreter would have been available if an accused party or a witness did not speak either of the two official languages, but only for the purpose of interpreting the evidence and not the rest of the proceedings. Thus, the accused and complainant would be unable to follow the proceedings if they were unable to understand English or Afrikaans. As a result, the language used in the record had a significant impact on how justice was administered and even who had access to it.

According to Roberts (1935), the absence of translation into the native tongue exacerbates the natives' misunderstanding of a law's intentions. There seems to be little engagement from both parties involved in Sityodana Mseswa's case, i.e., the accused and the plaintiff, and their records are limited to giving evidence. This speaks to the statement of Docrat et al. (2021) that an interpreter would have been available if an accused party or a witness was unable to speak either of the two official languages, but only for the purpose of interpreting the evidence and not the rest of the proceedings. This illustrates the fact that interpretations of the evidence were only made available to accommodate the judge. The accused and complainant were never considered to ensure that they understood and were able to follow the court proceedings.

Despite the substantial amount of South African legislation that allows citizens of the Republic of South Africa the right to be spoken to and speak in their native language or a language they fully understand and comprehend, the Heads of Court under former Chief Justice Mogoeng Mogoeng (South African Judiciary, 2018) decreed English as the only language to be used for record in all the country's courts. The former Chief Justice has stood by this decision although Section 35 (3) (k) of the Constitution confers the right to a fair trial, thus implying a counterproductive effort to uphold this right. To date, the South African justice system uses only English as the language of record, which is rather alarming, given that only 8.7% of the country's' population speaks English as a first language. It is also only the fifth most spoken language in the country, according to the 2022 Statistics South Africa census results (Stats SA, 2022). This reveals that at least 91.3% of the South African population are non-English first language speakers, thus disadvantaging them during court cases because they will be unable to properly follow the records, judges' language (most of whom most likely speak English) and proceedings.

The law during colonial and Apartheid rule imposed English as the language of record and language used throughout all court proceedings, except when an African language (isiXhosa in this case) speaker and interpreter exchanged speech needing to be translated into English for evidence purposes. There are instances where African words or references were used in the trial record of Sityodana Mseswa's case. This makes it quite evident that either the translator or transcriber failed to understand or find the equivalent word in English. This created a certain level of inconsistency in truly maintaining the use of English as the only language of record during court proceedings and leaves one to question the legitimacy and relevance of this directive. This further raises concerns about the interpreter's competences, which could have significantly impacted the verdict. The denial of culture and traditions embedded in the

Witchcraft Suppression Act and the Western courts reveals the cultural nuances that were overlooked in Sityodana Mseswa's case.

Lexicographical perspective

This inquiry makes use of a lexicographical approach to analyse the words, terms and jargon used in the archival document. These terms touch on important cultural aspects embedded in the beliefs of AmaXhosa, thus highlighting how some evidence was lost because the judge and interpreter were not culturally knowledgeable.

Two of the earliest isiXhosa lexicographical works are used to define these terms. However, it is worth noting that these early works were produced only as a means of preserving a language that was expected soon to cease to exist. Some, not all, definitions are limited to the colonisers' understanding and often do not capture the African conceptualisation or meaning of isiXhosa words/terms.

IsiXhosa dictionaries that existed in 1959 and at the time of the court case had significant European influences, in that some of the cultural terms were not properly defined (Moropa & Kruger, 2000). This is supported by the words of the late Mr Andrew Smith's proposal during a United Missionary conference held at King Williams Town in 1889: 'the lexicons should be printed, if only as a memorial of the Kaffir language which would soon be supplanted by English' (Kropf & Godfrey, 1915).

This statement speaks volumes about why the record keeping of isiXhosa lexicography was merely a tool that missionaries used for their undertakings and for record keeping purposes for a language that, according to their predictions of the future, would soon disappear (Nkomo & Wababa, 2013). One could argue that none of these works were made or produced for isiXhosa academics, speakers, and learners, but for the convenience of the missionaries. These findings contribute to our understanding of how limited the linguistic correctness was of the earliest isiXhosa dictionaries. The fact that these dictionaries were not compiled by indigenous language speakers also factors into the accuracy of their language. The use of these dictionaries during the court trial could have hindered translations of evidence.

Lexicographical analysis

According to the GDX (Great isiXhosa Dictionary), the Oxford English online dictionary, and the concise Kaffir-English Dictionary, the following definitions are given:

> Kraal – a traditional African village of huts, typically enclosed by a fence.
>
> Kraal – an enclosure for cattle or sheep.

Although the word '*ubuhlanti*' is not explicitly mentioned in the case record, it must be included for an understanding of the reference to the kraal. As per the second definition of the word 'kraal', we learn that it is an enclosure for cattle and sheep. When translating or defining this word and concept in isiXhosa it is '*ubuhlanti*'.

> *ubu-Hlanti*, n. 7. A cattle fold; loc. ebuhlanti, in the cattle kraal. The men assemble and feast in the kraal and have their corn pits in it. (Women married into the village are not allowed to enter the kraal. This is not because of inferiority, but out of respect to their departed fathers-in-law who are considered the heads of that village and kraal. The kraal is considered sacred.) (Kropf & Godfrey, 1915)

Cultural and traditional nuances

Gcingca-Ndolo (2008: 19) describes *ubuhlanti* as a sanctuary, sacred space, and a symbol of unity where rituals are performed to connect the living and the dead, where *lobola* negotiations that aim to bring families together have historically taken place, and where umbilical cords are buried in the kraal/*ubuhlanti*. The exclusion of women in the kraal/*ubuhlanti* is justified by biological factors, such as menstruation, which makes them 'impure' to enter this sacred place. It is also claimed that menstruation prevents the growth of livestock. Witchcraft beliefs are further used as justification for this action.

The assertion that women married into the village were not allowed to enter the kraal shows Magibisela Mseswa's (plaintiff's) cultural and traditional disobedience. It goes without saying that if this case had been conducted in traditional courts the deed of entering her brother-in-law's kraal/*ubuhlanti* would have been questioned and undoubtedly linked to witchcraft conduct because this act represented cultural and traditional disobedience.

This finding highlights the ways in which common law undermined the culture and traditions of the native people and produced unsatisfactory results and verdicts in all cases involving accusations of and convictions for witchcraft.

The court's and judges' failure to interrogate this evidence regarding the reference to the kraal could imply that Magibisela Mseswa did go into the kraal/*ubuhlanti* of Sityodana Mseswa. This would implicate her in witchcraft in accordance with the AmaXhosa beliefs that a woman married into a family is not allowed into the kraal/*ubuhlanti*. If seen there, they could be implicated in acts of witchcraft. Ultimately, Magibisela Mseswa might have been interrogated and possibly found guilty, had her case been heard in a traditional court under traditional laws; thus, possibly overturning the court and judge's verdict.

Misinterpretation analysis

> *Impundulu - Uhlobo lwentaka olungumlingo, ekuthakathwa* ngalo (Xhs. definition - GDX).
>
> *Impundulu* - The lightening bird (Eng. Definition - GDX).
>
> *Mpundulu* - The lightening bird (Eng. Definition - A concise Xhosa-English dictionary).
>
> *Tokiloshe* - A dwarf-like river spirit, a play mate of children and a familiar witchcraft agent of women (GDX).

Although '*Tokoloshe*' and '*Mpundulu*' both belong to the same sorcery and spiritual realm, none can be used to define the other as they differ in meaning, concept, and function. The linkage used in the court record between these two speaks to the fact that the court participants who had the duty to translate, interpret, or define the meaning of *Tokoloshe* misled everyone in court. This reveals and proves that the interpreter, judge, transcribers, and all other court personnel were far removed from the cultural context and meaning of these terms.

These findings imply that the interpreter was untruthful in his definitions to the court. None of these could have been corrected because there was an obvious language barrier among all the participants in the hearing. Such imprudent errors make one wonder how many other misinterpretations took place and did not make it to record as the record only covers evidence and verdict. These instances require deep reflection about traditional and cultural laws that were justice centred in comparison to common law that is solely law driven. This also emphasises the importance of working towards a justice system that uses all official languages as record languages.

Justice versus law

According to Squadrin (2019), the concepts of justice and the rule of law are often misunderstood and harmonised. Although closely related, the two are not the same. The concept of justice is built on ideals and ideas that are fundamental to human nature, even though they are not always universally accepted. Justice is a comprehensive notion that is based on fairness, morality, and the equality of all rights. Justice is not something that is created; it is a broad concept that connects all ethical and moral principles. Laws, in contrast, are established rules that govern the conduct of individuals and of the government itself in all aspects. Politicians or ruling administrations draft laws that go through a protracted process of checks and balances before being implemented.

In Sityodana Mseswa's case it is easy to determine the identity of the lawmakers, based on the date of the trial. The hearing happened at a time when both colonial and Apartheid regimes undermined the indigenous/traditional legal system and imposed the Roman-Dutch legal system in their efforts to colonise and oppress the South African native people. The authority of traditional courts was reduced because these courts were not courts of record, and cases were reopened at magistrate's courts in South Africa that utilised the foreign Roman-Dutch legal system. This compromised the handling of cases that had historically been dealt with by traditional courts and traditional leaders, serving no justice according to native beliefs, traditions, and culture.

Although the concepts law and justice are closely related, there are some important distinctions that should not be disregarded:

1) When we talk about a law, we mean a real, concrete collections of rules that the ruling government at the time has put in place to oversee and supervise its citizens' actions (Squadrin, 2019). In Sityodana's case, we note how laws were biased and exclusionary towards native South Africans. Common law was solely 'law' and lacked any form of justice at the time of Sityodana's hearing.
2) The concept of justice, on the other hand, is universal; moral principles and ethical standards sometimes take precedence over national boundaries and geographical divisions (Squadrin, 2019). This speaks to how customary and traditional laws are embedded in justice more than they are in common law.

The way justice was achieved in Western law helps us recognise how wisdom from traditional chiefs, leaders, and diviners was compromised. This reveals the dire need to revisit the ancient way of doing things when dealing with intricate traditional cases and to undo how common law criminalised traditional laws.

Undermining the wisdom of native South African justice

According to Hund (2000), bewitchment was a concern prior to the act's introduction, but like all concerns, it had solutions. The seeds of anarchy were planted by criminalising traditional courts and customary laws that worked as remedies on the grounds that they were opposed to the 'civilising mission' of the white, Eurocentric, Apartheid administration.

Previously, chiefs, traditional leaders, and diviners would oversee institutional responses that adhered to common African conceptions of reality. Multiple procedures were devised by traditional courts to deal with witchcraft's manifestations (Ludsin, 2004). State courts in South Africa lack the resources, however, and have never been able to convict someone of a crime for which there is no tangible proof in a court of law.

Regarding Sityodana Mseswa's case, every individual accused of practising witchcraft who is brought before the court under common law gets freed for a lack of conclusive proof (Ludsin, 2004: 92). In theory, although the complainant, Magibisela Mseswa, won the case, it is fair to argue that the outcomes and verdict would have been different had the case been heard in a traditional court.

The procedures of traditional laws and traditional leaders were completely different from those of Western law. A trial would begin after someone approached a traditional leader or chief with a complaint about harm caused by witchcraft. Upon carefully analysing and deliberating on the matter, the chief would decide whether this was a conflict issue which simply needed mediation to help eliminate allegations. If the chief became aware of or sensed witchcraft, the chief would call upon a diviner who would help determine whether the harm thought to be witchcraft was caused by angry ancestors or whether it was indeed witchcraft. It is significant that the chief always chose a diviner who lived far away from the community to help ensure objectivity, absence of bias, and to eliminate prior knowledge which might influence the process (Ludsin, 2004).

Chiefs did not rely solely on the evidence given by the diviner but considered all statements by the accused and the complainant against all traditional beliefs and customs. The chief would ultimately decide upon the conviction. The conviction for being found guilty of witchcraft ranged from ostracism to payments of a fine to death. Many other strategies existed in dealing with defamation of character resulting from witchcraft accusations.

This reveals that prior to the implementation of the WSA there existed a formula for dealing with witchcraft cases that worked for the native people. Although not always humane, it captured their beliefs and often left communities, accused, and complainants relatively confident with the manner in which the matter had been dealt with.

Ludsin (2004) stresses that the dismissal of traditional laws in dealing with witchcraft and the implementation of the Witchcraft Suppression Act 3 of 1957 led to traditional and customary laws losing their legitimacy and relevance in communities, and led people to taking the law into their own hands. Over time, this resulted in an increase in witchcraft-related violence and mob murders. In the name of keeping their power, many traditional leaders complied with the Witchcraft Suppression Act by getting permission from the relevant authority on Native Affairs under the Black Administration Act 38 of 1927. This also meant they were excluded from witchcraft trials and so were their traditional beliefs. Communities started feeling that chiefs and traditional leaders were now protecting witches and siding with the government. This led to the collapse of indigenous systems and traditional laws.

Ityala Ngumphikwa - a charge is a thing denied

The isiXhosa proverb '*Ityala ngumphikwa*' suggests that when one is faced with guilt, the automatic response is complete and utter denial, regardless of how obviously guilty one may be.

> *Ityala ngumphikwa* - a charge or accusation is a thing which is denied.
>
> *i-Tyala* - 2. Guilt, debt, fault, offence, misdemeanour, crime:

Ukupika/*Ukuphika* is defined as the act of denying, contending, and opposing the next person's views or, in this case, any accusations.

This proverb is not and should not be exclusively analysed or understood in Sityodana's case, or solely cases under the Witchcraft Suppression Act 3 of 1957 but rather as a general principle held by anyone who may be faced with criminal accusations (WhiteZulu, 2016).

These facts bring us to the assertion of how the proverb *ityala ngumphikwa* can also imply acts of incrimination and vindication.

Incrimination is defined clearly by Prinsloo et al. (2015) as 'Accusation of the commission of a crime'. The definition adds that an incriminating statement is one that 'connects the accused with wrongdoing', among other things (Prinsloo et al., 2015).

Incrimination, according to the Cambridge Essential English Dictionary, is the act of making someone appear guilty of a crime. Referring to the definition given by Garner (2014), this concept is defined as accusing someone of a crime, exposing someone to an accusation or charge of crime, and involving oneself or others in a criminal investigation or the danger thereof, particularly when the rule that a witness is not required to provide testimony that would tend to incriminate him/her is in effect (Ralarala & Rodrigues, 2019).

By denying an accusation, one in turn incriminates the complainant, and this is reflected in Sityodana Mseswa's case. Sityodana denied all the accusations brought against him in court, thus implying that the complainant was the guilty party when looking at the case through the incrimination lens. The denial from both parties regarding verbal evidence provided by both the accused (Sityodana Mseswa) and complainant (Magibisela Mseswa) in court is indicative of how the proverb is enabled through incriminating each other.

Conclusion

The current status of indigenous languages in the South African legal system contradicts the commitment made to the nation in the Constitution to 'take practical and positive measures to elevate the status of all previously ignored indigenous languages'. In keeping with Section 6 of the Constitution, the usage of language in court is a human right. Therefore, the decision to limit court proceeding documents to one language, namely English, goes against citizens' constitutional rights. These assertions magnify the dire need for introducing other official languages as languages to be used in records. The case of Sityodana Mseswa emphasises that such experiences in South Africa are reminders of how much change in the legal system is necessary to elevate African languages.

Chimhundu (1998: 63), a Zimbabwean scholar, poses the following pertinent questions as far as language policy in Africa is concerned. It is these very questions which the South African Government's Language Implementation Plan seeks to address: 'How can you guarantee democracy where the law of the country is not understood in the language of the people? How do you abide by what you do not know? How can you use information to which you have only limited access? How can you fully participate in anything, or compete, or learn effectively or be creative in a language you are not fully proficient or literate in? Above all, how can a country develop its human resource base to full potential without the language of the people?'

Concluding remarks

The words of Sindiwe Magona's (1991) preface from her book titled *To my children's children* capture the significance of this study: 'How will you know who you are if I do not or cannot tell you the story of your past?'

In the quest to mend the historical injustices to the native people of South Africa, we need to immerse ourselves in our history, regardless of how painful it is. It is through the understanding of your history and knowledge of your past that you are able to move forward towards building a democratic nation.

The significance of forensic linguistics in the legal system has been demonstrated by the linguistic study of the court case. The evidence provided by this analysis emphasises the importance of cementing the presence of forensic linguistics in the judiciary system to help decipher the identified disadvantages. The contribution from these findings can also be used to back recommendations that speak to why the WSA needs to be repealed, as it perpetuates these linguistic, cultural and traditional limitations in courts. This exemplifies how little, if any, change has happened within the South African judicial system in creating a just legal dispensation.

Recommendation

Forensic linguistics plays a crucial role in the judicial system by providing linguistic expertise to analyse language evidence in legal cases. Overall, forensic linguistics enhances the judicial process by providing valuable insights into language-related evidence, contributing to the pursuit of justice and fair legal outcomes. This is particularly important for culturally diverse countries that are home to people of different beliefs and traditions. It highlights the need to cement the presence of forensic linguistics in the justice system, especially for cases that require such skills.

To this end, Quinot (2012) advocates for transformative legal education. The hybrid South African legal system highlights the need to integrate law with other disciplines such as economics, philosophy, political science, sociology, psychology, public administration, and linguistics. The work being done by forensic linguists in South Africa is also proving that there is a gap for this discipline to help aid the legal and judicial dilemma in South Africa.

Equipping law students with multilingual skills enhances their professional development and prepares them to serve diverse clientele. Legal personnel who can communicate effectively in multiple languages are better equipped to navigate cross-cultural legal contexts and provide more accessible legal services (Rautenbach & Bekker, 2021).

To address these needs, efforts may include offering courses in indigenous languages, providing language support for students, and promoting bilingual legal education programs. Ultimately, language transformation in South African legal education is essential for fostering inclusivity, cultural relevance, and equal access to justice in a linguistically diverse society. The incorporation of forensic linguistic courses in law courses could also be beneficial.

Language and culture are inseparable, each influencing and shaping the other in a complex way. It is not just a means of communication; it also reflects the values, beliefs, history, and social norms of a particular group of people. Language can bear the imprint of historical events and societal structures, hence the importance of incorporating and highlighting some of the recommendations set out in the revised discussion paper by the South African Law and Reform Commission (SALRC) on the review of the WSA.

The Witchcraft Suppression Act 3 of 1957 is often criticised for its vague and outdated language, which can lead to the persecution of individuals accused of witchcraft, particularly in Africa where such accusations are still prevalent. Repealing the act would signal a commitment to upholding human rights and protecting individuals from unjust persecution.

For instance, the witchcraft litigation used in the analysis of the archival case demonstrates how witchcraft differs in Western and African perspectives. This calls for the need to repeal the Witchcraft Suppression Act 3 of 1957, as it is an artefact of colonialism and is discriminatory to the cultural and traditional beliefs of some sections of the population (Louw & Duvenhage, 2016). This act goes against the constitutional right to religious freedom, expression, equality, liberty, dignity, security, and the right to choose and practice their occupation within South Africa.

The following arguments may be made in favour of its repeal:

Research and awareness: Non-legislative interventions are important. This entails educating communities on this subject. Further research to help understand the implications and effects of the Witchcraft Suppression Act and raise awareness among the public about its negative consequences for indigenous cultures and human rights would be valuable.

Community mobilisation and international support: Mobilise affected communities, religious leaders, and traditional healers who may be adversely impacted by the act to advocate for its repeal. Seek support from international human rights organisations and bodies, as well as diplomatic pressure from countries that support human rights and cultural diversity, to encourage the government to repeal the act.

Alternative legislation*:* Propose alternative legislation that addresses concerns related to harmful practices while respecting cultural traditions and human rights. Many argue that the Witchcraft Suppression Act is not compatible with modern legal principles and international human rights standards. Repealing the act would allow for the development of more appropriate legal frameworks to address issues related to harmful practices while respecting individual rights and freedoms.

Repealing the Witchcraft Suppression Act 3 of 1957 could contribute to a more just and equitable society by promoting human rights, religious freedom, and the rule of law. The South African Law Reform Commission (SALRC) and many of its stakeholders support the notion of repealing the existing WSA entirely. The commission and its stakeholders deem the act to be in contravention of the following sections of the Constitution: Section 15 (right to freedom of conscience, religion, thought, belief, and opinion), 16 (right to freedom of expression), nine (right to equality before the law), ten (right to human dignity), 12 (right to freedom and security of the person), and 22 (right to choose trade, occupation, or profession freely).

The SALRC has circulated a revised discussion paper that reviews the WSA. The paper was first published on 16 January 2016, followed by a revised version published on 24

June 2022. This paper also serves as a basis for the commission's deliberations. Although the paper has many progressive views and recommendations, none should be regarded as the commission's and state's final stance. The revised discussion paper is to enable the public and everyone who wishes to make comments, recommendations, or share their views for reform purposes to do so with sufficient information prior to submitting anything to the commission.

Legal challenges and advocacy: Work with legal experts and human rights organisations to challenge the act in court on grounds of its discriminatory nature or its violation of constitutional rights, such as freedom of religion and cultural rights. This goal can be achieved through lobbying lawmakers and government officials to review and repeal the act, highlighting its outdated and discriminatory provisions and advocating for legislation that respects cultural diversity and human rights. The work done by SALRC, SAPRA (South African Pagan Rights Alliance), and many other stakeholders who are against the WSA is in line with this suggestion (SALRC, 2022).

References

Chimhundu, H. (1998). *Language policies in Africa*. Intergovernmental conference on language policies in Africa, 17–21 March, Harare, Zimbabwe. Accessed @https://ich.unesco.org/doc/src/00245-EN.pdf [Date accessed: 2 September 2023].

Docrat, Z., Kaschula, RH. & Ralarala, MK. (2021). *A Handbook on Legal Languages and the quest for linguistic equality in South Africa and beyond*. Stellenbosch: African Sun Media.

Garner, BA. (2014). *Black's Law Dictionary*. (tenth edition). St Paul MN: Thomson Reuters Legal.

Gcingca-Ndolo, ZC. (2008). *Amasiko nezithethe neendlela zokuziphatha kwaXhosa*. [Unpublished master's thesis]. Pretoria: University of South Africa.

Grobler, C. (2014). *An analysis of the cultural difference in South Africa*. [Unpublished master's thesis]. Accessed @https://repository.up.ac.za/bitstream/handle/2263/46121/Grobler_Analysis_2014.pdf?sequence=1&isAllowed=y [Date accessed: 10 October 2022].

Hund, J. (2000). Witchcraft and accusations of witchcraft in South Africa: Ontological denial and the suppression of African justice. *Witchcraft in South Africa*, 33(3), pp. 366–389. Accessed @ https://journals.co.za/doi/pdf/10.10520/AJA00104051_242 [Date accessed: 28 July 2022].

Inko-Tariah, C. (2010). Black History Month. *History.com*, A&E Television Networks. Accessed @https://www.history.com/topics/black-history/black-history-month [Date cccessed: 1 October 2022].

Inventory of the archives of the Magistrate and Bantu Affairs Commissioner of Port St Johns. 1/PSJ – 1/1/11. Sityodana Mseswa (1959).

Kobo, F. (2016). *Umfazi akangeni ebuhlanti emzini...* A womanist dialogue with Black Theology of Liberation in the 21st century. *HTS Teologiese Studies/Theological Studies*, 72(1), a3268. Accessed @https://doi.org/10.4102/hts.v72i1.3268 [Date accessed: 22 September 2023].

Kropf, A. & Godfrey, R. (1915). *Kafir-English Dictionary* (second edition). South Africa: Lovedale Mission Press.

Louw, G. & Duvenhage, A. (2016). *Is the Witchcraft Suppression Act (No.3, 1957) doing an injustice to the neo pagans in South Africa?* [Preprint]. Accessed @http://ensovoort.co.za/index.php/2016/11/08/is-the-witchcraft-suppression-act-no-3-1957-doing-an-injustice-to-the-neo-pagans-in-south-africa/ [Date accessed: 13 September 2023].

Lubbe, H. (2009). *The right to language in court: A language right or a communication, right?* [Preprint]. Accessed @ https://dialnet.unirioja.es/descarga/articulo/3199505.pdf [Accessed: 25 August 2022].

Ludsin, H. (2004). Cultural denial: What South Africa's treatment of witchcraft says for the future of its customary law. *Berkeley Journal of International Law,* 21(1), 62 - 110. Accessed @https://lawcat.berkeley.edu/record/1118657 [Date accessed: 12 February 2024].

Magona, S. (1991). From a Xhosa grandmother. In *To my children's children*. Cape Town: David Philip.

Malan, KJ. (2009). Observations of the use of official languages for the recording of court proceedings. *Tydskrif vir die Suid-Afrikaanse Reg*, 1, pp. 141–155.

Moropa, K. & Kruger, A. (2000). Mistranslation of culture-specific terms in Kropf's Kafir-English dictionary. *South African Journal of African Languages*, 20(1), pp. 70–79. Accessed @ https://www.tandfonline.com/doi/abs/10.1080/02572117.2000.10587414 [Date accessed: 18 September 2022].

Nkomo, D. & Wababa, Z. (2013). IsiXhosa lexicography: Past, present and future. *Lexikos*, 23(1), pp.1–23. Accessed @ https://www.researchgate.net/publication/273635910_IsiXhosa_Lexicography_Past_Present_and_Future#:~:text=The%20history%20of%20isiXhosa%20lexicography,the%20current%20language%20policy%20dispensation [Date accessed: 19 September 2022].

Prinsloo, M., Alberts, M. & Mollema, N. (2015). *Legal Terminology: Criminal Law, Procedure and Evidence*. Cape Town: Juta.

Quinot, G. (2012). Transformative legal education. *The South African Law Journal*, 129, pp. 411–433. Accessed @https://scholar.sun.ac.za/server/api/core/bitstreams/04c7a21d-d50a-4f07-823b-eca965483d5b/content [Date accessed: 12 October 2023].

Rakate, PK. (1997). The status of traditional courts under the final Constitution. *The Comparative and International Law Journal of Southern Africa*, 30(2), pp. 175–189. Available at: https://journals.co.za/doi/pdf/10.10520/AJA00104051_345 [Date accessed: 13 September 2023].

Ralarala, MK. & Rodrigues, T. (2019). Incarcerated, incriminated or vindicated? An investigation into socio-pragmatic elements of police interviewing. In Ralarala, MK., Kaschula, RH. and Heydon, G (ed.) *New Frontiers in Forensic Linguistics: Themes and Perspectives in Language and Law in Africa and beyond* (pp. 15–32). Stellenbosch: African Sun Media.

Rautenbach, C. & Bekker, JC. (2021). Nature and sphere of application of African customary law in South Africa. In Rautenbacj, C. (ed.) *Introduction to legal pluralism in South Africa* (pp. 15–43). Durban, South Africa: LexisNexis.

Republic of South Africa (RSA). (1996). *Constitution of the Republic of South Africa Act 108 of 1996*. Pretoria: Government Printer.

Republic of South Africa (RSA). (1957). *Witchcraft Suppression Act 3 of 1957*. Pretoria: Government Printer.

Republic of South Africa (RSA). (1997). *Witchcraft Suppression Amendment Act 33 of 1997*. Pretoria: Government Printer.

Republic of South Africa (RSA). (1970). *Witchcraft Suppression Amendment Act 50 of 1970*. Pretoria: Government Printer.

Republic of South Africa (RSA). (1944). *Magistrates' Court Act 32 of 1944*. Pretoria: Government Printer.

Roberts, CC. (1935). Witchcraft and Colonial Legislation. *Africa,* 8(4), pp. 488–494. Accessed @https://doi.org/10.2307/3180596 [Date accessed: 12 September 2023].

Samuelson, M. (2007). *Remembering the nation, dismembering women?: Stories of the South African transition*. Scottsville, KY: University of KwaZulu-Natal Press.

South African Law Reform Commission (SALRC). (2022). *The review of the Witchcraft Suppression Act 3 of 1957*. SALRC Project 135. Accessed @https://www.justice.gov.za/salrc/dpapers/dp158-p135-Revised-Review-WitchcraftSuppressionAct.pdf [Date accessed: 15 January 2024].

South African Judiciary. (2018). *Special edition: Presentation of the judiciary annual report*. National Office: Midrand. Accessed @https://www.judiciary.org.za/images/Judiciarynewsletter/Judiciary_Newsletter_December_2018_v4.pdf [Date accessed: 10 February 2024].

Squadrin, G. (2019). *Difference Between Law and Justice*. Accessed @http://www.differencebetween.net/miscellaneous/legal-miscellaneous/difference-between-law-and-justice/ [Date accessed: October 4, 2022].

Statistics South Africa (Stats SA). (2022). *Census dissemination*. Accessed @https://census.statssa.gov.za/#/ [Date accessed: 01 February 2024].

Van Niekerk, G. (2015). Multilingualism in South African courts: The legislative regulation of language in the Cape during the nineteenth century. *Fundamina*, 21(2), pp. 372–391. Accessed @https://doi.org/10.17159/2411-7870/2015/v21n2a10 [Date accessed: 2 April 2023].

WhiteZulu, WZ. (2016). *icala ngumphikwa – a charge is a thing denied*. Accessed @ https://whitezulu.wordpress.com/2016/04/30/icala-ngumphikwa-a-charge-is-a-thing-denied/ [Date accessed: September 25, 2022].

17

THE TRANSLATION OF LEGALLY DRAFTED WILLS INTO INDIGENOUS AFRICAN LANGUAGES: A SOUTH AFRICAN PERSPECTIVE

Hlohlolo Sephiri

Introduction

Normally, if not always, beneficiaries in a legally drafted will are at times not fully literate or even illiterate, and they cannot understand the contents of the will. In most wills, there are words or phrases in Latin or legal English, for example, words such as 'testator', 'testatrix', or 'probate'. Drafting a legally binding will is a burning issue, based on culture, custom, and language used. Most wills in South Africa are written in English or Afrikaans. These languages are often used in wills even if the wills are drafted for people who do not speak these languages. The promotion of indigenous African languages is a very crucial and contentious issue, which also came to the fore during the Fees Must Fall Movement, wherein academics were accused of being intellectually colonised and academic thugs, among other things. They (lecturers) were called intellectually colonised and academic thugs because they continue lecturing in either English or Afrikaans, and these languages are regarded as colonisers' languages. They were also accused of not being committed to promoting South African indigenous languages. Furthermore, they were accused of not promoting indigenous languages at their respective universities. Makalela (2018) posited a continuation of an age-old struggle, with more focus on the negative effects of corporate African universities, whilst also raising issues around culture and language. He indicated that students were concerned that South African indigenous languages are marginalised, resulting in the ultimate marginalisation of indigenous cultures. Both language and culture are intimately connected, implying that one cannot understand culture without having direct access to its language. It must be known that learning a language could be equivalent to learning a particular society's behaviours, customs, and culture. The use of the Use of Official Languages Act 12 of 2012 (2012) is committed to the promotion of all languages in South Africa and to ensure constitutional language equity and language rights as required in a democratic dispensation.

Furthermore, the Use of Official Languages Act 12 of 2012 (2012) provides recognition of multilingualism as a resource to maximise collaborative partnerships in nation building, economic development, and social cohesion. The aim of this contribution is to assess the role of the Use of Official Languages Act 12 of 2012 (2012) in the drafting of legal wills, particularly ones written in indigenous African languages of South Africa. The relegation of indigenous South African languages affects their development and their use in drafting legal wills. In relation to this is an argument that the marginalisation of South African indigenous African languages constitutes a barrier to justice and miscarriage of justice. Therefore, possible solutions will be discussed in this paper with the aim to ensure that South African indigenous African languages are used during the drafting of a legal will, and to contribute to the debate that currently preoccupies many people (especially intended beneficiaries of wills). The introduction or inclusion of South African indigenous African languages, which are key to the future development and inclusiveness of South African citizens who are so diverse, will be addressed in the contribution as a possible solution.

Problem statement

Currently, there are some language difficulties faced by citizens around the world. For this study, South Africa, where legally binding wills are written in either English or Afrikaans, shall be the focus. Very few citizens have these languages as their first language; they are commonly either second or third languages. As a result of this language misunderstanding, beneficiaries will not understand the contents of the will, and unfairness and unnecessary fights may break out. Therefore, if legal wills were to be drafted in South African indigenous African languages, this could provide better understanding and appropriate distribution of property. Harris (2008) postulated that it is helpful not to use English as first language or to write legally binding wills, whilst Kamwangamula (2016) posited that language practices in the family domain suggest that English is gradually replacing indigenous African languages in virtually all spheres including in the drafting of legal wills. Therefore, this study seeks to address the situation where during the drafting of legal wills care should be taken, and the use of South African indigenous African languages is encouraged. All the indications are that ordinary people do find legal language difficult to understand. Furthermore, there are very few people who have difficulties understanding statutory language.

Background and meaning of a legally drafted will

The main reason people need a legally drafted will is to decide who gets your property upon your death. Suppose one has a spouse and children; this can be very important as the interstate statute may not distribute your property as you may wish. Though no single document could likely resolve every issue that arises after your death, a will, officially known as a last will and testament, can come close. A will should be written for the client's eyes, of course, it must be technically sound. However, it need not be written in 'legalese' (language of lawyers that they would not otherwise use in ordinary communications but for the fact that they are lawyers). There is a belief that everyone 16-years-old and above can draft a legal will.

A last will is a legal document that lets you decide what happens with your estate after your death. A legally drafted will serves as a document that expresses a person's wishes as to how their property is to be distributed after their death, and which person is to manage the property until its final distribution. A legal will is a document that coordinates the distribution of one's assets after his/her death and can appoint guardians for minor children. A legal will is important to have, as it allows one to communicate their wishes clearly and precisely.

Research questions

1) How can indigenous African languages be introduced into the drafting of legal wills in South Africa?
2) Why is it important that legal wills are written in indigenous African languages?

Types of wills

It is imperative to know and have a better understanding of the type of will one may decide to draft. The following types (not limited to) that will be discussed are: simple, testamentary, joint, and living wills. Simple will: sometimes known as 'basic', which is the type most people have, where one can decide who will receive your assets and name a guardian for any minor children. This type is intended for distributing assets, property, and guardianship for basic estate planning. Testamentary trust will: places some assets into a trust for the benefit of beneficiaries and names a trustee to handle it. Through this type of will, assets can be put in a trust and place conditions on the inheritance which may be gradual based on age or other factors. Joint will: two testators sign a joint will, and create a shared estate plan. It includes executor, beneficiaries, and other provisions, and it cannot be changed even after the death of one testator. This type of will is intended for domestic partners or spouses who want the other will maker to receive their assets upon death. Living will: has nothing to do with distributing property after your death; instead, it allows one to choose what medical treatment one wants to have if you become incapacitated. In a living will, one may also name someone to make decisions on your behalf. It is intended for individuals who want to plan for medical contingencies.

Literature review

South Africa's Constitution (Act 108 of 1996) is underlined by convictions of good governance, in which 12 official languages are recognised and can be used for communication within different institutions, including charismatic churches. It must be noted that the 12th official language (South African Sign Language) was introduced into the Constitution of South Africa on 19 July 2023. Section 32 of the Constitution deals with access to information by all citizens in the Republic. It (Section 32 of the South African Constitution) further indicates that everyone has the right to the following: a) any information held by organisations, such as churches;and b) any information that is held by the other person and that is required for the exercise or protection of any rights.

This Section 32 of the RSA Constitution also stipulates that such information (for this study, legal fraternity) should be made available in multiple languages, including African indigenous languages. Section 3 (b) of the Constitution of the Republic of South Africa (Act 108 of 1996) focuses on the language of preference by citizens in a particular area of residence. It suggests the use of different languages (regional African indigenous languages) to be of utmost importance. This study, therefore, attempts to close the language gap wherein legally drafted wills are mostly written in languages such as English and sometimes Latin. Thus, citizens who are not literate in these languages are left behind, and possibly ignored, when some legal expressions are written in Latin, or at times do not follow or distribute assets accordingly. Therefore, it could be appropriate if the wills are written in regional African indigenous languages to enable proper distribution of assets. Section 8.2 of the Constitution of the Republic of South Africa (Act 108 of 1996) protects citizens against discrimination based on race, culture, language, gender, sex, ethnicity, social origin, colour, sexual orientation, age, disability, religion, and conscience. Similarly, Sections 3.3; 3.6, and 3.7 of the Constitution of the Republic of South Africa (Act 108 of 1996) acknowledge the right of citizens to address and be addressed by institutions as well as parliament(s) in the language(s) of their choice. Mandela (1989) posited that if someone is talking to you in your language, that goes into your heart. Therefore, the reaction of people becomes positive when hearing their African indigenous languages spoken to them or forming part of their discussion or any written documents (for this study, legally drafted wills).

Methods and study design

The study adopted Mixed Method Research. Both qualitative (interviews with illiterate citizens) and quantitative (questionnaires with other citizens) approaches were mixed by engaging a descriptive, cross-sectional approach to explore and describe the value of providing relevant information to all citizens using all South African languages, including indigenous African languages. Polit and Beck (2017) posited that a study's design is the plan for addressing a research question, including specifications for enhancing the study's integrity.

Population and sample

Polit and Beck (2017) defined population as the complete combination of cases in which the researcher is interested; consequently, a population is not chosen for the purpose of generalisability, but rather to establish the kinds of individuals that are suitable to take part in the study. For this study, the target population comprised of South Africans, mostly illiterate citizens. This population was difficult to find as illiterate citizens were afraid to participate in the study for fear of being stigmatised and labelled. At last, on discovering that the study will help them address their plight, they voluntarily availed themselves for the study. Polit and Beck (2017) refer to sampling as the procedure of selecting a subset of the population to represent the whole population. This study managed to have 100 participants (within a population of 160 532; Stats SA: 2011), sourced from the Free State Province, South Africa. Most research studies do not depend on how big the sample is; only a reasonable number may suffice. The sample was randomly selected from different shopping complexes in the Free State (within Moqhaka Local Municipality, towns: Kroonstad, Viljoenskroon, and Steynsrus). For qualitative research, participants were randomly selected. A purposive sampling, and a non-probability sampling method where the researcher selected participants based on his personal judgment of which of them would be most informative, were used. The researcher combined purposive sampling and non-probability methods to generate more data.

Instrument and data collection procedure

Saris and Gallhofer (2014) postulate that a questionnaire is the main instrument for collecting data in survey research, with a set of standardised questions, often called items, which follow a fixed scheme to collect individual data about one or more specific topics. The questionnaire was composed of sections that capture demographic information as well as sections on assessment (education level), educational experience, and social experience with both closed and open-ended questions. In ensuring the validity of the research tools (questionnaire and interview) a scholar on education issues was consulted to help with language and scope. Above all, the research tools were administered to citizens who consented to participate in this study.

Ethical considerations

Mark (2015) refers to ethical considerations as a branch of philosophy that deals with the conduct of participants and guides norms or standards of behaviour of participants and their relationships with each other. Moral behaviour must be considered when conducting research. The researcher indicated that at no stage will his participants be known to any person. Furthermore, the researcher indicated that participants' rights and privacy will be considered and protected, permission will be obtained to record the session, and they will have an option of disclosure or non-disclosure of their identification. Of importance to note is that participants were made aware that, should they feel offended at any point, they are free to discontinue the research, as they took part willingly. Over and above, adhering to principles of voluntary participation and informed consent, participants were also requested to fill in the consent forms and were also guaranteed confidentiality of their responses and anonymity of their identities. The ethical considerations are not limited to the above-mentioned only.

Data analysis

Wiid and Diggines (2013) define data analysis as how the researcher spells out the purpose and logic of analysing, explaining the way gathered information will account for variations in some of the quality of responses. Furthermore, Saris and Gallhofer (2014) maintained that data analysis is a process conducted to sift, reduce, organise, and give purposeful meaning to data, helping to respond to research questions. Data was summarised and presented. Thematic analysis was used to analyse qualitative data, especially in exploring relationships between responses to different questions. Thematic analysis emphasised identifying and interpreting patterns of meaning within qualitative data. Thematic analysis allows the researcher to focus on different ways of analysing the data. This approach is flexible, and analysis can deal with the entire dataset or deal with a particular phenomenon in depth (Braun & Clarke, 2006). The results revealed that IALs (indigenous African languages) have not been adequately used in drafting legal wills. 80%, or 40 participants, indicated that no indigenous African languages were used in drafting legal wills. These participants (80%) further expressed their displeasure, indicating that the languages used in legal wills (legal English and a bit of Latin) are foreign to them as they are either semi-literate or illiterate in these languages. 15%, or eight participants (literate participants), indicated that they do not have problems with the use of English, whilst five percent, or two participants, decided to be non-committal, preferring to say 'no comment'. The significance of the results is that IALs form an integral part in helping South Africans (illiterate, semi-literate, literate) to understand the contents of legally drafted wills.

Qualitative analysis

Punch (2013) refers to qualitative analysis as a collection and analysing of non-numerical data (e.g., text, videos, or audio) to understand concepts, opinions, or experiences.

Furthermore, qualitative analysis is about emotions or perceptions of people, what and how they feel. It is concerned with gaining insights, reasoning, and motivations. The interviewer used a voice-recorder to conduct the interviews with respondents. For this study, the interview was informal and unstructured/conversational, wherein most open-ended questions were asked spontaneously. With these spontaneous questions, the interviewer was letting the flow of the interview dictate the questions to be asked. A voice-recorder was used in analysing data, as the interviews were recorded on it. The interviewer experienced some problems with some residents who are very suspicious of strangers, but some responded positively and felt free to be interviewed. Therefore, the information was collected and analysed to provide the results in this study.

Discussion

The United Nations (2004) acknowledged that illiterate people are entitled to exercise their political, civil, social, cultural, as well as linguistic rights on an equal basis with other people. Furthermore, it must be noted that the South African Constitution (Act 108 of 1996) stipulated a philosophy of political pluralism. This implies that the positioning of languages in South Africa had to do with accommodating every citizen's language. García and Wei (2014) referred to linguistic pluralism as a situation where there is more than one language spoken in an area, and more than one language is acceptable within a country or community. Linguistic pluralism as enshrined in the Constitution of the Republic of South Africa (Act 108 of 1996); the former language dispensation was based on official bilingualism, and now is replaced by official multilingualism. Furthermore, the Constitution of the Republic of South Africa (Act 108 of 1996) emphasises that equal language rights are extended to all 11 spoken languages.

Indigenous African languages were to be promoted by the South African government after the dawn of democracy in 1994. In doing so, the government had to introduce acts to achieve its aim of mainly promoting previously disadvantaged indigenous African languages. The South African government introduced the Use of Official Languages Act 12 of 2012 (2012) and this act has indicated that provincial governments must introduce their respective Use of Official Languages Act to promote the use of African indigenous languages within their provinces. The Use of Official Languages Act 12 (2012), among other things, is aimed at promoting the equitable use of the twelve South African official languages and facilitate access to government services. The supreme law of the country (the Constitution of the Republic of South Africa) demands accessibility and recognition, as well as the use, of all official languages as enshrined in the Bill of Rights. The Bill of Rights is the cornerstone of democracy in South Africa. It protects both rights and freedoms of all the citizens of the Republic of South Africa.

García and Wei (2014) postulated that language rights concern the rights of individuals, countries, and communities to use their indigenous languages for certain purposes and in certain circumstances. Furthermore, Zuanelli (1991) posited that there are two major language rights: 1) individual language rights, which refer to those rights the individual possesses to use only as an individual; and 2) communal language rights, which refer to those rights a group has to establish its institutions and for the promotion of language and culture for a group. Communal language rights support this study, in that citizens in one environment are likely to use a common regional language. Both individual and communal language rights are enshrined in the Constitution of the Republic of South Africa (Act 108 of 1996), but these rights are not being implemented.

Linguistic rights versus the sole language of record policy

Faingold (2004) posited that linguistic rights are human and civil rights concerning the individual and collective right to choose the language, or languages, for communication in a private or public space. Importantly, there are parameters for analysing linguistic rights, including the degree of territoriality, amount of positivity, and orientation in terms of maintenance or assimilation, as well as overtness. Linguistic rights include, among others, the right to an individual's own language in legal, administrative, and judicial acts. Moreover, these rights include the right to speak one's own language in legal spheres, or have personal documents held in custody for your safety in an individual's preferred language (for this study, an indigenous African language). The Universal Declaration of Linguistic Rights (ULDR) (1996) supports linguistic rights, especially those of endangered languages, such as indigenous African languages in South Africa. Its objective was to define equality in linguistic rights, regardless of differences in political or territorial statuses. It further serves to promote international commitment in respecting the rights of linguistic groups, especially those of historicity. The UDLR (1996) regards several policies that motivated the respect of linguistic rights.

The mandate that English should be the sole language of record in South African courts as a policy, passed by the former South African Chief Justice in 2017, has had a negative impact on the other 11 South African Languages. This policy puts English as the sole language of record in South African courts. This policy clashes with other South African acts, for example the Use of Official Languages Act 12 of 2012, which specifically helps to provide for the regulation and monitoring of official languages by national government for government purposes, reporting on use of official languages by government (including judicial entities, such as courts of law). Again, the use of the Republic's official languages must be promoted and pursued in accordance with the Constitution of the Republic of South Africa (1996).

Section 6 of the Constitution of the Republic of South Africa provides for 12 official languages, recognises the diminished use and status of indigenous African languages, and requires that the state take practical and positive measures to elevate the status and advance the use of indigenous African languages. It must be noted that the 12th official language (South African Sign Language) was introduced into South Africa's Constitution on 19 July 2023. Furthermore, the Constitution of the Republic of South Africa (1996) requires that all official languages enjoy parity of esteem and be treated equitably. As a result, Section 6 (4) of the Constitution provides that national government must regulate and monitor its use of official languages through legislation and other practical measures. As a result, the sole language of record policy is in contravention of Gazette Acts, as indicated above. Therefore, this policy could have been imposed without considering other South African official languages. It is imperative that individuals are within their linguistic rights to have their legally drafted wills in their indigenous African languages.

A time to change

It is understandable that lawyers should have their specialised terminology, like any other field of career. It must also be noted that lawyers, like other professionals, rely on the broader public they serve. For most lawyers, talking with non-lawyers is as important as talking with each other. Lawyers can talk with non-lawyers only if legal language and ordinary language are not too removed from each other. In legal conversations, there is usually a client who is not a lawyer, and the client wants to understand why the law operates as it does. The law is not, sometimes tragically, the only way of settling a dispute. If the gulf between legal language and ordinary languages (for this study, indigenous African languages) becomes too wide, the lawyer will not be able to explain why the law is as it is. The convenience of traditional legal language must give way to the requirements of better communication (for this study, communication in any indigenous African language). Codification came into the picture; codification involves reform of the substantive law, but it was also about the reform of legal language. Codification also took special care to use language ordinary people would understand. There is a need for a periodic return to the language of the ordinary people (for this study, indigenous African languages). This could promote language and human rights within the legal fraternity.

Will-related disputes

A will is an important legal document. It sets out the wishes of the deceased as to the distribution of their assets. It is commonly thought that an individual can dispose of their assets as they see fit. In fact, there is legislation that can be relied on to contest or dispute a will if a family member, or another individual, believes that the deceased has not made adequate provision for them. A disputed will is when the validity of a will can be contested if people believe it was created under one or more of the following conditions (not limited to the mentioned): the person who passed away did not have sufficient knowledge or understanding of English at the time of drafting a will; the deceased did not have sufficient mental capacity at the time the will was drawn up. The following are some examples of wills that have been contested.

- Will Contested by Estranged Daughter

Mary was the mother of two adult children, a son and daughter. She had been estranged from her daughter for over seven years before she died. Mary did not mention her daughter in her will at all and left her entire estate to her son. The daughter contested the will, claiming that her mother had a moral duty to provide for her, as she had significantly fewer financial resources than her brother, and suffered from a debilitating condition that made it difficult for her to find continuing employment. The daughter was awarded nearly half of her mother's estate. This example of a contested will demonstrates two significant points: firstly, that an individual may make a successful inheritance claim even if they are estranged from the testator; secondly, that evidence of financial need is a significant factor in determining whether a will has made adequate provision for the children of the deceased, even adult children.

- Will Contested Because of Prior Contribution to Assets

Frank, a widower, died leaving behind an estate consisting of the family home and proceeds from the sale of a family-owned business. His will divided his assets equally amongst his eight children. Frank's eldest son contested the will, requesting an increased proportion of the inheritance as he had materially assisted in building the family business. The court awarded the eldest son a significantly larger proportion of the estate, reducing the provision for the other seven children accordingly. This case study demonstrates that if an individual has contributed financially or in kind to an asset distributed in a will, they may have greater claim to the estate than other beneficiaries.

- Will Contested through Contribution to the Support of the Testator

Linda died leaving behind three children. She bequeathed everything to her youngest daughter, who was also appointed as executor of the estate. The youngest daughter had provided Linda with emotional and economic support for the last 15 years of her life. She had paid off the small

mortgage on Linda's house and made improvements and renovations to her property. She had also cared for Linda's physical and emotional wellbeing, assisting with doctor's appointments, and visited regularly. Linda's son returned for his mother's funeral after many years abroad. He made a claim for a portion of the estate, even though he had not seen his mother for many years and had not provided material or emotional support to her. Linda's third child did not make a claim for an increased inheritance, because she was financially secure and felt that it was fair for her sister to inherit the estate after providing ongoing care for her mother. As Linda's son was able to demonstrate financial need, he was awarded one-third of Linda's estate. The remaining two-thirds of the estate was awarded to Linda's youngest daughter. This case study shows first that a claimant has an opportunity to contest a will even when they have had limited contact with the deceased. Second, it demonstrates again that the financial need of the claimant is a significant factor in applications for increased inheritance. Finally, this case also demonstrates that when one beneficiary has provided significant financial and practical support to the deceased, this will be a consideration in determining the distribution of the estate. Although Linda's youngest daughter had to share the estate with her brother, she was allocated twice the portion in recognition of her closer relationship with, and contributions to, her mother's life.

- Will Contested by ex-wife of Nelson Mandela - Former South African President

When Mandela died at the age of 95, he left nothing of his estimated £2.5 million estate to his ex-wife Winnie. She was demanding ownership of the ancestral home of Mandela in Qunu. Before Mandela died there was plenty of bickering and family divisions. Whilst the former South African president was still in hospital fighting for his life, a case was fought in court between his grandson, Mandla, and 16 other relatives. The battle was over the three bodies of Mandela's children. The 16 relatives wanted these bodies to be exhumed and reburied. They won. Mandla thought they were being vengeful and trying to control his grandfather's legacy.

- Michael Jackson - King of Pop

Since the death of the King of Pop in June 2009, his family has been embroiled in a plethora of legal and financial disputes. The people feeling upset are his siblings, who were left out of the will. Some of the siblings joined together to write and sign a letter claiming the will to be fake. In 2012, they asked the executors of the estate to resign. However, one of the signatories, Jermaine Jackson, later retracted his signature. There was also a lot of arguing over the custody of Jackson's three children: Prince, Paris, and Blanket. Their grandmother, Michael's mother, was named legal guardian, but briefly lost her guardianship when she went missing for a short period of time in August 2012. After a bit of mishap, she was later reinstated as guardian.

Will-related language

There are no language restrictions when writing a will. A will can be written in any language, provided that the words are clear and unambiguous so that the intention of the testator is reflected in his/her will. For example, 'I direct that any inheritance bequeathed herewith shall be free from the operation of the consequences of any marriage in community of property. Such inheritance shall also not form part of any accrual operative in the South African law or any law elsewhere where a beneficiary may arise'. Furthermore, a will can either be a verb or a noun. As a verb, a will can be the main verb when designating that the subject wishes or desires something or a situation. 'Will' can be an auxiliary verb that works with another main verb. When used as noun, 'will' can indicate someone's wish or desire.

Again, words and meaning in a will play a significant role, namely: testate, a person who has died and has left a valid will behind; testator, the owner of a will/testament (still living); estate, after someone dies all the money, properties, other assets, and debt that they have left behind; executor of the estate, the person who is responsible for keeping the estate safe until the assets or money can be properly allocated to the people listed in the will; and liabilities, a person's or company's financial debts, e.g. a car or a house one is paying off .

Implications/recommendations

- There are many reasons for wanting to reform legal language. The most compelling reason is that obscure legal language could deprive ordinary people of their legal, equal, and human rights.
- If they are unable to do this, ordinary people do not have access to their full range of rights and are at the mercy of whoever claims to know what the language means.
- Processing information is a cognitive exercise; having to process information in a language that you are not most acquainted with becomes even more challenging.
- The language of communication has challenged us in more ways than one, not the least of which is how we relate to each other, and language used in legally drafted wills is no exception.
- Now is the time for legally drafted wills and their entities or agents to take the language agenda to the next level.
- The state (as the RSA constitutional guardian) is urged to note that the language matter has become more crucial for effective attempts to save our people from the discrepancies that occurs during the reading of legally drafted wills.
- The legal fraternity is encouraged to try to translate legally drafted wills into indigenous African languages.
- The state, with its political power and will, must take the lead in promoting indigenous African languages and realise the parity of esteem as envisaged by the Constitution.
- Constitutional changes taking place in South Africa call for changes in the language and style in which legal documents are available in indigenous African languages.

Conclusion

From the findings of this study, there is an extensive gap among different languages, as the different institutions or individuals in the legal profession (e.g., lawyers) have opted to use English as the medium of communication between themselves and citizens. To date, illiterate and semi-literate people, in general, are still being discriminated against because legally drafted wills are, to date, written in English and sometimes Latin, with little effort from the government through laws and policies to end this, despite opposition from advocacy groups. Democratic South Africa cannot be involved in the perpetuation of the cultural annihilation of African heritage which involve language.

References

Austrian Federal Government. 2020. Aus Verantwortung für Österreich. Regierungsprogramm 2020 2024. https://www.bmeia.gv.at/fileadmin/user_upload/Vertretungen/Bern/Dokumente/Regierungsuebereinkommen_Kurzfassung.pdf. Accessed 7 Februar 2024.

Austrian Parliamentary Administration. 2024. Begutachtungsverfahren Wissenswertes zum vorparlamentarischen und parlamentarischen Begutachtungsverfahren. https://www.parlament.gv.at/beteiligen/wissenswertes/begutachtungsverfahren/index.html. Accessed 7 Februar 2024.

Braun, V. & Clarke, V. (2006). Using thematic analysis in psychology. *Qualitative Research in Psychology* (3): 77-101. https://doi.org/10.1191/1478088706qp063oa.

Faingold, ED. (2004). Language rights and language justice in the constitutions of the world. *Language problems & Language Planning*, 28 (1): 11-24.

Fredericks, INA. (2011). The protection of languages and language rights is enshrined in the South African Constitution. [Doctoral dissertation] South Africa: University of Western Cape Press.

García, O. & Wei, L. (2014). *Translanguaging: Language, Bilingualism and Education.* London: Palgrave Macmillan Publishers.

Green, Daniel. 2023. The Discursive Construction of Antisemitism in Nazi Children's Books: Elvira Bauer's Trust No Fox (1936) and Ernst Hiemer's The Poisonous Mushroom (1938). International Journal for the Semiotics of Law - Revue internationale de Sémiotique juridique 36, 2355-2396.

Green [Leisser] & Kager. 2021. Die partizipative Lücke im österreichischen Mandatsverfahren: Handlungswissen und Einstellungen bei Akteuren der Strafverfolgung. In Toke Hoffmeister , Markus Hundt und Saskia Naths (eds.). Laien, Wissen, Sprache Theoretische, methodische und domänenspezifische Perspektiven. Berlin: De Gruyter, 569-591.

Harries, TE. (2008). *Applied Organisational Communication: Theory and Practice in a Global Environment.* (third edition). Oxfordshire. United Kingdom. Routledge Publishers.

Jones DA. & Skarlick DP. (2012). How perceptions of fairness can change: A dynamic model of organisational justice. *Journal of Applied Psychology*, 33. Colombia: University of British Colombia Press.

Kamwangamula, NM. (2016). Language Policy and Economics: The Language Question in Africa. *Language Problems & Language Planning,* 43(3).

Koester, Almut. 2022. "Building small specialised corpora". In: Anne McCarthy O'Keeffe, Michael J. (eds). The Routledge Handbook of Corpus Linguistics. London: Routledge, 48-61.

Makalela, LM. (2018). 'Our academics are intellectually colonised': Multi-languaging and Fees Must Fall. *Southern African Linguistics and Applied Language Studies*, (46):1–11.

Mandela, RN. (1989). *Long Walk to Freedom: The Autobiography of Nelson Mandela*. USA: Little, Brown and Company.

Mark, I. (2015). *Research Ethics and Integrity for Social Scientists*. (second edition). London, Los Angeles: SAGE Publishers.

Mwaniki, M. (2012). *Multilingualism and the Public Sector in South Africa.* Bloemfontein: African Sun Media.

Polit, DF. & Beck, CT. (2017). *Nursing Research: Generating and Assessing Evidence for Nursing Practice.* (tenth edition). Philadelphia: Academic Publishers.

Punch, KF. (2013). *Introduction to Social Research: Quantitative and Qualitative Approaches.* London: SAGE Publishers.

Republic of South Africa (RSA). (1996). *Constitution of the Republic of South Africa.* Pretoria: Government Printer.

Republic of South Africa (RSA). (2011). *Statistics South Africa*. Pretoria: Government Printer.

Republic of South Africa (RSA). (2012). *Use of Official Languages Act 12 of 2012*. Pretoria: Government Printer.

Saris, WE. & Gallhoffer, IN. (2014). *Design, Evaluation, and Analysis of Questionnaires for Survey Research*. (second edition). Hoboken: Wiley Publishers.

Thompson, JB. (2007). *Ideology and Modern Culture: Critical Social Theory in the Era of Mass Communication*. Cambridge: Wiley Publishers.

United Nations (UN). (2004). *The Convention on the Rights of Persons with Disabilities.* Geneva: Department of Public Information.

Universal Declaration of Linguistic Rights. (1996). www.https://culturalrights.net>drets_culturals389

Wiid, J & Diggines, C. (2013). *Marketing Research.* Cape Town: Juta.

Zuanelli, E. (1991). *Italian in the European Community: An Educational Perspective on the National Language and New Language minorities.* Berlin: Prospects and Quandaries

18

DISSECTING PUBLIC LEGAL DISCOURSES ON THE AMENDMENT OF THE AUSTRIAN NAZI PROHIBITION ACT: A DISCOURSE ANALYSIS OF STATEMENTS DURING PARLIAMENTARY REVIEW

Daniel Green

Introduction

Various countries around the globe have legislation in place that bans the public display of National Socialist symbolism, such as the Swastika, Nazi flags, or the so-called Hitler salute. Some other countries have enacted or tightened such existing anti-Nazi legislation. For instance, in 2022 the Victorian Government in Australia passed the Summary Offences Amendment (Nazi Symbol Prohibition) Act 29 of 2022. The amendment of the criminal code led to various laws directed at preventing the intentional public display of Nazi symbols if the perpetrator 'knows, or ought reasonably to know, that the symbol is associated with Nazi ideology' (Commonwealth of Australia, 2022). Unlike in the case of the legislation passed in Australia, the Austrian Nazi Prohibition Act 1947 is in constitutional rank. It does not solely focus on preventing public displays of Nazi symbolism and gestures, but aims to ban the Nazi party, its subsidiaries, and any kind of re-engagement with (neo-)Nazi activities in the present and the future. The Australian and the Austrian approaches to prevent Nazi activities differ, since the former focuses on the prevention of public displays of Nazi symbolism, while the latter is concerned with the evil of Nazism itself, the ideology of which is sought to be combated by a defensive democracy (see also the Basic Law of the Knesset (Section 7A)). The case for the necessity of a democracy defending itself by means of legislation as opposed to a form of democracy that is tolerant of intolerance and brings about its self-destruction is best illustrated by the notorious words of the so-called Reich Minister of Propaganda, Joseph Goebbels:

> 'When democracy granted democratic methods for us in the times of opposition, this was bound to happen in a democratic system. However, we National Socialists never asserted that we represented a democratic point of view, but we have declared openly that we used democratic methods only in order to gain the power and that, after assuming the power, we would deny to our adversaries without any consideration the means which were granted to us in the times of opposition (Joseph Goebbels 1935, cited in Florida Center for Instructional Technology, 2005).

As is unambiguously clear in the quote above, Nazi ideology is hostile to democracy and used democratic methods in the past to gain power but had no intention of upholding democratic principles once in power. Instead, the Nazis planned to suppress any opposition and deny democratic rights to their political adversaries, wherever they were located on the political spectrum. This merits legislative action against any activity in the present that seeks to establish a national socialist order of society in Austria and in any other part of the world. However, this paper is not concerned with a comparative analysis of anti-Nazi legislation around the globe. Instead, it seeks to offer new insights into the public legal discourse operative in the statements published as part of the legislative process of the changes made to the Austrian Nazi Prohibition Act 1947. It aims to provide answers to the question as to how the tightening of the Prohibition Act 1947 is discursively negotiated in the statements made throughout the legislative process. Throughout the parlaimentary legislative process, citizens, institutions, and organisations may submit statements on all legislative initiatives. While the relevant federal ministry typically requests other federal ministries, state governments, and interest groups to submit statements on a ministerial draft, all citizens and institutions are entitled to submit their views on ministerial drafts. Citizens can also submit their views on parliamentary citizen initiatives or petitions (Austrian Parliamentary Administration, 2024).

The intention of the Austrian Federal Government to amend the Prohibition Act 1947 can be traced back to the government programme for the years 2020 to 2024, which includes the task of engaging in the 'Fight against Antisemitism – Revision of the Prohibition Act – Evaluation and possible legislative revision of the Prohibition Act with regard to domestic jurisdiction, particularly regarding the offences of sections 3g and 3h of the Prohibition Act and closing further gaps (e.g., partial denial) – Examination of the possibility of confiscating Nazi memorabilia independently of the commission of a punishable act and evaluation of the Badge Act'(Austrian Federal Government, 2020). In 2021, a National Strategy against Antisemitism was presented. The Federal Ministry of Justice then established a working group in the same year to evaluate the Prohibition

Act 1947, within which the need for revision was discussed, the needs of practice were assessed, and the historical and constitutional foundations were addressed. The working group commenced its activities in autumn 2021 and comprised representatives from academia, civil society, practice, and religion. Four meetings were held by the working group, and it concluded its work in autumn 2022. The final report of the working group was then presented to the public in November 2022 and suggested that various kinds of legislative action should be taken. For instance, the working group suggested that there is a need to extend Austrian jurisdiction to certain conduct abroad that falls under the Prohibition Act 1947 but simultaneously rejected Austria's worldwide jurisdiction. The working group also critically assessed the penalties under the Prohibition Act 1947 and advised towards differentiation of provisions to increase efficiency and practicability. The working group endorsed diversionary resolutions of criminal proceedings under the Prohibition Act 1947, particularly in the low-threshold area of speech offences. In Austrian criminal law, such a diversionary resolution constitutes:

> '... the possibility for the prosecution or the court (...), when the facts are sufficiently clarified, to refrain from conducting a formal criminal proceeding. In the case of diversion, the accused or the defendant is offered the opportunity to undergo a burdensome measure (e.g. community service). (...) The imposition of a fine or imprisonment is thus no longer the only possible reaction of the state to a clarified criminal offense. (...) When a criminal proceeding is terminated by means of diversion, there is no guilty verdict and no formal conviction. There is also no entry in the criminal record; however, the diversion is stored internally within the justice system for ten years' (Ministry of Finance, 2024 (author's translation). See also section 198 Austrian Criminal Procedural Code, 1975).

While the working group did not identify significant legal gaps, it stated that clarifications and specifications regarding section 3g and section 3h of the Prohibition Act 1947 were sensible. For instance, section 3h of the Prohibition Act 1947 should be clarified by removing the word 'grossly' to make it punishable to trivialise the Holocaust in any way, not only when gross trivialisation takes place. Finally, the working group took note of the necessity that it should be possible for Nazi memorabilia to be confiscated even without a connection to a specific act of Nazi re-engagement. In other words, Austrian legislation took a clear stance regarding the necessity to prevent the rise of Nazism on Austrian territory and not only sought to ensure Nazi symbolism and gestures are not displayed. Being mindful of this wider sociopolitical context to the normative text with which the statements under analysis engage, this paper makes a clear distinction between legislation aiming to prevent the public display of Nazi symbols, and gestures and legislation seeking to prevent reactivation of Nazi ideology in its entirety. It argues that it is an important characteristic of defensive democracies to fight ideologies that seek to do away with the democratic order of society. Hence, the legislation does not only seek to prevent the display of Nazi symbols and gestures only, but is concerned with protecting social peace and keeping down destructive forces residing in the simmering (neo-)Nazi movements around the globe. The following section will offer a brief overview of the Austrian Prohibition Act 1947 and aims to demonstrate why the amended Prohibition Act 1947 is likely to serve as an effective model for combating Nazi ideology, rather than merely prohibiting the display of Nazi symbolism and gestures in public.

'... to prevent all Nazi activity and propaganda in Austria' – the Nazi Prohibition Act 1947

Article 9 of the Austrian State Treaty of 1955 decreed the enactment of laws against any fascist and Nazi activity on Austrian territory (see also Lichtenwagner & Zatloukal 2018). It states explicitly that "Austria will also continue its efforts to eradicate all traces of Nazism from Austrian political, economic, and cultural life to ensure that the aforementioned organisations are not revived in any form and to prevent all Nazi or militaristic activity and propaganda in Austria" (author's translation). In order to meet this promise, the Prohibition Act 1947, the Badge Act and the Introductory Act to the Administrative Procedures Act were enacted (see Lichtenwagner & Zatloukal, 2018). Today the normative content of these legislative texts relates to prohibited conduct and legal issues in the context of Nazi re-engagement and Holocaust denial (Bailer, 2018), the promotion of Nazi propaganda (Salimi, 2018), the delineation between punishable conduct under Article III para 1 Z 4 EGVG and the Prohibition Act 1947 (Merli, 2018), the display of Nazi badges (Lichtenwagner, 2018), subsidiarity and prohibition of double jeopardy (Birklbauer, 2018), the tension between Nazi prohibition and freedom of expression (Wiederin, 2018), and Nazi symbolism online (Wagrandl, 2018). However, the question remains whether focus should be placed on preventing by prohibiting the display of Nazi symbols and gestures, or on preventing reactivation of Nazi ideology as a threat to democracy. The proposition to focus solely on the public display of Nazi symbols and gestures overlooks a significant risk, as neo-Nazi groups may manage to operate discreetly, for instance, by potentially undermining democratic institutions from within, e.g. (see Höcke's rhetoric in Germany, see Tottmann 2022). Due to space limitations, this paper cannot provide an exhaustive discussion of the various legal ramifications of concentrating on preventing the display of Nazi symbols and gestures. However, it is a relevant point to make that the danger from Nazism does not only emanate from symbols and/or gestures, but primarily from the ideology itself, which promises megalomaniac superiority to some to the dehumanising detriment of others. For instance, as eloquently phrased in Australia's Summary Offences Amendment (Nazi Symbol Prohibition) Act 2022, 'the *Hakenkreuz* (meaning 'twisted or hooked cross' in German) (...) became a symbol of the Third Reich, under which heinous crimes were perpetrated against humanity, particularly the Jewish people. The *Hakenkreuz* is a symbol of antisemitism and hatred and of an ideology fundamentally incompatible with Victoria's multicultural, multiethnic and democratic society'. In Austria, the law punishes any propagandistic expression of Nazi ideology which the symbols and gestures (see Green, 2024), such as the swastika and the Hitler salute, represent. This continuous struggle against the poison cabinet emanating from and operating within Nazi ideology is best illustrated by sections 1 and 3a to 3o of the Prohibition Act 1947 (see Table 18.1):

TABLE 18.1: Regulatory content of sections 1 and sections 3a to 3o of the Prohibition Act 1947

Section	Legal content
1	Revival or maintenance of the Nazi Party (NSDAP) and its affiliated organizations.
3a	Attempting to maintain or reestablish dissolved Nazi organisations or establishing connections with such organisations.
3b	Participation in or support of Nazi organisations through financial contributions or other means.
3d	Public incitement to Nazi activities, glorification of Nazi goals or institutions, or solicitation to engage in prohibited actions.
3e	Conspiring to commit serious crimes such as murder, robbery, or arson in furtherance of Nazi objectives.
3f	Attempting or committing serious crimes as a means of promoting Nazi ideology.
3g	Engaging in activities in support of Nazi ideology through means other than those specified in previous sections.
3h	Denial, trivialisation, or justification of Nazi genocide and other crimes against humanity.
3i	Failure to report prohibited activities to authorities.
3j	Jurisdiction of courts for prosecuting offences under the Prohibition Act.
3k	Automatic dismissal from public office upon conviction under the Prohibition Act.
3l	Extraterritorial application of the law to offences committed abroad by Austrian citizens or residents.
3m	Extraterritorial application of specific provisions to offences committed abroad that threaten public order or safety in Austria.
3n	Confiscation of objects capable of facilitating prohibited activities under the Prohibition Act.
3o	Implementation of educational programmes for offenders as an alternative to prosecution.

As can be seen from the summary of provisions above, the purpose of the Prohibition Act 1947 does not only encompass preventing the display of Nazi symbols or gestures but also fighting Nazism at the grassroots. The provisions target various forms of Nazi activity, including any attempts to revive or maintain Nazi organisations (section 1, section

3a), participation in or support of Nazi organisations (section 3b), public incitement to Nazi activities (section 3d), conspiracy to commit serious crimes in furtherance of Nazi objectives (section 3e), and the commission of crimes to promote Nazi ideology (section 3f). The law also addresses the denial, trivialisation, or justification of Nazi genocide and other crimes against humanity (section 3h), failure to report prohibited activities (section 3i), and provides for the confiscation of objects facilitating prohibited activities (section 3n). It also includes provisions for the extraterritorial application of the law to offences committed abroad by Austrian citizens or residents (section 3l, section 3m) and the implementation of educational programmes for offenders (section 3o). It becomes clear that the legislative intent seeks to address and prevent any form of Nazi ideology and activity at its core and does not tolerate Nazism 'in the quiet chamber'. This is why the legislative body has performed a stronger differentiation of offences under Sections 3g and 3h of the Prohibition Act 1947 and enacted a selective increase in penalties. These amendments aim to differentiate between various forms of offences covered by the relevant provisions and divide them into a basic offence and two (more severe) qualifications, with the second qualification now carrying a minimum penalty of ten years. The jurisdiction of Austrian courts is also expanded to cover offences outlined in Sections 3a, 3b, 3g, and 3h of the Prohibition Act 1947, including if these offences are committed outside the country. As a result of the amendment, Austrian officials face automatic dismissal upon conviction for offences falling under the Prohibition Act 1947, with a corresponding provision for contract employees (*Vertragsbedienstete*, amendment to the Contract Employees Act of 1948). Finally, Nazi propaganda materials can now be confiscated without a specific criminal offence being committed, which was a relevant prerequisite for any confiscation before the amendment took effect. This amendment of the Prohibition Act 1947, which was proposed by the government, also caused public debate regarding the breadth and depth of its normative content, which is, inter alia, reflected in the statements published throughout the legislative process. These statements, submitted by various agents, is the focus of the qualitative analysis presented in this paper. The following chapter presents the method underlying the analysis and interpretation of findings.

Methodology

This paper seeks to provide insights into public legal discourse assumed to be operative in the statements published regarding the changes made to the Prohibition Act 1947. In the investigation, focus is placed on how the tightening of the Prohibition Act 1947 is discursively negotiated in all publicly available statements. To this end, a specialised snapshot corpus (see Köster, 2022; McEnery & Hardie 2011) of 51 published and accessible statements addressing the amendment of the Prohibition Act 1947 was constructed. The statements were submitted to the Austrian Parliamentary Administration (*Parlamentsdirektion*) between 8 June 2023 and 20 July 2023. First all statement were categorised according to whether they are publicly available or not, leading to exclude the inaccessible ones, i.e. eight statements. All statements that were made available publicly were then copied into a TXT file, split into a formatted header and a body, and categorised according to whether the agent submitting the statement was writing as an academic (A), a religious community (RC), a legal institution (LI, e.g. a court, a prosecution office), a government agency (GA), a non-government organisation (NGO), or a private individual (PI). Building on previous research, XML annotation was applied including the metadata of the statement, the day, month and place of publication, and the applicable category and subcategory, e.g. <court>, <Upper Regional Court>, <Vienna>. The statements were then split into sentences, using the tag<s>,and were analysed regarding predication strategies directed at the tightening of the Prohibition Act 1947. Gläser's and Laudel's four-step approach to content analysis served as the basis of the analysis of the statements, which was successfully applied in previous research projects (Green, 2024; Green 2023; Green [Leisser] & Kager, 2021) and included preparation of data extraction, data extraction, data processing, and analysis. The open category system consists of five categorie: 1) legal and legislative considerations; 2) ethical concerns; 3) practical implementation and resource management; 4) political discourse and freedom of expression; and 5) historical revisionism. As the extraction phase progressed, new emerging themes were identified and used to produce a more detailed system of inductive categories. All public statements provided by private individuals were anonymised in this paper but can be accessed via the website of the Parliamentary Administration at https://www.parlament.gv.at/.

Findings

In total, 59 statements were submitted to the Parliamentary Administration. 51 of these statements were made publicly available. The following subsections show the themes that were found to be operative in the seven groups of academics, religious communities, legal institutions, government agencies, non-governmental organisations, public-law bodies, and private individuals.

Academics

Four criminal law experts have submitted review statements regarding the planned amendment of the Prohibition Act 1947, all of whom are affiliated with the Institute of Criminal Law and Criminology based in the University of Vienna: Alexander Tipold, Jakob Hajszan, Susanne Reindl-Krauskopf, and Farsam Salimi. All experts take an analytical approach to the amendment of the Prohibition Act 1947 and seem to support the proposed changes to the legislation, with the majority of authors suggesting various adjustments to the ministerial bill. The public legal discourse operative in the statements reveals different themes in relation to legislative drafting and parliamentary review, such as the historical context of the proposed legislation for the interpretation of its contemporary significance, the degrees of text-internal amendability, the degree of disambiguation of intertextual meanings, the degree of transparency and expected effectiveness of the proposed legislation, the degree of the legislation's responsiveness to practical issues (e.g. internet-related crimes), existing or projected gaps in legislation, the degree of consistency within the Prohibition Act 1947 and its wider legislative context, and the degree of harmonisation of criteria and terminology to ensure uniform application, inter alia.

Religious communities

The Jewish Community of Vienna (*Israelitische Kultusgemeinde Wien* or IKG) was the only religious community in Austria submitting a statement in parliamentary review. The public legal discourse operative in the IKG's statement shows various themes in relation to legislative drafting, such as the degree of the legislation's effectiveness regarding the prevention of the trivialisation of Nazi crimes and dissemination of Nazi propaganda, the degree of implementability and effectiveness of the legislation regarding local and global prosecution and alignment with international legal frameworks, the degree of restrictiveness and inclusiveness of the legislation, the degree of closure of existing legal gaps (e.g. regarding the confiscation of Nazi memorabilia), the degree of appropriateness and necessity of loss of office for civil servants (*Beamte*) and contract employees (*Vertragsbedienstete*), the degree of alignment of the legislation regarding fundamental legal principles (e.g. proportionality and constitutional safeguards) as well as principles of justice and human rights, and the degree to which the legislation reflects perspectives and legitimate interests of stakeholders, such as minority communities, inter alia.

Legal institutions

In total, nine legal institutions submitted statements on the amendment of the Prohibition Act 1947: the Supreme Court (OGH), the Office of the Attorney General at the Supreme Court, the Upper Regional Court Vienna (OLG Wien), the Regional Court for Criminal Matters Graz (LG Graz), the Regional Court for Criminal Matters Klagenfurt (LG Klagenfurt), the Chief Public Prosecutor's Office Vienna (OStA Wien), the Chief Public Prosecutor's Office Linz (OStA Linz), the Public Prosecutor's Office Vienna (StA Wien), the Public Prosecutor's Office Wels (StA Wels). The statements made by the Courts, the Attorney General, and the Public Prosecutor's Offices show varied and partly diverging positions towards the amendment of the Prohibition Act 1947. The professional public legal discourse (see Green [Leisser] & Kager 2021) shows nuanced positions regarding the degree of evaluability of the legislation's (in) coherence and (in)consistency with legal standards and frameworks in force, the degree of interpretability of legal concepts, the degree of qualifiability of offences (e.g. genuine qualifications and abstract endangerment offences), the degree to which diversionary measures and the formation of distinct penalty scales for different types of offences can be accommodated, the degree of judicial discretion provided by the legislation, the incorporability of provisions regarding the confiscation of Nazi propaganda materials and administrative penalties, the degree of feasibility concerning the workload of judicial personnel and the (in)adequacy of existing resources in the justice system, the degree of implementability of professional training and resource allocation in the justice system, the maintainability of the right to a fair trial, efficiency, and transparency in the judicial process, the degree of freedom of expression, privacy rights, and the right to criticise political figures, the degree of adequacy in relation to the prevention of hate speech and the preservation of public order, the degree of expectability of an increase in conviction rates, the degree of expandability and enforceability of domestic jurisdiction, the determinability of in-country jurisdiction for offences committed online, the degree of implementability of measures to address the dissemination of foreign print media, the degree of applicability of past legal interpretations, the degree of clarifiability and specification of the proposed legislative text, and the degree of (legal) certainty and effectiveness, inter alia.

Government agencies

Five out of nine local government agencies submitted statements regarding the proposed ministerial draft. These were the Offices of the Lower Austrian State Government, the Vorarlberg State Government, the Tyrol State Government, the Salzburg State Government, and the Vienna State Government. Notably, the Lower Austrian State Government submitted a statement according to which it 'has decided that no statement will be provided on the draft federal law amending the Prohibition Act 1947, the Contract Civil Servants Act 1948, and the Introductory Act to the Administrative Procedure Acts 2008 (Prohibition Act Amendment 2023)' (59/SN-279/ME). The Salzburg State Government briefly stated 'that it has no fundamental objections to the draft law referred to in the subject matter' (37/SN-279/ME). Similarly, the Tyrol State Government only briefly responded to the proposed amendment by stating 'regarding the aforementioned draft law, no objections are raised from the perspective of the State of Tyrol' (44/SN-279/ME). Other government agencies contributing statements were the Constitutional Service Section in the Federal Chancellery, the Federal Ministry for Climate Protection, Environment, Energy, Mobility, Innovation, Technology, and the Ministry of Finance. The public legal discourse operative in the statements may thus be described as pertaining to the degree of interpretability of the legislation, the degree of clarity and consistency of legal argumentation, the degree of clarity and consistency of legal concepts in the legislative text, the degree of potential ambiguities or inconsistencies of the amendment, the degree of impact the legislation may have on federal, state, and local authorities, the degree of feasibility regarding administrative procedures and responsibilities, the degree of increased workload and resource allocations for administrative bodies, the degree of feasibility regarding budgetary allocations and resource management, the degree of the legislation's alignment with existing legal frameworks and principles, the degree of clarity and transparency of communication strategies employed by the government, and the degree of feasibility and effectiveness of enforcement, inter alia.

Non-Government Organisations

In total, seven non-government organisations submitted statements on the amendment of the Prohibition Act 1947. These are the Documentation Archive of the Austrian Resistance (DÖW), the Mauthausen Committee Austria, the Association of Austrian Judges, ZARA – Civil Courage and Anti-Racism Work, the Public Service Union, the Austrian Trade Union Federation, and the Austrian Association for Legal Linguistics (ÖGRL). The public legal discourse operative in the statements reflects a varied picture of positions across the organisations, such as the amendment's degree of refinement of diversion eligibility criteria and implementation guidelines, the degree of feasibility and impact on the effectiveness and fairness of the legal framework, the degree of relevance of satire and caricature exemptions, the degree of clarity, legal coherence and consistency in relation to the text of the amendment, the adequate degree of freedom of expression and the prohibition of Nazi propaganda, the degree of applicability of international legal norms and obligations under international human rights treaties, the degree of feasibility of implementation in relation to training programmes for law enforcement and judicial personnel, the degree of identifiability of legal gaps and effective enforcement, the degree of adaptability of the legal framework to address modern forms of propaganda dissemination (e.g. in digital spaces.), the degree of adequacy of measures for combating online neo-Nazi propaganda, the degree of protection awarded to vulnerable populations from radicalisation, the degree of harmonisation of penalties for the display of Nazi symbolism with penalties for other extremist symbols, the degree of deterrence effectiveness, the degree of inclusiveness/ exclusiveness of the working group regarding the development of the legislation, the degree of (in)adequacy of the differentiation of offences, penalties, and other relevant provisions, the degree of (un)clarity and (in)effectiveness of legal concepts addressing

National Socialist atrocities, the degree of relevance of historical memory, Holocaust education, and commemoration efforts, the degree of (un)suitability of diversion programmes and educational initiatives with youth, the degree of potential ambiguities and inconsistencies in the legislative text, the degree of successful communication of memorial sites and legal institutions, the degree of availability of resources, funding sources, and long-term sustainability, the degree of (un)enforceability of extraterritorial jurisdiction in relation to Austrian interests or nationals, the degree of feasibility regarding evidence collection, jurisdictional boundaries, and coordination among law enforcement agencies, the degree of balance between combating hate speech, Holocaust denial, and extremist propaganda while safeguarding freedom of expression, the degree of workload and resource requirements of state prosecutors and courts, the degree of efficient enforcement of new provisions, the degree of stakeholder engagement in the legislative process, the degree of involvement of jury courts to lay judge panels, the degree of comparability of jury courts in Austria with those in other continental European countries, the degree of fair and effective trials, the degree of democratic legitimacy and transparency of judicial decision-making processes, the degree of the legislation's influence on public perception of the judiciary and court decisions, the degree to which proposals for constitutional reforms, particularly regarding judicial structures, have been discussed and debated within the political sphere, the degree of optimal composition and functioning of judicial bodies, the degree of transparency and accountability of the legal system, the degree of the legislation's impact in relation to prosecution strategies, sentencing guidelines, and diversion programmes, the degree of necessity for the amended legislation due to rising antisemitism and hate speech in online spaces, the degree of suitability of definitions of offences and thresholds for prosecution, the degree of balance between security and civil liberties, the degree of potential unintended consequences of the legislation, the degree of proportionality, and the rights and obligations of public servants and the degree of perceived integrity and reputation of the public sector, inter alia.

Public-law bodies

Three statements on the amendment of the Prohibition Act 1947 were submitted by public-law bodies (*Körperschaften öffentlichen Rechts*). These statements were submitted by the Austrian Bar Association, the Austrian Union of Students, and the Federal Workers' Chamber.

The public legal discourse tangible in the statements reflects different positions, such as the amendment's degree of sufficient penalties for propagating national socialist ideologies and the denial or trivialisation of the Holocaust, the degree of balance between combating extremism and protecting individual rights, the degree of appropriacy of legal language used with regard to the definitions of offences (e.g. the use of 'public' in section 3h), penalties, procedural aspects such as the handling of diversionary resolutions and the criteria for determining culpability, the degree to which the legislation addresses contemporary societal challenges effectively, the degree of fairness, accountability, and the protection of minority rights, the degree of enforcement difficulties, resource constraints, the degree of unintended consequences, the degree of limitation on freedom of expression related to satire and caricature, the degree of necessity of training prosecutors and judges in relation to the inclusion of digital Nazi collections in the scope of confiscation, the degree of suitability of diversionary measures for adult offenders, the degree of relevance for criminal liability for acts abroad, and the degree of involvement of various stakeholders in the legislative process.

Private individuals

In total, 17 individuals submitted statements to the parliamentary administration, part of which may be described as critical, others outright revisionist. Many statements show intersection between legal and political discourse and seek to delegitimise the Prohibition Act 1947 and/or all amendments under discussion. The discourse operative in many statements still shows a varied picture of positions, such as a perceived degree of political bias in the government proposing the legislation, a perceived degree of intentional arbitrariness of political and legal institutions, a perceived degree of subjectivity of judges influenced by societal, political, ideological, and religious biases, a perceived degree of political agendas, a perceived degree of influence of the anti-fascist movement (Antifa) on legislative processes, a perceived degree of abuse of the law to suppress dissenting voices, a perceived degree of reframing of Nazi ideology as 'left-wing', a perceived degree of necessity to preserve legal neutrality in the law, a perceived degree of historical revisionism in legal argumentation (e.g. a perceived degree of maintainability of objectivity and fairness in the interpretation and application of the law, irrespective of political ideology), a perceived degree of governmental overreach in the context of the amendment of the Prohibition Act 1947, a perceived degree of criminalisation of individuals for speech acts, a perceived degree of inconsistency in relation to law enforcement, a perceived degree of endangerment of democracy and free speech as a result of the legislation, a perceived degree of similarity between historical events and regimes and COVID-19 measures and climate change policies, a perceived degree of similarity between Nazi atrocities and contemporary political discourse, a perceived degree of uncertainty in relation to vague or broadly defined provisions, a perceived degree of negative impact on civil liberties and societal norms and values, and a perceived degree of necessity to explore alternative approaches to addressing concerns related to extremism and hate speech, inter alia. A clear majority of statements submitted by private individuals seek to express disdain and aversion against the Prohibition Act 1947 and the legislative efforts made to eradicate national socialist ideology at the grassroots. Many statements appear to relativise the necessity of the ministerial draft, with one disappointed author, speaking explicitly from their personal experience as an affected person that was 'unjustly sanctioned', describing the amendment as something 'to be strictly rejected due to historically verifiable findings' (Statement of private individual 1, (13/SN-279/ME)). There are various implicit attempts to redefine the meaning of *national socialism* and *national socialist* (see 15/SN-279/ME) which may be interpreted as part of the endeavour to establish a comparison between the Nazi leadership and the democratically elected government of Austria. This clearly constitutes a trivialisation of the Nazi crimes against humanity which is the objective the legislative body sought to accomplish by amending the Prohibition Act 1947.

Discussion

The findings of the qualitative analysis of the statements submitted in parliamentary review show a nuanced landscape in public legal discourse. While members from most groups express a concern for the effectiveness, fairness, and clarity of the amendment of the Prohibition Act 1947, it is reasonable to assume that agents refer to different types of interpretabilities, coherence, consistency, and alignment with legal standards. Each group considers the potential impact of the amendment on society, including the amendment's effectiveness in combating extremism, protecting civil liberties, promoting minority rights, and maintaining social cohesion. There seems to be a shared recognition of potential challenges across some groups in implementing the amended legislation, such as resource constraints, enforcement difficulties, and the need for training programmes for law enforcement and judicial personnel, to name a few. Some groups emphasise the importance of historical memory, Holocaust education, and commemoration efforts in shaping the legislative response to Nazi ideology and ensuring societal awareness of past atrocities. Different groups hold varying perspectives on the necessity, adequacy, and implications of the proposed amendments to the Prohibition Act 1947. While some groups support specific changes, others raise concerns or objections regarding the linguistic realisation of legal content. Each group foregrounds different aspects of the amendment, which seems to corroborate Widdowson's argument that the 'the textual features that are activated in interpretation are only those which are perceived, consciously or not, to be contextually and pretextually relevant' (Widdowson, 2004: 166). For instance, legal institutions tend to focus on issues related to legal interpretation, qualification of offences, jurisdiction, and penalties. In comparison, NGOs prioritise human rights, protection of minorities, freedom of expression, and the amendment's societal impact. Religious communities such as the IKG clearly emphasise the prevention of hate speech and Holocaust denial, while government agencies tend to focus on administrative feasibility and coordination. Groups with high legal expertise, such as academia and legal institutions, may provide more detailed analysis of legal concepts, terminology, and procedural aspects compared to other groups. Table 18.2 shows the inductive variables as developed based on the statements of all groups.

TABLE 18.2: Inductive variables and examples as developed based on the statements of all groups

Inductive variables	Examples
Legal and legislative considerations	• Degree of effectiveness and necessity of legislative changes • Interpretability, coherence, and consistency of legal frameworks • Alignment with international legal norms and human rights principles • Impact on judicial processes, fairness, and trial procedures • Clarity and transparency of legislative text • Balance between security measures and civil liberties
Ethical concerns	• Prevention of trivialisation of Nazi crimes and dissemination of Nazi propaganda • Protection of minority rights and vulnerable populations • Historical memory, Holocaust education, and commemoration efforts • Fairness, accountability, and integrity in legal processes
Practical implementation and resource management	• Feasibility of enforcement and administrative procedures • Impact on workload and resource allocation for judicial and administrative bodies • Training programmes for law enforcement and judicial personnel • Coordination among law enforcement agencies
Political discourse and freedom of expression	• Perceived political bias, subjectivity, and governmental overreach • Perceived influence of societal, political, ideological, and religious biases on legal processes • Perceived concerns about potential abuse of the law to suppress dissenting voices
Historical revisionism	• Revisionist interpretations of historical events and ideologies • Comparison between Nazi atrocities and contemporary political discourse • Perception of legislation based on historical revisionism

While the analysis aimed to capture as many detailed aspects as possible, it does not claim to represent the entire public legal discourse of and around the Prohibition Act 1947. It aims to provide a solid basis for future empirical analyses of these constituents of discourse. Importantly, the study has shown how different agents in legal discourse bring into perspective the Prohibition Act 1947 generally, and the proposed amendments specifically, from their respective positions as a legal scholar, a judge, a prosecutor, a lawyer, a Holocaust educator, a student representative, a convict, etc. This leads to the assumption that the notion of legal discourse cannot be tied to a narrow understanding of legal contexts, but that legal discourse can and will emerge in unexpected contexts and have multiple intersections with other discourses. Critical applied legal linguists (CraLL) can turn to the discourses in and around legislative processes to identify, analyse, and critique the relationship of public legal discourse and society along the boundaries of permissible and impermissible expressions of ideology.

The analysis of the statements from the different groups also provides useful insights into repeated considerations in legislative processes. For instance, the perceived relevance of the historical context of proposed legislation, the focus on disambiguation of meanings within the text, the projected effectiveness of the legislation and its responsiveness to practical issues, the consistency within existing laws, that is, with the web of interwoven legal meanings and discourses, and finally, the harmonisation of criteria and terminology for uniform application of legislative texts, particularly in the domain of criminal law. It seems legislative discourse revolves around the effectiveness of proposed legislation in achieving its objectives, alignment with international legal frameworks and standards, and adherence to fundamental legal principles such as proportionality, constitutional safeguards, justice, and human rights. In legislative discourse, potential challenges in implementation are also negotiated, including resource constraints (see Yang, 2016), feasibility of enforcement (see Guillery, 2018), impact on civil liberties, public order, and societal norms (see Amnesty International, 2024), and anticipating unintended consequences (see Fucik, 2021). Similarily, legislative discourse reflects negotiations of the protection of minority rights, the fairness of trials, and notions of the democratic legitimacy, transparency, and accountability of the legal system. It appears that what sets the Prohibition Act 1947 apart from other pieces of legislation is fierce criticism, claiming a perceived political bias and governmental overreach, drawing on historical revisionism, and expressing unspecified concerns about the state's infringement on free speech (for genocide denial and the limits of free speech, see Hennebel & Hochmann, 2011). Nazism is a threat which extends beyond symbols and gestures to the ideology of hatred itself, which promotes an unfounded superiority for some at the expense of dehumanising and annihilating others. Of course, criminal law is designed to address criminal conduct, but the underlying purpose of the Prohibition Act 1947 is to eradicate

Nazism before it creates deeper roots in Austria once more. Therefore, the enforcement of the Prohibition Act 1947 serves not only as a necessary tool to combat the rapidly increasing instances of antisemitism and Nazi-inspired hate speech online, but also as a robust legal instrument to deter any resurgence of Nazism in the future.

Obiter dictum, it may be useful to draw comparisons between Austria's and South Africa's legal responses to extremist ideology. Both legal orders seek to suppress extremist ideologies and prevent their resurgence. This raises broader questions, such as what constitutes an effective defensive democracy in the context of criminal justice, how historical accountability is negotiated, and where the limits of free speech should be drawn. Austria follows a bright-line rule that criminalises Nazism with a view to safeguarding its democratic system. South Africa has also implemented legislation against racial hate speech as well as shameless Apartheid denialism. Both jurisdictions face various challenges regarding the appropriate balancing of legal restrictions with freedom of expression when enforcing prohibitions. Whilst I was unable to consider these parallels in this paper, which focused on the Austrian context, it is reasonable to draw on comparative analyses and learn from one another when refining legislation in both jurisdictions. Critical applied legal linguistics (CrALL) and critical forensic linguistics (CrFL) have the potential to provide new theoretical as well as methodological perspectives regarding the defences democracy applies in and around legal discourse.

Conclusion

In conclusion, the analysis of the statements on the amendment of the Prohibition Act 1947 shows that public legal discourse largely revolves around the endeavour of combating the resurgence of Nazism. The legislation clearly goes beyond merely targeting the public display of Nazi symbols and gestures, aiming to root out Nazism at its core by prohibiting any form of Nazi activity. The statements from academia, legal institutions, government agencies, non-government organisations, a religious community, and various private individuals show that citizens have differing perspectives on the necessity, adequacy, and implications of the proposed amendments. While some groups support specific changes, others raise concerns regarding the specific linguistic expression of legal content or unintended consequences. The legislative discourse operative in relation to the Prohibition Act 1947 reveals the negotiation of the projected effectiveness of the proposed measures in achieving its objectives, alignment with international legal frameworks and standards, and adherence to fundamental legal principles such as proportionality, constitutional safeguards, justice, and human rights. Moreover, considerations regarding the historical context, disambiguation of meanings, consistency within existing laws, and harmonisation of criteria are foregrounded in legislative discussions. Despite criticism and opposition particularly by authors classified as private individuals, the significance of eradicating Nazism and preventing its resurgence may be viewed as a service to democracy. The ongoing threat posed by Nazism and right-wing extremism in Austria, and potentially elsewhere, extends beyond symbols and gestures to the ideology itself. The enforcement of the amended Prohibition Act 1947 serves as an important legal mechanism in combating antisemitism, hate speech, and right-wing extremism, safeguarding democratic values, and ensuring a more inclusive and tolerant society in Austria. Employing comparative legal analyses with other jurisdictions, such as South Africa, can provide valuable insights for refining legislative approaches.

References

Amnesty International. (2024). Freedom of expression. Accessed @https://www.amnesty.org/en/what-we-do/freedom-of-expression/. [Date accessed: 7 February 2024].

Austrian Parliamentary Administration. (1955). *Article 9 Austrian State Treaty 1955.* (1955). Accessed @https://www.ris.bka.gv.at/Dokumente/BgblPdf/1955_152_0/1955_152_0.pdf. [Date accessed: 7 February 2024].

Austrian Parliamentary Administration. (2023). *Statements on the Prohibition Act Amendment 2023, Amendment (279/ME).* Accessed @https://www.parlament.gv.at/gegenstand/XXVII/ME/279?FP_142_vhgBEZUG_GP_CODE=XXVII&FP_142_vhgBEZUG_ITYP=ME&FP_142_vhgBEZUG_INR=279&FP_142_vhgpage=3&selectedStage=101. [Date accessed: 7 February 2024].

Austrian Parliamentary Administration. (2024). *Begutachtungsverfahren Wissenswertes zum vorparlamentarischen und parlamentarischen Begutachtungsverfahren.* Accessed @https://www.parlament.gv.at/beteiligen/wissenswertes/begutachtungsverfahren/index.html. [Date accessed: 7 February 2024].

Austrian Parliamentary Administration. (1947). *Federal Constitutional Law on the Prohibition of the NSDAP (Prohibition Act 1947 – Verbotsgesetz).* Accessed @https://www.ris.bka.gv.at/GeltendeFassung.wxe?Abfrage=Bundesnormen&Gesetzesnummer=10000207. [Date accessed: 7 Feb 2024].

Bailer, B. (2018). Gegen nationalsozialistische Wiederbetätigung und Holocaustleugnung. Das NS-Verbotsgesetz 1947 bis heute. In Lichtenwagner, M. & Reiter-Zatloukal, I. (ed.). *‚... um alle nazistische Tätigkeit und Propaganda in Österreich zu verhindern' – NS-Wiederbetätigung im Spiegel von Verbotsgesetz und Verwaltungsstrafrecht.* Graz: Clio, 13–26.

Birklbauer, A. (2018). Subsidiarität und Doppelbestrafungsverbot bei Verstößen gegen das Verbotsgesetz und das Verwaltungsstrafecht. In Lichtenwagner, M. & Reiter-Zatloukal, I. (ed.). *‚... um alle nazistische Tätigkeit und Propaganda in Österreich zu verhindern' – NS-Wiederbetätigung im Spiegel von Verbotsgesetz und Verwaltungsstrafrecht*. Graz: Clio, 59–66.

Commonwealth of Australia. (2022). *Offences Amendment (Nazi Symbol Prohibition) Act 29 of 2022.* Federal Register of Legislation.

Florida Center for Instructional Technology. (2005). Means Used by the Nazi Conspiractors in Gaining Control of the German State. *A Teacher's Guide to the Holocaust.* Accessed @https://fcit.usf.edu/holocaust/resource/document/DOCNAC7.htm. [Date accessed: 7 February 2024].

Fucik, R. (2021). Recht und Sprache in der Gesetzgebung. In Kohl, G. & Nimmerfall, P. (ed.) *Recht und Sprache in der Praxis.* Vienna: Facultas, 106–135.

Green, D. (2024). Gesetzliches und übergesetzliches Sprachenrecht in Österreich. In De Cillia, R., Reisigl, M. & Vetter, E. (ed.) *Sprachenpolitik in Österreich: Bestandsaufnahme 2021* (bd. 50). De Gruyter.

Guillery, D. (2018). States and the limits of feasibility: enforcement, morality and possibility. [Doctoral dissertation] University College London.

Hennebel, L. & Hochmann, T. (ed.). (2011). *Genocide Denials and the Law.* Oxford: Oxford University Press.

Koester, A. (2022). Building small specialised corpora. In McCarthy O'Keeffe, A. & Michael, J. (ed) *The Routledge Handbook of Corpus Linguistics.* London: Routledge, 48–61.

Lichtenwagner, M. (2018). ‚… den Geist der Organisation verpflanzende Wirkung' Das Abzeichengesetz als Mittel im Kampf gegen NS-Symbole. In Lichtenwagner, M. & Reiter-Zatloukal, I. (ed.). *‚… um alle nazistische Tätigkeit und Propaganda in Österreich zu verhindern' – NS-Wiederbetätigung im Spiegel von Verbotsgesetz und Verwaltungsstrafrecht.* Graz: Clio, 47–58.

McEnery, T. & Hardie, A. (2011). *Corpus Linguistics: Method, Theory and Practice.* Cambridge: Cambridge University Press.

Merli, F. (2018). Unfug' im Einführungsgesetz zu den Verwaltungsverfahrensgesetzen. In Lichtenwagner, M. & Reiter-Zatloukal, I. (ed.). *‚… um alle nazistische Tätigkeit und Propaganda in Österreich zu verhindern' – NS-Wiederbetätigung im Spiegel von Verbotsgesetz und Verwaltungsstrafrecht.* Graz: Clio, 35–46.

Ministry of Finance. (2024). Allgemeines zur Diversion. https://www.oesterreich.gv.at/themen/gesetze_und_recht/strafrecht/4/Seite.2460601.html. [Date accessed: 7 February 2024].

Salimi, F. (2018). Zur Reichweite der Strafbarkeit nationalsozialistischer Propaganda. Eine Analyse der §§ 3g und 3h Verbotsgesetz. In Lichtenwagner, M. & Reiter-Zatloukal, I. (ed.). *‚… um alle nazistische Tätigkeit und Propaganda in Österreich zu verhindern' – NS-Wiederbetätigung im Spiegel von Verbotsgesetz und Verwaltungsstrafrecht.* Graz: Clio, 27–34.

Statement of the Constitutional Service Section in the Federal Chancellery (39/SN-279/ME)

Statement of the Federal Ministry for Climate Protection, Environment, Energy, Mobility, Innovation, and Technology (23/SN-279/ME)

Statement of the Federal Workers' Chamber (28/SN-279/ME)

Statement of the Ministry of Finance (41/SN-279/ME)

Statement of Alexander Tipold (27/SN-279/ME)

Statement of Farsam Salimi (19/SN-279/ME)

Statement of Jakob Hajszan (26/SN-279/ME)

Statement of private individual 1 (13/SN-279/ME)

Statement of private individual 2 (15/SN-279/ME)

Statement of Susanne Reindl-Krauskopf (25/SN-279/ME)

Statement of the Association of Austrian Judges Association (58/SN-279/ME)

Statement of the Austrian Association for Legal Linguistics (ÖGRL) (57/SN-279/ME)

Statement of the Austrian Bar Association (53/SN-279/ME)

Statement of the Austrian Trade Union Federation (36/SN-279/ME)

Statement of the Austrian Union of Students (55/SN-279/ME)

Statement of the Chief Public Prosecutor's Office Vienna (52/SN-279/ME)

Statement of the Documentation Archive of the Austrian Resistance (DÖW) (49/SN-279/ME)

Statement of the Jewish Community of Vienna (60/SN-279/ME)

Statement of the Mauthausen Committee Austria (43/SN-279/ME)

Statement of the Office of the Attorney General at the Supreme Court (35/SN-279/ME)

Statement of the Office of the Lower Austrian State Government (59/SN-279/ME)

Statement of the Office of the Salzburg State Government (37/SN-279/ME)

Statement of the Office of the Tyrol State Government (44/SN-279/ME)

Statement of the Office of the Vienna State Government (31/SN-279/ME)

Statement of the Office of the Vorarlberg State Government (45/SN-279/ME)

Statement of the Public Prosecutor's Office Vienna (30/SN-279/ME)

Statement of the Public Prosecutor's Office Wels (47/SN-279/ME)

Statement of the Public Service Union (48/SN-279/ME)

Statement of the Regional Court for Criminal Matters Graz (40/SN-279/ME)

Statement of the Regional Court for Criminal Matters Klagenfurt (20/SN-279/ME)

Statement of the Supreme Court (OGH) (50/SN-279/ME)

Statement of the Upper Regional Court Vienna (38/SN-279/ME)

Statement of ZARA - Civil Courage and Anti-Racism Work (54/SN-279/ME)

Summary Offences Amendment (Nazi Symbol Prohibition) Act 2022

Tottmann, Berit. 2022. Strategisches Framing bei Björn Höcke – wie ein rechtsextremer Politiker den Rahmen sprengt. Zeitschrift für Rechtsextremismusforschung 2(1), 128–140.

Wagrandl, U. (2018). Digitale wehrhafte Demokratie. Verbotene politische Symbole im Internet. In Lichtenwagner, M. & Reiter-Zatloukal, I. (ed.). ‚... um alle nazistische Tätigkeit und Propaganda in Österreich zu verhindern' – NS-Wiederbetätigung im Spiegel von Verbotsgesetz und Verwaltungsstrafrecht. Graz: Clio, 79–92.

Widdowson, HG. (2004). *Text, Context, Pretext: Critical Issues in Discourse Analysis.* Oxford: Blackwell.

Wiederin, E. (2018). Das Verbotsgesetz und die Meinungsfreiheit. In Lichtenwagner, M. & Reiter-Zatloukal, I. (ed.). ‚... *um alle nazistische Tätigkeit und Propaganda in Österreich zu verhindern' – NS-Wiederbetätigung im Spiegel von Verbotsgesetz und Verwaltungsstrafrecht.* Graz: Clio, 67–78.

Yang, CS. (2016). Resource Constraints and the Criminal Justice System: Evidence from Judicial Vacancies. *American Economic Journal: Economic Policy* 8(4): 289–332.

ABOUT THE CONTRIBUTORS

Karien Brits is a lecturer in Sepedi and Language in Practice at Akademia. She holds a master's degree (cum laude) in Setswana from the North-West University (NWU). Her research focuses on multilingualism, linguistic rights, and language learning, but she is also interested in morphology, language technology, and onomastics. Her great passion for language learning is evident in practice; she has proficiency in several languages, and she is still learning. She gained linguistic experience in various fields as a language practitioner, court interpreter, lecturer, and language advocate for NGOs.

Endurance Midinette Koumassol Dissake is a lecturer of Linguistics in the Department of Linguistics and African Language at the University of Bamenda in Cameroon. Her research is situated in the field of applied linguistics, with a particular focus on forensic linguistics, discourse analysis, and language documentation. She is the author and co-author of various scientific publications, including the book titled *Language and Legal Proceedings: Analysing Cameroon Courtroom Discourse* (2021).

Daniel Green is the founding president of the Austrian Association for Legal Linguistics (AALL) and a lecturer at Sigmund Freud University Vienna, the Vienna University of Economics and Business (WU), and the University of Vienna. He holds an LLM in Law from the University of Edinburgh and a Mag. phil. in English, American Studies, and History from the University of Vienna. His research focuses on the intersection of language, law, and business, with a particular interest in legal discourse and applied legal linguistics.

Mabilo Thabo Jonas holds a master's of Language Practice degree from Tshwane University of Technology (TUT). He is currently a PhD candidate at the University of the Western Cape (UWC) in African Languages. Some of his work includes being an assistant language educator in various schools in Tshwane West District, and a few in Limpopo Province, Sekhukhune District. He is currently a part time lecturer at TUT, Department of Applied Language, where he teaches English and Northen Sotho.

Wellman Kondowe is a senior lecturer in the Department of Language, Cultural and Creative Studies at Mzuzu University in Malawi. He holds a master's degree and a PhD in Applied Linguistics from Central China Normal University. He has published three books: *Multilingualism in Southern Africa*; *Discrimination and Access to Justice in Africa*; and *Forensic Linguistics in Southern Africa: Origins, Progress and Prospects.*

Precious Lungu is working at Mzuzu University as a lecturer in the Department of Language, Cultural and Creative Studies. He holds a Bachelor of Education Degree specialising in Language Studies, obtained in 2014 from Mzuzu University. He also holds a master's degree in Translation obtained in 2021 from the University of Buea in Cameroon. Some of his research interests are forensic linguistics (courtroom discourse, multilingualism in the courtroom, and legal language), community translation, and interpreting.

Stanley Madonsela is professor and chair of the Department of African Languages at the University of South Africa (Unisa). He is a co-manager of Unisa's research node of the South African Centre for Digital Language Resources (SADiLaR). He is Unisa's representative in the Community of Practice for the Teaching and Learning of African languages (CoPAL) under the patronage of the Universities South Africa (USAf). He also served as the deputy chairperson of the Gauteng Provincial Language Committee (GPLC).

Linidle Mali is a master's student at the University of the Western Cape. He has an honours degree in African Language Studies. He is a professional teacher, a freelance language practitioner (specialising in interpreting, translation, subtitling, and language editing), an interpreter, translator, and a member of both the isiXhosa National Language Body and the African Association of Forensic and Legal Linguists (AAFLL).

Nomfundo Mali is the current Western Cape Pan South African Language Board (PanSALB) Provincial Manager since 2006. She has acted in both the executive management and as PanSALB CEO. She holds a PhD in Literature in Language Teaching and Literacy (DLitt). She is currently enrolled for her second PhD in African Languages with a focus on forensic linguistics. She was presented with the prestigious award for succeeding against the odds for two consecutive years by the University of Stellenbosch Rector. She is the treasurer of the African Association of Forensic and Legal Linguistics (AAFLL).

Qhamani Masiki is a master's student at the University of the Western Cape with a research focus in forensic linguistics.. He holds an honours degree in African Language Studies.

Lloyd Matenga holds a Master of Laws degree in International Trade (by full dissertation) from the University of Fort Hare. He also completed his Bachelor of Laws degree from the same university. He is an aspiring legal practitioner. He has done his practical legal training (PLT), Articles of Clerkship for Attorneys, and has passed all his board exams for admission as a legal practitioner. He is currently a legal researcher for Advocate Donovan Pitt.

Josephate Mutangadura holds a PhD of Technology in Language Practice from Tshwane University of Technology and a PhD in Communications Science from the University of South Africa. His research interests include visual language and photojournalism, forensic linguistics, sociolinguistics, social media and development communication, and African literature. He is an experienced university lecturer for Professional Communication, Sociolinguistics, English for Journalists, African Literatures, and Development Communication, with over 20 years experience in six universities across three countries in Southern Africa.

Indiphiwe Mxakaza is a master's student at the University of the Western Cape with a research focus in forensic linguistics. She holds an honours degree (cum laude) in African Language Studies.

Tasneemah Nordien attained a BA degree in Social Work at Stellenbosch University and followed it up with an international master's degree in Social Work as an exchange student at Gothenberg University, Sweden. She obtained her PhD in Social Work from Stellenbosch University in 2019, which focused on empowerment services to sexually abused children. Before starting an academic career at Stellenbosch University, Tasneemah worked in the fields of child abuse prevention and sexual offences, where she attained vast experience in counselling exposure with the sexual offence court. As part of her lecturing duties, she teaches at undergraduate level to first-, second- and third-year students, coordinates the first-year Practice Education Programme, and supervises several postgraduate students at both masters and PhD levels.

Gerald Nthala is a lecturer in Applied Linguistics and Communication Studies at Mzuzu University, Malawi. He holds a Master of Arts degree in Applied Linguistics from the University of Malawi obtained in 2010. The book chapter contribution in this volume is his first academic publication.

Donovan Pitt holds a Diploma Juris and BProc from the University of Transkei (UNITRA), and an LLB from the University of Fort Hare. He is a practising advocate and chairperson of the Bhisho Society of Advocates. He previously practiced as an attorney and worked as a forensic lawyer with the Special Investigating Unit. He was recently appointed as an acting judge in the Eastern Cape Division of the High Court of South Africa.

Keneilwe Radebe is a senior lecturer, admitted attorney of the High Court, and commissioner for the South African Law Reform Commission. Her teaching and research areas are constitutional law and media law. She has published work on the subjects of media law (freedom of expression), customary law, and constitutional law. Her research focuses on the transformation of legal education and legal practice. Before working as an academic, Dr Radebe served her Articles of Clerkship at a law firm in Pretoria and worked for the North West High Court (Mahikeng, Mmabatho) as a law researcher.

Tebogo Rakgogo is an National Research Foundation (NRF) Y2-rated researcher, senior lecturer, and the Head of the Department of Applied Languages at the Tshwane University of Technology (TUT). He possesses a Diploma, B-Tech, and a master's degree in Language Practice from Tshwane University of Technology, a Postgraduate Certificate in Education (PGCE), an Honours Bachelor of Education in Educational Management, and an Honours Bachelor of Arts in Translation Studies from Unisa. He has a PhD from the University of the Witwatersrand. He is the Deputy Chairperson of the African Languages Association of Southern Africa (ALASA). He chairs the National Terminology Policy Steering Committee instituted by the Department of Sport, Arts, and Culture.

Happyness Nokwatu Raselabe is currently a master's student at the University of the Western Cape. She holds a B.Soc.Sci. from Rhodes University and BA Honours (cum laude) degree in African Languages and Literature from the University of Cape Town. She teaches isiXhosa and English, and works as a researcher. She has been a recipient of the Rhodes top 100 award, Deputy Vice Chancellor bursary, and the National Institute for Humanities and Social Science (NIHSS) Dr. Sindiwe Magona Research assistant scholarship.

Hlohlolo David Sephiri is a lecturer in the Department of Communication Sciences at Central University of Technology (CUT), Free State, South Africa. He holds a PhD in Communication and Language Practice (CUT), and is a member of both the Faculty Research and Innovation, and Language Committee at CUT. His research focus is on linguistics, language rights, and language equality. He is the recipient of the three minutes thesis discussion award at CUT. He has published articles on language rights and communication.

Aliziwe Sidiki is a master's student at the University of the Western Cape with a research focus in forensic linguistics. She holds an honours degree in African Language Studies.

Corle Smith holds a PhD. She is an Associate Professor in the Department of Applied Languages at Tshwane University of Technology. She has published many journal articles and supervised at Masters and Doctoral level.

Fiona Van Wyk has been a court intermediary with the Department of Justice and Constitutional Development for the past 19 years. After obtaining a BA(HDE) degree, (majoring in Afrikaans and Linguistics & English Language) from Rhodes University, she went on to teach languages in secondary schools for 12 years. She obtained a BAHons (Psyc) degree and a certificate in Victim Empowerment from the University of South Africa. She has worked at the Cape Mental Health Society. She is particularly interested in how children use language to express themselves when testifying and focuses on how their 'meaning' may become lost or misinterpreted by role players in court who do not share knowledge or understanding of the child's form and level of linguistic expression.

Natasha Venter is a law lecturer at Akademia where she teaches the modules Criminal Law, and English and Afrikaans Language Proficiency in the Legal Context. She holds an LLB degree and a master's degree in Criminal Law and Criminal Procedure from the North-West University, as well as a BA degree in Linguistics and Psychology from the University of South Africa (cum laude). She is currently registered for her LLD (Doctorate of Law) at the University of Pretoria. Natasha worked at the Private Prosecution Unit, under the leadership of Adv. Gerrie Nel. She is also an admitted attorney of the High Court of South Africa.

www.ingramcontent.com/pod-product-compliance
Lightning Source LLC
Chambersburg PA
CBHW061352240926
51846CB00007B/1385
* 9 7 8 1 9 9 1 2 6 0 9 4 9 *